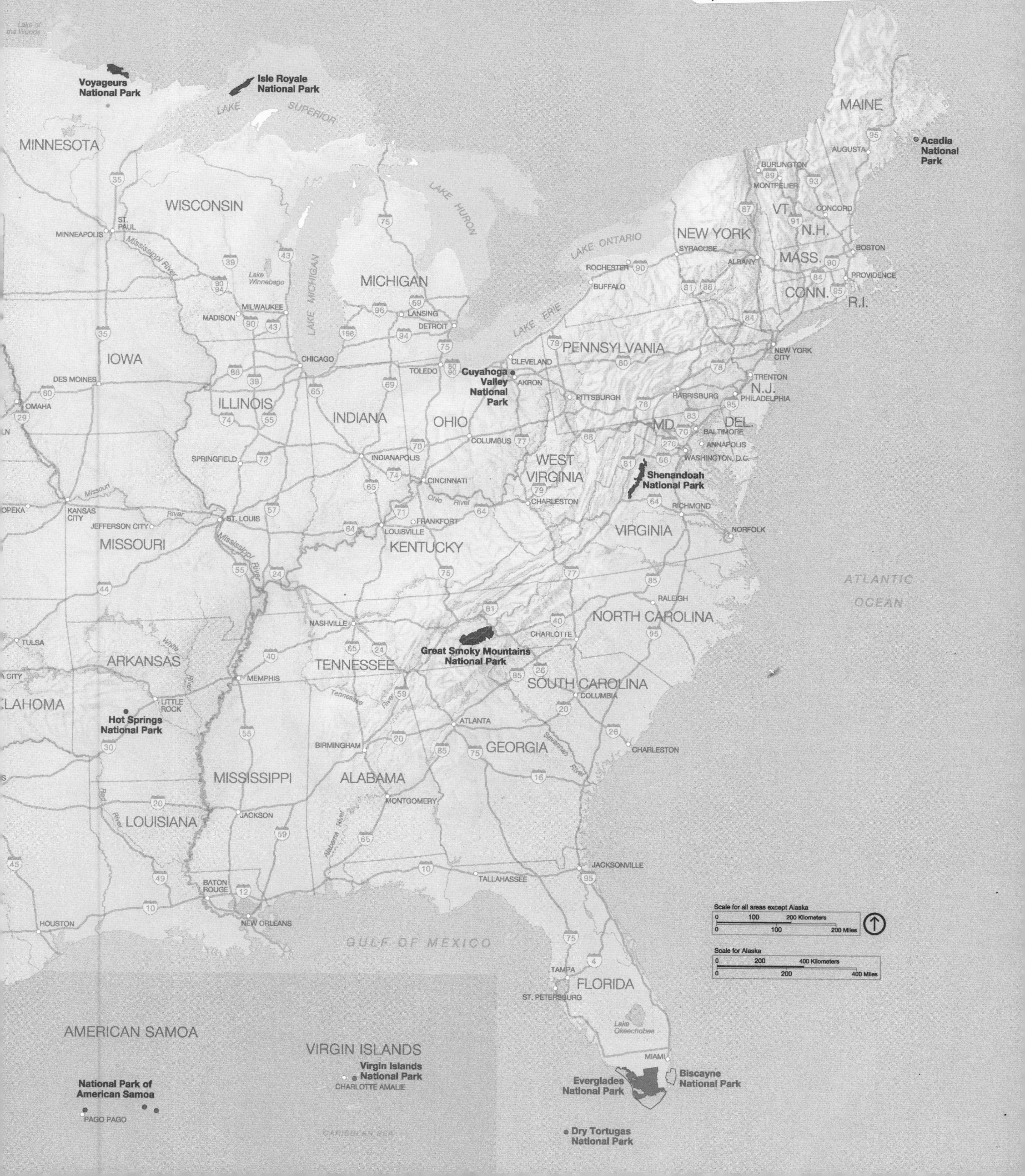

Voyageurs National Park
Isle Royale National Park
Acadia National Park
Cuyahoga Valley National Park
Shenandoah National Park
Great Smoky Mountains National Park
Hot Springs National Park
Everglades National Park
Biscayne National Park
Dry Tortugas National Park

MINNESOTA
WISCONSIN
MICHIGAN
IOWA
ILLINOIS
INDIANA
OHIO
PENNSYLVANIA
NEW YORK
MAINE
VT.
N.H.
MASS.
CONN.
R.I.
N.J.
DEL.
MD.
WEST VIRGINIA
VIRGINIA
KENTUCKY
MISSOURI
ARKANSAS
TENNESSEE
NORTH CAROLINA
SOUTH CAROLINA
GEORGIA
ALABAMA
MISSISSIPPI
LOUISIANA
FLORIDA

LAKE SUPERIOR
LAKE MICHIGAN
LAKE HURON
LAKE ERIE
LAKE ONTARIO
Lake of the Woods
Lake Winnebago
Lake Okeechobee
ATLANTIC OCEAN
GULF OF MEXICO
CARIBBEAN SEA
Mississippi River
Missouri River
Ohio River
Tennessee River
White River
Red River
Alabama River
Savannah River

AMERICAN SAMOA
National Park of American Samoa
PAGO PAGO

VIRGIN ISLANDS
Virgin Islands National Park
CHARLOTTE AMALIE

Scale for all areas except Alaska
0 100 200 Kilometers
0 100 200 Miles

Scale for Alaska
0 200 400 Kilometers
0 200 400 Miles

America's National Parks

PROUD PARTNERS OF
AMERICA'S NATIONAL PARKS

A TEHABI BOOK

AMERICA'S NATIONAL PARKS

THE SPECTACULAR FORCES THAT SHAPED OUR TREASURED LANDS

BY PAUL SCHULLERY

Discovery CHANNEL

Tehabi Books developed, designed, and produced *America's National Parks* and has conceived and produced many award-winning books that are recognized for their strong literary and visual content. Tehabi works with national and international publishers, corporations, institutions, and nonprofit groups to identify, develop, and implement comprehensive publishing programs. Tehabi Books is located in San Diego, California. www.tehabi.com

President: Chris Capen
Senior Vice President: Sam Lewis
Vice President and Creative Director: Karla Olson
Director of Corporate Publishing: Chris Brimble
Editor: Sarah Morgans
Art Director: Sébastien Loubert
Author: Paul Schullery
Naturalist Copywriter: Thomas Schmidt
Illustrator: Brian Battles
Geology Consultant: Gary H. Girty, Ph.D.
Copy Editor: Camille Cloutier
Proofreader: Lisa Wolff
Indexer: Ken DellaPenta
Production Artist: Monika Stout
Production Artist: Gina Sample

DK Publishing
LONDON, NEW YORK, MUNICH, MELBOURNE, DELHI

Publisher: Sean Moore
Editorial Director: Chuck Wills
Art Director: Dirk Kaufman

First American Edition, 2001

4 6 8 10 9 7 5 3

Published in the United States by
DK Publishing Inc.
95 Madison Avenue
New York, NY 10016

Library of Congress Cataloging-in-Publication Data

America's national parks.– 1st American ed.
p. cm.
Includes index.
ISBN 0-7566-1020-6 (alk. paper)
1. National parks and reserves—United States—Pictorial works. 2. Natural history—United States—Pictorial works. 3. United States—Pictorial works.
E160 .A5794 2001
917.304'931–dc21

2001042261

The paper used in this publication meets the minimum requirements of the American National Standard for Information Sciences—Permanence of Paper for Printed Library Materials, ANSI z39.48-1984.

Printed in China

The Spectacular Forces
Six spectacular geo-eco forces have shaped America's national parks. Featured in the opening spreads are Volcanic and Geothermal, pages 2–3; Mountain Building, pages 4–5; Waves, Caves, and Currents, pages 6–7; Glacial Carving, pages 8–9; Wind and Water Erosion, pages 10–11; and Climatic Extremes, pages 12–13. Right: A gray wolf stares through a snowstorm. Page 16: The Merced River washes among snowclad boulders on the floor of Yosemite Valley.

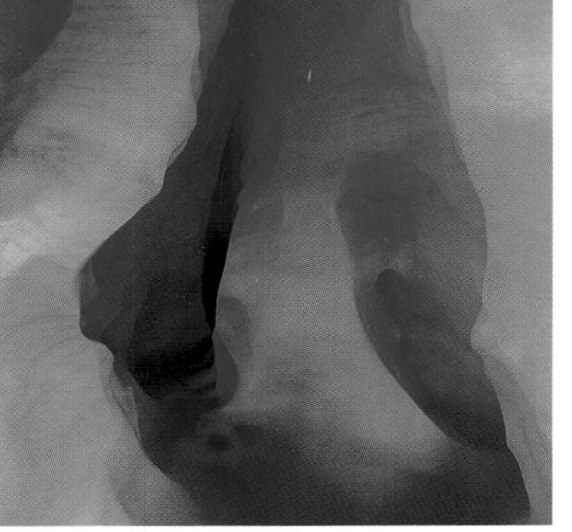

Ice Cave
The ghostly interstices of an ice cave wind back into the toe of Holgate Glacier, a lobe of the great Harding Icefield in Kenai Fjords National Park in Alaska.

OUR TREASURED LANDS

The American national parks celebrate the timeless earth-shaping and life-giving forces of nature. In these magnificent landscapes, so rich in human legend and natural diversity, we witness the planet's inexhaustible creative energies and satisfy our longing for the perfect beauty of wild nature. As the parks are shaped by great forces, so do they shape us—calming us as they thrill us, and humbling us as they fill us with pride.

Ask a few of your friends to name the most important American invention. You will get some lively and confident answers. Sports fans will say baseball. Music buffs will champion jazz, or bluegrass. Other enthusiasts will offer other quirky and even brilliant creations—the telephone, or DNA fingerprinting, or rodeo, or the cheeseburger—as the most uniquely American gift to the planet. We are passionate about many different things, and there are many definitions of "important."

One answer you probably will not get is "the national parks." And yet the parks may be the most far-reaching institution we Americans have brought to the long pageant of human society. Since Yellowstone was established in 1872, almost every nation on the planet has embraced the national park idea. Of course as the world conservation movement has grown, each nation's park system has found its own unique direction, reflecting the needs of its equally unique culture. Nowadays, America's parks are as likely to benefit from the wisdom of park professionals elsewhere as vice versa.

But the American contribution stands. By creating the first parks, we led the way to a world of parks. And by creating such a comprehensive national park system, we discovered new meanings for parks. Once seen only as resorts or

Life Force
A wood lily, left, lays itself open to cross-pollination. Above: Two bull elk square off during the autumn rutting season in Yellowstone National Park.

Coastal Silhouettes
Wave-battered sea stacks rise against the setting sun along the 60 miles of pristine Pacific coastline protected by Olympic National Park.

Subterranean Marvels
Dripstone columns adorn the Great Hall in Carlsbad Caverns, which is renowned for both the variety and extent of its delicate dripstone formations.

Acadian Autumn
Hardwood foliage responds to autumn in Acadia National Park, where all of the park's land was donated in the interests of conservation.

Denali's Mountains
The Alaska Range cuts through the heart of Denali National Park. The park straddles the highest portion of the 600-mile range, which is home to Mount McKinley.

Break Time
An endangered sea otter yawns while reclining in a kelp bed along the Pacific Coast. The otters live along the coast of Alaska and off Washington's Olympic Peninsula.

Saw-Whet Owl

A Northern Saw-whet owl roosts in a sumac bush. A relatively small owl, it thaws out frozen prey by sitting on it as if incubating an egg.

Death Valley Dunes

Sculpted by desiccating winds, several large dune fields augment Death Valley National Park's tremendous variety of desert landscapes.

Channel Islands

A crush of wildflowers, including paintbrush and giant coreopsis, carpet a canyon on San Miguel Island in Channel Islands National Park off southern California.

Colossal Trees

The enormous trunk of a giant sequoia dwarfs those of mature white firs in Sequoia National Park. Sequoias are Earth's largest living things.

Light Show

Visitors at Hawaii Volcanoes National Park watch one of Kilauea's frequent and relatively gentle eruptions of fluid lava.

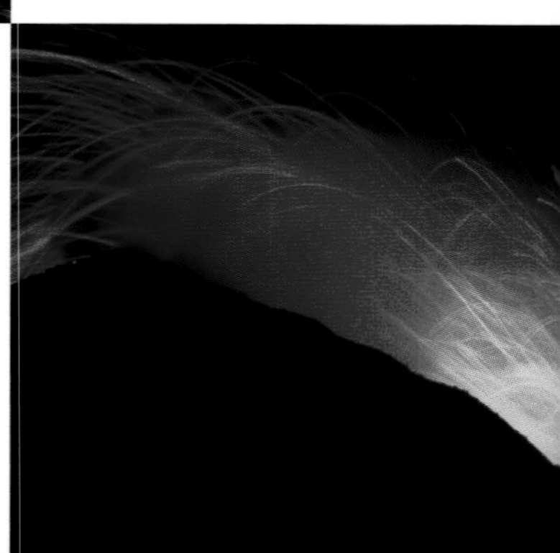

Wisp of Mist

One of Zion National Park's many waterfalls spills from the cliffs as a delicate wisp of mist above the Emerald Pools Trail in the heart of Zion Canyon.

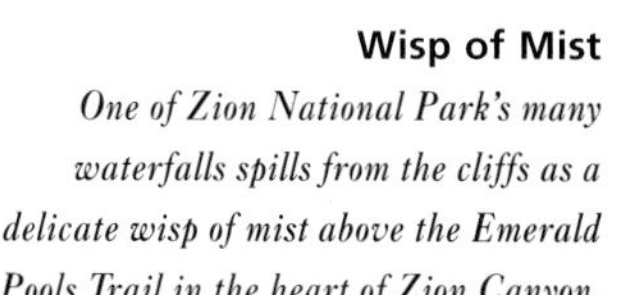

oddities of nature, parks are now recognized as irreplaceable treasuries of life's variety. They are hailed as great outdoor universities, and essential barometers of our world's health. And, despite all these weighty responsibilities, parks are still terrifically fun.

But it won't do for us to get too puffed up about what we have accomplished here. After all, nature did most of the work. We get credit for having the good sense to set these places aside. But the real creators of the parks were already hard at work when our ancestors had their hands full inventing the pointy stick. The creative forces of the parks—the forces that literally built them from the ground up and then blessed them with life at its most riotously wild—had much bigger plans, and are still at work today.

This book is organized to illuminate the forces behind the parks as much as to honor the parks themselves. The better we understand the natural events that brought a landscape to form and life, the better and deeper we can engage that landscape's wonder. The chapters of this book focus on six of those forces: volcanism, mountain building, waves and currents, glaciation, erosion, and climate. Each force is profoundly complex and never creates quite the same landscape twice. That is why each park is unique, and especially deserving of our attention.

Of course nature is neither simple nor orderly. Most parks show the traces of many if not all of these forces, and the forces themselves blend into each other. But there is both sense and satisfaction in singling out a most influential force—the one behind our decision that this place should be a park. Besides, it's good for some delightful surprises when you discover that a park isn't quite what you thought it was.

So make yourself comfortable—it's a great ride. You will see the earth at its rawest and gentlest, its most accessible and most demanding. You may be surprised at the number of visitors who, over long millennia, have preceded you. Be also prepared for some alarms; the parks face many perils in a swiftly changing world.

May you find abundant wonder and beauty beyond expression. May you also find gratitude—for nature's creation of such a magical world, and for our invention of the way to save and enjoy that magic.

Clam Digger

An Alaskan brown bear noses a razor clam it has just dug from the sand.

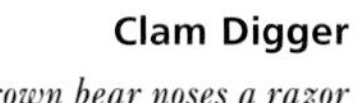

Following spread: A herd of bison move through Yellowstone National Park.

VOLCANIC AND GEOTHERMAL FORCES

A RECENT GEOLOGY TEXT, with typical scientific understatement, describes volcanic eruptions as "compelling events." In the other extreme, one vividly realistic disaster movie referred to the terrifying pyroclastic cloud of a full-scale volcanic eruption as "God's Big Show." Either description is correct, but even the latter falls short of capturing the violent immediacy, the riotous complexity, or even the actual magnitude of the thing in question.

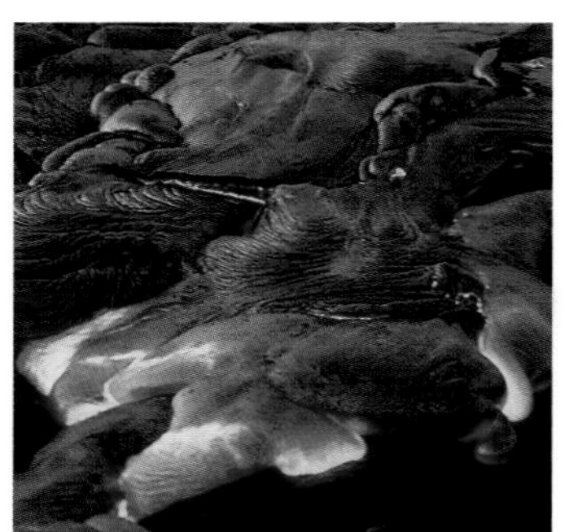

Molten Rock
Fluid pahoehoe lava flows down Kilauea at Hawaii Volcanoes National Park.

Past cultures had their own answers to the whys, wherefores, and whens of volcanoes. The twentieth-century realization that our planetary surface is composed of about twenty drifting slabs or plates—some immense, some only enormous—that bang and scrape against each other with frequently explosive consequences has not only overwhelmed all previous views, but has showcased just how volcanoes work.

Calderic Lake
Crater Lake occupies a caldera at the top of Mount Mazama in south-central Oregon.

THE ROILING LAND

And what a showcase volcanic power is: The roiling tower of flame, the shower of rocks, the glowing tide of lava—these are the staples of volcano terror. But there is so much more. Collapsing ramparts generate cyclonic winds that flatten forests and towns beyond counting. And earthquakes—everywhere there are rifts and slumps, tremors and landslides. In a hundred ways, the Big Show has its sideshows, all irresistible and wondrous. They incinerate, shear, and smother the life from a landscape—and, thus, they precisely define the terms on which life will inevitably return. For life, too, is irresistible and wondrous, and its fire is, at last, even harder to quench.

Incandescent Streams
Streams of incandescent lava spill over steaming cliffs and into the Pacific Ocean at Hawaii Volcanoes National Park.

THREATENING BEAUTY

Beautiful, foreboding, and sometimes quite deadly, volcanoes have created some of the most compelling landscapes in the National Park system. Yellowstone, with its myriad geothermal features, encompasses a huge, collapsed volcanic structure known as a caldera. Other parks, such as Mount Rainier, illustrated here, and Crater Lake, take in massive stratovolcanoes. The Hawaiian parks lie atop colossal shield volcanoes. Elsewhere, volcanism leaves its mark in the form of cinder cones, volcanic domes, and lava flows.

Vent
Stratovolcanoes
Most of the Earth's active stratovolcanoes, also known as composite cones, occur along a narrow zone known as the Ring of Fire, which encircles the Pacific Ocean. They are large, nearly symmetric structures built by alternating eruptions of relatively viscous lava and pyroclastic materials such as dust, ash, pulverized rock, glass, and lava fragments. Stratovolcanic eruptions can be unexpected and catastrophic. Examples include Vesuvius, Mount Fuji, Mount Saint Helens, and Mount Rainier.
Secondary conduit

Lassen's Cinder Cone
Standing 10 miles northeast of Lassen Peak, Cinder Cone was built up by a succession of ash eruptions during the past few centuries. It measures about a half mile in diameter.

YELLOWSTONE'S GEOTHERMAL FEATURES

GEYSERS

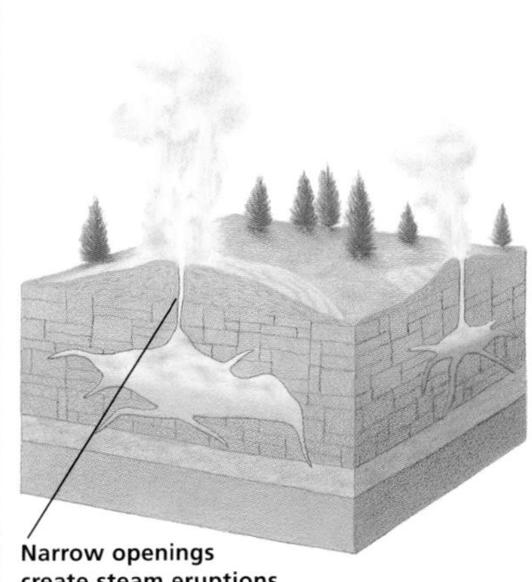

Like all of Yellowstone's ten thousand geothermal features, its geysers operate on heat released from a large body of hot igneous rock that lies very close to the surface of the ground. Water percolating through the ground collects in each geyser's intricate plumbing system and in connected areas of porous rock. There—under great pressure—the water is heated to temperatures well above the normal boiling point. As some of the water is forced out at the surface, pressure at the bottom of the system is reduced and a portion of the superheated water flashes into steam. This flings the remaining water out the surface vent in a sudden rush. After the eruption, more water percolates into the system and renews the cycle.

Old Faithful
Old Faithful erupts to an average height of 130 feet every 75 to 80 minutes. It used to erupt nearly every hour, but three major earthquakes seem to have rejiggered its plumbing.

HOT SPRINGS

Hot springs work in a manner similar to geysers. They are fed by water that seeps down through the ground, gets heated by a body of hot rocks, and then rises again to the surface. But because the plumbing systems of hot springs contain fewer constrictions than those of geysers, pressure does not build to the point of eruption. The hot water simply flows from the ground, often collecting into pools ringed by colorful microorganisms.

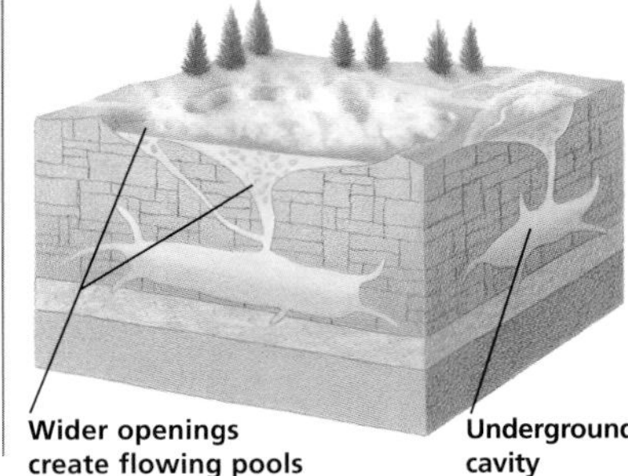

FUMAROLES

Fumaroles, or steam vents, are found throughout Yellowstone's geyser basins. They release steam and various gases—often quite acidic gases. Sometimes the acids break down enough of the surrounding rock and soil to form small mudpots. When the water table rises sufficiently, some fumaroles can become small geysers.

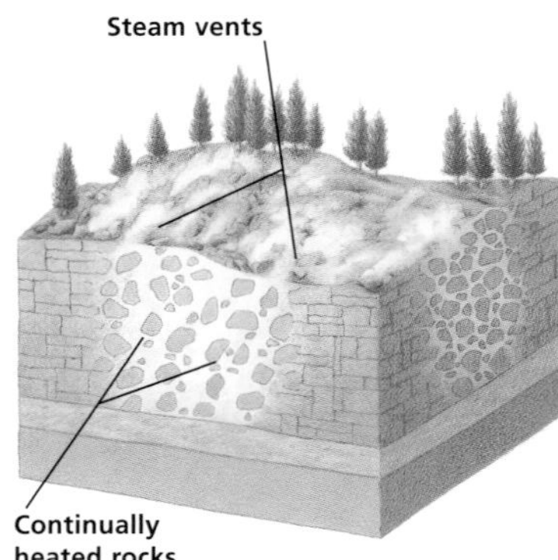

MUDPOTS

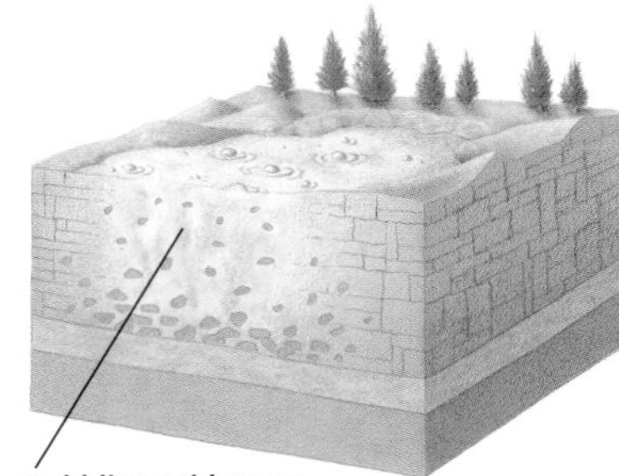

Pools of bubbling muck, mudpots are simply hot springs that lack enough water to flush out sediment as it accumulates. They contain boiling mud and other dissolved compounds that hot water and steam transport from the rocks below. Hydrogen sulfide gas, converted to sulfuric acid by microorganisms, decomposes the rock into wet clay mud and gives mudpot areas their characteristic "rotten egg" aroma. Sulfur compounds also color the mud in varying hues of yellow and gray.

Bubbling Mudpot
Acidic vapor bursts a bubble of muck in a mudpot at Artist's Paint Pots, a group of colorful mudpots south of the Norris Geyser Basin in Yellowstone National Park.

TRAVERTINE TERRACES

When water from geysers and hot springs flows across the surface, material in solution often precipitates. When the water contains calcium carbonate, a type of limestone called "travertine" is deposited. At Yellowstone's Mammoth Hot Springs area, thick travertine terraces cover an area of nearly 1 square mile. There, more than 2 tons of calcium carbonate bubble to the surface daily. As the warm waters trickle over the existing terraces, particles of calcium carbonate precipitate and add to the stairstepping pile of rock. Colorful algae living in the water streak the terraces with shades of brown, yellow, red, orange, and green.

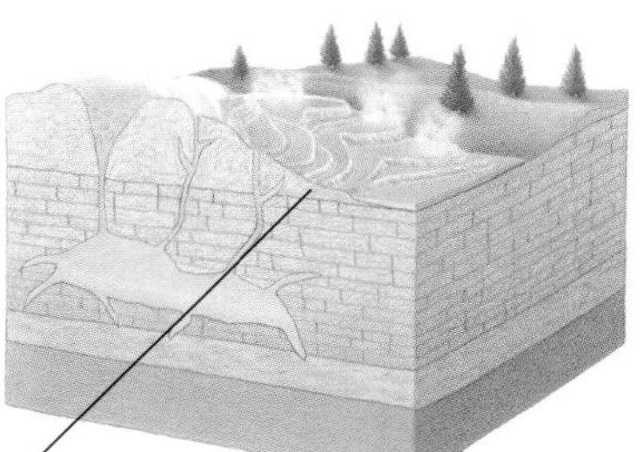

Minerva Terrace
Minerva Terrace is part of the vast travertine deposit at Mammoth Hot Springs in Yellowstone National Park, which is the largest carbonate-depositing spring system in the world.

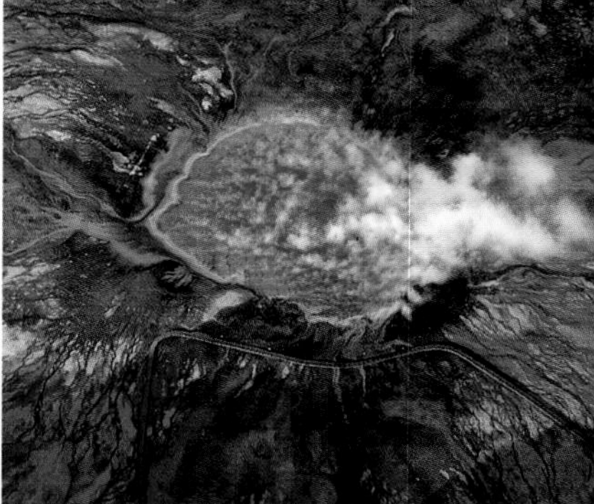

Hot Colors

Grand Prismatic Hot Springs in Yellowstone owes its colorful perimeter to algae, which reflect different water temperatures: The cooler the water, the darker the algae.

Crater Lake Caldera

The Crater Lake caldera formed about seven thousand years ago when Mount Mazama erupted and collapsed. Rain and groundwater slowly filled the caldera to form the lake.

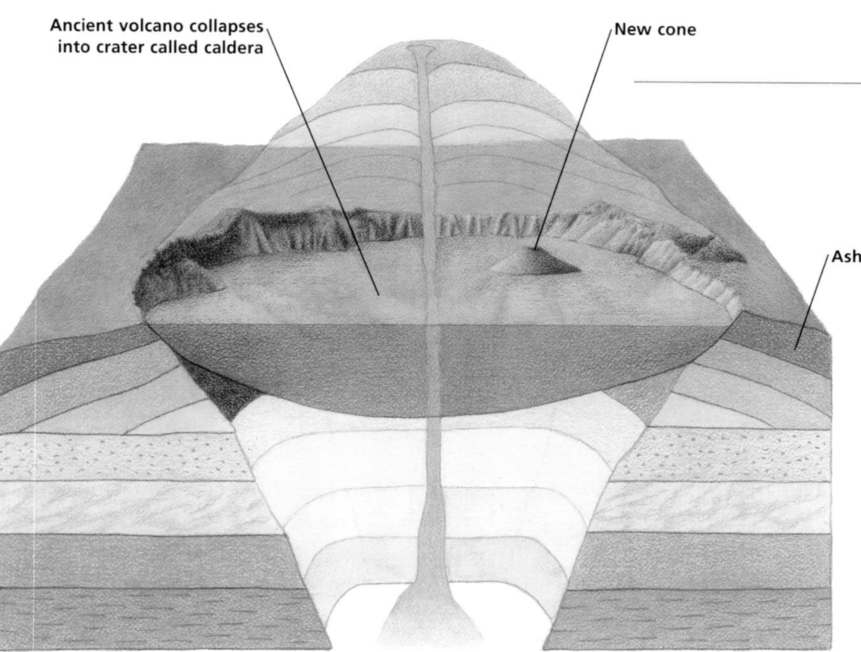

CALDERAS

Most volcanoes have a crater, and calderas are simply large versions of volcanic craters. Specifically, craters with diameters exceeding 1 kilometer (or a little more than half a mile) are referred to as calderas. Most form after an explosive eruption when the summit of a volcanic structure collapses suddenly into a partially emptied magma chamber, as the illustration at left shows. But Mauna Loa's caldera formed by gradual subsidence as magma from summit chambers drained gradually during flank eruptions.

LAVA DOME

Volcanic domes, also called lava domes, are relatively small, bulbous structures of congealed lava that usually form within the crater of a stratovolcano after an explosion of gas-rich magma. They are made of lavas so viscous they barely flow from the vent and usually turn into rhyolite or obsidian as they cool.

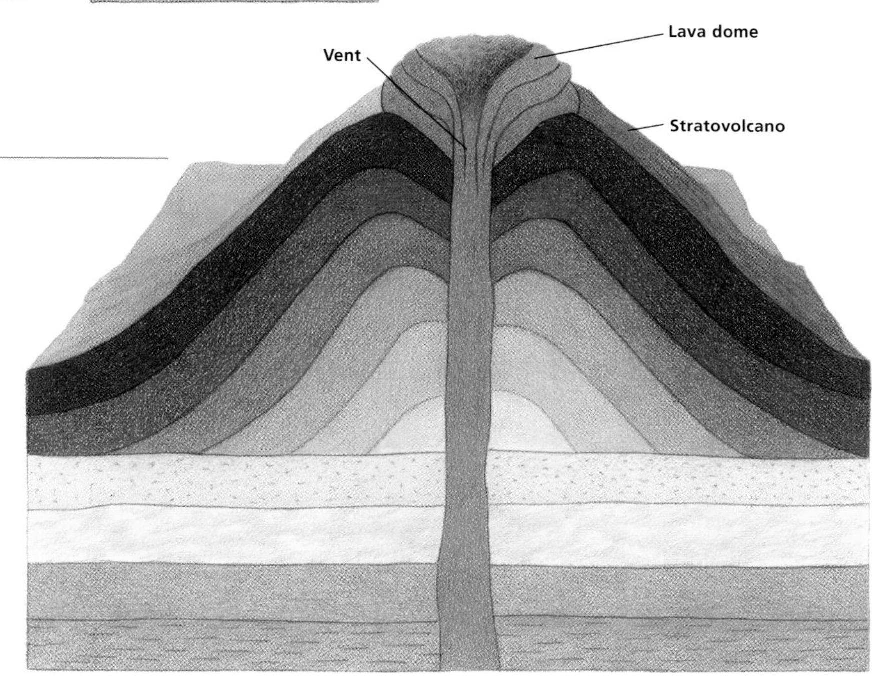

SHIELD VOLCANO

This diagram compares the relative magnitudes of the two basic types of volcanoes. Shield volcanoes are substantially larger than stratovolcanoes. Broad, very gently sloped, and massive, shield volcanoes build up slowly from successive eruptions of fluid basaltic lava flows. Mauna Loa, one of five shield volcanoes that make up the Hawaiian Islands, when measured from its base on the sea floor, is the tallest mountain on earth. Mount Rainier is dwarfed by comparison.

Mauna Loa

Mount Rainier

Pacific Ocean
19,000 feet deep

120 miles

LIQUID ROCK UNDER HEAT AND PRESSURE

FIRE IN THE EARTH'S BELLY

Volcanoes are the products of plate tectonics—processes at once so elegant and messy, so vast and deep, that they force us to reimagine the volcano as little more than an aftereffect. They also make us wonder if geology might at times be more a conjectural art than a hard science, and if today's scientific analysis may be tomorrow's embarrassing bad guess. For the moment, we can take great comfort in knowing that our understanding of how the planet builds its landscapes has advanced tremendously over even fifty years ago, and that we are learning more all the time.

Crater Lake

Hawaii Volcanoes

The earth's lithosphere, that brittle outer layer of the planet that is at most only a few dozen miles thick, is composed of plates that slide and override and jostle one another like hotcakes jammed too tightly on a griddle. In a planetary drama on a scale almost beyond our comprehension, the collisions and frictions of these plates generate enormous amounts of energy, heat, and movement.

An Emergent Land
A cloud of steam rises where fresh lava meets the Pacific Ocean in Hawaii Volcanoes National Park.

The great majority of our volcanic national parks are associated with the Pacific Ocean, especially its hot spot island chains and its famous Ring of Fire. Haleakala, Hawaii Volcanoes, and American Samoa are the products of hot-spots on the tops of columns of molten rock that rise to the Earth's crust from deep within the planet. These "plumes" of magma probably originate at the outer edge of the Earth's core, some 1,800 miles below the surface. The great crustal plates whose upper surfaces make up the continents and sea bottoms slide over the athenosphere, the outermost part of the earth's mantle. The athenosphere is often warm and permeable enough that molten rock can rise through it from below and create a "lubricated" surface over which the plates can move in a motion that scientists liken to a conveyor belt or treadmill.

Where plumes of molten rock from deep within the planet break through the plates they become volcanoes, and disgorge huge quantities of lava onto the surface. The Pacific island parks are the result of this process.

Yellowstone, far inland from the Pacific, is also the site of a hot spot that has recurrently erupted for millions of years, leaving a long trail of volcanic features across the landscape. There is no other continental area on the planet with a record of volcanic activity equal to Yellowstone's.

But hot spots are by no means the grandest volcano factories. For wholesale volcanism, it's hard to beat subduction, where one plate slides under another. Along the Pacific shore of the United States, subduction has produced the long mountain chains that include most of our other volcanic parks—Katmai, Lake Clark, Mount Rainier, Crater Lake, and Lassen.

Katmai and Lake Clark, on the Alaska Peninsula, rise from

Enrichment
Tall silversword, a rare native plant, grows in the rich soil of Haleakala.

American Samoa

Haleakala

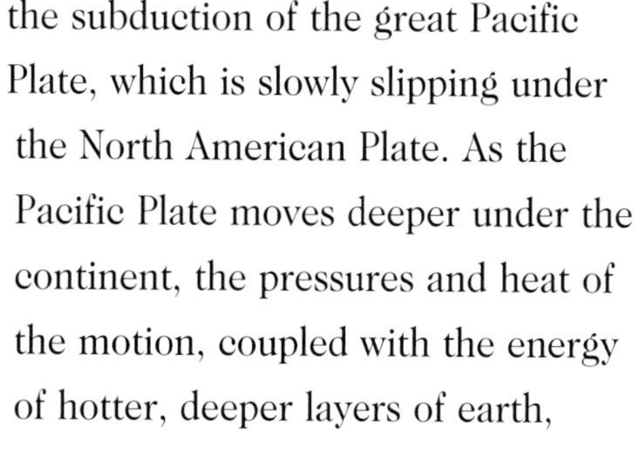

Wizard Island

Cinder cone Wizard Island rises 800 feet above the surface of Crater Lake.

the subduction of the great Pacific Plate, which is slowly slipping under the North American Plate. As the Pacific Plate moves deeper under the continent, the pressures and heat of the motion, coupled with the energy of hotter, deeper layers of earth, reduce the solid rock of the plates to magma. This magma is then buoyed back toward the surface, either bulging straight up toward the surface or oozing and angling up through existing faults and passages to become erupting volcanoes.

The same effect is produced in Washington, Oregon, and California. There, huge oceanic plates are sliding under North America. Sometimes the result is just an ominous reminder of the planet's instability—earthquakes. But over the long geological haul, earthquakes aren't enough to ease the pressures and energies of this friction. Landscapes shiver, bulge, and subside, but ultimately nothing short of a volcano, or several volcanoes, will settle the earth for a while. The leading edge of plate-melting action in this region seems to be directly underneath the famous volcanic peaks of the Cascade Range.

Hot Springs

Katmai

Lake Clark

Lassen Volcanic

Mount Rainier

Yellowstone

In the southeastern United States there is one more representative volcanic park, Hot Springs, where what we see on the surface is an especially mild effect of the earth's internal fires. Water, having seeped only a mile or two below the surface, is heated and purified for its return to us as a mild but persistent reminder that even in quiet lands, the deep fires are not gone.

In Hot Water

Steaming water runs down Tufa Terrace into a thermal pool at Hot Springs National Park.

AMERICAN SAMOA

POLYNESIAN PARADISE

At 2,300 miles southeast of Hawaii, American Samoa is the only United States territory south of the equator. The result of a hot spot in the earth's crust, the islands constitute the upper reaches of interconnected shield volcanoes that have mounded up from the ocean floor, some 3 miles deep. The national park protects a variety of rain forests, near-pristine coral communities, beaches, volcanic mountains, and some of the world's highest sea cliffs.

No two national parks are managed identically. Each, because of its unique attributes and the legislation creating it, has its own sense of direction. But even among the other parks in the national parks system, the National Park of American Samoa is an extraordinary experiment in creative administration. No land is owned by the federal government. Instead, the parkland on all three islands is leased from the nine villages that are contained in the park, and from the territorial government of American Samoa.

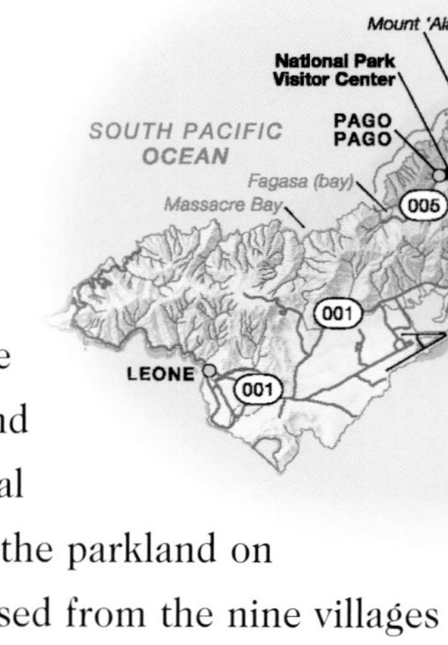

All the implied wonders and delights of terms like "tropical paradise" are right in front of you in Samoa. The several types of rain forests that blanket almost all of the land host a slowly earned diversity of species that found their way here with or without the help of humans. Among the animals, perhaps the most striking and attention-getting for tourists are the two species of bat, the Samoan flying fox and the white-collared flying fox. Both have wingspans of about 3 feet, and live on fruit and pollen. They are Samoa's only native mammals, though introduced species such as pigs do considerable harm to vulnerable natural landscapes.

The wonders and delights of National Park of American Samoa include native culture and the warm hospitality of modern Samoans. Samoa was among the first Pacific island groups colonized by seafaring Asians about 3,000 years ago. Saua, a sacred site in the park on the island of Ta'ū, is honored in Samoan cultural tradition as the launching point for Polynesian settlement throughout the Pacific.

Volcanic Islands
The volcanic islands of Samoa formed over a hot spot under the floor of the Pacific Ocean.

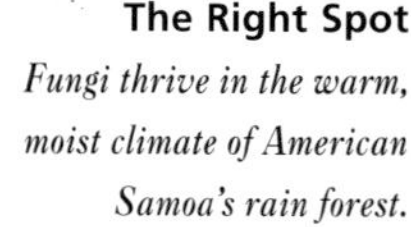

The Right Spot
Fungi thrive in the warm, moist climate of American Samoa's rain forest.

Watery Cleaver

Streams have cut deeply into Samoa's easily eroded basalts, right, chiseling steep peaks, knife-edged ridges, and many closely spaced stream valleys. Sea cliffs on Tutuila Island, below, attract seabirds.

NATIONAL PARK OF AMERICAN SAMOA

History Note: The deep-water port of Pago Pago, a flooded caldera, was used by the United States Navy as a coaling and repair station as well as a staging area during World War II.

Flora: Lush paleotropic rain forests, including coastal, lowland, montane, and cloud forest communities that preserve rare plants.

Fauna: Many species of birds, including tropical honey birds, seabirds, and shorebirds; fruit bats, endangered hawksbill sea turtles, green sea turtles, and 890 species of fish (twice the number found in Hawaii).

Visitor Tip: To learn firsthand about Samoan culture and lifestyle, consider avoiding the hotels and arranging instead to stay in a village with a Samoan family. Contact the park in advance to book a "home stay."

Leviathan Levitates

A humpback whale breaches in the Pacific, below. Humpbacks frequent Samoa's balmy waters during September and October. Following spread: Surf breaks against rugged Ta'ū Island.

Volcanic Lakebed

Crater Lake, left and below, lies in the caldera of Mount Mazama, a stratovolcano that erupted and collapsed 7,700 years ago. The caldera measures roughly 5 miles across.

CRATER LAKE

NATIONAL PARK IN OREGON

PLACID BEAUTY

In the Pacific Northwest's Cascade Range, a stupendous volcanic eruption barely seven thousand years ago blasted 25 cubic miles of lava, rock, and ash onto the surface and into the atmosphere. The ejection of such a volume of material caused the collapse of the entire upper cone of Mount Mazama, creating the caldera that now holds the deepest lake in the United States. The park is a showcase of glacial effects that predated this great eruption and of related volcanic effects that characterize the entire Cascade Range.

Accompany, if you will, prospector John Wesley Hillman and his companions on a prospecting trip out of Jacksonville, Oregon, in 1853. Tantalized by stories of a secret gold mine, you find your way into the rugged Cascade Mountains in early June. There, you toil up a steep, broad slope. As you climb, more and more of the forested lowlands and neighboring peaks come into view. But then you top the ridge and are brought up short, stunned by what you see.

Beneath you is an impossibly blue, impossibly large circle of water. It's a huge lake 5 miles across, cupped in the crater of what was apparently once the base of a great mountain. As the others catch up, you gawk and jabber, trying to think of more convincing ways to say "blue." Someone suggests "Deep Blue Lake" as a passable name, and you move on.

Amazingly, the name you give the lake, and your exhilarated descriptions of it, have little effect on the pioneering communities far below. They have more urgent treasures on their minds, and they don't care to come and see. But those of you who stood there in the glory of that brilliant color will never forget. There is no need to regret not having been with Hillman. The lake will still be your discovery. The great advantage of the 33-mile Rim Drive is that it allows you to reaffirm the unlikely reality of the lake from different angles, framing it with rocky outcrops and forested foregrounds. To help convince you, the island known as Phantom Ship provides some contrast against the perfect sheet of blue. And a trip on the tour boat out to Wizard's Island, the volcanic cone that rises

Phantom Landmark
Twisted branches frame Phantom Ship, an island and landmark just off Crater Lake's south shore.

Stocking the Larder
Golden-mantled ground squirrels, right, cache food all summer to survive the eight-month winters at Crater Lake, above.

hundreds of feet above the water, gets you right down on the blue.

But tear yourself away from the lake for a while. The plant and animal communities common to these elevations in the Cascades are flourishing here, but it's hard work, made all the harder when winter brings 50 feet of snow. The park's harshest world, even less hospitable than the high crater rim or the peaks, is the Pumice Desert on the north side of the park. The pumice is too deep and loose to hold moisture, and its high silica content prevents the production of soil. Only a dozen or so plant species have sparsely colonized a few spots.

Columns of Ash
The Pinnacles, columns of ash fused by hot gases, stand along the rim of Sand Creek Canyon.

Or go to the southeastern corner of the park to see yet another variation on the volcanic theme. In a little-celebrated canyon region you will find the Pinnacles—tall spires of fused volcanic ash. At every turn, even where life has successfully blanketed the landscape, the legacy of Mazama is not far beneath the surface.

Wind-Battered Thicket
A thicket of whitebark pines stunted by severe alpine conditions, below, huddles high on the flank of Mount Mazama. Right: Mount Scott rises over the eastern shore of Crater Lake.

America's Deepest Lake

A clump of rabbitbrush blooms above Crater Lake. The lake ranks as the deepest in the United States, reaching a maximum depth of 1,932 feet.

Ring of Fire

The Cascade Range is part of the volcanic belt that encircles the Pacific Ocean and marks the boundaries where oceanic crust is subducted beneath continental crust.

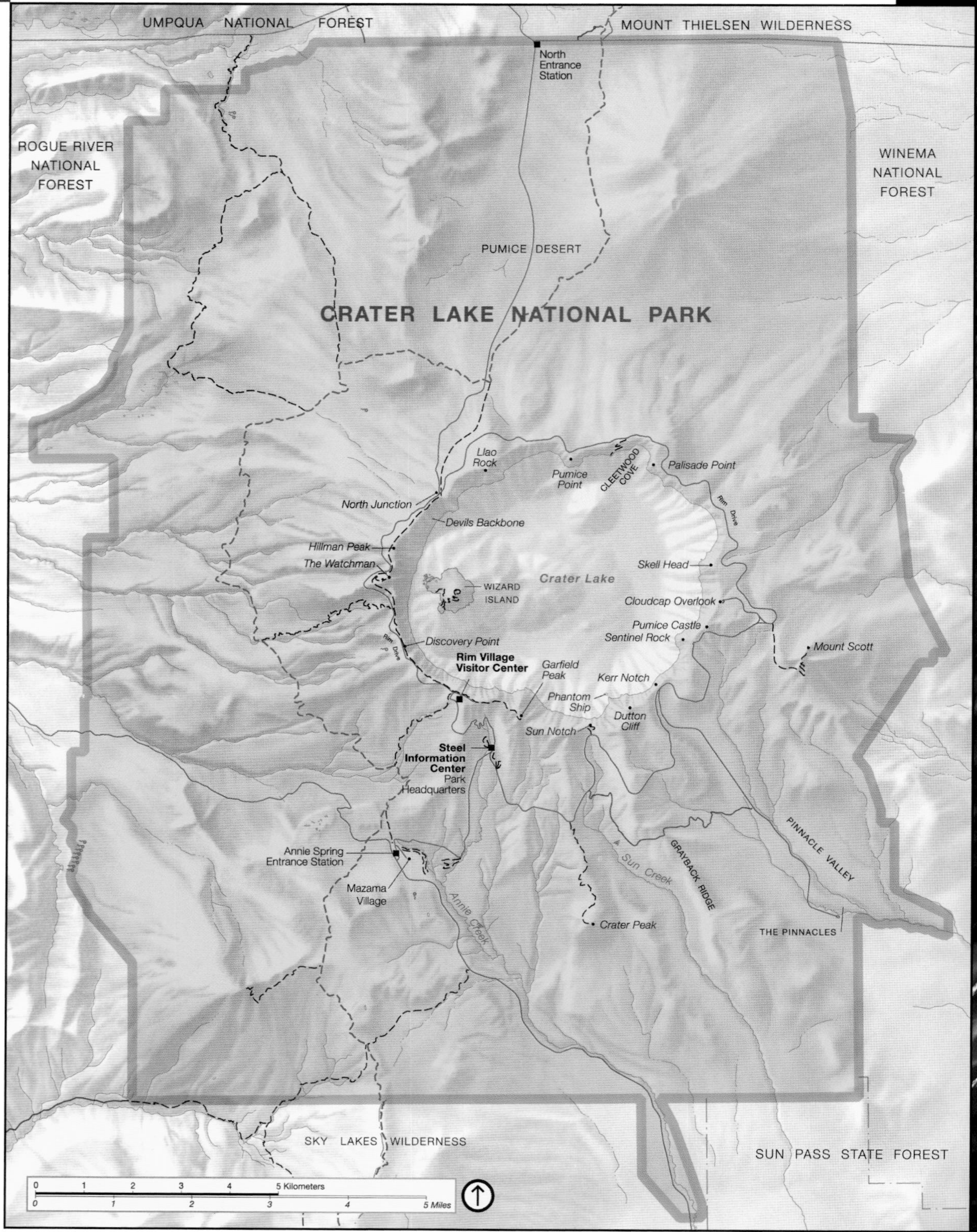

Gnarled Sentinel

A whitebark pine stands along the rim of the caldera. Whitebark pines, usually found near tree line, produce seeds that are an important food source for birds, squirrels, and rodents.

Clark's Nutcracker

A Clark's nutcracker perches in a mountain hemlock. Each bird caches 22,000 to 33,000 conifer seeds each year, carrying as many as ninety-five seeds in a pouch under its tongue.

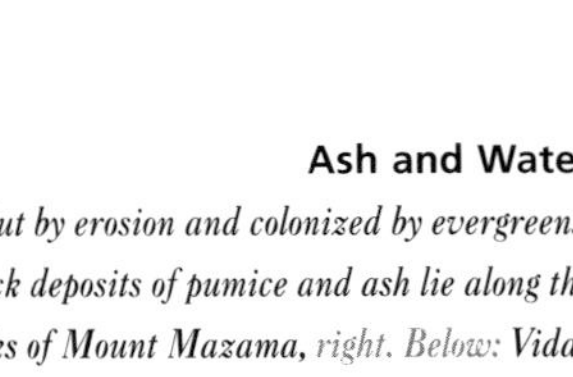

Ash and Water

Cut by erosion and colonized by evergreens, thick deposits of pumice and ash lie along the flanks of Mount Mazama, right. Below: Vidae Falls cascades behind a patch of red columbine.

CRATER LAKE NATIONAL PARK

History Note: Humans probably witnessed the cataclysmic eruption of Mount Mazama. Archaeologists have found sandals and other artifacts buried under the layers of ash, pumice, and dust ejected during the eruption.

Flora: More than six hundred plant species, including pumice paintbrush, Crater Lake currant, and ancient whitebark pines.

Fauna: More than fifty mammals, including Roosevelt elk, mule deer, marmots, pikas, snowshoe hares, and big brown bats; 160 species of birds, including golden and bald eagles.

Visitor Tip: For the most comprehensive vista of the lake and caldera, climb Mount Scott, the highest point in the park (5 miles roundtrip).

Wildflowers

A singular sprig of lupine, one of more than six hundred wildflower species found in Crater Lake National Park, blossoms in a park meadow.

HALEAKALA

NATIONAL PARK IN HAWAII

EXOTIC DIVERSITY

Less than a million years ago, the island of Maui, the upper reaches of an enormous submerged volcano, rose in fire and steam above the Pacific Ocean. Now, on the summit of the island's higher peak, the ragged walls of Haleakala enclose a raw, fractured landscape of cinder cones and the convoluted results of millennia of erosion. Farther down the slope, the jumbled topography is blanketed by a fabulously diverse set of ecological communities whose richness is exceeded only by their fragility.

Mark Twain called Hawaii "the loveliest fleet of islands that lies anchored in any ocean." Haleakala contains within its boundaries an incredible array of lovely things. Descending from the stark, raw rockscapes of the volcano, the park protects alpine, subalpine, rain forest, dry forest, streamside, and coastal habitats, all in 46 square miles of mountainside.

The tropical lushness you encounter when you back away from the active volcanic areas is the result of millions of years of slow, painstaking, accidental colonizations—many thousands of years passing between the arrival of successful species. Each native plant and animal you see is a product of this arduous exercise in making life fit. Most exist only here. Because of an epidemic of introduced species, you are witness to one of the world's most urgent conservation efforts at Haleakala. The human spirit simply cannot afford the loss of so much beauty and wonder.

Go to the highlands and find the Haleakala silversword, as lovely as the islands themselves. On the whole Earth this subspecies is found only here, with a total range of less than 2,500 acres. The silversword matures slowly, taking up to fifty years. Then it suddenly raises a tall flowering stalk, offers its seeds to the world, and dies. In a landscape thick with unusual species, the silversword is a hallmark conservation victory.

From a conservation standpoint, having Haleakala as a sample of the landscape's pre-development condition provides a priceless benchmark by which to measure the health of other parts of the archipelago.

Monk Seal
Monk seals are one of just two native land mammals on the Hawaiian Islands.

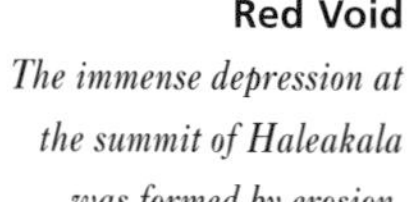

Red Void
The immense depression at the summit of Haleakala was formed by erosion.

Sea and Stone
Rugged lava outcrops along Maui's eastern shore contain rocks formed during Haleakala's widely spaced eruptive periods, right. Below: Lava cliffs face the sea at Kipahula.

HALEAKALA NATIONAL PARK

History Note: Polynesian migrants colonized the Hawaiian Islands 1,500 years ago, arriving in large, double-hulled canoes after sailing across 2,500 miles of open ocean.

Flora: Native rain forest, dry forest, subalpine shrubland, and riparian and coastal zones contain an incredibly rich diversity of plants, including ohia and koa trees, silverswords, lobelias, ferns, and many shrubs and grasses found nowhere else in the world.

Fauna: Many birds, including seven endangered species such as the nene (Hawaiian goose); bats, monk seals, spiders, insects, and a host of alien species such as mongooses.

Visitor Tip: For a short jaunt topped off by a refreshing swim, head for the Kuloa Point Loop Trail, which leads from the Kipahulu Visitor Center to several pools and waterfalls overlooking the ocean.

Rainbow of Bark
Multicolored strips of bark adorn a eucalyptus tree trunk at Hosmer Grove in Haleakala, below. Following spread: Cascades connect several pools in Oheo Gulch at Kipahula.

HAWAII VOLCANOES

NATIONAL PARK IN HAWAII

FIERY FOUNTAINS

In Mauna Loa, volcanism has created one of the world's largest mountains, an immense, gentle-sloped shield volcano more than 56,000 feet from base to tip. Hawaii Volcanoes National Park protects the heights of this gargantuan landform, where Mauna Loa and Kilauea continue their fiery earthbuilding. On this dynamic geological stage, a no less spectacular community of plants and animals has developed—a unique and imperiled world of life forms found nowhere else on the planet.

There is something almost comical in the contrasts that nature has arranged in Hawaii. Here on the one hand is a landscape so young it is literally still on fire, fuming and simmering side-by-side with a delicate ecological community so rich, diverse, and distinctive that it is a Biosphere Reserve of world renown. The hot spot that has built the Hawaiian archipelago has created land so remote and so ideally situated for a hospitable climate that even the slow parade of arriving species was sufficient to build an amazing new world.

Given the easy pace and relatively little to worry about (no mammalian predators or grazers to speak of, for example), these long-distance colonists had plenty of time and opportunity to evolve into every suitable niche. Hawaii has one hundred endemic (unique to this one place) landbirds alone. There are native plants, fish, insects, and mollusks beyond hope of acquaintance, in a paradisiacal setting that to the uninitiated must seem perfect.

But it is not.

Because of the actions of humans, Hawaii has been labeled the extinction capital of America. This is not the kind of world leadership we prefer, so it is modest consolation that our efforts to prevent an ecological catastrophe are heroic. Nature in crisis may be an even more stirring and inspiring sight than nature undisturbed. In Hawaii, you see the fate of a beautiful world held in our hands.

For centuries—starting long before the arrival of Europeans—humans have changed the pace of change here, introducing new species that were violently hostile to the ancient natural

Ferns
The "fiddlehead" of a fern unrolls on the floor of a park rain forest. Many types of ferns grow in the park, including three species of ferns that can grow 20 feet high.

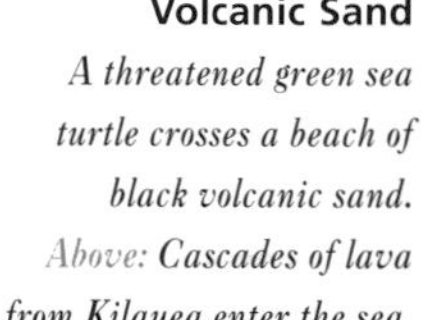

Volcanic Sand
A threatened green sea turtle crosses a beach of black volcanic sand. Above: Cascades of lava from Kilauea enter the sea.

Fiery Fountains

A fountain of molten lava spews from the flank of Kilauea, below. Right: Mauna Kea, elevation 13,796 feet, is the world's highest peak on an island.

setting. The nene, a native goose and the Hawaiian state bird, exemplifies this process. When the first Polynesians arrived here 1,600 years ago, they found seven species of geese. Most of them were flightless, and soon succumbed to overharvest. The one surviving species faced increased pressure after Euro-Americans arrived in the late 1700s—from introduced mongooses, dogs, and cats, and increasing encroachment on its habitat. The nene now symbolizes hope that Hawaii can keep its native wildness. Visitors soak up responsibility with the beauty, and learn humility along with the wonder.

Ribbon of Fire

A ribbon of molten lava streams down Kilauea. When lava is quite fluid, it can rush along at velocities of 10 to 25 mph.

The park offers one of the most extreme variations in altitude possible in an American park. It is almost 14,000 feet up from the ocean to the top of Mauna Loa. You move easily in and out of the lower climate zones, and if you have the time and energy, you can climb clear to the summit and stand 11 miles above the mountain's base. Even while driving, you will see the park's diverse vegetation communities, then cross the lava flows that have recently incinerated and smothered others of their kind.

Kilauea Rain Forest

A dense tropical rain forest of tree fern and 'ohi'a cloaks the eastern rim of Kilauea left. Over a thousand flowering plants have evolved on the islands. The slopes of Kilauea are pockmarked with craters and overlain with lava from many different eras, below.

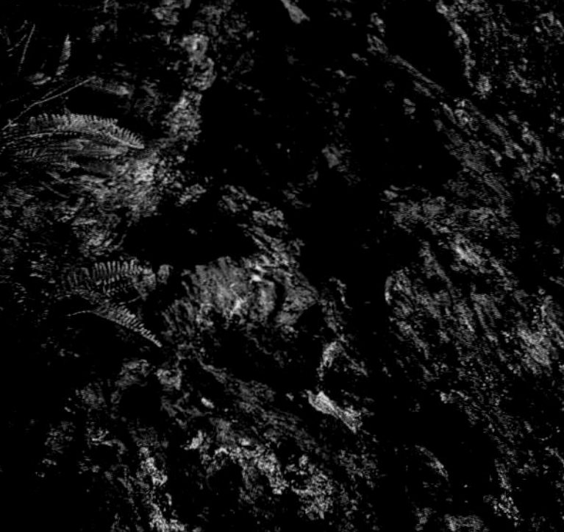

A Clean Slate

Ferns and mosses grow on a formerly barren lava surface, one of many such clean slates found throughout the park in a variety of climates.

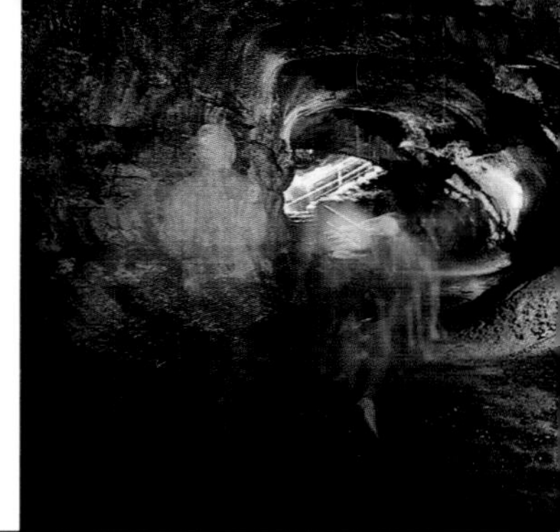

Lava Tubes

Lava tubes, such as the park's Thurston Lava Tube, form beneath the congealing surface of pahoehoe flows and act as conduits for moving fresh, hot lava downslope.

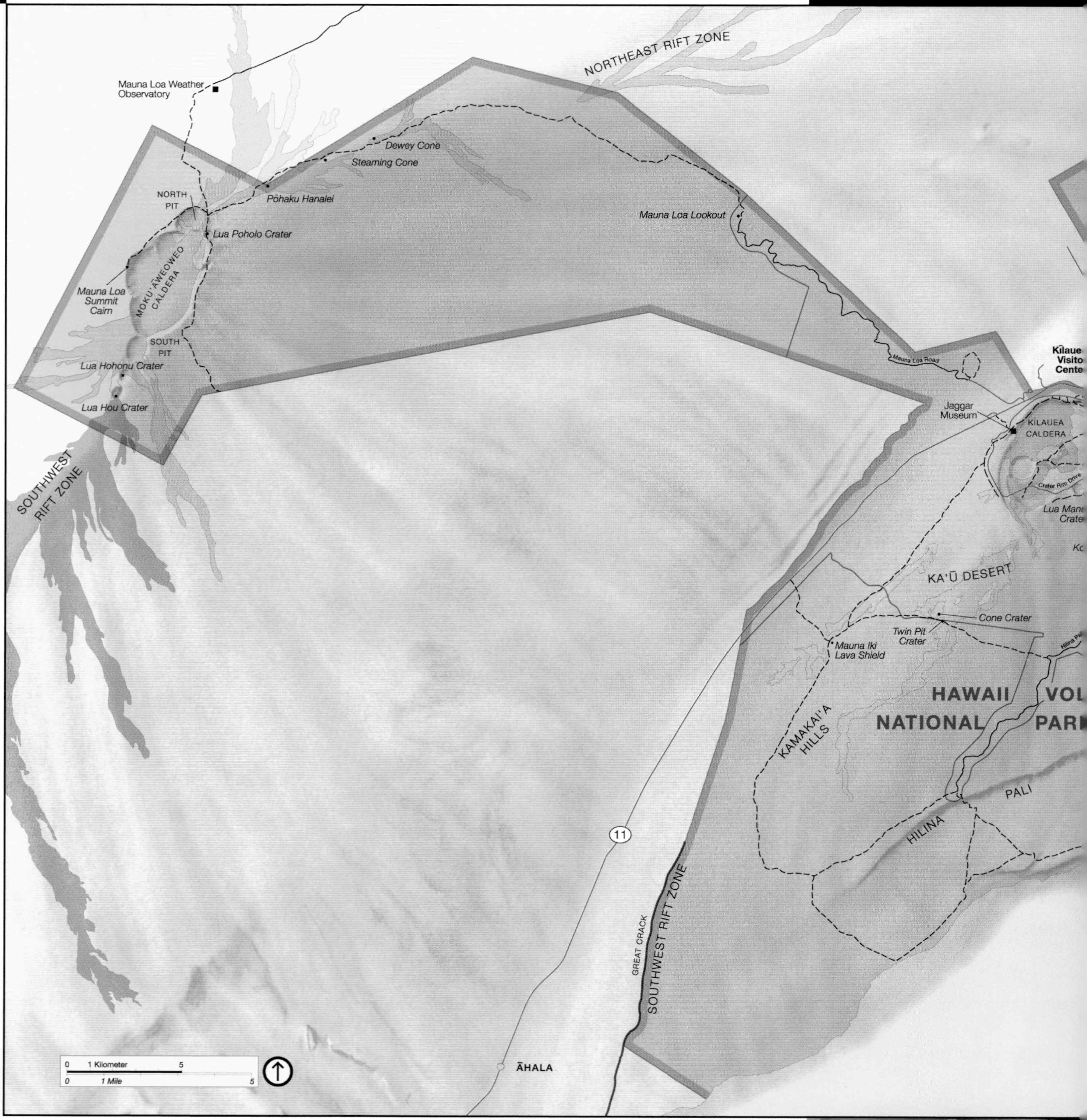

NORTHEAST RIFT ZONE
Mauna Loa Weather Observatory
Dewey Cone
Steaming Cone
NORTH PIT
Pōhaku Hanalei
Lua Poholo Crater
Mauna Loa Lookout
MOKU'ĀWEOWEO CALDERA
Mauna Loa Summit Cairn
SOUTH PIT
Lua Hohonu Crater
Lua Hou Crater
Mauna Loa Road
Kīlaue
Visito
Cente
Jaggar Museum
KĪLAUEA CALDERA
Crater Rim Drive
Lua Mani
Crate
SOUTHWEST RIFT ZONE
KA'Ū DESERT
Cone Crater
Twin Pit Crater
Mauna Iki Lava Shield
HAWAII
VOL
NATIONAL
PAR
KAMAKAI'A HILLS
PALI
HILINA
11
GREAT CRACK
SOUTHWEST RIFT ZONE
ĀHALA
0 1 Kilometer 5
0 1 Mile 5

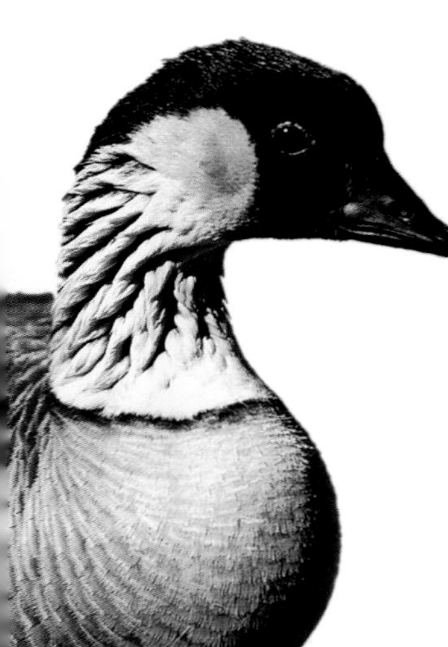

Sole Survivor

Hawaii's state bird, the nene, is the sole surviving species of at least seven species of geese that originally existed on the islands.

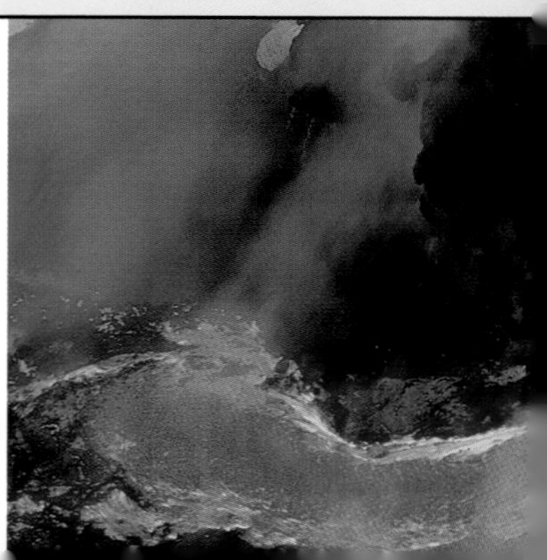

Fluid Lavas

The high temperatures and low silica content of Hawaiian lava allow gases to escape easily rather than build up to explosive pressure.

Forest Threat

Second only to land development as a threat to Hawaii's native forests, feral pigs destroy vulnerable plants such as orchids as they dig for roots and earthworms.

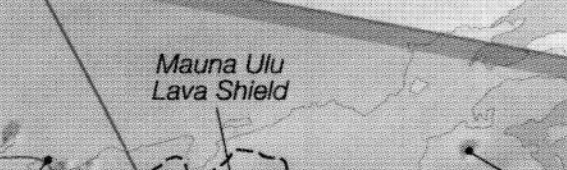

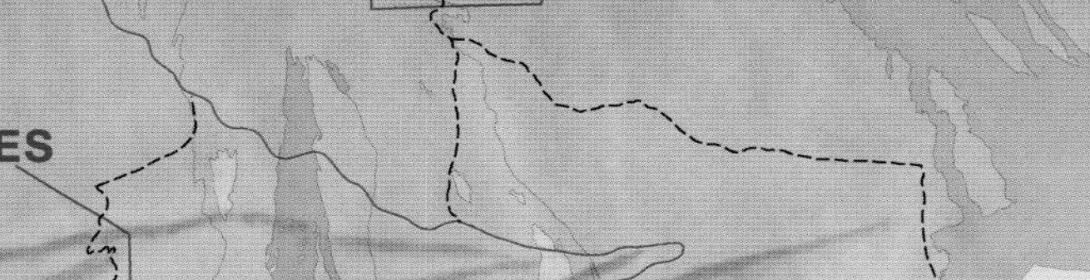

HAWAII VOLCANOES NATIONAL PARK

History Note: In 1790, an ash explosion on Kilauea killed a band of Hawaiian warriors. Their footprints are still visible on the ash surface.

Flora: Habitats range from arid expanses of lava to lush rain forests. Many of the island's 1,000 endemic plant species have been forced into extinction by land clearing and the introduction of alien plants and animals.

Fauna: Introduced species such as pigs, mongooses, cats, and rats have wreaked havoc on the islands' rain forests and on endemic populations of landbirds. Endangered species include the monk seal, the nene (Hawaiian goose), hawksbill turtles, and the 'Io (a beautiful raptor).

Visitor Tip: Consider spending a day hiking around the rim of the Kilauea caldera. The 11-mile hike follows an easy trail through rain forests and warm deserts.

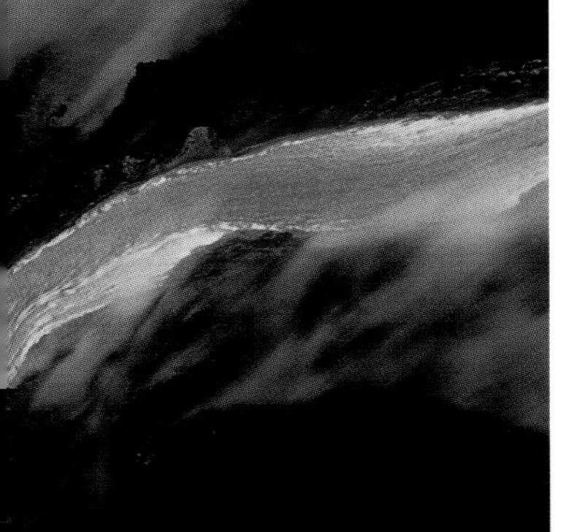

Grassy Foothold

Hawaii Volcanoes National Park has been overrun with nine hundred alien plant species. Here, tufts of an alien grass invade a lava field.

HOT SPRINGS

NATIONAL PARK IN ARKANSAS

SOOTHING WATERS

These highly civilized hot springs display a consistency not expected of geothermal systems. No fiery volcanoes here—not even the deep molten pockets that keep so many other hot springs steaming along. Instead, the heat that drives these springs originates in the gradually warmer rock typical deep in the earth's crust. Ancient water slowly works its way thousands of feet down, is heated, and—once thus energized—returns quickly to the surface and emerges from dozens of vents.

Forget for a moment all you've learned about Yellowstone, Yosemite, and the other "grand old parks" of America. Set them aside, and meet the original. Though not officially designated a national park until 1921, these remarkable hot springs so enchanted and concerned the young United States that in 1804, President Thomas Jefferson sent one of his least-known expeditions of discovery to investigate them. And in 1832, at the urging of President Andrew Jackson, the springs became what the National Park Service now calls "the first U.S. reservation made simply to protect a natural resource."

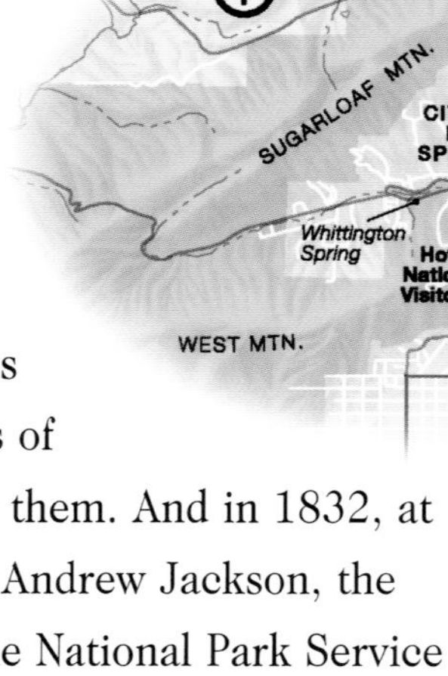

The water is the story, a story known for millennia by Native Americans, and entering Euro-American consciousness in the early 1500s. Whether or not the water has the almost magical therapeutic qualities so often attributed to hot springs, it is without question extraordinary. For four thousand years or more, moving only a matter of inches a year, rainfall has slowly filtered down through minute passages in the porous rock. At depth, the water is heated, and because it has passed through so few soluble minerals, it is oderless and tasteless, qualities that have attracted both bathers and drinkers.

Now almost totally contained and managed for the use of commercial bathers, the springs are still aggressively protected for their historic purity, and still have a combined winter flow of 950,000 gallons a day. The park celebrates the geological processes that create such a perfect liquid, and the accumulation of cultural features that both exploited and protected such a simple, priceless gift.

Ancient Waters
As with all the park's hot springs, water issuing from Display Springs fell as rain 4,400 years ago.

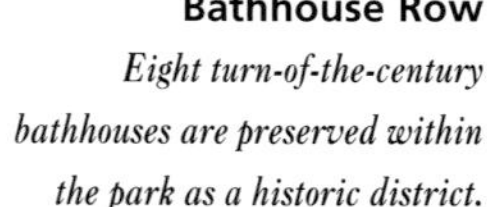

Bathhouse Row
Eight turn-of-the-century bathhouses are preserved within the park as a historic district.

Historic Quapaw

An intricate rotunda caps the red tile roof and ornate entryway of the historic Quapaw Bathhouse in downtown Hot Springs, Arkansas.

HOT SPRINGS NATIONAL PARK

History Note: In 1541, a contingent of Hernando de Soto's army of Spanish conquistadors traveled through the park area, relaxing in the park's hot springs and leaving behind disease that helped bring the demise of the native inhabitants.

Flora: Landscaped grounds with flowering trees and shrubs, woodlands, and rugged hill country.

Fauna: A host of small mammals, including raccoons, opossums, and squirrels; deer, fox, and wild turkey; and many birds, including crows, owls, and songbirds.

Visitor Tip: For a panoramic vista of the Ouachita Mountains surrounding the park, visit the observation tower on top of Hot Springs Mountain.

Peaceful Strolls

Dogwood and Redbud blossom on the Grand Promenade, below. Left: A federal park since 1832, Hot Springs preserves forty-seven thermal springs, including the landscaped cascade of Tufa Terrace. Following spread: Fall foliage frames a graceful stone bridge on the park's landscaped grounds.

KATMAI

NATIONAL PARK AND PRESERVE IN ALASKA

TUNDRA TREASURE

More than a dozen historically active volcanoes make this upper portion of the Aleutian Range one of the most restless segments of the Pacific Ring of Fire. Almost a hundred years ago, a little-known mountain in this great volcanic arc erupted so impressively, and left such a stark and alien landscape, that the area was made a national monument. But it would be the wildness and ecological richness of the surrounding setting that propelled Katmai to prominence as a great nature preserve.

Near the base of the Alaska Peninsula, an hour's flight southwest of Anchorage, Katmai National Park and Preserve encompasses more than 4 million acres of wildland—a magnificent reserve that owes its existence to a single natural event. On June 6, 1912, with only a handful of people residing close enough to witness it, a volcano eruption covered some 40 square miles of country with hundreds of feet of cinder and ash, and another 3,000 square miles with at least a foot of such material. About 650 miles to the northeast on the Klondike River in the Yukon, and 750 miles to the southeast at the little mining community of Juneau, puzzled heads turned to listen to a remote and persistent booming.

Fortunately, few people were nearby, and they made harrowing escapes through the blinding ash and terror. The ash and fine particles, blasted high into the atmosphere, smogged the skies of Virginia, Europe, and North Africa. The sulfurous air ruined clothes hanging on lines in Vancouver, British Columbia.

So remote was the region that it took four years for a National Geographic Society expedition, under Dr. Robert Griggs, to even reach the site of the eruption. There, they were stunned by "one of the great wonders of the world," the Valley of Ten Thousand Smokes, where more than 10 miles of former river valley had been flooded by ash hundreds of feet thick. The still superheated ash and rock continually simmered off the precipitation and groundwater through a jumble of steam vents giving the area its name.

Explosive Beauty
The jagged peaks of Katmai's volcanic mountains rise roughly 7,000 feet above Alaska's Shelikof Strait. Above: Boreal spruce forests carpet sections of the park.

Journey's End

Every year, a bevy of Alaskan brown bears gathers at Brooks Falls, below, to feast on sockeye salmon as the fish, right, return to their birthplace streams in Katmai.

The National Geographic Society teamed up with the National Park Service in 1918 to create a national monument around this fantastic scene, and visitors ever since have witnessed the gradual carving away of ash by the local streams, which have excavated colorful winding canyons penetrating back down to the original valley floor.

Carving a New Face
Streams quickly erode the deep ash flows that bury the floor of the Valley of Ten Thousand Smokes.

As the valley's steam vents quietly died out, administrators of the original monument gradually enlarged it to include not only more geological wonders but also great stretches of wild Alaska, creating an ecological treasure-house.

Modern visitors arrive by air, some to visit various isolated backcountry lodges and campsites, but most to travel the road to the great ash valley or to witness the aggregation of brown bears at Brooks Falls, where salmon fishing occupies both bears and humans for much of the short summer. Looking for bears and smokes, Katmai's visitors also find a huge and beckoning northern wilderness and a lifetime's supply of utterly wild nature.

Valley of Ashes
The spectacular pyroclastic ash flows that buried the Valley of Ten Thousand Smokes cover 40 square miles.

Katolinat
Mount Katolinat, elevation 4,730 feet, looms over a pond in Katmai. Its summit overlooks the Valley of Ten Thousand Smokes and stands about 15 miles northwest of Novarupta.

Fattening Up

A brown bear bites into a salmon during Katmai's short summer. The bears must gain several hundred pounds before winter drives them into hibernation.

Kaguyak Crater

A lake-filled caldera lies at the top of Mount Kaguyak, an inactive volcano that stands 40 miles northeast of Mount Katmai in Katmai National Park.

0 10 20 Kilometers
0 10 20 Miles
ILIAMNA LAKE
KAMISHAK BAY
KUKAKLEK LAKE
NATIONAL PRESERVE
NONVIANUK LAKE
McNEIL RIVER STATE GAME SANCTUARY
Kvichak River
Alagnak River
Kvichak Bay
American Creek
Mount D
KATMAI NATIONAL PARK
Fourpeak Mounta
NAKNEK
Naknek River
King Salmon Park Headquarters and Visitor Center
Lake Camp
NAKNEK LAKE
Lake Coville
Lake Grosvenor
Brooks Camp
Visitor Center
Savonoski River
Swikshak Bay
Iliuk Arm
Brooks Lake
Mount Katolinat
Ukak River
Rainbow River
Hook Glacier
•Devils Desk
•Kukak Volcano
•Mount Steller
Mount Denison•
Hallo Bay
Hallo Glacier
VALLEY OF TEN THOUSAND SMOKES
BUTTRESS RANGE
Mount Griggs
Serpent Tongue Glacier
Baked Mountain
Knife Creek Glaciers
•Snowy Mountain
•Mount Katmai
Kukak Bay
Novarupta
Crater Lake
•Katmai Pass
Kaflia Bay
King Salmon River
Mount Martin•
Mount Megeik
Katmai River
Kinak Bay
BECHAROF NATIONAL WILDLIFE REFUGE
Angle Creek
Amalik Bay
SHELIKOF STRAIT
Katmai Bay
Dakavak Bay
BECHAROF LAKE
Kejulik River
Kashvik Bay
ALASKA PENINSULA WILDLIFE REFUGE
Upper Ugashik Lake

Emergent Coast

Fjords and high cliffs, like those along Kukak Bay, continue to emerge as the Pacific plate subducts beneath the North American plate.

Chilling Out

Cool now, the Valley of Ten Thousand Smokes once hissed and roared as great columns of steam jetted from its hot, ashen floor.

Lakeshore to Summit

Old gravel beaches line the shore of Kukaklek Lake, right. Below: Mount Denison, elevation 7,606 feet, is the highest point in the park.

KATMAI NATIONAL PARK AND PRESERVE

History Note: The ashfall from the 1912 eruption of Novarupta was so thick that for days radio communication was silenced and a lantern held at arm's length could not be seen. When the skies cleared, ash a foot deep covered an area of 3,000 square miles.

Flora: Treeless tundra; forests and woodlands of spruce, birch, poplar, aspen, and balsam; shrublands; bogs; and meadows.

Fauna: Largest protected population of brown bears on the continent; caribou; songbirds, shorebirds, waterfowl, and seabirds, including tundra swans, arctic terns, bald eagles, and falcons; moose; otters; sea lions; and whales.

Visitor Tip: A viewing platform at Brooks Lodge offers visitors an unparalleled opportunity to watch brown bears fish for salmon.

Hot Pink Pioneers

A cluster of vivid wildflowers pioneers volcanic soil in the Valley of Ten Thousand Smokes.

Volcanic Peaks

The park's mountains, above, are part of a 1,600-mile volcanic arc that curves inland along the Alaskan Peninsula. Two active volcanoes stand within the park's boundaries. One of many glaciers in Lake Clark National Park, right, bites into a rugged peak at the southern end of the Alaska Range.

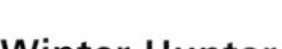

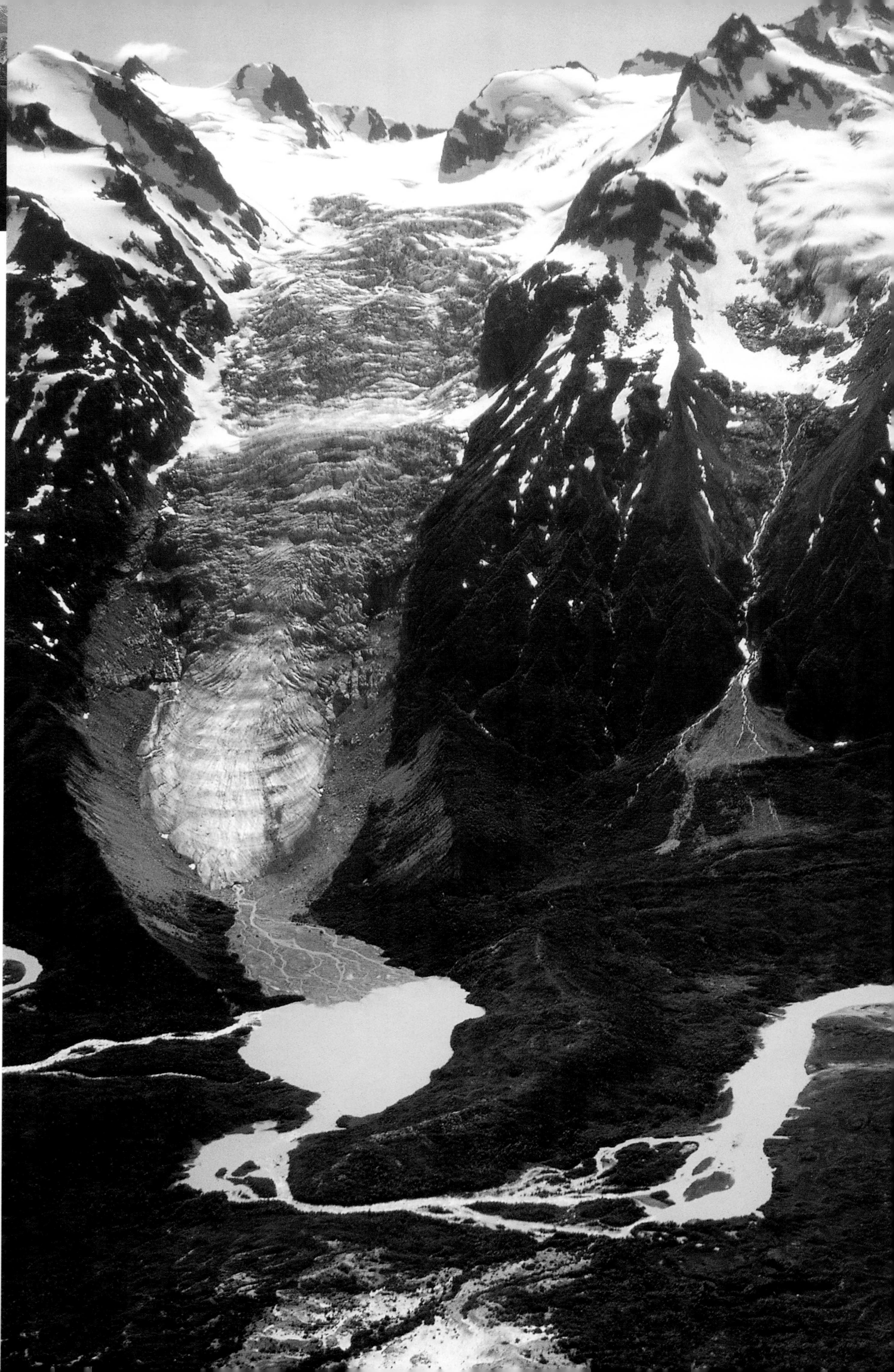

Winter Hunter

Foxes remain active during Lake Clark's long winter, patrolling home ranges of up to 100 square miles for small rodents. When hunting is good, they cache surplus animals.

LAKE CLARK

NATIONAL PARK AND PRESERVE IN ALASKA

BECKONING WILDERNESS

The boundaries of Lake Clark encircle the junction of three mountain ranges. The Alaska Range curves down from Mount McKinley to the northeast, running up against the Chigmit Mountains along the park's east side. Farther south, the Chigmits blend into the Aleutian Range, on its way southwest to Katmai and beyond. Lake Clark's eastern boundary includes many miles of ocean shore, while across the mountains, the western boundary captures extensive tundra plains.

Because of its diversity of landscapes, Lake Clark is a kind of sampler. And for good reason. It is, in the words of Alaskan adventurer and writer John Kauffmann, "the essence of Alaska."

The park is a meeting of ecosystems, those difficult-to-define but essential combinations of species and conditions that determine and sustain life. For a few species, Lake Clark is at the edge of things: The ecological conditions required by the black bear and the Dall sheep, both common farther north and east, stop here.

For many others this country is part or all of their home. Herds of caribou drift through their annual migration cycles on and beyond the park's tundra plain. Moose slosh contentedly through deep ponds seeking out succulent aquatic plants.

It could be, though, that the creature that best symbolizes this park is not a mammal but the sockeye salmon. Sockeyes hatch in freshwater but migrate to the sea, where they spend most of their lives gathering fat and energy in the deep ocean. When fully grown, they ascend their native rivers determined to spawn, but in the end they satisfy many appetites besides their own. Dozens of terrestrial species, including brown bears and eagles, cash in on the bounty.

Conservationists rightly point out that these salmon are a perfect example of how a park's needs and benefits can extend far beyond its boundaries—in this case far out into the ocean. Bristol Bay sockeye salmon support a giant commercial fishery, as well as substantial sport and subsistence harvests. Perhaps the real lesson the salmon are teaching us is to recognize that parks themselves are only part of a much larger ecosystem.

Volcanic Forms
The ramparts of the Alaska Range rise above Lower Twin Lake, left. Above: The Tusk, a volcanic neck.

Burrowing Birds
Tufted puffins burrow into cliffs along the coast, creating tunnels that reach as far as 9 feet before opening into nesting chambers.

Bellowing Bull
A bull moose bellows during the rut. Moose forage throughout the tundra and boreal forests along the western flank of the Chigmit Mountains.

LAKE CLARK NATIONAL PARK AND PRESERVE

History Note: The Lake Clark region has been continuously inhabited by humans for at least ten thousand years and includes Alaska's single-largest Athabascan archaeological site.

Flora: Coastal forests of Sitka and white spruce, boreal forests, tundra-covered foothills, marshes, and bogs; summer wildflowers, including fireweed, lupine, blueberry, and bearberry.

Fauna: Brown and black bears, caribou, moose, and Dall sheep; whales and seals along the coastline.

Visitor Tip: This park is remote in the extreme. The only access is by plane or by boat, and there are no roads or trails. Visitors must arrive self-sufficient or hire an outfitter.

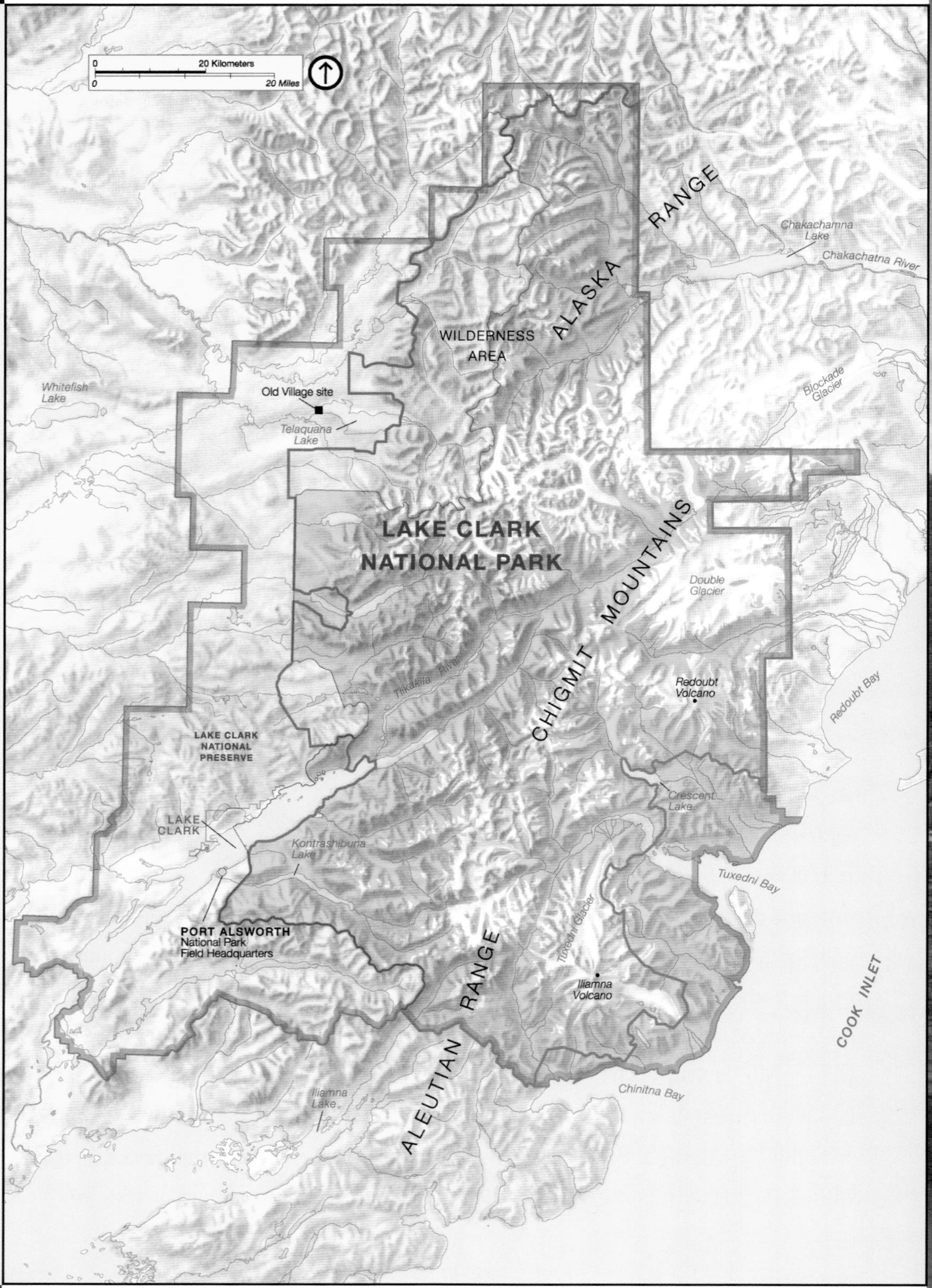

Setting Fruit
Berries must ripen quickly between Lake Clark's protracted winters, which start in October and end in April.

Faulty Lake
Waves break against the shore of Lake Clark, which stretches for more than 40 miles along an active fault zone.

LASSEN VOLCANIC

NATIONAL PARK IN CALIFORNIA

VOLCANIC LEGACY

Lassen Volcanic National Park is the former site of a massive volcano, 11,500-foot Tehama, that experienced a catastrophic collapse. Lassen Peak was one of several smaller volcanoes, or vents, to develop in the area since the collapse. The Lassen area was obscurely known for its volcanic activity until the early twentieth century. A spectacular period of eruptions between 1914 and 1921, when hundreds of separate events were observed, cured the obscurity.

Lassen Volcanic National Park offers visitors a tour through the stages of natural recovery from volcanic activity. The "Devastated Area" is perhaps the most famous roadside evidence of the Lassen Peak eruptions of the earlier twentieth century. As you drive through, compare the vegetation in nearby areas that were unaffected by the eruptions of the early 1900s with the modest, struggling growth in the Devastated Area. Wild nature is resilient, but it needs time to put itself back together.

Along the same road, farther south, you may find a more compelling experience of the volcano's power at Sulphur Works, Little Hot Springs Valley, and Bumpass Hell. Here are vivid examples of old Tehama's legacy of fiery earthmaking. Thanks to the mountain's inner reserves of heat, there is a sufficient supply of energy, moisture, and volatile chemistry to maintain a pungent vignette of the Inferno. Hydrogen sulfide—"rotten egg gas"—lingers potently in the air like a bad joke, evoking gasps and grimaces from unexpecting visitors. But for the modest toll of a few unsavory whiffs, you get to see a natural paintbox—chemically altered rocks, now soft clays, resplendent in shades of ochers, reds, yellows, and tans. There are also baked soils, slowly roiling mudpots, churning hot springs, thickly steaming fumaroles—in short, every appearance of evidence that Tehama sleeps only uneasily. As you stand in the earthy fragrances of Bumpass Hell, and consider the banked fires that must smolder somewhere below, it is not hard to imagine there is more to come.

Fuming

Steam vents from a fumarole in Bumpass Hell, where strong sulfur vapors are as striking as the scenery.

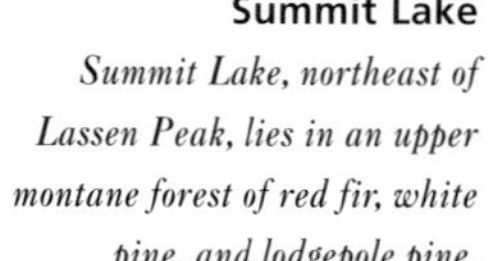

Summit Lake

Summit Lake, northeast of Lassen Peak, lies in an upper montane forest of red fir, white pine, and lodgepole pine.

Deer Hunter

Mountain lions—superb ambush hunters—help keep Lassen Volcanic National Park's deer population in check. Below: Thermal area Bumpass Hell covers 16 acres.

LASSEN VOLCANIC NATIONAL PARK

History Note: Though settlers, politicians, and scientists at the turn of the twentieth century considered the Lassen Peak volcano extinct, local Indians told them the mountain was full of fire and water and that it would explode some day. In 1914, they were proved right.

Flora: Diverse plant communities, including low-elevation mixed conifer forests; mountain chaparral; juniper-pine woodlands; dense upper montane forests of red fir; subalpine forests of whitebark pine and mountain hemlock; alpine tundra; and wildflower meadows.

Fauna: Mule deer, pronghorn, black bears, coyotes, bobcats, mountain lions, marmots, pikas, many rodents, three species of hummingirds, several hawks, golden and bald eagles.

Visitor Tip: Don't miss the Loomis Museum, which chronicles the 1914–15 eruptions with historic photos and informative exhibits.

Lassen History

Lassen Peak, below, last roared to life in 1914–15, with a series of steam explosions and eruptions of lava, ash, and pumice. Following spread: Lassen Peak stands guard over Manzanita Lake at sunset.

Dawn's Mirror
Dawn glimmers in Reflection Lake, near Paradise. Dozens of such small, alpine lakes dot the flanks of Mount Rainier.

MOUNT RAINIER NATIONAL PARK

History Note: In 1870, Hazard Stevens and P. B. Van Trump made the first recorded ascent of Mount Rainier. Benighted, they survived freezing temperatures by warming themselves beside fumaroles they found in an ice cave near the summit.

Flora: More than seven hundred species of plants in four major vegetative zones that include a rare inland example of a temperate rain forest; lush lowland forests of cedar, hemlock, and old-growth Douglas fir; silver fir forests; and vast subalpine wildflower meadows.

Fauna: Fifty-four mammal species, including mountain goats, elk, deer, and black bears; 126 species of birds.

Visitor Tip: To see the powerful effects of even a "minor" volcanic event, hike the self-guiding Kautz Creek Nature Trail, a 2-mile trail that investigates a 1947 mudflow that buried the highway 30 feet deep.

Snow-fed Streams
Fairy Falls tumbles over its rocky bed on the south flank of Mount Rainier, below. Water melting from the volcano's glaciers and snowfields feeds the park's numerous cascades. Right: One of the park's celebrated wildflower meadows displays its glory.

MOUNT RAINIER

NATIONAL PARK IN WASHINGTON

GRAND PEAK

Mount Rainier, casually named in 1792 by the explorer Captain George Vancouver for an officer friend of his, is the highest and most commanding of the Cascades volcanoes. Its present height of more than 14,410 feet is about a thousand feet less than its summit was before an eruption 5,700 years ago removed the top. Today, a glacial cap drapes the upper contours. Ongoing studies indicate that under its icy cap the volcano is more active than previously imagined.

Approach from any direction, and Mount Rainier will not merely dominate the horizon; it will seem to hover above it, free-floating and independent. As you move through its domain, it will loom there, haunting your vision's edge, giving you your bearings, and demanding that you look again, if only to convince yourself such a stupendous thing could exist.

Several tribes of Native Americans in the region called it "Takhoma" or "Takoma." Some whites doubted the worth of that name, pointing out that it was just a generic Indian term for mountain. But one early writer noted that though the native people described every other mountain by the combination of some specific name and the term Takoma, they used only the one word for Rainier. Yes, there were many mountains, but this was The Mountain.

From the summit, John Muir did almost as well when he called the Cascades volcanoes "islands in the sky." And, with more ecological emphasis, an early geologist called Mount Rainier an "arctic island in a temperate zone." Today it seems an island of wildness in an increasingly tame region, and its popularity has only indirectly to do with that unforgettable, ever-distracting summit. But it is still The Mountain.

During the last ice age, glaciers covered almost all of the present park area, and they still constitute the most impressive unified glacial field in the lower forty-eight states. Though they were larger during the cooler years of the "Little Ice Age" (roughly 1350 to 1850), Rainier's glaciers have not shrunk as much as so many others. The notoriously damp, cool climate of

Dormant Giant
At 14,410 feet, Mount Rainier, above, is the highest volcano in the Cascade Range. Left: A Steller's Jay.

Emergent Eden
A tangle of false hellebore emerges from Rainier's moist earth in early spring.

the Pacific Northwest even promoted some modest advances in the mid-1900s.

Downslope, below the raw rock and the creeping ice, are the reasons two million people come here each year. At least since the late 1880s, when James Longmire first developed his little hotel to serve users of the local "medical springs," visitors have flocked to the foothills and lower slopes of the mountain.

Court of Elders
Ancient western red cedars hold court in the Grove of the Patriarchs, a stand of old-growth forest along the Ohanapecosh River.

They come for the forests of Douglas fir and western hemlock, redolent with the wild scents of old growth and fresh decay. They will likely see some black-tailed deer, perhaps some elk, though probably not the resident black bears. They may even see spotted owls, silently gliding along, happily oblivious of the bitter controversy that has swirled around protection of their habitat in the Pacific Northwest.

But even more, they come for the meadows. Mount Rainier is wildflower heaven, especially in the aptly named Paradise area, where visitors walk the trails with all the intensity, wonder, and excitement of botanists at a formal garden. With the mountain and its bright glaciers rising beyond, the brilliant flower meadows seem, like the mountain itself, almost too lavish and beautiful a gift to be real.

Tiger Lily
Moisture-loving tiger lilies thrive in Rainier's damp valleys and woodlands.

Ice and Forest
One of Mount Rainier's twenty-five glaciers grinds down the volcano's slopes.

After the Thaw

Mount Rainier National Park is renowned for its spectacular displays of wildflowers, including arnica, lupine, and asters, in the spring.

Paradise River

Fed by snowmelt and runoff from a clutch of glaciers, the Paradise River in Mount Rainier National Park rushes past a thicket of Lewis monkey flower.

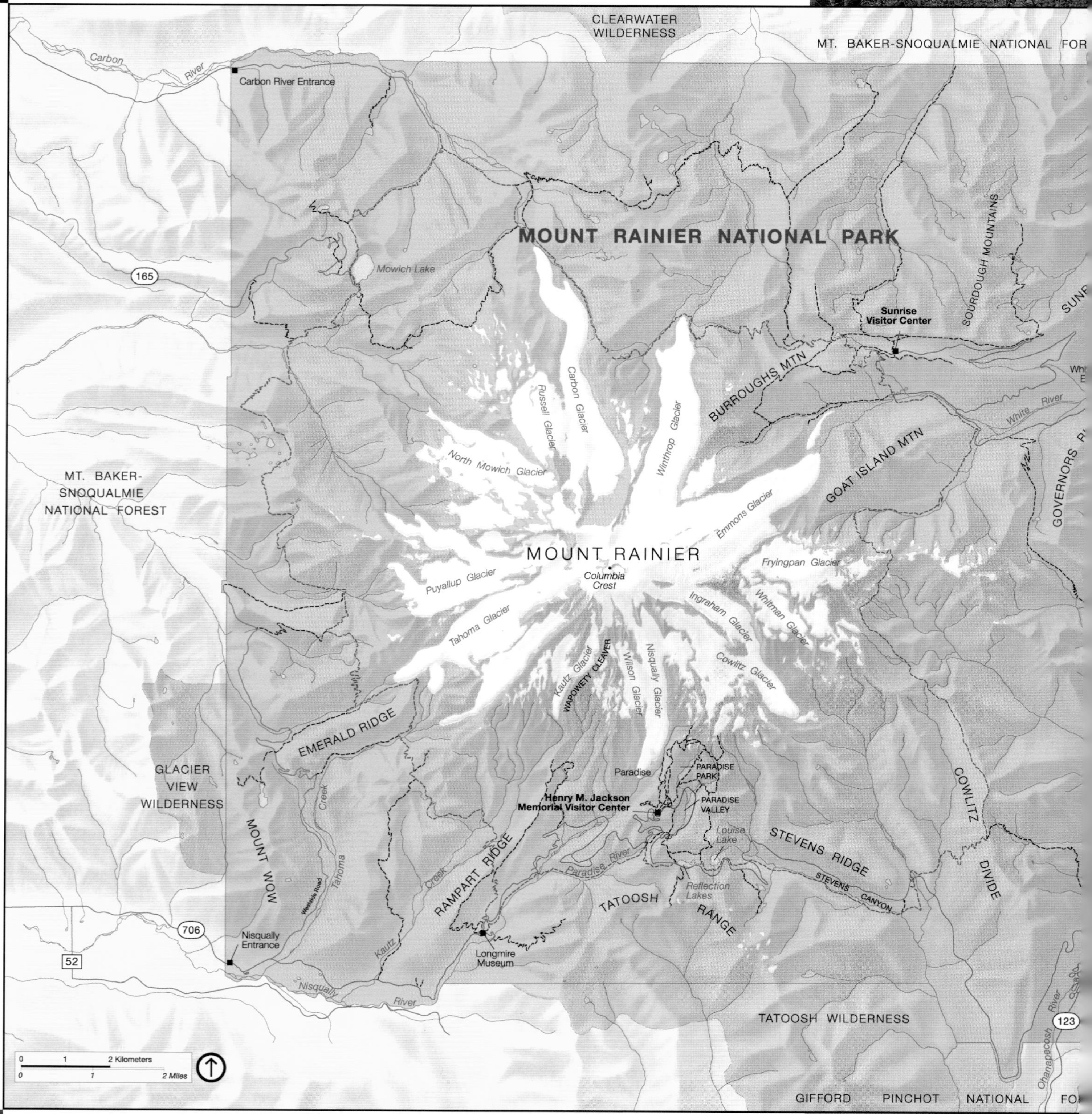

CLEARWATER WILDERNESS
MT. BAKER-SNOQUALMIE NATIONAL FOR
Carbon River
Carbon River Entrance
MOUNT RAINIER NATIONAL PARK
165
Mowich Lake
SOURDOUGH MOUNTAINS
Sunrise Visitor Center
SUN
BURROUGHS MTN
Carbon Glacier
Russell Glacier
Winthrop Glacier
White River
North Mowich Glacier
GOAT ISLAND MTN
GOVERNORS R
MT. BAKER-SNOQUALMIE NATIONAL FOREST
Emmons Glacier
MOUNT RAINIER
Columbia Crest
Fryingpan Glacier
Puyallup Glacier
Ingraham Glacier
Whitman Glacier
Tahoma Glacier
Cowlitz Glacier
Kautz Glacier
WAPOWETY CLEAVER
Wilson Glacier
Nisqually Glacier
EMERALD RIDGE
Paradise
PARADISE PARK
GLACIER VIEW WILDERNESS
Henry M. Jackson Memorial Visitor Center
PARADISE VALLEY
Louise Lake
COWLITZ
MOUNT WOW
Creek
Tahoma
Westside Road
STEVENS RIDGE
DIVIDE
RAMPART RIDGE
Paradise River
Reflection Lakes
STEVENS CANYON
TATOOSH RANGE
706
Nisqually Entrance
52
Kautz
Longmire Museum
Nisqually River
TATOOSH WILDERNESS
123
Ohanapecosh River
0 1 2 Kilometers
0 1 2 Miles
GIFFORD PINCHOT NATIONAL FO

Chip off the Old Block

Rainier's present summit stands about 1,000 feet lower than its previous summit, which blew apart 5,700 years ago.

Volcanic Neighbor

The Tatoosh Mountains and Mount Adams, far right, rise south of Mount Rainier and are part of the Cascade Range volcanic chain.

A Misty Veil

Comet Falls, right, streams down just a mile or so off the park's main road west of Paradise. Below: Autumn drapes the slopes of Paradise Valley with vibrant colors.

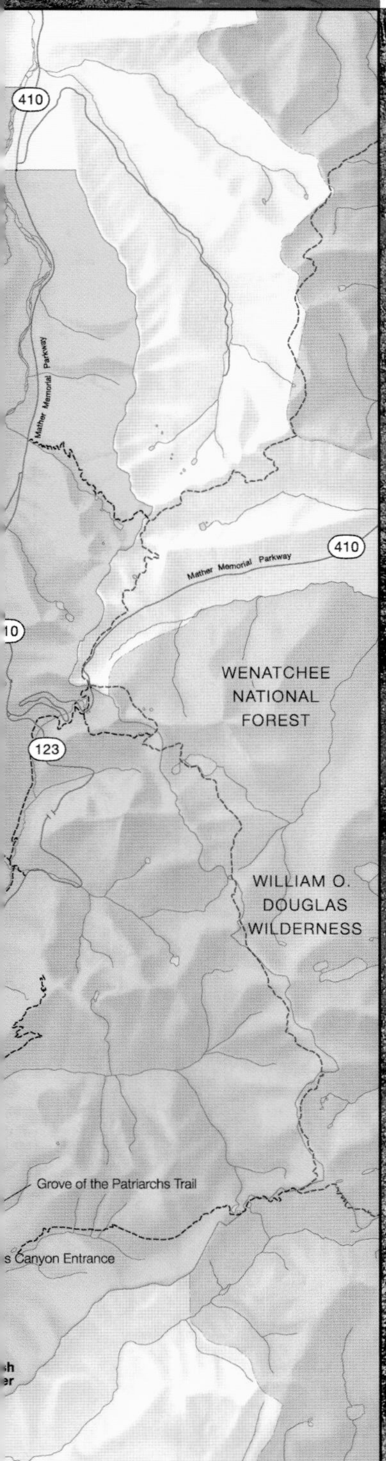

Show of Strength

Bighorn sheep rams, right, battle for dominance. Following spread: The south face of Mount Rainier greets the dawn.

Canyons and Castles

Pillows of snow soften the rim of the Grand Canyon of the Yellowstone, above, a deep gorge carved by the Yellowstone River. Yellowstone encompasses an enormous calderic depression where cataclysmic explosions have rocked the land three times in the past two million years. Castle Geyser, right, provides a less monumental but more frequent display of geothermal force.

Camp Robber

Bold, curious, intelligent, the gray jay's brazen pilfering of campers' food has earned it the nickname "camp robber." Yellowstone boasts three hundred species of birds.

YELLOWSTONE

NATIONAL PARK IN WYOMING, IDAHO, AND MONTANA

WONDERS ABOUND

The first national park, Yellowstone has served as a model and inspiration for hundreds of similar preserves around the world. Out on its topographically gnarled landscape, approximately 290 waterfalls and the majority of the world's geysers reside. The park hosts seven native ungulate species, including the world's largest elk herd and the last free-ranging bison herd in the United States. Yellowstone is the only place in the lower forty-eight states where every species of native large mammal survives today.

For all its renowned wonders, Yellowstone's foremost role in human society may be as a testing ground for our relationship with nature. Established in 1872 to protect a unique collection of geothermal features and scenic wonders, the park's mission was soon expanded to include the conservation of its large populations of grazing animals, including elk, moose, bighorn sheep, mule and white-tailed deer, pronghorn, and bison. For almost 130 years, Yellowstone has continually demanded reinvention, either to better protect some element of the setting or to restore an element that was ignorantly neglected or mistreated.

In the park's first decades, activities such as publicly feeding bears, destroying wolves and other predators, fighting naturally caused fires, and pumping water from geothermal features for public bathing all reflected social attitudes of the day. But as values changed, and people began to understand how a wild ecosystem worked, Yellowstone was given the finer mission of providing the public with the increasingly rare opportunity to witness wild nature functioning freely.

In today's Yellowstone, despite three million visitors a year, the natural setting is remarkably robust. The famous geysers erupt on their own schedules, and the hot springs and mudpots burble and roil without interruption or plumbing. Each fall, thousands of ungulates migrate from high country meadows to valley winter ranges as the weather, the forage, and their own urges dictate. In a scene that has been aptly described as "the American Serengeti," the grizzly bears, black bears, mountain lions, coyotes, and

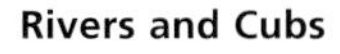

Rivers and Cubs

At Fishing Bridge, left, the Yellowstone River meanders north from Yellowstone Lake. Above: Grizzly cubs play.

Verdant Firescape

Wildflowers blossomed all over Yellowstone following the wildfires of 1988. Here, charred lodgepole trunks stand among heartleaf arnica.

wolves (finally restored in 1995) attend them through the seasons, culling the weaker animals with almost textbook precision.

The park's own history has become a memorable part of the Yellowstone experience. Century-old hotels, the Fort Yellowstone Historic District (from which the U.S. Cavalry patrolled the park from 1886 to 1918), and the Museum of the National Park Ranger provide glimpses of an earlier Yellowstone and how it was enjoyed by our ancestors. There is a growing awareness of the role that Native Americans played on this landscape. One of the most surprising lessons of Yellowstone history is that significantly less of the park's land is developed for roads and facilities now than was fifty or even eighty years ago.

Yellowstone's legacy and responsibility only grow richer and more complex. The long-protected hot springs are now yielding treasures unimagined by the park's founders—the entire industry of DNA fingerprinting, with all its medical, scientific, and criminological applications, was made possible by a tiny organism discovered in an obscure Yellowstone hot spring. More broadly, the park is recognized as the heart of a grander conservation challenge, the protection of the 12- to 18-million-acre Greater Yellowstone Ecosystem. Yellowstone's service to human society seems only to grow with age.

Cones and Terraces

Steam rises from stairstepping terraces of travertine, right, at Mammoth Hot Springs. Left: Liberty Cap, an extinct travertine hot-spring cone.

Trumpeters

A trumpeter swan spreads its wings on the Madison River. Weighing 20 to 30 pounds and with wingspans up to 8 feet, trumpeters are the largest waterfowl in North America.

Celebrity Plume

Old Faithful, the world's most famous geyser, erupts in midwinter. Recent earthquakes have lengthened the average time between its eruptions from seventy-four to eighty-eight minutes.

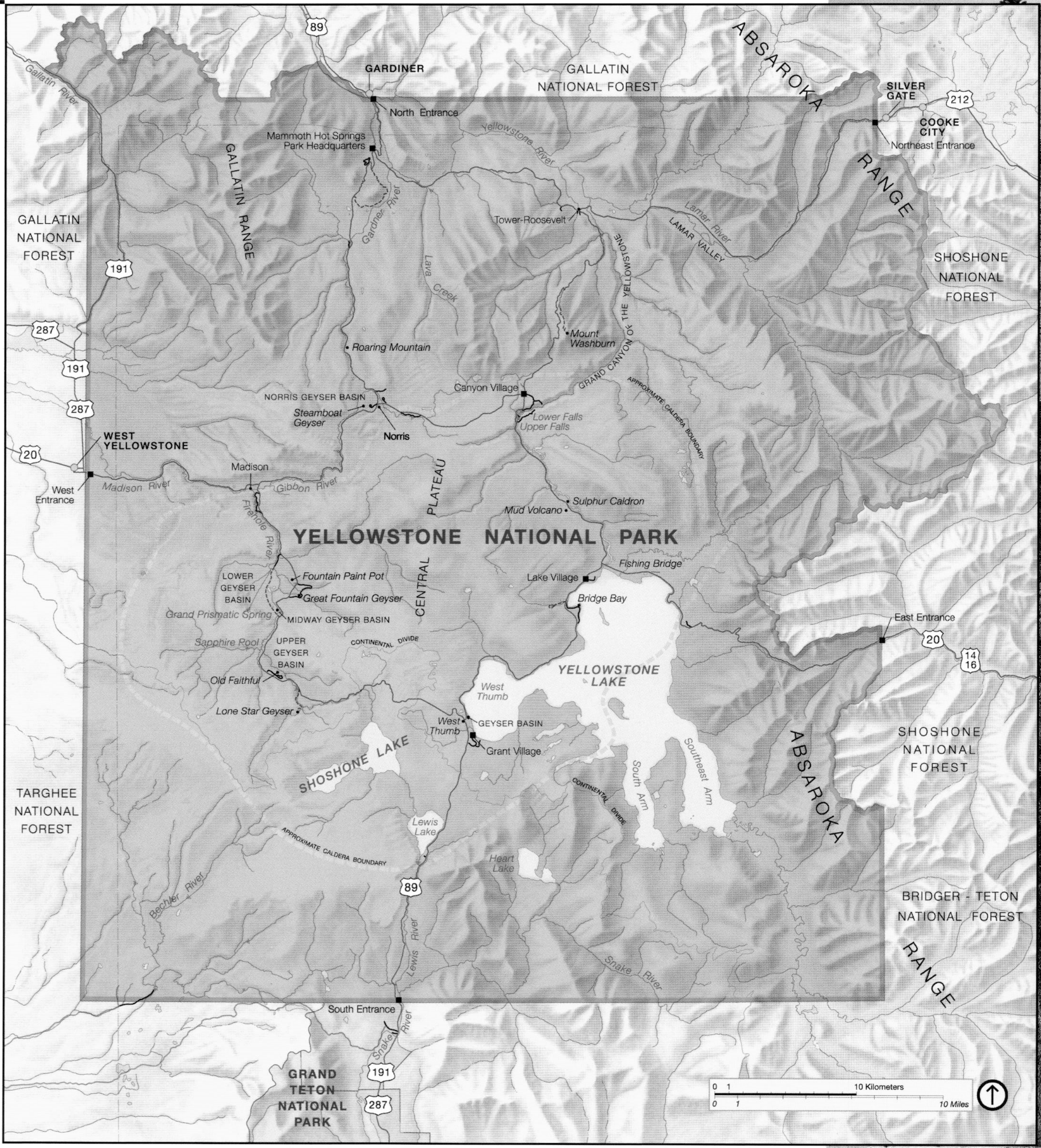

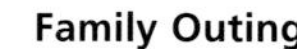

Prairie Giant

An animal of the grasslands, bison stand roughly 6 feet tall and sometimes weigh upward of 1,800 pounds.

Family Outing

A pair of elk cows and their calves step through one of Yellowstone's thermal areas.

Stunning Views

Lower Falls plummets 308 feet over a ledge of resistant rhyolite, below. Right: A light snow dusts boulders and a fallen juniper along the Gardner River near Mammoth Hot Springs.

YELLOWSTONE NATIONAL PARK

History Note: John Colter, a fur trapper who had crossed the continent with Lewis and Clark, may have seen Yellowstone's geothermal areas in 1807.

Flora: More than 1,700 native plant species, ranging from semiarid grasslands to alpine tundra; vast stands of lodgepole pine; vibrant wildflower meadows.

Fauna: Some fifty-nine species of mammals, including wolves, grizzly bears, black bears, bison, elk, deer, moose, bighorn sheep, and antelope; over three hundred species of birds, including golden and bald eagles, hummingbirds, songbirds, shorebirds, and spectacular waterfowl such as trumpeter swans and pelicans.

Visitor Tip: Though Yellowstone is notorious for its crowded summer roads, most of the park is deserted. Just stroll a mile or two off the pavement anywhere in the park and you're bound to find a pristine nook virtually unchanged since the last ice age.

Cloud of Steam

Clepsydra, a constantly erupting geyser, puffs its cloud of steam in the Fountain Paint Pot area.

WILDFIRES FOR WILD FORESTS

To casual observers, forest fires often seem to be purely destructive. Flames sweep across the land under a pall of smoke, leaving behind charred tree trunks, blackened slopes, and the lingering scent of soot in the air. What's left is all too often described as a "veritable moonscape," as if fire had so altered the place as to render it alien to life as we know it.

Blackwoods Pond
A secluded pond reflects a stand of charred lodgepole pines.

Actually, fire is creative as well as destructive. Endemic and beneficial to natural forest ecosystems, it is an integral force that has been part of the natural system of checks and balances in forests for as long as there have been trees.

Nothing Wasted
Rotting trees, such as this old snag, recycle as homes and food for insects.

Whether it burns in forests young or old, whether the flames hug the ground or leap through the canopy, fire cleanses, culls, regenerates, recycles, and sows the seeds for rebirth. Without it, forests become uniform, stagnant, and far more prone to diseases and parasites.

Fire moving across a forest floor cleans out dead fuels and enriches the soil by accelerating the release of nutrients bound up in accumulated litter. Flames in the canopy open the forest floor to sunlight and thus to a myriad of sun-loving wildflowers, grasses, and broad-leafed shrubs that provide forage for grazing animals such as elk, moose, and deer.

In 1988, Yellowstone experienced the most intense drought in its recorded history. The dryness of fallen branches was compared with that of kiln-dried lumber. The huge conflagrations of that summer burned 36 percent of the park, overwhelmed the efforts of 25,000 firefighters, grabbed headlines, yet did remarkably little damage.

The fires killed many lodgepole pines and other trees, but merely burned the tops of most plants, leaving the roots intact for regeneration. Growth of new plants and entire plant communities began almost immediately. The wildflower season of 1989 was one of the most vibrant and lush in living memory, and today millions of young lodgepole pines carpet the hills among the charred trunks of their elders.

Regeneration
Fire killed this stand of lodgepole pines and opened up the forest floor to sunlight, which nourishes a carpet of wildflowers, grasses, and shrubs.

A BRIEF HISTORY OF YELLOWSTONE

The land, rivers, lakes, and geothermal wonders of Yellowstone were known intimately by native peoples for thousands of years before Europeans set foot in what is now the park. Beginning at least 11,500 years ago, small groups of hunters roamed Yellowstone, hurling spears at bison, deer, and mountain sheep. Over time, people increased their use of the Yellowstone region, building pit houses and, later, erecting tepees, wickiups, and lean-tos.

Though many tribes made use of Yellowstone, the people most associated with the park are the Shoshone, who were living there in small bands when Euro-American trappers began exploring the region.

John Colter is believed to be the first trapper to see Yellowstone. A veteran of the Lewis and Clark Expedition, he walked through the region in 1807. Later, other trappers saw the park and told vivid tales of its geysers, mudpots, and hot springs. Few believed their stories until the 1860s, when the first reputable scientific expeditions began to chronicle Yellowstone's wonders.

In 1870, the Washburn Expedition spent a month in the park. In 1871, the geologist Ferdinand V. Hayden led a large, multifaceted expedition into Yellowstone. Hayden's report helped to convince Congress that Yellowstone's unique attributes deserved a unique form of protection. On March 1, 1872, Congress established Yellowstone as the world's first national park, granting it protection from commercial exploitation and explicitly calling for the retention of its wonders "in their natural condition."

Winter on the Firehole
Bison amble along the Firehole River, left. Following spread: Colorful bacteria ring the blue waters of Grand Prismatic Pool in the park's Midway Geyser Basin.

Rolling Meadows
Wildflowers blossom among the rolling meadows of the Yellowstone Valley.

Toward the end of the nineteenth century, railroads promoted the park, established an elegant carriage trade, and built luxury hotels for wealthy visitors at convenient intervals. Automobiles were first admitted to the park in 1915, but it wasn't until after World War II that cheap gas, cheap cars, and an improved national road system put Yellowstone National Park within reach of millions. And millions came.

Coyotes
Coyotes eat just about anything, from rodents to rabbits to roadkill.

Today, the park attracts three million visitors each year from all over the world.

THE POWER OF MOUNTAIN BUILDING

EVER SINCE WE first stood up on our hind legs and scanned a landscape, we have had to deal with mountains—often as obstacles, just as often as homes, and always as imposing and beckoning ramparts. We carried the emotional load of their brooding presence—some seventeenth-century theologians believed that a smooth-surfaced Earth fresh from creation was made jumbled and chaotic by man's sins—before modern science began to unravel the origins of mountains. It is no wonder that we still view rugged high country with more awe than analysis, and with more romance than reason. Science may have made mountains more understandable, but it has yet to diminish their magic.

Great Smokies
The Great Smoky Mountains are America's loftiest range east of the Black Hills.

Alaska Range
A rainbow forms over the Teklanika River Valley, north of the Alaska Range.

With luck, we will never stop viewing mountains in unrigorous but inspiring ways. But we have also become skilled at interpreting their biographies. We now understand them as the products of titanic forces operating in such a profusion of directions, and working with such a diversity of raw materials, that their very variety inspires more wonder.

THE BROKEN CRUST

For mountains are made in many ways, and unmade in many more. If, as one popular metaphor has it, the Earth's surface is its skin, then our planet is covered in scar tissue. No sooner is a wound healed than another is opened elsewhere. No sooner does a mountain range rise than it is undermined and, eventually, brought down. We have made mountains symbols of great permanence only because we have not yet watched them long enough.

Vast Wilderness
Denali National Park straddles the central and highest portion of the Alaska Range.

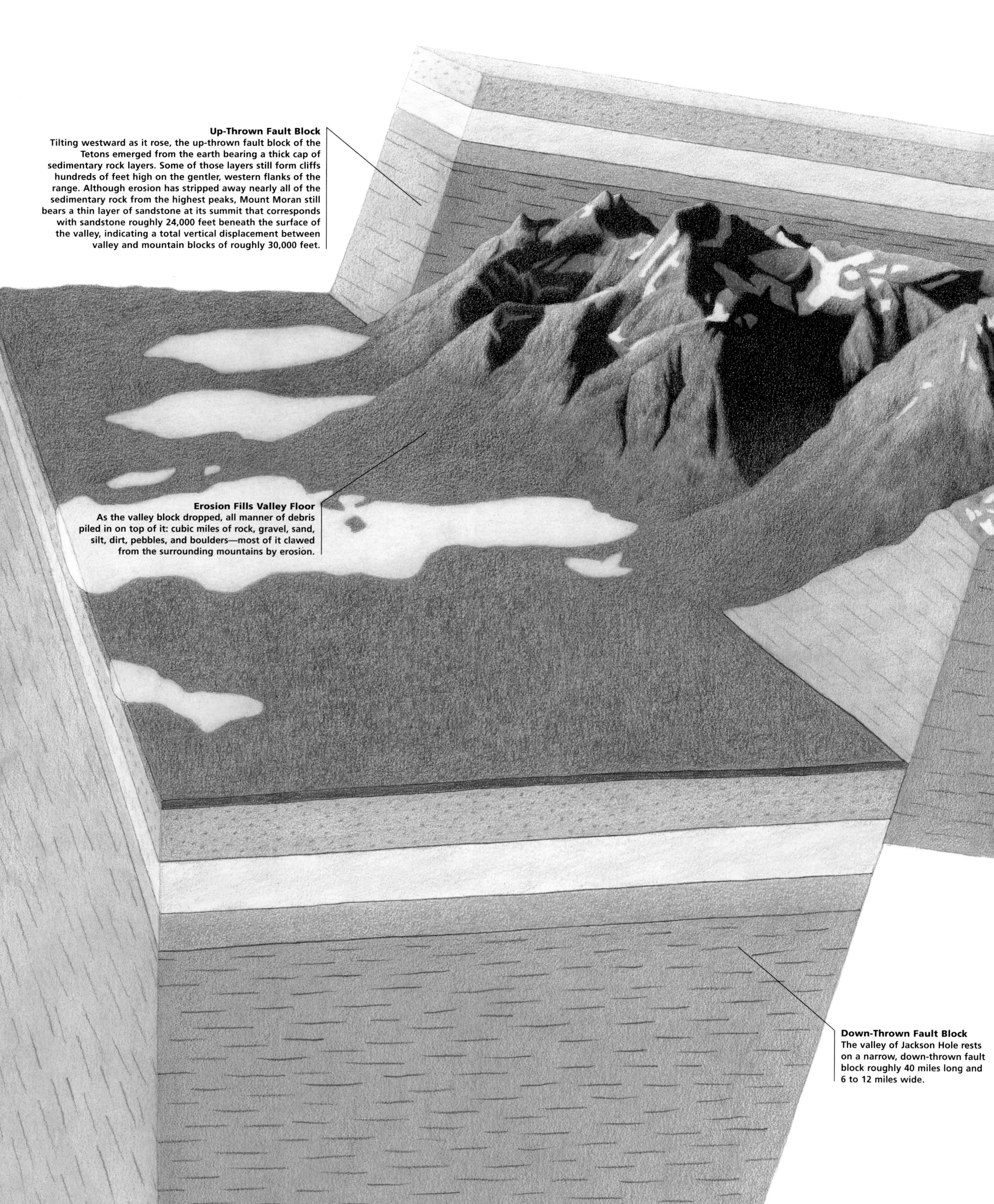
Up-Thrown Fault Block
Tilting westward as it rose, the up-thrown fault block of the Tetons emerged from the earth bearing a thick cap of sedimentary rock layers. Some of those layers still form cliffs hundreds of feet high on the gentler, western flanks of the range. Although erosion has stripped away nearly all of the sedimentary rock from the highest peaks, Mount Moran still bears a thin layer of sandstone at its summit that corresponds with sandstone roughly 24,000 feet beneath the surface of the valley, indicating a total vertical displacement between valley and mountain blocks of roughly 30,000 feet.
Erosion Fills Valley Floor
As the valley block dropped, all manner of debris piled in on top of it: cubic miles of rock, gravel, sand, silt, dirt, pebbles, and boulders—most of it clawed from the surrounding mountains by erosion.
Down-Thrown Fault Block
The valley of Jackson Hole rests on a narrow, down-thrown fault block roughly 40 miles long and 6 to 12 miles wide.

Erosion Carves the Tetons
As the mountain block rose, the forces of weathering and erosion attacked the upper layers of sedimentary rock, stripping the central peaks down to the Precambrian core of gneiss, schist, and granite. Then, during the past one million years, several glaciations carved the mountains into today's familiar shapes.

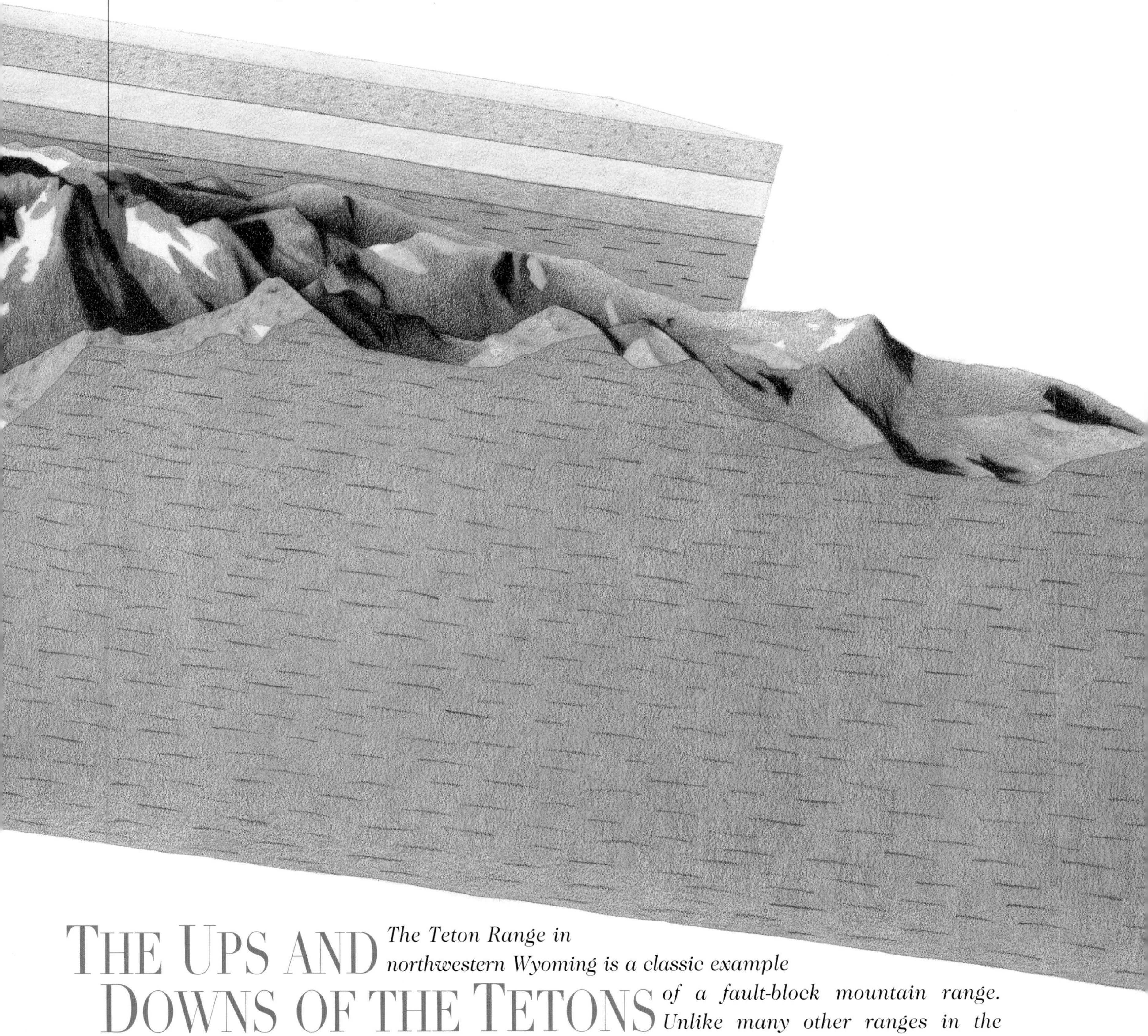

THE UPS AND DOWNS OF THE TETONS

The Teton Range in northwestern Wyoming is a classic example of a fault-block mountain range. Unlike many other ranges in the Rockies, which formed as the continent's crust was compressed, the Tetons formed as the crust was pulled apart. This strong tensional force produced a steep normal fault along what would become the eastern front of the range. The mountain block slid upward along the fault, and the valley block slid down.

Teton Range

Composed of ancient gneisses, schists, and granites as old as 2.75 billion years, the Tetons broke through the surface of the Earth within the past ten million years.

PUSHING AND SHOVING, FOLDING AND FAULTING

A RANGE OF FOLDS

During the mountain-building process, sedimentary rock layers are often severely deformed. Originally deposited horizontally, the layers develop unlikely bends, folds, warps, and even startling interruptions of the geologic sequence.

These arresting patterns—seen in cliff faces, in road cuts, and on geologic maps—are the result of intense compressional forces exerted by converging tectonic plates. Like a fender bender in extreme slow motion, the plates push against one another, crumpling the rock strata.

Bends and folds occur deep beneath the surface at pressures where solid rock becomes ductile and flows plastically. In near-surface environments, rocks are brittle and fracture under stress. creating faults. Sometimes, compressional forces raise ancient beds of rock along a fault and then shove or thrust them over much younger layers of rock. Just such an overthrust fault pushed Glacier National Park's mountain block 50 miles eastward.

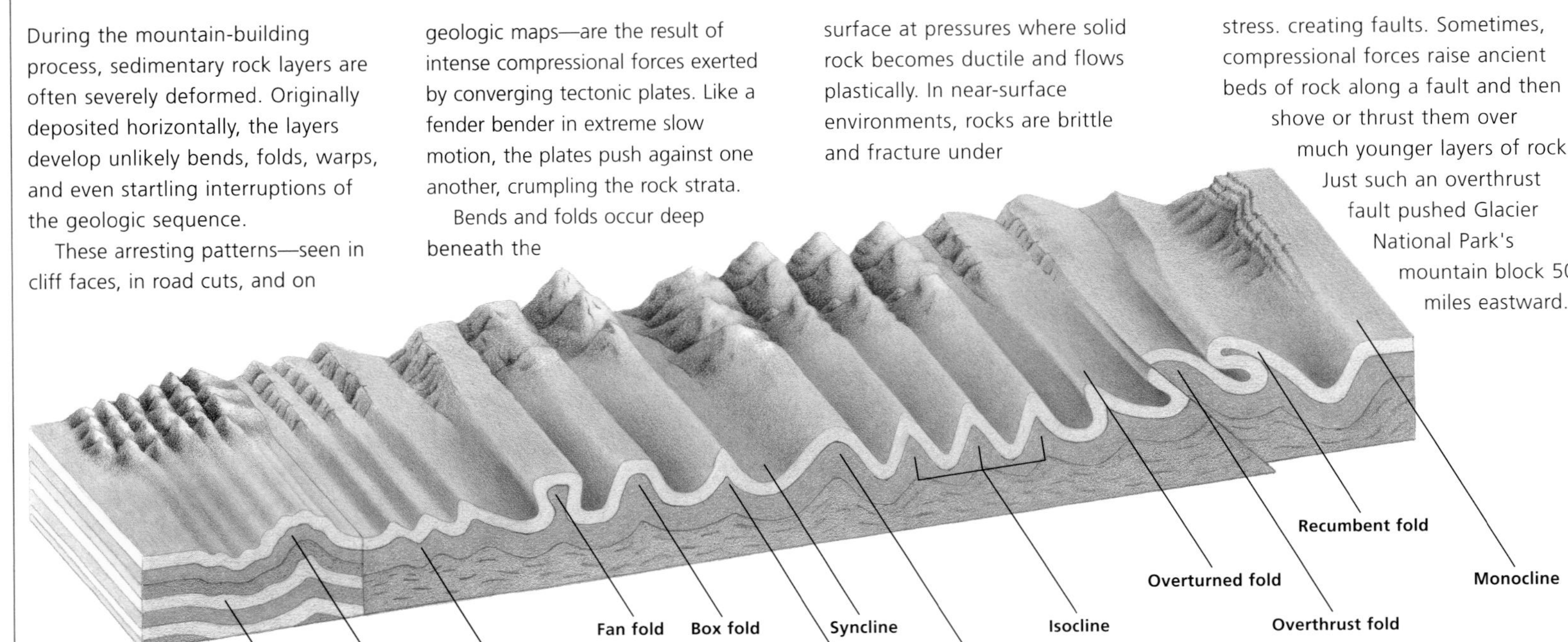

NORMAL FAULT

A normal fault is a fault in which the rock surface immediately above the fault (called the hanging wall) moves downward relative to the rock surface immediately below (called the footwall). Normal faults are associated with tensional forces.

REVERSE FAULT

In reverse faults, the hanging wall moves up relative to the footwall. Thrust faults work the same way, but at lower angles. Both are associated with compressional forces.

STRIKE-SLIP FAULT

A fault in which the two rock surfaces move laterally, or slide past one another horizontally, is called a strike-slip fault. California's San Andreas Fault is a large-scale strike-slip fault involving

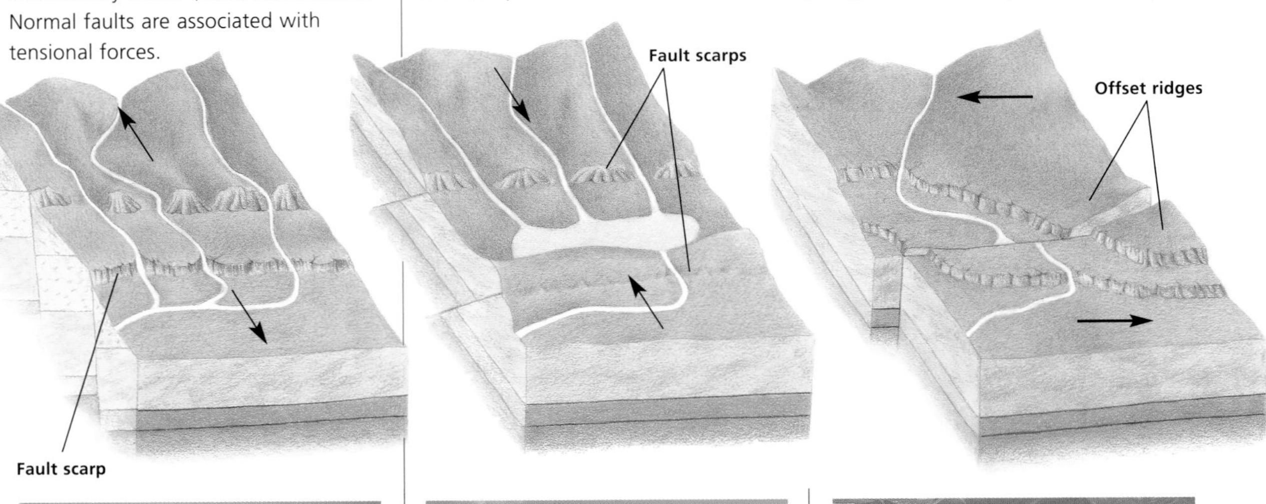

Finding Faults

The Teton Range, left image, rose along a 40-mile normal fault, while Glacier National Park's mountain block, center image, slid for roughly 50 miles along a thrust fault. In Denali, far right image, a major strike-slip fault runs the length of the park.

Rocky Mountains
The Rockies stand as roughly parallel ridges of folded and faulted sedimentary and volcanic rocks.

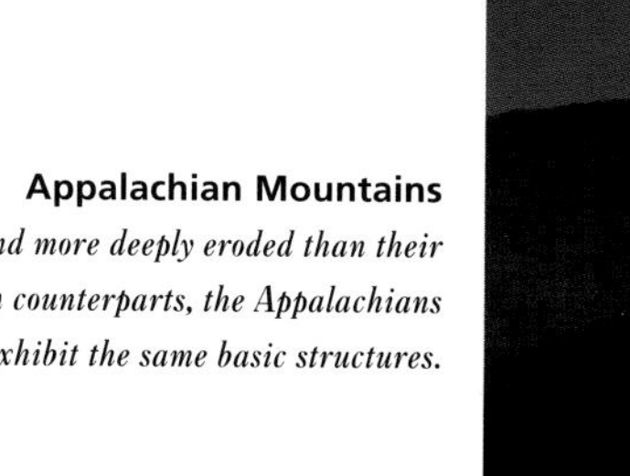

Appalachian Mountains
Older and more deeply eroded than their western counterparts, the Appalachians exhibit the same basic structures.

BUILDING THE ROCKIES

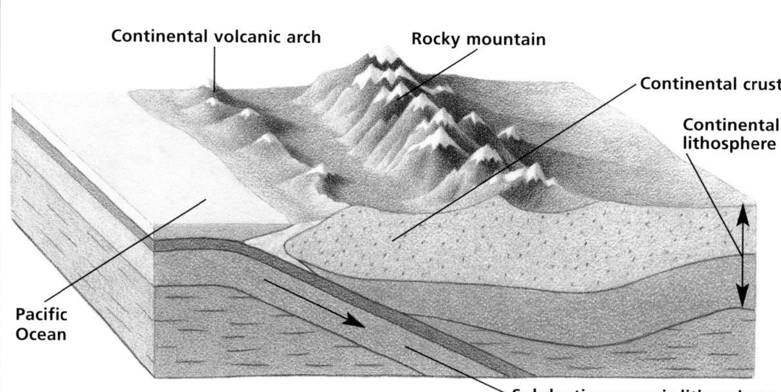

Broadly speaking, the Rocky Mountains were built by a tectonic plate collision between the North American continent and the floor of the Pacific Ocean. Starting roughly 200 million years ago, the continental plate began to move slowly westward, overriding the oceanic plate. Eventually, the continuing effects of this collision were felt throughout what is now the Rocky Mountain region, with most, but not all, of the mountain building occurring between sixty million and ninety million years ago.

In the northern Rockies, intense horizontal forces produced ranges of mountains composed of thick sequences of severely deformed sedimentary rock layers that were shoved eastward on low-angle thrust faults. These great blocks of folded rock jammed against one another from western Wyoming far north into Canada, thickened the continental crust, and rose against the sky.

The structure of the southern Rockies is quite different. There, the mountains were pushed upward almost vertically as part of a regional upwarping of the crust. Millions of years of erosion have stripped most of the overlying sedimentary strata, exposing the ancient igneous and metamorphic core of ranges from the Bighorns of Wyoming to the Sangre de Cristos of New Mexico.

BUILDING THE APPALACHIANS

Like the Rockies, the Appalachians resulted from a tectonic plate collision. Here, though, the convergence involved continental plates only, those of North America, Europe, and Africa. The mountain-building lasted for nearly 300 million years, involved several distinct episodes, and intensely metamorphosed and deformed the central core of the range.

The final episode occurred 250 million to 300 million years ago, when North America, Europe, and northern Africa were juxtaposed as part of the supercontinent of Pangaea. As these continental plates jammed against one another, masses of rock were shoved landward onto North America for distances up to 155 miles. Shallow-water sediments that had fringed North America were severely deformed, and show up today as the folded and faulted sandstones, limestones, and shales of the range's Valley and Ridge Province.

Erosion explains why the Appalachians appear smoother, rounder, and less imposing than the Rockies. Running water, the freeze-thaw cycle, weathering, and gravity have all simply had much more time to work on the Appalachians.

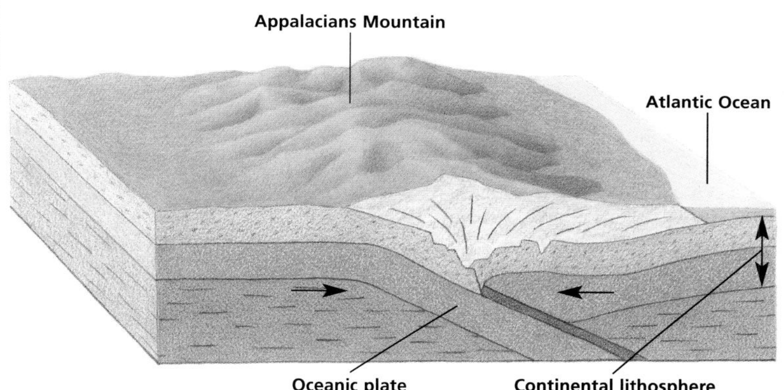

The High One
Mount McKinley, elevation 20,320 feet, is North America's highest mountain.

UPTHRUSTS AND FAULT LINES

The mountain ranges of North America swing in a wide arc down from Alaska and Canada, through the western United States and on to the highlands of northern Mexico. In southwestern Texas, they make a tentative link with eastern ranges on the other side of the Mississippi—ranges that form the rounded ridges of the Appalachians and complete the arc of highlands up into New England. This arc features a series of national parks with mountain ranges young and old, sharp and weathered, barren and lush. They are the continent's great open geology book.

Denali

Great Smoky Mountains

At the high northwestern end of the arc is North America's foremost mountain, Mount McKinley, in Denali National Park. It dominates the Alaska Range, a complex tangle of rock forms, some brought great distances across the landscape, others the result of local volcanic activity and erosion. The same collision and slithering around of tectonic plates that causes so much volcanic action down on the Alaska Peninsula powers the Denali fault system. Not only is there a clear record of many miles of horizonal slippage along the local faults but also massive uplift. The mountains rise raw and jagged, and glaciers and other erosive processes slowly trim them back down.

A Great Relief
Denali National Park's Mount McKinley has the greatest vertical relief of any mountain in the world.

The same forces put on very different performances, with strikingly different results, all along the arc of North American mountain ranges. Follow the mountains down—the length of the Alaska Range to the east, then south through the Canadian Rockies to Grand Teton National Park in Wyoming. Here, a single, straight fault permits the dramatic vertical slippage of mountains climbing up from a subsiding valley and gives us the sheer wall of the Teton Range and the flats and river benches of Jackson Hole. And here as well, the mountains are being eroded and glaciated back onto the valley floor.

To the south, in Colorado, the same forces build the mountains enclosed in Rocky Mountain National Park. Complex alternating episodes of uplift, erosion, and even oceanic sedimentation have built the current front range of mountains. These mountains emerged into the view of ancient eyes some seventy million years ago, rising from the sea that then covered Colorado.

The proportions of the forces in action were dramatically different in Guadalupe Mountains National Park in western Texas. An extended 250-million-year-old fossil limestone reef, uplifted in a block, is the centerpiece of a mountain range composed of the remains of ancient sea-bottom formations. Farther south along the Texas-Mexico border, at Big Bend National Park, the proportions are again different. Sedimentation from seas is still abundant, but volcanic influences are more evident.

Captain of the Cactuses
Guadalupe Mountain's El Capitan rises above a foreground of Claret Cup cactus.

Big Bend

Grand Teton

Guadalupe Mountains

Rocky Mountains

Shenandoah

The Big Bend country is a kind of symbolic junction of North America's two mountainous regions. From here, the American mountain arc swings east and then north in the worn and ecologically rich Appalachian Range. Great Smoky Mountain National Park in Tennessee and North Carolina and Shenandoah National Park in Virginia are built primarily of sedimentary rock, but their construction was different.

Appalachian Cascade
A waterfall spills over a cliff in Great Smoky Mountains National Park.

Unlike so many of the volcanic parks, where the mountains are the result of collision and subduction of tectonic plates, the Appalachians received their final boost as mountains from the opposite process. More than two hundred million years ago, all the continents had merged into the supercontinent now known as Pangaea. As Pangaea began to break up, the North American continental plate drifted free from the ancient African coast. The gradually expanding space between the two filled with an early form of the Atlantic Ocean.

As the continents widened the gap, the intervening crust stretched and thinned. Huge blocks of rock that had been compressed and weighed down during the time of Pangaea were freed and gradually buoyed up, rising to form the original southern Appalachians. As with all other planetary engineering, there was no break between creation and destruction. Erosion continues its patient work even today, perhaps at a faster pace than the buoying up of the mountains can compensate for.

None of this is done; none of these parks is a finished landscape. These are mountains built by the imperceptible bulging of the Earth's crust and then dismantled on the scale of each grain of silt washing down some untraveled gulley, into a lowland river, and finally to the sea, where it will await the next round of tectonic construction to return it to the heights.

Bighorn
As nimble on flat land as on steep, a bighorn ram steps behind a row of bull thistles.

BIG BEND

NATIONAL PARK IN TEXAS

RANGE OF SURPRISES

Big Bend is a landscape of boundaries and edges. The park is on the southeastern end of the basin-and-range province of the American West, and it contains northern portions of the Chihuahuan Desert. Many plants and animals end—or begin—their native ranges here, ranges that extend in all directions into different ecological worlds, blessing the park with twenty distinct plant communities. It is the only park to contain an entire contiguous mountain range.

John Steinbeck once complained that, "Once you are in Texas it seems to take forever to get out, and some people never make it." Not leaving is easier to understand once you've seen Big Bend. Texas folklorist J. Frank Dobie once described the Big Bend country as "the most Texan part of Texas."

As you may recall from history class—or from Davy Crockett movies—Texas entered the Union differently than the rest of the states. One effect of being a republic before becoming a state was that there is essentially no federal land in Texas. This meant that it was just that much harder to dedicate any large piece of land, no matter how deserving, as a national park. Considering that (and the state's traditional unwillingness to establish such reserves), the creation of Big Bend National Park in 1944 was a heroic achievement.

But it is, admittedly, not necessarily a place you take to at first glance, especially if you are from someplace green, or if your idea of desert is some postcard-colorful southwestern park. At midday in a Big Bend summer, when the temperature of the ground may reach 180 degrees, it would be especially easy to disregard it as "just a desert." Don't fall for that, here of all places. Deserts are harder work to enjoy at first, but they are correspondingly more rewarding when you try. As historian-naturalist Dan Flores has put it, "You gotta love the desert. Ten billion creosote bushes can't be wrong."

And the desert is only one of three remarkable worlds here. There is also the river, with its own distinct, water-loving plant and animal communities, and its long history as a

Chisos Mountains
The jagged crest of the Chisos Mountains, below, cuts across the heart of Big Bend National Park in southwest Texas. Above: Ringtails prey upon small rodents in the park's pinyon-juniper woodlands.

Prickly Pear

Prickly pear cactus blossoms in Big Bend's arid wilderness, right. Below: Like the rest of the Chisos Mountains, Casa Grande Peak is composed of igneous rocks emplaced within the Earth's crust forty to sixty million years ago.

human homeland, a highway, a boundary, and a magical canyon wilderness. There are the mountains, the Chisos, which are haunted by white-tailed and mule deer, black bears, mountain lions, ringtails, and many smaller predators and their prey.

Any one of the three—desert, river, mountains—would be enough to justify the trip, but with their extraordinary assortment of habitats, they constitute a huge biological surprise. It will shock no one that there are more varieties of cactus (seventy or so) here than in any other park. But more bird species (upwards of four hundred) visit or live here than in any other park. There are at least sixty-seven native species of reptiles and amphibians (the Everglades, which most people think of as Creepy-Crawly Central, has sixty-six) and twenty species of bats. The place is quite literally crawling with life. Much of it, like the javelina, the roadrunner, and the black-tailed jackrabbit, can instantly charm you out of your preference for other landscapes.

Rio Grande Canyons

The Rio Grande carves three major limestone canyons in Big Bend. The Rock Slide lies in Santa Elena Canyon.

Smooth Sailing

The smooth surface of the Rio Grande bends placidly beneath high limestone walls along the southern perimeter of the park, left. Below: The Chisos Mountain range is entirely contained within Big Bend National Park.

Mostly Desert

Chihuahuan Desert vegetation—yuccas, agaves, lechuguillas, cactuses, and creosote bushes—covers about 80 percent of the park, surrounding the mountain core like a desert sea.

Javelinas

Collared peccaries, known locally by their Spanish name, javelinas, are commonly seen at dawn and dusk in Chisos Basin and around Panther Junction and Rio Grande Village.

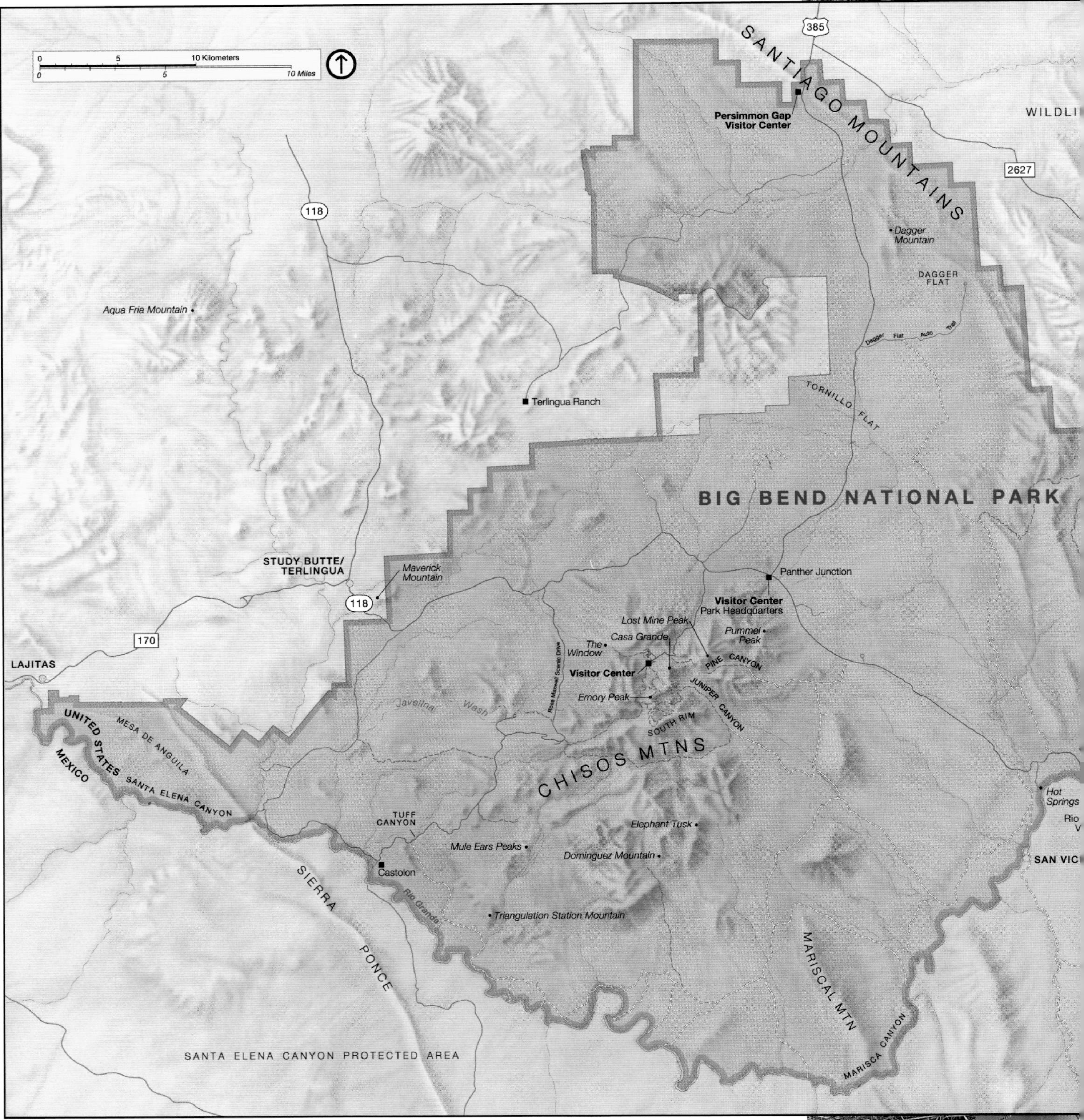

Night Eyes

Mountain lions, whose retinas contain more rods than cones, have excellent night vision. In Big Bend they prey on deer, mice, rabbits, and ground squirrels.

Strawberry Cactus

Magenta blossoms of the strawberry cactus bloom amid a bristling nest of spines. A common Chihuahuan plant, the cactus is named for its sweet, fleshy fruits.

Oak Creek Cliffs

Big Bend National Park's Oak Creek slips over a low drop-off and gathers in a copper-colored pool between sinuous cliffs.

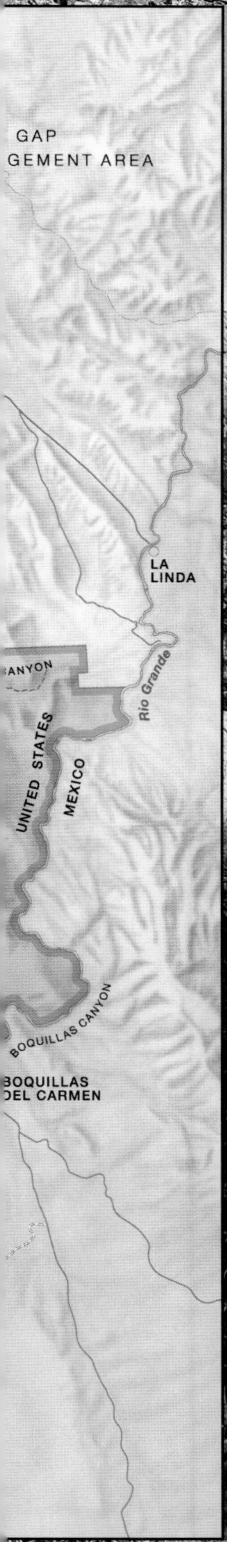

BIG BEND NATIONAL PARK

History Note: At the close of the ice age ten thousand years ago, Big Bend was a temperate, well-watered region where nomads hunted elephants, camels, and bison.

Flora: Mostly desert, but abrupt elevation changes create diverse habitats where more than one thousand flowering plants find their niches. Cactuses, desert shrubs, century plants, yucca, pinyon-juniper woodlands, and oak thickets abound.

Fauna: Seventy-five mammals, including coyotes, mule deer, white-tailed deer, mountain lions, javelinas, and jackrabbits; roughly 450 species of birds—more than any other national park.

Visitor Tip: Plan a stargazing dip at Hot Springs, near Rio Grande Village. Remote from city lights, Big Bend lies beneath one of the most vivid night skies in the country.

Balancing Act

In addition to a fabulous array of vegetation, Big Bend National Park brags some interesting rock formations in the park's Grape Vine Hills area.

Mercury Mines

An abandoned ore cart recalls the 1890–1940 mining era of Big Bend, when mercury, or quicksilver, was extracted from the mineral cinnabar.

Snow-white Sheep

A Dall sheep, left, rests on a rocky ledge. Denali National Park straddles the central and highest portion of the 600-mile Alaska Range, below, which was built up along a major fault zone that slices across southern Alaska.

DENALI

NATIONAL PARK AND PRESERVE IN ALASKA

PARAMOUNT PEAK

Still called its original Athabaskan name, Denali, by many locals, Mount McKinley hangs above the park more like a permanent cloud than an extension of the earth. Denali National Park and Preserve protects more than six million acres of wild interior Alaska. The south side of the reserve is dominated by the mountain and its acolyte peaks in the Alaska Range, while to the north the park includes a vast range of taiga and tundra lands, home to a wealth of animal life.

The section of the Alaska Range containing Mount McKinley would deserve protection merely for the magnificence of its other peaks, ranging between 12,000 and 17,000 feet in elevation. But those peaks are dwarfed and forgotten in the presence of Mount McKinley, a pile of rock so massive that its own local gravity field was strong enough to defeat standard surveying instruments. Its true height, 20,320 feet, was eventually determined using satellite technology. Mount McKinley's vertical relief of 18,000 feet makes it the tallest mountain in the world when measured from base to summit.

And yet the park was not created because of the mountain. Unlike Yellowstone, which was created to protect geological features and only later made a wildlife sanctuary, Denali started out as a game refuge and grew into a mountain refuge. With the expansion of the park in 1980, it also became far better able to protect the wildlife of concern to the founders, especially the winter ranges and calving grounds of migrating caribou herds.

The park, like some other Alaskan parks, also represents an important and controversial step in the evolution of the very idea of national parks—subsistence hunting. The enlargement legislation of 1980 allowed for traditional users, both native and non-native, to continue their use of wildlife in the expansion, and also accommodates sport hunting and other activities on some portions of the expansion lands. The integration of human predation into the park scene has been a fascinating new twist in the saga of Alaskan park management.

Winter Resident
Well-adapted to Denali's long winters, ptarmigans, left, turn pure white in late autumn. Above: The Tokasha Mountains.

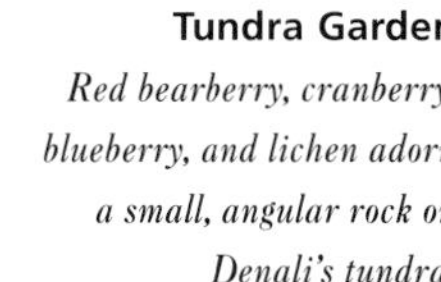

Tundra Garden
Red bearberry, cranberry, blueberry, and lichen adorn a small, angular rock on Denali's tundra.

Denali has also pioneered an impressively nonintrusive style of visitor experience. The park's one major road, a mostly unpaved 90-mile route from the entrance on the east side to a small development at Kantishna in the center of the park, is open for private vehicles only for the first 15 paved miles. From there, traffic is limited to a generous system of shuttle buses that cruise through mile after mile of wild Alaska. Black spruce bogs, braided glacier streams, sparse taiga forests of spruce, aspen, and birch, and stretches of cushiony tundra roll by.

Rock and Snow

Windblown snow fills gullies and ravines along the stony flanks of the Alaska Range in Denali National Park.

As the bus moves along, hikers climb off, starting more personalized excursions; others climb on, full of what they've just seen. Eager bus passengers call out each new wildlife sighting—a dozen Dall sheep shining from a high slope, a herd of caribou drifting across a tundra flat, a moose half-hidden in the willows, a family of grizzly bears shuffling along a gravel bar. It is wild Alaska's great treasure hunt, and someone is always looking farther off, waiting for a gap in the foothills to reveal the grand prize, Denali itself, honoring us with a glimpse of its broad white flanks through the infamously fickle cloud cover that shrouds it for weeks on end.

The High One

Mount McKinley, below and right, rises to 20,320 feet from a base of 2,000 feet—more vertical relief than any mountain in the world. The Athabascans named it Denali, meaning the "High One."

Alaska Range

A shimmering Denali river streams down from the Alaska Range, which forms a drainage divide between the coastal lowlands and the Alaskan interior.

Spectacular Skies

The northern lights or aurora borealis, a nighttime display caused by magnetic disturbances from the sun, blaze over a high valley in the Alaska Range.

DENALI NATIONAL PARK AND PRESERVE

History Note: The north peak of Mount McKinley, the true summit, was reached for the first time in 1913 by three American climbers. They included Harry Karstens, the park's first superintendent.

Flora: More than 650 species of flowering plants in wet and dry tundra and in taiga forests, where black and white spruce intermingle with poplar, aspen, larch, and birch; small shrubs, including many types of berry bushes.

Fauna: Dall sheep, caribou, grizzly bears, gray wolves, moose, and thirty-two other mammals; 159 species of birds, including gyrfalcons, hawk owls, goshawks, golden eagles, and arctic terns.

Visitor Tip: Though most of the park's road is closed to private motorized vehicles, you can mountain bike the length of it undisturbed by passing cars.

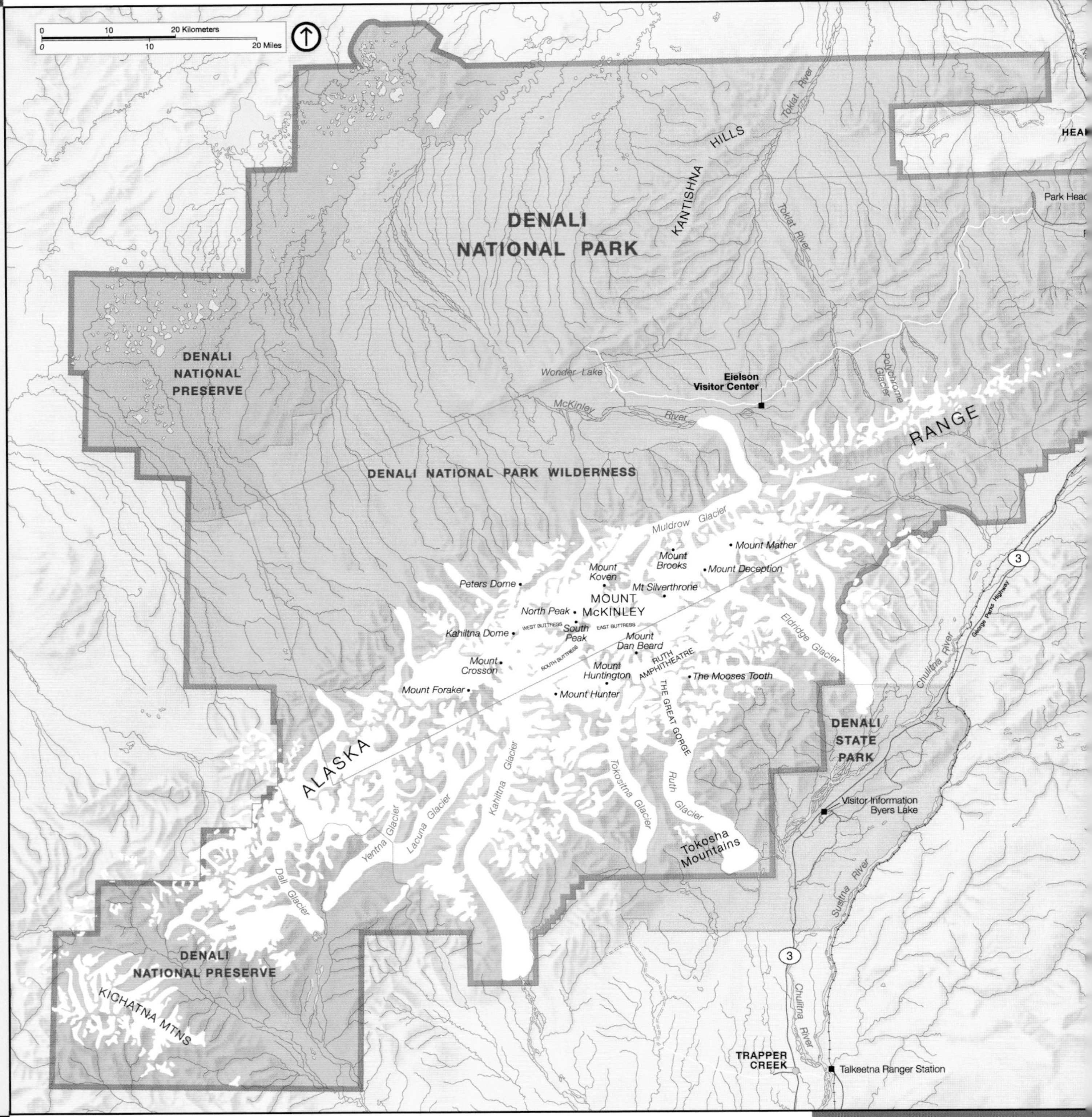

0 10 20 Kilometers
0 10 20 Miles
DENALI NATIONAL PARK
KANTISHNA HILLS
Toklat River
Park Head
DENALI NATIONAL PRESERVE
Wonder Lake
McKinley River
Eielson Visitor Center
Polychrome Glacier
RANGE
DENALI NATIONAL PARK WILDERNESS
Muldrow Glacier
Mount Mather
Mount Brooks
Mount Deception
Mount Koven
Peters Dome
Mt Silverthrone
MOUNT McKINLEY
North Peak
WEST BUTTRESS
South Peak
EAST BUTTRESS
Kahiltna Dome
Mount Dan Beard
Eldridge Glacier
Mount Crosson
SOUTH BUTTRESS
RUTH AMPHITHEATRE
Mount Huntington
The Mooses Tooth
Mount Foraker
Mount Hunter
THE GREAT GORGE
Chulitna River
George Parks Highway
3
DENALI STATE PARK
ALASKA
Yentna Glacier
Lacuna Glacier
Kahiltna Glacier
Tokositna Glacier
Ruth Glacier
Visitor Information Byers Lake
Tokosha Mountains
Dall Glacier
Susitna River
DENALI NATIONAL PRESERVE
KICHATNA MTNS
TRAPPER CREEK
Talkeetna Ranger Station

Mushing

Denali National Park's rangers still rely on dogsleds to carry them around parts of the park's six million acres when making winter patrols.

Autumn Landscape

Thickets of willow and berry bushes stretch across the tundra at the foot of the Alaska Range. Cow moose take their calves to feed on willows in the spring.

Caribou Antlers

Caribou, right, of both sexes grow spectacular racks of antlers, the only members of the deer family to do so. Below: Dawn breaks near the Teklanika River.

Gray Wolves

Seldom seen, Denali's gray wolves roam territory of 200 to 600 square miles. They hunt in packs for moose, caribou, and Dall sheep; individually for hares, beaver, and birds.

Fishing Birds

A bald eagle sweeps over the water in search of fish, left. Pelicans on the Snake River, below, glide across the reflection of Mount Moran, which stands nearly 6,000 feet above the Jackson Hole valley.

GRAND TETON

NATIONAL PARK IN WYOMING

CITADELS OF STONE

The peaks of the Teton Range form a dark, jagged rampart along the west side of the valley known as Jackson Hole. Centered on the Teton Fault that divides them, the mountains have climbed and the valley dropped more than 4 miles over the last thirteen million years. But erosion works to neutralize the opposing motions, eating away at the mountains and hauling them out onto the valley floor below. Today, the mountains are little more than a mile ahead of the valley in this struggle.

They are the mountains of our childhood—storybook-perfect peaks that zigzag across crayoned horizons and frame the background in the old Western films many of us grew up with. They are also the mountains of the modern West's childhood, beacons to the first Euro-Americans struggling to find their way through the jumbled ranges of what would become northwestern Wyoming. And they are in fact mountains in their own childhood, among the youngest of all American mountain ranges.

They are so flawless, so photogenic, so accessible to our easy admiration and use (in cigarette billboards, amateur paintings, magazine covers, and travel posters beyond counting), that they have become a kind of clichéd idea of a landscape, rather the way Shakespeare's brilliance was dulled by centuries of unattributed, secondhand overuse. But, as with Shakespeare, the original has kept its magic. When you stand at the foot of the peaks, hike the glacial troughs between them, or climb onto their shoulders, all sense of weary stereotype fades.

When Grand Teton National Park was established, in 1929, it contained only the Teton Range and the six glacial lakes at the foot of the mountains. Because of local resistance to protecting additional lands, it was twenty-one years later before the park was enlarged to include much of the valley of Jackson Hole. But the valley had to be included; it is essential to the story of how this unforgettable landscape came to be.

Much of that story is in human history. Archaeological investigations reveal evidence of

The Grand

The Grand Teton, left, elevation 13,770 feet, noses above its companion summits at the scenic center of the Teton Range, below. The young mountains expose gneisses 2.8 billion years old. Above: A bull moose bellows.

thousands of years of human activity here, hunting, fishing, and otherwise making homes among the plenty of the summer meadows. Jackson Hole was routinely visited by the famed mountain men of the trapper era, followed by the prospectors, and, at about the time of the Civil War, the first official government parties—"exploring" a land known and crisscrossed by previous visitors for millennia.

Canyon and Basin
A rocky slope of wildflowers adorns the glacially carved floor of Cascade Canyon in Grand Teton National Park.

What they saw is still there. Thousands of elk make long seasonal migrations through their ancestral ranges. Bison and pronghorn dot the flatlands of the valley floor. Moose have achieved informal mascot status among locals, who have attached this unlikely animal's name and image to a happy array of businesses and products.

Despite the airport, the ranches, and even the pricey suburban sprawl nearby, there is a prevailing sense of authenticity to the landscape. Perhaps most satisfying, from both the historical and an ecological perspective, is that the great predators of the mountain-man days—grizzly bears, mountain lions, and wolves—are returning. These animals bring a mysterious power to this park's message—at least in a few places older, wilder forces of nature still endure and are still honored for what they bring to human imagination.

Tough Row to Hoe
An old barn glows at the foot of the Tetons, below. Harsh winters and porous soils made cattle ranching difficult, so many of the valley's settlers turned instead to dude ranching. Right: The Alaska Basin retains layers of sedimentary rock that have eroded from the Tetons' central peaks.

Lush Crush

A vibrant cluster of lupine blossoms in a meadow near Jenny Lake. Grand Teton National Park supports a great diversity of wildflowers and other plants.

A Gentler Side

The central peaks of the Tetons jut above the gentler slopes of the range's west side. The more famous eastern face of the Tetons lacks foothills, because it stands along an active fault zone.

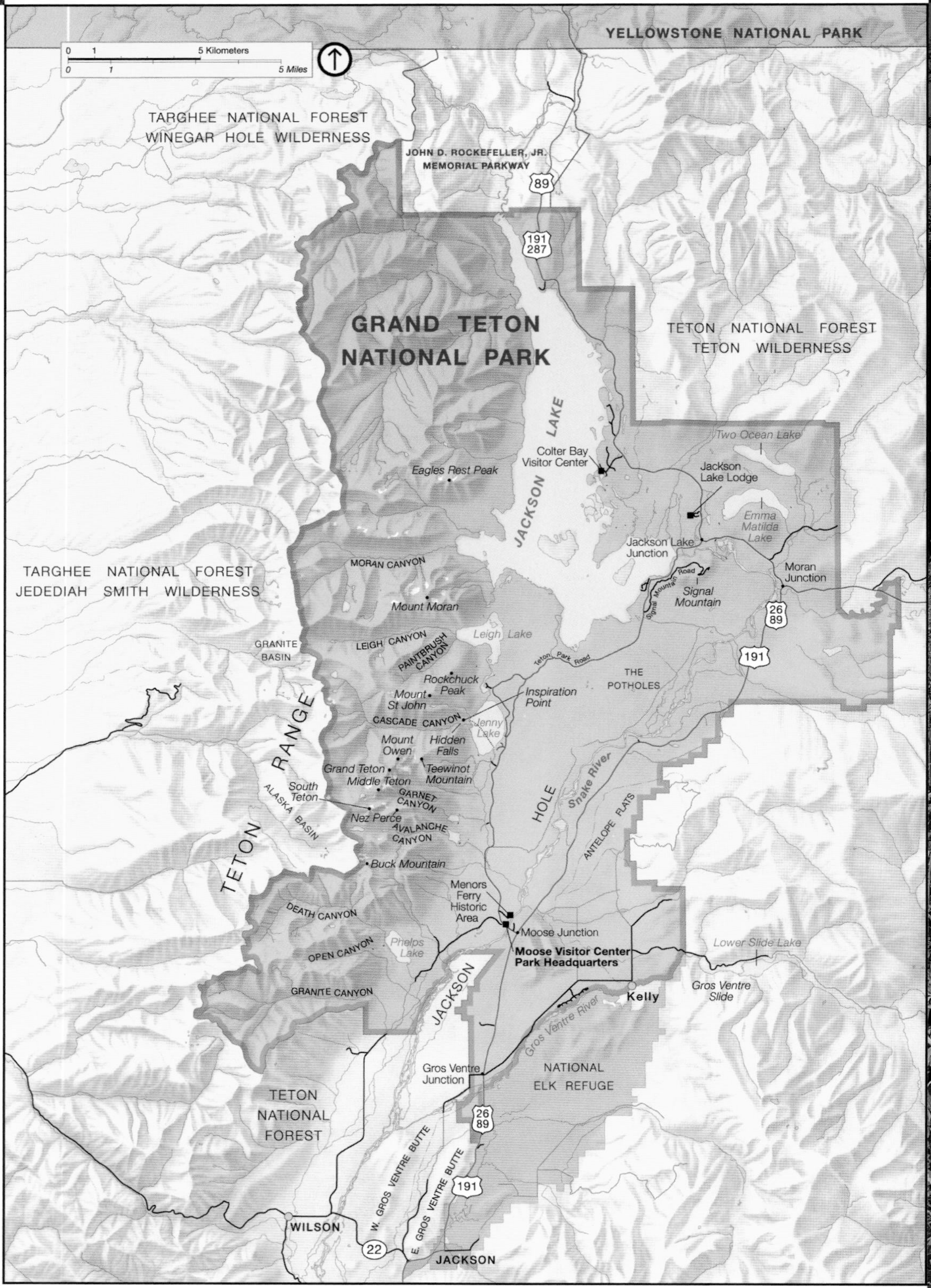

Pronghorn

Known locally as antelope, or goats, pronghorn browse among the sagebrush flats on the floor of the Jackson Hole valley.

Snake-Eyed View

The Snake River carves a narrow, meandering trough across much of the valley floor and occasionally opens up spectacular vistas of the central Teton peaks.

Mirrors for the Peaks
Several glacially formed lakes lie along the base of the Tetons. The biggest, Jackson Lake, was enlarged by a dam across the Snake River.

GRAND TETON NATIONAL PARK

History Note: Legendary mountain man Jedediah Smith named the valley of Jackson Hole after his trapping partner, David Jackson, who dearly loved the place.

Flora: Sagebrush flats, pockets of prairie grasses and wildflowers, wetlands, lodgepole forests, aspen groves, subalpine forests of Engelmann spruce and subalpine fir, subalpine and alpine wildflower meadows.

Fauna: Moose, elk, deer, pronghorn, bison, river otters, black bears, grizzlies, cougars, wolverines, and nearly three hundred species of birds, including peregrine falcons, bald eagles, and trumpeter swans.

Visitor Tip: Don't miss the drive up Signal Mountain, which offers a comprehensive vista of the Tetons, Jackson Lake, the valley, and its surrounding mountain ranges.

Carpet of Flowers
Wildflowers such as sticky geranium, lupine, and Indian paintbrush blanket a meadow bordering Jackson Lake, left.

Prairie Plants
Prairie wildflowers, right, thrive on the floor of the valley, where porous soils confront plants with semiarid conditions similar to those found on the Great Plains.

JACKSON HOLE: FROM FURS TO DUDES

The broad, flat-floored valley known as Jackson Hole got its name during the Rocky Mountain fur-trade era of 1824–40. To the trappers who followed the mountain streams looking for beaver, the term "hole" referred to a deep valley completely encircled by mountains. No wonder they applied the term to this spectacular valley, in which the Tetons form a 6,000-foot wall on the west. They added "Jackson" for David Jackson, a fur-trade leader who had a special fondness for the place.

Jackson, of course, was by no means the first to see the valley. Native Americans had used it as a seasonal hunting ground for thousands of years, and John Colter had wandered through it during his 1807 reconnaissance of the Yellowstone country. Many other trappers followed, including such legends as Jim Bridger, William Sublette, and Jedediah Smith.

Settlement began in the late nineteenth century, when several small but lively communities sprang up in the valley: Wilson, Jackson, Kelly, and Moose. Characters as colorful as the landscape included Bill Menor, who ran a general store and ferryboat operation along the Snake River; and Ed Trafton, who made history in 1914 by going up to Yellowstone Park and robbing fifteen stagecoaches full of tourists in less than an hour.

Chilly Vista
The Snake River bends through Jackson Hole as dawn breaks across the wintry crest of the Tetons.

Trafton wasn't the first resident to try his hand at something new. Ranching in Jackson Hole was tough, due to porous soils and long,

Beavers
Beavers, America's largest rodents, paddle among the park's lakes, ponds, and streams.

harsh winters. Early on, locals began to cater to a growing clientele of visitors, or "dudes" as they were called. These outsiders, generally well-heeled, came to experience the valley's natural setting and to tour the new national park, Grand Teton, established in 1929.

Tourism continued to grow in Jackson Hole until it formed the single largest

First Light
The Grand Tetons' summit stands 7,000 feet above the water in the valley below.

industry in the valley. Today, nearly everyone's income is linked in some way to what many locals still call "the visitor trade."

Gristmill

Many of the park's historic structures, including this old gristmill, left, stand in the historic enclave of Cades Cove. Shot Beech Ridge, below, overlooks Deep Creek Valley in the Great Smoky Mountains.

GREAT

GREAT SMOKY MOUNTAINS NATIONAL PARK

History Note: During the nineteenth century, the farming community of Cades Cove was also a center for regional music performance and training. Its Sacred Harp singing school drew hundreds of outsiders.

Flora: Richest biodiversity in temperate North America, with five major forest types, 130 species of trees, 1,500 species of flowering plants, and four thousand species of other plants.

Fauna: Sixty-five mammals, including white-tailed deer, opossums, foxes, and black bears; more than 230 species of birds; snakes, turtles, lizards, skinks, frogs, and thirty-one species of salamanders, including one that can grow 2½ feet long.

Visitor Tip: Take the spur road to Clingmans Dome and hike a half mile to the summit of Tennessee's highest peak, elevation 6,643 feet.

A Lofty Range

The Little Pigeon River tumbles through forested slopes on the north flank of the Great Smokies.

SMOKY MOUNTAINS

NATIONAL PARK IN NORTH CAROLINA AND TENNESSEE

STORIED RIDGES

Located in the southern end of the 2,000-mile-long Appalachians, Great Smoky Mountains National Park is a geologically ancient land. The original mountains here were long ago flattened by erosion. It is still rugged country, but thanks to a climate of rare hospitality, it is also blessed almost beyond measure with life. Even without the topographic extremes required to give some other parks their biodiversity, Great Smoky Mountains is the hands-down winner in the species abundance contest.

Long before there were "mountain men," there were "mountain people," and the Appalachians were their home. For many years, American society caricatured and—perhaps worse—pitied them for the perceived deprivations they suffered and the seemingly narrow lives they led. There is still a lingering bias against anyone with a twangy accent and a rural mountain heritage, but smart people know better. Humans are just as able to find good homes and good lives in the mountains as anywhere else.

The Great Smoky Mountains demonstrate that not only humans but also life in general can thrive, almost beyond belief, in the mountains. Strange as it may seem in a nation with so many parks of greater topographical and climatic variability, this half-million-acre reserve is world-famous as the most richly diverse of all.

It has to do with the "smoke" in Great Smoky Mountains, which isn't really smoke, but is without question great. Moisture, generously provided by the Gulf of Mexico, combines with terpene vapors given off by the park's forests to lay a diffuse "smoky" haze over the landscape and to help ensure ideal growing conditions for everything beneath. A recently initiated "All Taxa Biodiversity Inventory" is to identify all known forms of life in the park—from fungus to insects to plants to birds and mammals. It will probably tally at least one hundred thousand species.

That is an amazing number. There are more tree species in this park—about 130—than in all of northern Europe. There are already more than 5,000 other known plant species, 1,500 of

Sights and Sounds
Giving the Smoky Mountains their descriptive name, moist air settles as a "smoky" haze in Cades Cove, above. In the spring, male ruffed grouse, left, can be heard drumming for mates.

Damp Understory
A spray of wildflowers embellishes the understory of a Great Smoky forest. Abundant moisture from the Gulf of Mexico supports the forests within the park.

which flower (Smokies regulars time their visits to coincide with their preferred flower shows). There are eighty-two reptiles and amphibians, including thirty-one salamanders (making it a kind of salamander capital of the world). It is a fabulous, intensely packed zoological treasure-house.

Stony Bed
The stony bed of a dry creek heads off through the forest near Greenbrier in Great Smoky Mountains National Park.

But let's pretend otherwise for a minute. Let's pretend it is so boring that biologists driving through the area fall asleep at the wheel. Even then, we would still need to set it aside, as a monument to the beauty, misery, and dreams of human culture.

For a thousand years, the Cherokee lived here. Then, in the early 1800s, Euro-American settlers wanted more land, so in 1832, thousands of the Cherokee were sent on a brutal forced march, the infamous Trail of Tears, to reservation lands in Arkansas and Oklahoma. Those who stayed settled on a reservation, where they have flourished.

Weathered Trunks
The trunk of an old white pine tree weathers in the depths of a Great Smokies pine-oak forest.

The Euro-American mountaineers who displaced them very quickly adapted to life here, nurturing a regional subculture of their own. Ironically, they, too, eventually had their turn at displacement—when the park was established in 1934. The park service energetically interprets these past human residents and their complex heritage in this mountain landscape.

Diversity of Trees
Great Smoky National Park's forests support 130 species of trees, including maples that turn yellow and gold in the fall.

Wildflowers

Hundreds of species of wildflowers such as lance-leaved coreopsis blossom throughout the park during spring and summer.

Smoky Formula

The characteristic haze of the Smoky Mountains softens a forest near Newfound Gap. The haze is a combination of mist, wisps of fog, and vapors from resins and plants.

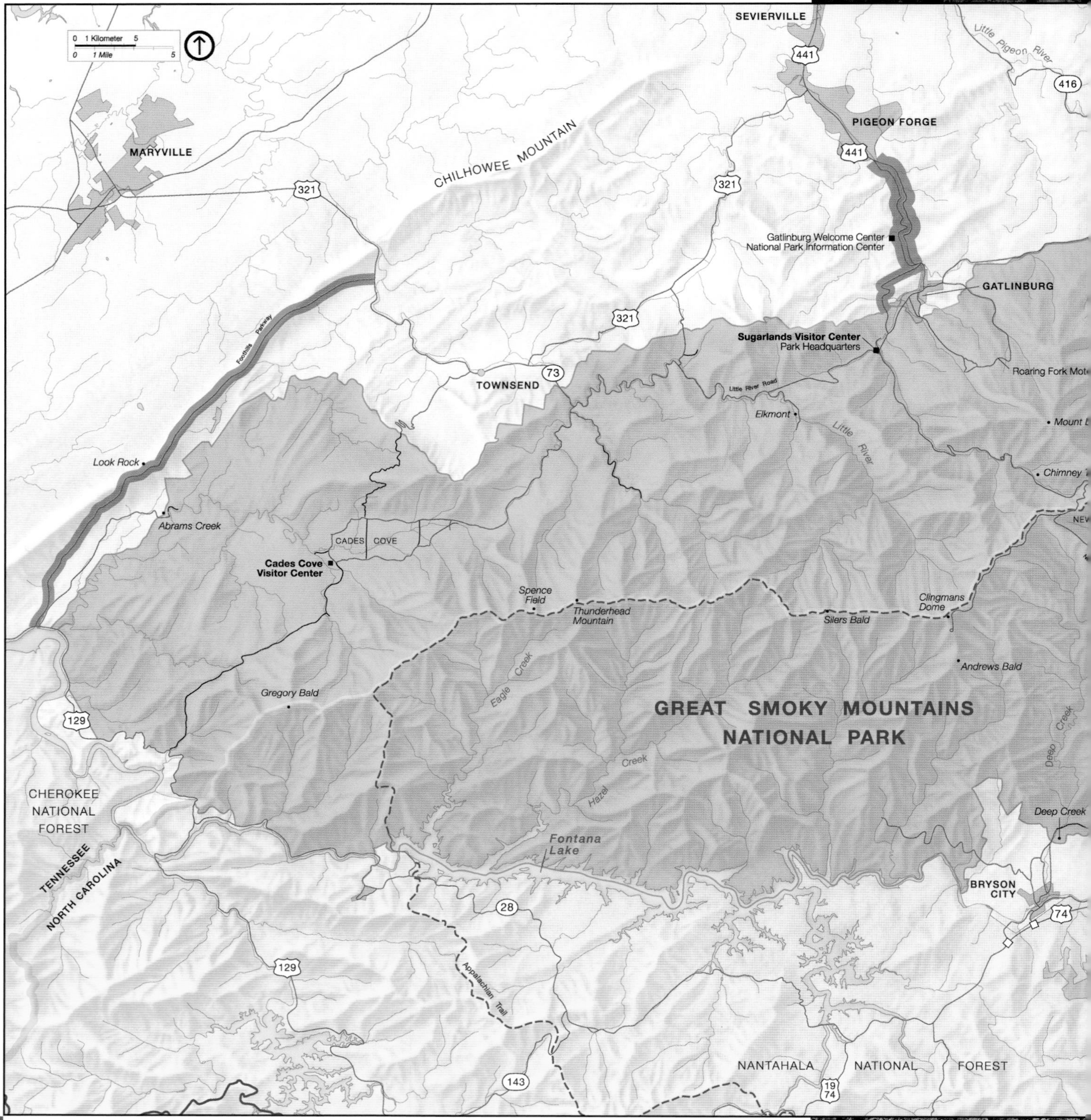

0 1 Kilometer 5
0 1 Mile 5
SEVIERVILLE
441
Little Pigeon River
416
PIGEON FORGE
441
MARYVILLE
CHILHOWEE MOUNTAIN
321
321
Gatlinburg Welcome Center
National Park Information Center
GATLINBURG
Foothills Parkway
321
Sugarlands Visitor Center
Park Headquarters
Roaring Fork Mot
TOWNSEND
73
Little River Road
Elkmont
Little River
Mount
Look Rock
Chimney
Abrams Creek
CADES COVE
Cades Cove Visitor Center
Spence Field
Thunderhead Mountain
Silers Bald
Clingmans Dome
Andrews Bald
Eagle Creek
Gregory Bald
129
GREAT SMOKY MOUNTAINS NATIONAL PARK
Deep Creek
CHEROKEE NATIONAL FOREST
Hazel Creek
Deep Creek
TENNESSEE
NORTH CAROLINA
Fontana Lake
BRYSON CITY
28
74
129
Appalachian Trail
143
NANTAHALA NATIONAL FOREST
19 74

Ravens

Among the most adaptable of birds, the raven is a quick learner capable of hunting cooperatively. Groups of ravens have even been seen harrying cats to make them drop mice.

Northern Hardwoods

A northern hardwoods forest responds to the coming of autumn in the Great Smokies. The park protects the largest remaining old growth forest in the eastern United States.

Falling Water

Deep Creek tumbles down ledges of bedrock to form Toms Branch Falls along the park's Deep Creek Trail in Great Smoky Mountains National Park.

COSBY
Foothills Parkway
Pigeon River
Cosby Creek
321
Big Creek
40
Mount Sterling
Mount Guyot
BALSAM MTN
Appalachian Trail
PISGAH NATIONAL FOREST
Charlies Bunion
Cataloochee
Oconaluftee River
Balsam Mountain
Smokemont
BLACK CAMP GAP
Blue Ridge Parkway
MAGGIE VALLEY
19
Oconaluftee Visitor Center
Mountain Farm Museum
441
CHEROKEE INDIAN RESERVATION
CHEROKEE
19
441
Blue Ridge Parkway
23
74
SYLVIA
441
23

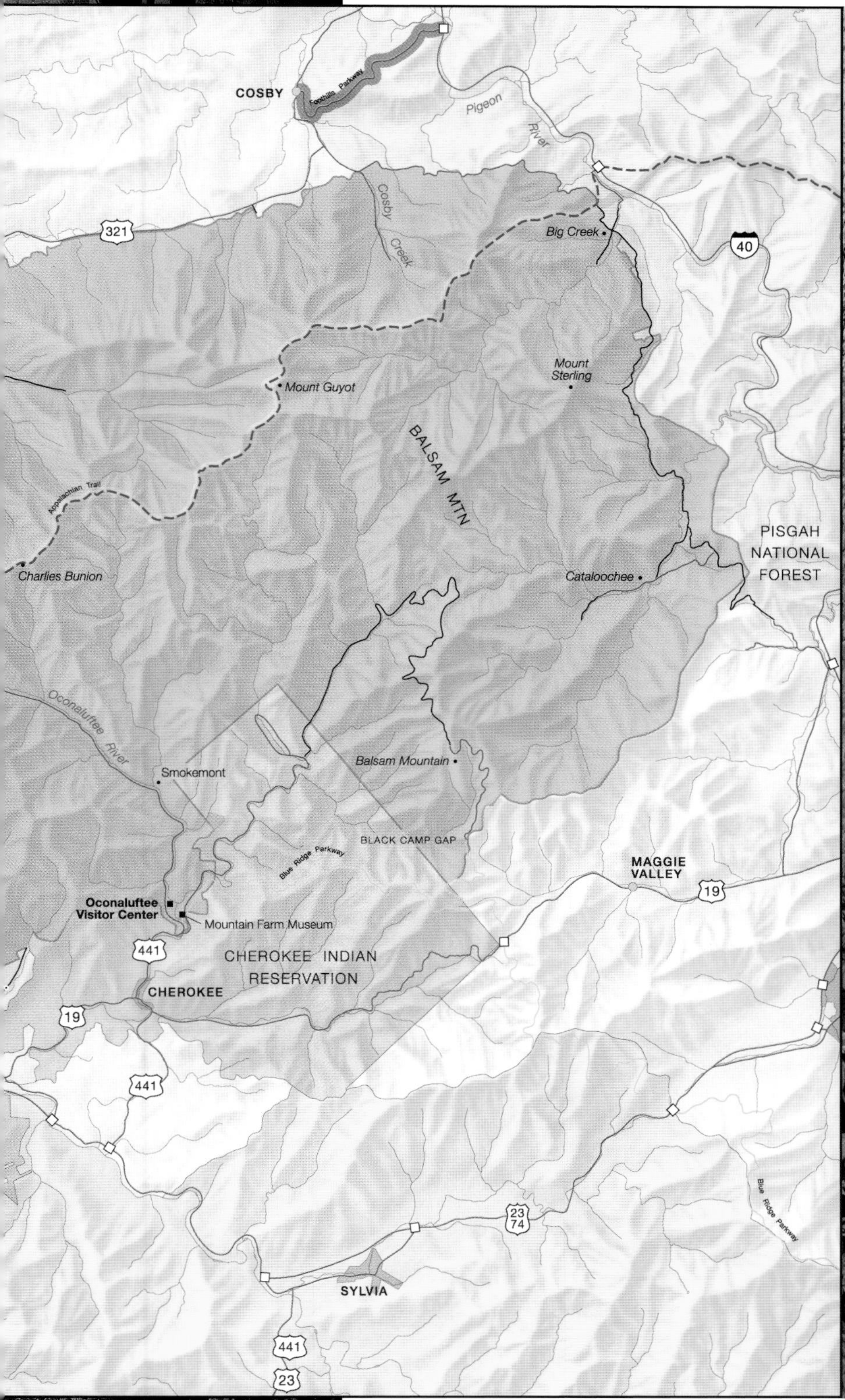

Lush Life

Ferns form a lush understory in Great Smoky Mountains National Park.

Smoky Bears

A black bear sow relaxes with her cubs, right. Following spread: A tangle of hepatica and spring beauties carpets a forest floor in Great Smoky.

GUADALUPE MOUN

NATIONAL PARK IN TEXAS

DESERT AND REEF

The Guadalupes, a 250-million-year-old marine fossil reef, rise abruptly over the West Texas desert, a landmark visible for great distances. One spectacular portion of the Guadalupes, known as Capitan Reef, is one of the largest known fossil reefs on the planet and has been studied by geologists from all over the world. The mountains are surrounded on three sides by Chihuahuan Desert similar to that in Big Bend National Park. Guadalupe Peak, at 8,749 feet, is the highest point in Texas.

Unless they happen to have read Nevada Barr's absorbing mystery novel *Track of the Cat* (1993), most Americans almost certainly have never heard of this park. But on the insider grapevine of park rangers, they say that Guadalupe Mountains National Park is a hard place to get a job because anyone lucky enough to do so never wants to leave. Former secretary of the interior Stewart Udall, no stranger to the wild beauty of many parks, once exclaimed, "My Lord, what a paradise that place is!"

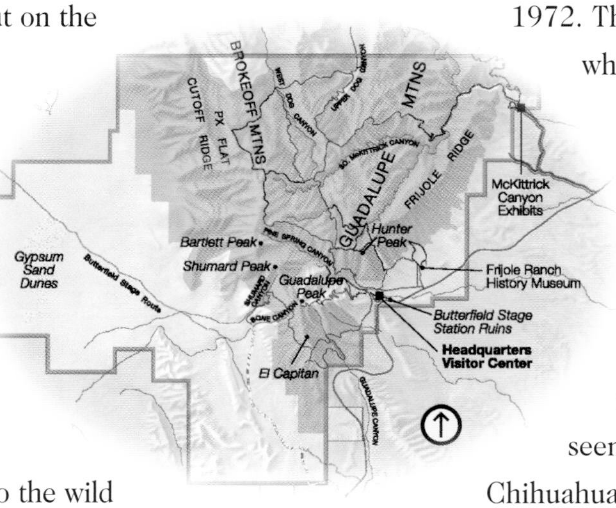

Part of its attraction may be that it also is a haunted paradise, home to Native Americans for untold millennia. For some years in the mid- to late 1800s, the Nde, or Mescalero Apaches, used the mountains as a base from which to fight a determined but losing battle with United States troops, as whites settled the West Texas region.

Not all the ghosts are human. The grizzly bear and the wolf are gone, exterminated from the region long before it became a park in 1972. The native elk, pronghorn, white-tailed deer, and bison were all either hunted or pressured out as well. (The elk were later replaced by Rocky Mountain elk.) But the magic of the Guadalupes hardly seems diminished. The Chihuahuan Desert is still there. The high pine and fir forest, relic of a cooler ice-age climate that once connected it to the Rockies, is still wild. The steep-walled canyons stairstep up through an amazing variety of woodland types. The plants, as well as the black bears, mountain lions, wild turkeys, mule deer, and a variety of raptors, suggest that wildness, like beauty, is still alive and well in this particular paradise.

Desert to Meadow
A limestone pinnacle in Guadalupe juts high above the Chihuahuan Desert of west Texas. In the high country, the park supports evergreen forests and an anomalous subalpine meadow.

Roadrunners
Roadrunners, capable of darting along at 15 mph, prey on insects, lizards, snakes, rodents, and other birds.

TAINS

Dry Slope
A mule deer crosses a brushy slope in Guadalupe. The deer are abundant within the park, where they are preyed upon by mountain lions.

GUADALUPE MOUNTAINS NATIONAL PARK

History Note: The nation's first transcontinental mail carrier, the Butterfield Overland Mail Company, routed its stagecoaches through Guadalupe from 1858 until August 1859.

Flora: Chihuahuan Desert plants, including cactuses, chollas, yuccas, and sotol; transitional woodlands of madrones, walnuts, and junipers; highland forests of ponderosa pine, white pine, Douglas fir, and aspen.

Fauna: Sixty species of mammals, including mule deer, elk, coyotes, rabbits, ringtails, javelinas, and sixteen species of bats; a variety of snakes and lizards; and more than 300 species of birds.

Visitor Tip: For a nice but rigorous hike and a look at all three of the major types of reef rock, head for McKittrick Canyon and the Permian Reef Geology Trail.

Gypsum Dunes
Wind-rippled dunes of gypsum sand, below, lie to the west of the Guadalupe Mountains. The mountains, left, expose the uplifted remains of a Permian reef that formed in an inland sea 250 to 280 million years ago.

Deep Sleeper

When the yellow-bellied marmot, left, hibernates, its body temperature drops from 95 degrees to the low 40s. Mills Lake, below, lies cradled in Glacier Gorge, a deep, glacially carved valley that flanks the west face of Longs' Peak (upper left).

ROCKY MOUNTAIN

NATIONAL PARK IN COLORADO

MILES-HIGH RAMPART

The Front Range of the Rocky Mountains make up one of the most abrupt changes of scenery to be encountered anywhere in the world. From the mile-high elevation along the western edge of the Great Plains, the Front Range suddenly climbs to more than twice that in a long, straight rampart. Rocky Mountain National Park protects a particularly impressive section of this range, including some sixty peaks that are at least 12,000 feet high.

In 1846, adventurer-historian Francis Parkman traveled along the eastern foothills of what would later be Colorado, across "a desert as flat as the outspread ocean." But along the western horizon, the towering clouds were behaving oddly. Mixed in with the rest was one that seemed darker—and it didn't move. Finally, he could no longer deny what he saw: "It must, thought I, be the summit of a mountain; and yet its height staggered me."

It was Long's Peak, the most celebrated of Rocky Mountain National Park's many high summits. It has that same effect today on travelers moving along Interstate 25, who catch sight of something improbable out of the corner of their eyes but take several looks before they come to terms with it. Long's Peak is the best and most persuasive invitation the park could offer to people who need a little relief, literally, from flatness.

Of the several parks in the Rocky Mountains, Rocky itself is perhaps the most fully representative of Rocky Mountain wilderness, but it is the ease of access that makes it so appealing to many nonclimbing, nonhiking visitors. Though any self-respecting veteran enthusiast of this landscape will insist you need at least a week, if not a lifetime, to do it justice, Rocky Mountain is also generous to the hasty traveler. In a short drive you climb 4,000 feet, at the same time moving from high prairie to the arctic (about a quarter of the park is above tree line), with stops for numerous intermediate landscapes and wild habitats.

This sort of experiential compaction carries with it the risk that something so easily gained

Long's Peak

Long's Peak, below, at 14,255 feet, is the highest mountain in the park and the most famous summit in the Front Range north of Pike's Peak. Above: The sun sets on Long's Peak and Trail Ridge in Rocky Mountain National Park.

will be poorly appreciated, but there is little chance of that. Stand at the windy and vertiginous overlooks along the Trail Ridge Road, the celebrated "roof of the Rockies," and discover what "panoramic" really means when nature puts its mind to it. Stretch out on the tundra (careful not to squash anything!) for a close look at the incredible array of tiny "bellyflowers." Glass the adjoining slopes for elk, bighorn sheep, and other native wildlife (patience pays off every time). It is almost impossible not to become fully engaged, and utterly enchanted, with the wildness of these first rows of the Rocky Mountains.

Rocky Landscape
A jumble of rock debris surrounds a pair of dead evergreens in Rocky Mountain National Park.

Naturalist and conservationist Enos Mills, who a hundred years ago led the struggle to have a portion of the Front Range set aside as a national park, saw it as a struggle on behalf of posterity: "In years to come when I am asleep beneath the pines, thousands of families will find rest and hope in this park." May he sleep at ease—it has happened. You may not feel like resting, though, and your fondest hope may be to come back.

Autumn Rites
Two bull elk square off in a stream during the autumn rut, below. The park is one of the most dependable sites in the Rockies for spotting elk. Right: Snow lingers in the park's high country for much of the summer.

Glacial Track

The brow of Hallet Peak, elevation 12,713 feet, overlooks Tyndall Gorge, a classic, U-shaped glacial trough within easy walking distance of Bear Lake.

Ponderosa Parkland

The snowy crest of the Front Range arcs over one of Rocky's parkland meadows. Several of these large openings of grass and widely spaced ponderosa pines grace the park's eastern foothills.

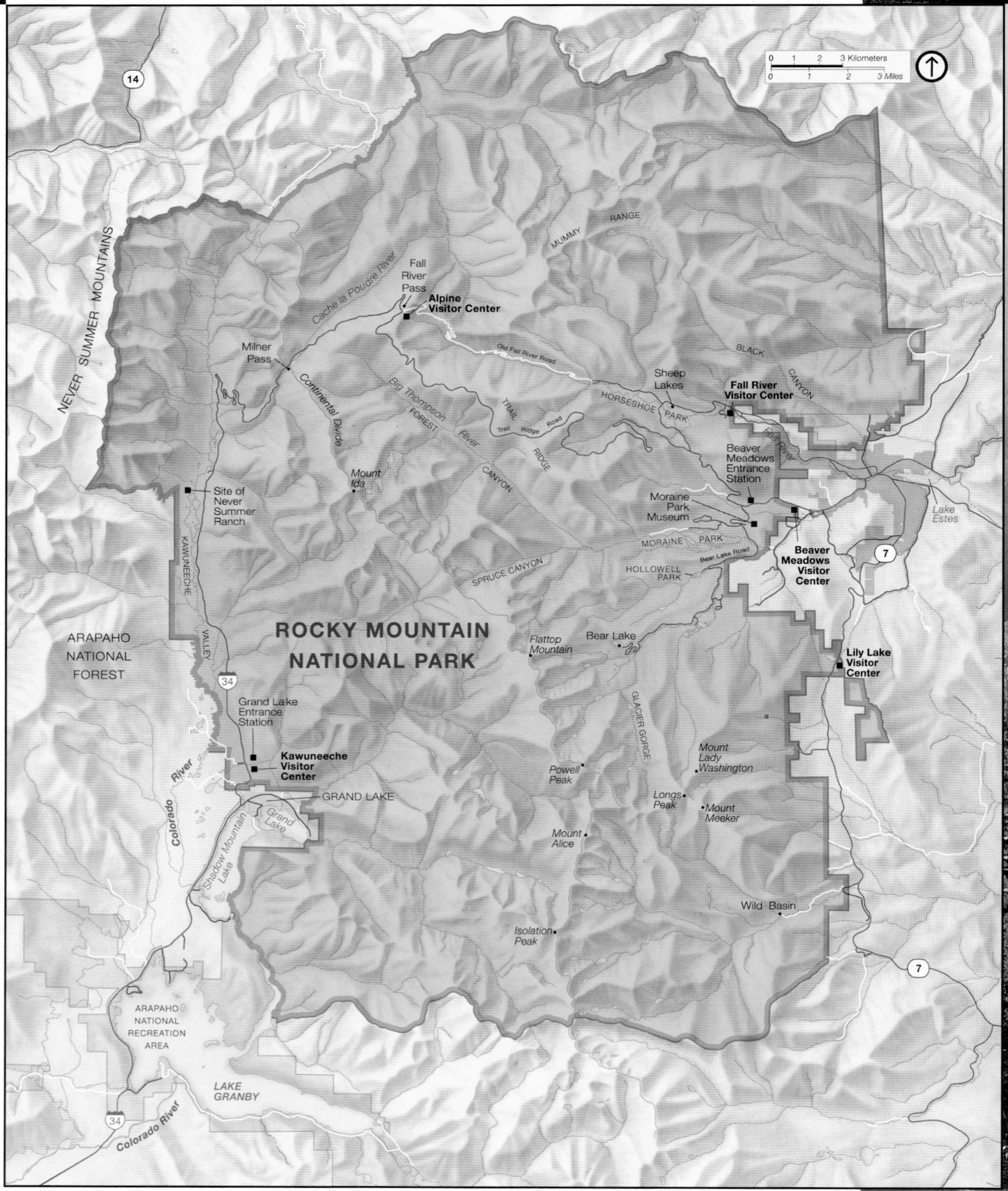

ROCKY MOUNTAIN NATIONAL PARK
0 1 2 3 Kilometers
0 1 2 3 Miles
14
NEVER SUMMER MOUNTAINS
MUMMY RANGE
Cache la Poudre River
Fall River Pass
Alpine Visitor Center
Milner Pass
Continental Divide
Old Fall River Road
Big Thompson River
FOREST CANYON
TRAIL RIDGE
Trail Ridge Road
BLACK CANYON
Sheep Lakes
Fall River Visitor Center
HORSESHOE PARK
Fall River
Beaver Meadows Entrance Station
Moraine Park Museum
MORAINE PARK
Bear Lake Road
Beaver Meadows Visitor Center
Lake Estes
7
Site of Never Summer Ranch
KAWUNEECHE VALLEY
Mount Ida
SPRUCE CANYON
HOLLOWELL PARK
ARAPAHO NATIONAL FOREST
Flattop Mountain
Bear Lake
Lily Lake Visitor Center
34
Grand Lake Entrance Station
Kawuneeche Visitor Center
GRAND LAKE
GLACIER GORGE
Mount Lady Washington
Powell Peak
Longs Peak
Mount Meeker
Colorado River
Grand Lake
Shadow Mountain Lake
Mount Alice
Wild Basin
Isolation Peak
ARAPAHO NATIONAL RECREATION AREA
LAKE GRANBY
Colorado River

Mallards

A mallard preens to keep its feathers well oiled and water resistant. Mallards are often seen around Sprague Lake, a trout pond created in 1914 by damming Glacier Creek.

Grand Ditch

The first of many irrigation projects along the Colorado River, Grand Ditch diverts meltwater from the Never Summer Mountains to the plains of eastern Colorado.

Roosting Tree

A ponderosa pine snag stands on a grassy parkland slope, right. Hawks and owls roost in such trees while hunting. Below: A dusting of snow frosts spruce trees.

ROCKY MOUNTAIN NATIONAL PARK

History Note: The sumptuous Stanley Hotel, on the outskirts of Estes Park, was built in 1909 by Freelan Stanley, inventor of the Stanley Steamer automobile and a strong backer of establishing the national park.

Flora: Ponderosa parkland meadows with prairie grasses and wildflowers; dense mountain forests of Douglas fir, limber pine, lodgepole pine, Engelmann spruce, and subalpine fir; extensive alpine tundra zone carpeted with tiny wildflowers.

Fauna: Elk, mule deer, bighorn sheep, moose, tassel-eared Abert squirrels, and many birds, including hawks, golden eagles, owls, and hummingbirds.

Visitor Tip: For a primer on the flora, fauna, and climate of the park's exquisite alpine tundra zone, drop by the Alpine Visitor Center, on Trail Ridge Road, and stroll the Tundra Nature Trail.

Night Shift Owl

Silent on the wing, the long-eared owl, like other nocturnal owls, is a formidable hunter. Active throughout the park, the long-eared owl uses its sharp sense of hearing more than sight to locate prey.

MAKING OF A MEADOW

Mountain meadows come in a wide variety of sizes, shapes, and types, but what they all share in common is a relative absence of trees. Conditions are either too dry, too wet, or too cold for vulnerable tree seedlings to get a foothold. In their place grows an abundance of grasses, sedges, and wildflowers, each species superbly adapted to its immediate surroundings.

In Rocky Mountain, these expansive oases of open space range from dry grassland basins dotted with prairie wildflowers to lush subalpine meadows full of moisture-loving plants, and finally to gardens of tiny wildflowers in the frigid alpine tundra zone. The meadows are located along the bottoms of glacially carved troughs, on gentle slopes, on rounded ridges, and along rivers and streams.

Dry meadows are generally larger than wet ones. While they hold abundant moisture in the form of snow during winter, meltwater quickly percolates through porous soils, confronting plants with semiarid conditions similar to those found on the plains. Wet meadows have a high water table and often form in poorly drained sites next to lakes, beaver ponds, or streams. Soils there are cold, soggy, and low in oxygen. Sedges, rushes, grasses, and willows thrive in such conditions, but not trees.

Rocky Mountain National Park's Horseshoe Park contains wet and dry meadow areas. In the foreground, willow thickets carpet the wet valley floor adjacent to Fall River. In the distance, the glacially carved valley opens up into a dry grassland with a fringe of ponderosa pines.

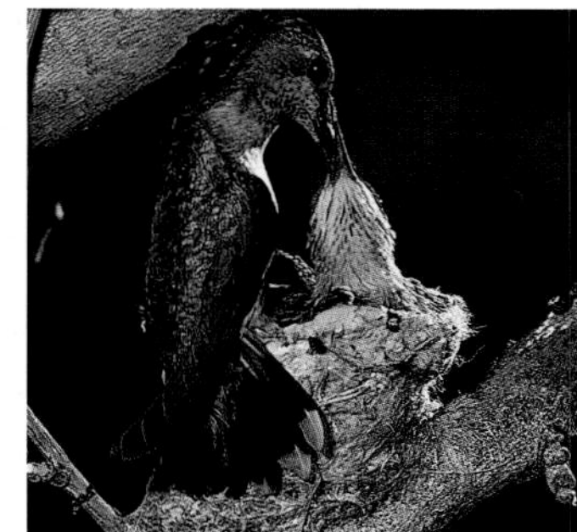

Home Delivery
A black-chinned hummingbird, common to the Rocky Mountains, feeds its young.

During the last ice age, Horseshoe Park lay beneath a glacier 1,500 feet thick. As the glacier melted, it left a terminal moraine that dammed the valley and created a lake.

The fine-grained mud, sand, and soil that filled in the lake discourages tree growth. Today, the valley's meandering river corridor, the abundance of grass, sedge, wildflowers, and browsable shrubs, and the protection of surrounding forests, draw a wide variety of animals such as bighorn sheep, elk, mule deer, coyotes, hawks, and songbirds.

Ponderosa Still Life
The needles and cones of a ponderosa pine lie on the ground.

Horseshoe Park
Horseshoe Park's diverse vegetation and lush riparian zone attract many large mammals, especially bighorn sheep.

SHENANDOAH

NATIONAL PARK IN VIRGINIA

BLUE RIDGE VISTAS

Shendandoah straddles part of the Appalachian province known as the Blue Ridge, which was named for the same moisture-heavy atmospheric conditions that gave the Smokies their name. Shenandoah launches many small streams down its sides, replete with countless cascades and waterfalls. The broad vistas from the Skyline Drive—the Shenandoah Valley to the west and the Piedmont to the east—contrast with the nearer views of a diverse and almost continuous forest.

There is something joyfully comforting, even cozy, about a hardwood forest. Think of the positive images and feelings evoked in our minds by descriptions of deciduous woods—ambling down a shady trail under a leafy sheltering canopy to a sun-dappled forest glen surrounded by grand old patriarchs of oak and maple. The clichés are rampant, but they're also irresistible. These are the places in nature that Europeans learned to love and inhabit long ages before they came to the New World. It is no wonder that we are raised to love them even yet. Unlike the desert, the prairie, the tundra, or the monochromatic western mountains, this is no work at all. It is instantly appealing, and reassuringly familiar.

Shenandoah accommodates those feelings with ease. Whether you wind along the Skyline Drive, hike the Appalachian Trail that parallels it, or go adventuring down the stream channels and hollows, you walk under such forests. You couldn't avoid them; they cover 95 percent of the park. Even in winter, without their leaves, bare and stark against the dark sky, these trees feel like home. And they are a glory beyond expression in the autumn.

They have stories to tell. The cycle of human tenancy here was roughly similar to that in the Smokies. Native people knew the Blue Ridge for thousands of years, but found themselves pushed aside by white settlement. Like the natives before them, the whites dug in, tuned in on their environment, and turned themselves into the new natives. Before the park was established in 1935, the Commonwealth of Virginia evicted them.

Deep Forest

Mist envelops a forest of yellow poplar, left. Above: Shenandoah is famous for its vistas.

May Flame

Pink azaleas blossom along Skyline Drive. When they fade, mountain laurel starts to bloom.

Hawksbill Lava

Like many high points along the Blue Ridge, the summit of Hawksbill Mountain, above, is composed of ancient lava flows that metamorphosed into greenstones. Hawksbill is the highest summit in the park, elevation 4,051 feet. Left: Many waterfalls, such as Doyle River Falls, spill from the heights.

Black Bears

Black bears live mainly in the park's backcountry but are sometimes seen in more heavily visited areas.

But after some 150 years of occupancy, these people had made some big changes. Large mammals were almost gone. Some—elk, bison, wolves, mountain lions—were probably gone forever. Others—deer, black bears—still hung on nearby. Two centuries of intermittent logging and clearing of land had changed the face of the forest, as did the chestnut blight of 1920s. When the chestnuts, the dominant species of tree and a unique contributor to the diet of wildlife, faded from the scene, yellow poplar and cove hardwoods swiftly occupied their vacant niche. Each change brings others, until all is a welter of cause and consequence, losses and gains.

Musky Denizen
A striped skunk trundles through a park meadow. It owes its distinctive odor to a powerful, sulfur-rich musk.

Removing people and creating the park didn't stop this. White-tailed deer, black bear, and many smaller species returned. As for the forest, it continues to adjust and react. New problems—gypsy moths and other exotic infestations, dirty air—appear. Losses and gains are weighed, watches are kept.

We are mindful of these things, and we wonder where this magical land might be headed, but Shenandoah never lets us forget that there is still a forest, and it still feels like home.

On the Blue Ridge
A thicket of shrubs, below, begins its annual turn toward autumn. Left: Dawn breaks over the Blue Ridge near Buck Hollow.

Appalachian Spring
In the depths of a Shenandoah hardwood forest, a flowering dogwood blossoms in the cool mist of early spring.

Coons
Found near water, raccoons forage at night during the warmer months but stay in their dens for weeks at a time during winter.

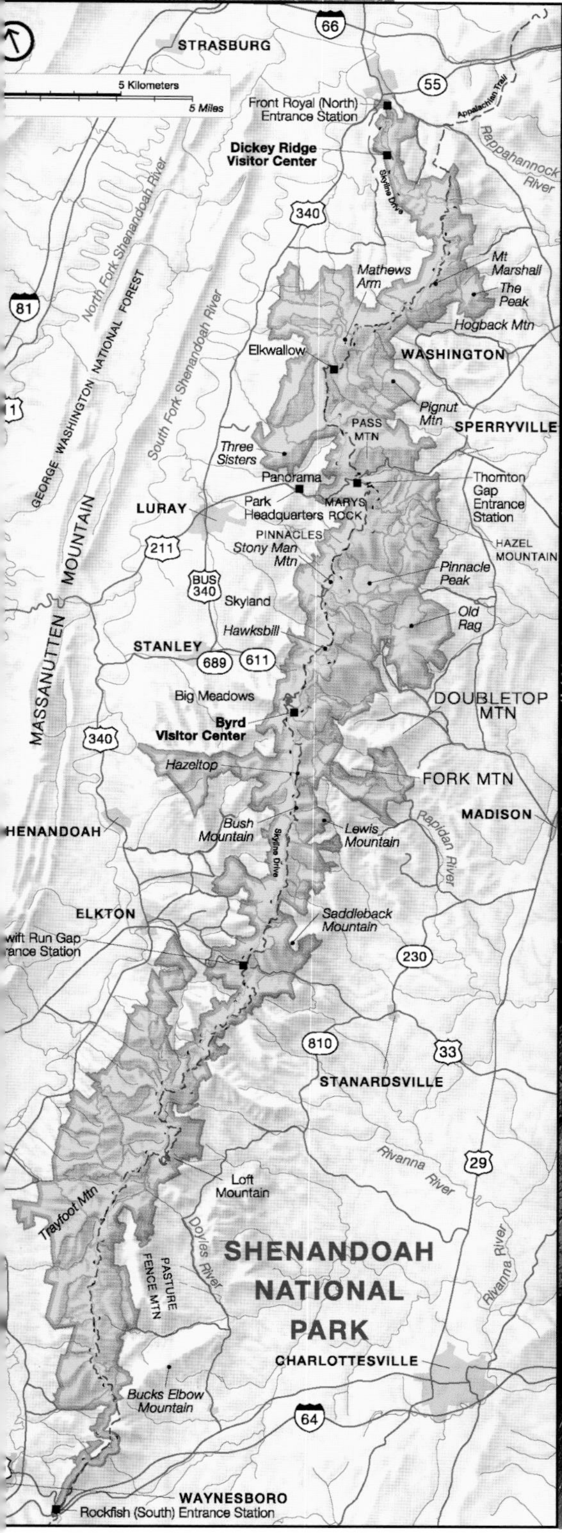

SHENANDOAH NATIONAL PARK

History Note: John Lederer explored the Blue Ridge region in 1669 and described the Monacan and Manahoac peoples living there as "peaceful and intelligent people who worshiped one god and followed a calendar." By 1730, most of them had died or moved away.

Flora: Roughly 1,600 species of vascular plants, including many wildflowers, flowering trees, and flowering shrubs. Forests, mainly deciduous, cover 95 percent of the park's area and include roughly one hundred species of trees.

Fauna: Black bears, white-tailed deer, bobcats, skunks; about two hundred species of birds, including wild turkeys, ruffed grouse, barred owls, and woodpeckers; snakes, frogs, and rare salamanders.

Visitor Tip: Fall colors usually reach their peak between October 10 and 25.

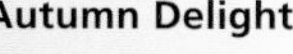

Autumn Delight
Water cascades 70 feet over greenstone at Dark Hollow Falls near the Byrd Visitor Center in Shenandoah National Park.

Leafed Out
Maple leaves, left, reach their peak of color in mid-October. Facing page: Once spring takes hold the green of leafing trees moves up the mountain slopes at a rate of 100 vertical feet each day, reaching the crest of the Blue Ridge by late May.

Big Meadows
The largest open area in the park, Big Meadows, right, supports more than 270 species of plants that cover ancient lava rock. Following spread: The rolling hills and farmsteads of Gibson Hollow greet another day.

WAVES, CAVES, AND CURRENTS

WATER DRIVES MANY subtle natural systems in which the scene is shaped—and life makes itself at home. These shaping processes are as diverse as they are persistent, and often enlist life itself as a primary builder of the landscape. And no matter what built the land, whether biology or geology, sometimes water then sets the land apart, in those unique little worlds we call islands.

Recumbent Reptile
In Everglades National Park, alligators, above, live side by side with crocodiles.

Far from sunlight, the strains of the ages leave bedrock fractured and split—all the invitation water needs. Great tangled networks of groundwater pour through this maze, dissolving rock to carve caves and depositing some dissolved minerals to furnish caves with fantastic sculpture.

Coral Reefs
A handful of national parks preserve beautiful, but supremely fragile, coral reefs.

Or the water may stay on the surface, and work in one dimension and direction. There are some wetlands so flat and water-dependent that a change in elevation of only inches might change the entire biological community. In coastal shallows, hospitable temperatures and depths welcome vast populations of earthbuilding organisms, the most prominent being coral reefs, colonized by a community of other creatures.

WATER DESIGNING LANDS

But even the most localized processes are at the mercy of planetary trends. Tectonic motions may deepen or raise the sea bottom. If the Earth's climate cools, northern ice consumes oceanic waters, and the shallow sea over the coral subsides. The community dies, but when warmth and water return it rebuilds itself.

Draped with Dripstone
A wonderful variety of dripstone formations adorn New Mexico's Carlsbad Caverns.

CHAMBERS BENEATH THE EARTH'S SURFACE

Strange yet alluring, labyrinthine cave systems lie beneath the surface in several of the country's national parks. Hollowed out over long periods by slightly acidic groundwater, the networks of passageways, chambers, and shafts can extend for many miles. Kentucky's Mammoth Cave, for example, boasts 350 miles of surveyed passageways and an estimated 600 miles of undiscovered passageways. Large or small, cave systems often contain elaborate flowstone formations and highly specialized life forms such as eyeless fish.

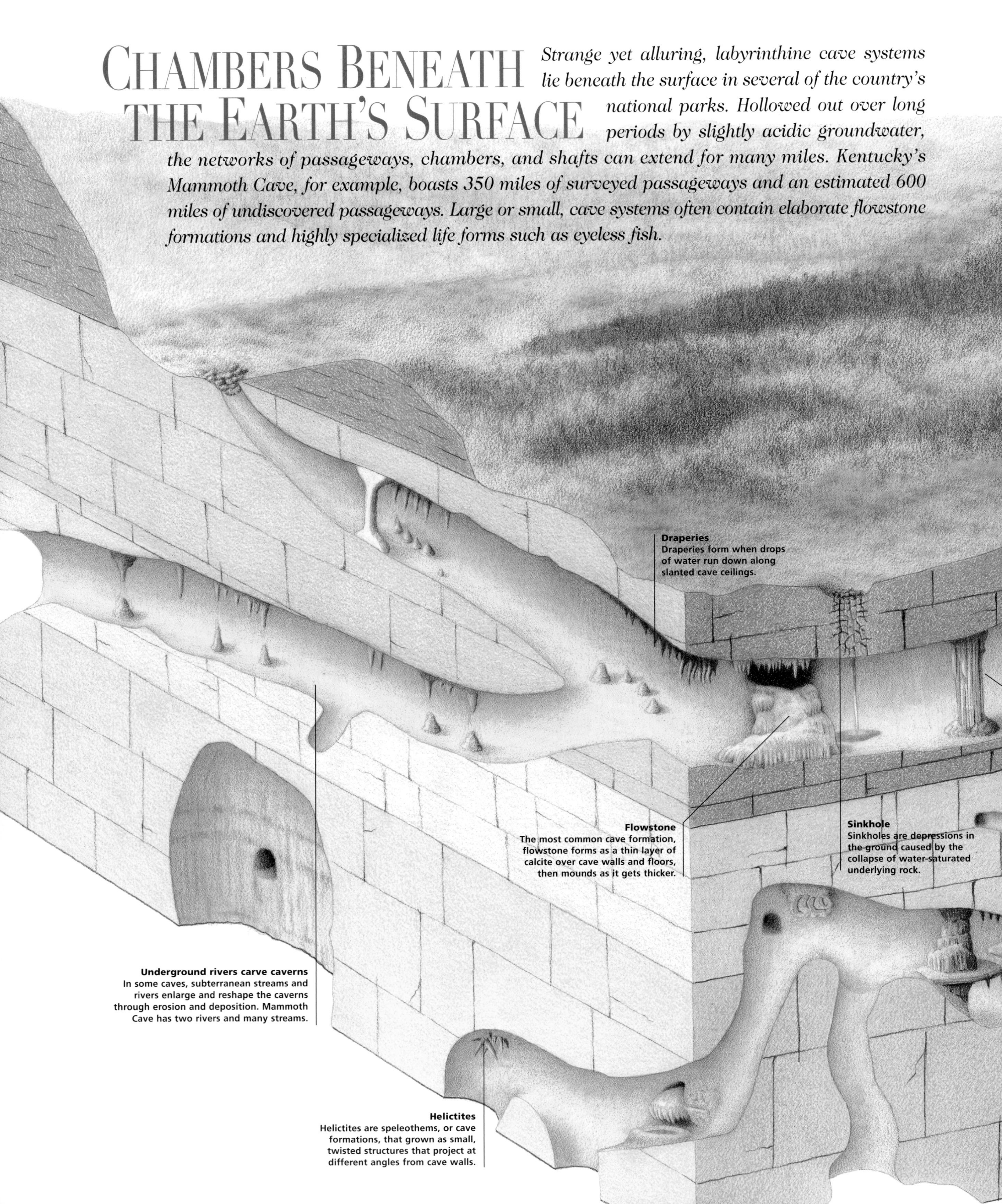

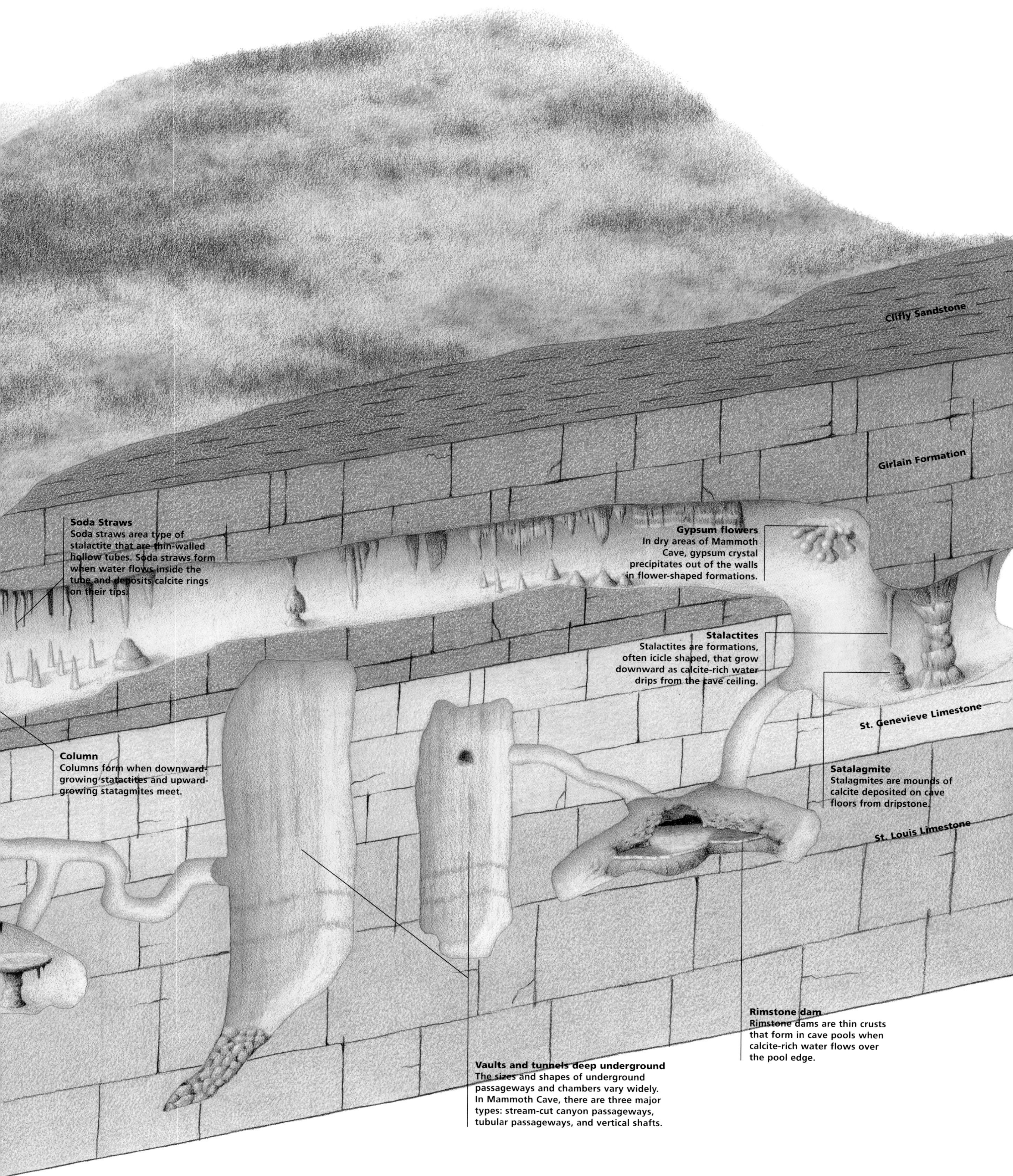

Clifly Sandstone
Girlain Formation
Soda Straws
Soda straws area type of stalactite that are thin-walled hollow tubes. Soda straws form when water flows inside the tube and deposits calcite rings on their tips.
Gypsum flowers
In dry areas of Mammoth Cave, gypsum crystal precipitates out of the walls in flower-shaped formations.
Stalactites
Stalactites are formations, often icicle shaped, that grow downward as calcite-rich water drips from the cave ceiling.
St. Genevieve Limestone
Column
Columns form when downward-growing statactites and upward-growing statagmites meet.
Satalagmite
Stalagmites are mounds of calcite deposited on cave floors from dripstone.
St. Louis Limestone
Rimstone dam
Rimstone dams are thin crusts that form in cave pools when calcite-rich water flows over the pool edge.
Vaults and tunnels deep underground
The sizes and shapes of underground passageways and chambers vary widely. In Mammoth Cave, there are three major types: stream-cut canyon passageways, tubular passageways, and vertical shafts.

Beach Builders

Longshore currents, combined with beach drift, are capable of moving large amounts of sand, even along relatively sedate beaches like those in Virgin Islands National Park.

HOW SEA WAVES BUILD LANDS

LONGSHORE DRIFT

Most waves break obliquely against their beaches, rushing up the slope with their loads of sediment at an angle, no matter how slight. The backwash, however, runs straight down the slope. This dual action transports sand and pebbles in a zigzag pattern of movement called beach drift, which is capable of moving sand thousands of feet a day.

Oblique waves also stir currents in the surf zone that run parallel to shore. Called longshore currents, they carry fine suspended sand, roll larger grains and gravel along the bottom, and are capable of moving much more sediment than beach drift.

Taken together, longshore currents and beach drift can move hundreds of thousands of tons of sediment along a particular stretch of shore each year, building and maintaining beaches, bars, and spits.

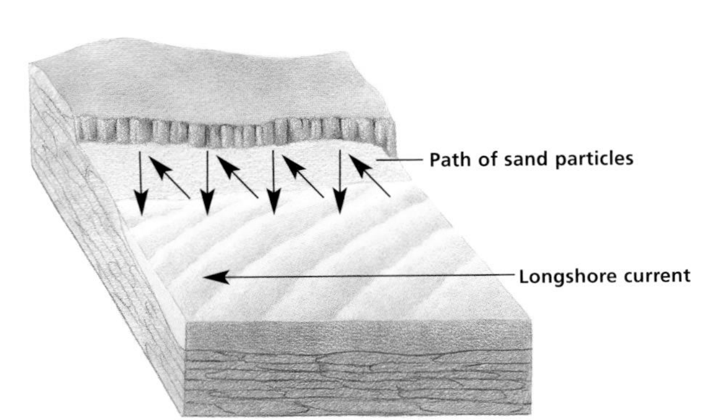

BAYHEAD BEACH

A bayhead beach forms at the head end of a bay, where wave action is weaker than it is along adjacent headlands. In bays, waves tend to diverge and to expend less energy, giving sediments a chance to settle and accumulate.

Bayhead beach

TOMBOLO

A tombolo is a ridge of sand extending from the mainland to an island, or from one island to another. They, too, are formed from sediments transported by beach drift and longshore currents.

Mainland
Tombolo
Island

BAYMOUTH BAR

A baymouth bar is a sandbar that completely crosses the mouth of a bay, sealing it off from the open ocean. Like spits and bayhead beaches, such bars form from sediment deposited by beach drift and longshore currents.

Baymouth bar

FRINGE REEFS

Fringe reefs are relatively small, linear reefs that parallel the shoreline. They form close to shore and often attach to the shore, usually without a lagoon. Fringe reefs are common in the Virgin Islands.

Fringe reef
Ocean currents move sea sediments to form fringe reef

Island Preserves

The sun sets over South Florida's Biscayne Bay, left. *Some thirty-three small coral islands dot the shallow bay.* Right: *Wave action hammers cliffs and builds beaches on Santa Cruz Island in Channel Islands National Park.*

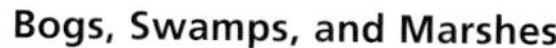

Wet-Footed Prairie
Wide expanses of saw grass prairie stretch for miles across the exceptionally flat landscape of the Everglades. Through the grass flows a broad sheet of shallow, slow-moving water.

Bogs, Swamps, and Marshes
Bogs, swamps, and other types of wetlands form in a variety of national park settings. The Everglades lies on shallow layers of muck and peat laid down on limestone bedrock.

WETLANDS

Wetlands, often divided into marshes, swamps, and bogs, are places where water saturates the soil for long periods of time. They often form where a layer of rock or other impervious material prevents groundwater from percolating deeply into the earth, thus maintaining a water table at, near, or above the surface of the land. This is the case in the Everglades, right, which lies atop a shallow limestone platform.

Marshes have no trees or shrubs and often include areas of open water surrounded by soft-stemmed plants such as cattails and rushes. Water lilies dot the open water, and tiny floaters, such as duckweed, cast a greenish hue across the surface.

Swamps have a lower water table than marshes and are dominated by trees and shrubs. They often form along major river courses or in wet basins. Typical Everglades swamps contain low islands supporting bald cypress draped with Spanish moss.

Bogs are acidic, appear relatively dry, but are spongy and wet to the touch. They often develop in former glacial lakes and are usually characterized by evergreen trees and shrubs underlain by deep deposits of peat. Black spruce and larch tend to dominate northern bogs; white cedar, southern bogs.

Wetlands play a crucial ecological role. They not only provide important habitat for a wide range of animals, especially waterfowl, but also control floods, purify and store water, and recharge the water table. Less than half of the original 215 million acres of wetlands still exist in the United States.

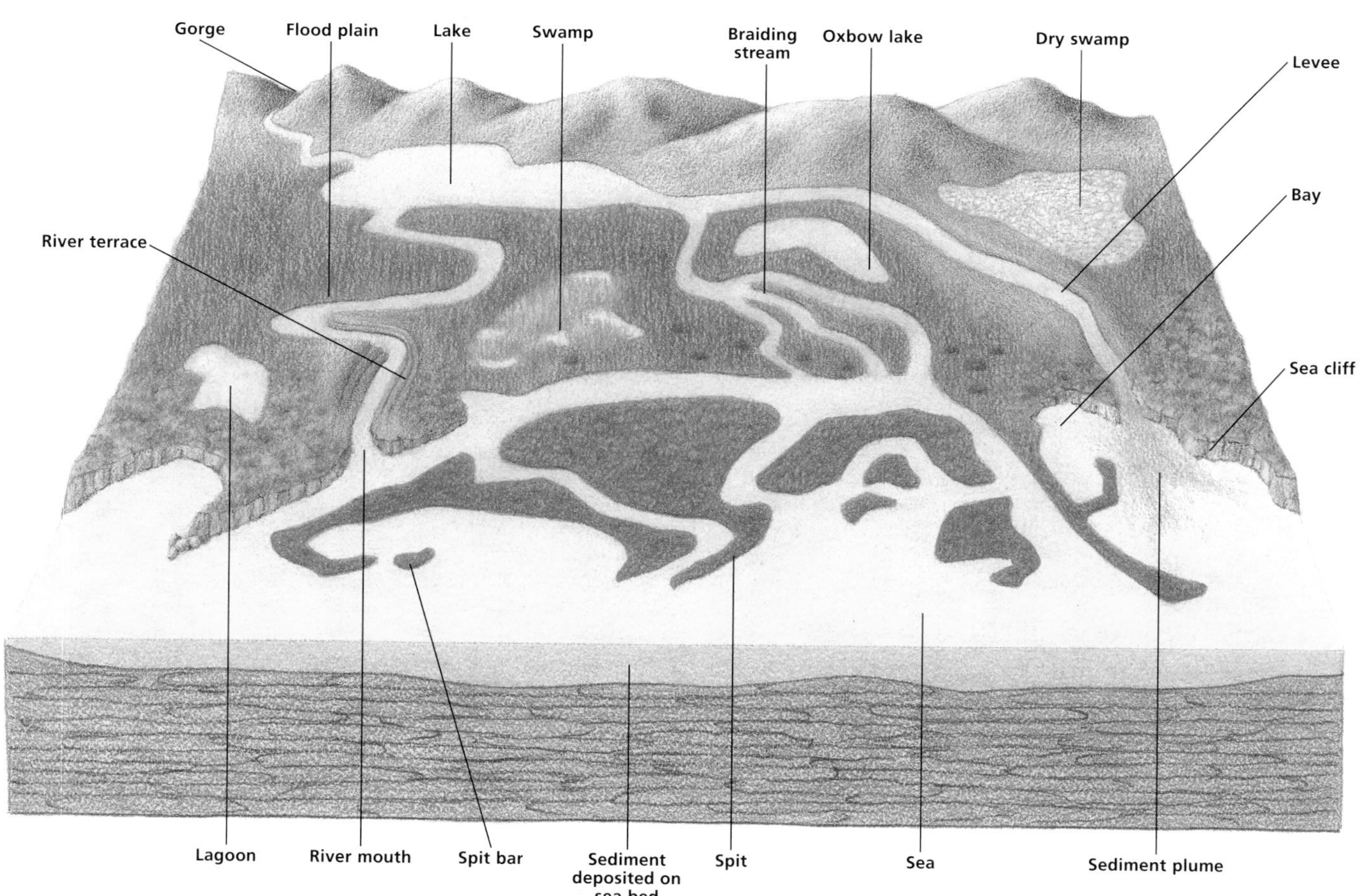

EBBING AND FLOWING

WATER'S GUIDING HAND

Borrowing a dubious but apt expression from the commercial recreation industry, we might call these the water parks. They honor places where water has played different roles than its accustomed ones in the conventional parks with their big mountains, big glaciers, big forests, and big animals. Water has many functions and attributes besides its widely advertised way with erosion and its equally well-known gift for fostering terrestrial life. There is subtlety in all nature, but in these parks, subtlety is a key to understanding and the pathway to wonder.

Carlsbad Caverns

Dry Tortugas

Start underground. Deep under the lovely hardwood forests of western Kentucky, water has made the world's longest cave. Mammoth Cave winds for hundreds of miles through a sprawling limestone region. Rain seeps through the soil into a flourishing and energetic set of aquifers that has spent millions of years dissolving fabulous passageways, chambers, and pits out of the rock. Much of the cave is dry, but where water still flows it continues to build the endlessly varied dripstone and flowstone formations (speleothems) so popular among visitors.

Water's Handiwork
Water seeping through beds of limestone hollowed out Carlsbad Caverns and slowly decorated its walls, ceilings, and floors.

New Mexico's Carlsbad Caverns rivals Mammoth Cave for subterranean spectacle, but there are fundamental differences. While the water that created Mammoth Cave's tunnels and halls was a very mild solution of carbonic acid, at Carlsbad, different underlying strata allowed the creation of sulfuric acid, which does the same job of dissolving its way through the earth. Carlsbad's extraordinary speleothems are both more diverse and more numerous than those of the longer Mammoth Cave. And there is nothing else anywhere under the surface of North America to compare with Carlsbad's "Big Room."

Wind Cave, in the Black Hills of South Dakota, is the product of other twists on this same process, with even more emphasis on the subtle. The cave system, mile after mile of narrow passageways, lacks the huge chambers and monumental speleothems of Mammoth and Carlsbad, but reveals a surprising array of smaller decorations to the attentive eye.

In contrast to these deep and convoluted excavations, consider water's role in the Everglades, often called the "river of grass." A thin layer of water is slowly spreading sediments and nutrients over south Florida. Belying the stereotypical movie image of a swamp as a stagnant, fetid place of death, this is a robust and dynamic ecosystem, continually renewed by the southward flow of fresh water from the north.

Water has taken on other construction and nurturing roles in Biscayne, Dry Tortugas, and Virgin Islands National Parks, with their keys, cays, reefs, and

Everglades Neighbors
An alligator basks on its soggy bed as a heron waits for a passing meal.

Biscayne

Channel Islands

Everglades

Mammoth Cave

Virgin Islands

Wind Cave

Coastal Defense
Eighteenth-century Fort Jefferson dominates Garden Key in Dry Tortugas.

other tropical treats so uncharacteristic of the mainland. Dry Tortugas is anything but. Less than 1 percent of this 67,700-acre Caribbean reserve east of the Florida Keys is above water, and then only a few feet. As at Biscayne, there are extensive coral reefs. The larger islands are sand, but the sand itself is largely made up of the remains of ancient corals and related organisms. And, as at Biscayne, a phenomenal diversity of life is attracted to this hospitable marine environment.

Virgin Islands National Park, not far southeast of Puerto Rico, shows obvious signs of its more complex geological legacy. The Caribbean was formed when Europe and Africa separated from the Americas, so the islands reflect the subductions, volcanism, and general restlessness associated with such dramatic tectonic action. The same magnificent coral architecture as at Biscayne and Dry Tortugas not only thrives here, but provides the raw material for the island's legendary beaches.

The five major islands and island groups of the Channel Islands, off the southern California coast, offer an even more complex setting. Not only are their individual geological biographies distinct (more evident volcanism here, more sedimentary rock there), but also they are being differently affected by ongoing plate tectonics. As the Pacific Plate passes northward along the edge of the North American Plate, the islands have been slowly rotating for many millions of years. Meanwhile, oblivious to all this motion and energy, native and nonnative life-forms have created remarkably distinct communities on these islands. Thanks to the water around them, they are just remote enough from each other and the mainland to develop into unique little worlds.

Wave Power
Powerful wave action formed Arch Rock off Anacapa Island in the Channel Islands.

BISCAYNE

NATIONAL PARK IN FLORIDA

STUNNING REEFS

Biscayne's land surface is derived from the remains of corals and calcareous algae. The park's four major ecosystems are nicely lined up, parallel to one another. Starting from the west, there is the narrow band of coastal shoreline, then Biscayne Bay itself, then the string of keys, and finally the offshore water with its many reefs. These four distinct worlds are inhabited by a kaleidoscopic array of life-forms—an enduring source of joy, wonder, and scientific inquiry, only minutes away from much tamer landscapes.

There is a very important forest in Biscayne, one that is little more than a thin vertical line along the park's western edge. This slight ribbon of vegetation has a parkwide reach. It begins not far south of Miami and runs down the coast for 22 shore-hugging miles. At first glance, you might be inclined to call it a thicket rather than a forest, but that is what a mangrove forest looks like.

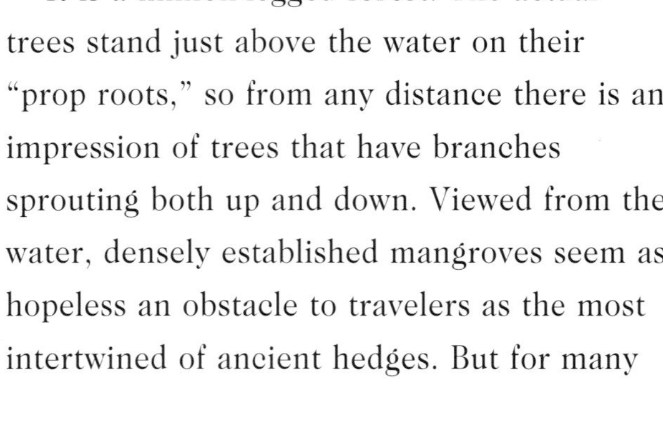

It is a million-legged forest. The actual trees stand just above the water on their "prop roots," so from any distance there is an impression of trees that have branches sprouting both up and down. Viewed from the water, densely established mangroves seem as hopeless an obstacle to travelers as the most intertwined of ancient hedges. But for many species it is a perfect place to live. Young fish and other sea creatures find food and shelter in among the roots. Birds find the same up above and make the rookeries on top, from which they can make long feeding forays to the rest of the park and beyond.

But the mangroves perform much grander services for this region. The millions of roots serve as a barrier against pollutants moving from the land into the estuary. From the other direction, they firmly hold shoreline soils and sands in place against winds and waves—even against hurricanes. And over time the silt they capture builds new soil. The mangroves are shelter, anchor, filter, and architect, all in one—an essential part of the superb wilderness they so unobtrusively border.

Brain Coral
Single mounds of brain coral can reach diameters of 9 feet after several centuries of growth.

Reef Denizen
A moray eel, left, found around Biscayne, above, lies in wait for his next meal.

Water Park

More than 95 percent of Biscayne lies underwater. There, divers can encounter more than three hundred species of fish, as well as many other marine life-forms.

Camouflaged Crab
The mottled colors of the spider crab help it blend in with its coral surroundings. Other crustaceans that live in the waters of Biscayne include the spiny lobster.

Biscayne Bay
The national park takes in most of Biscayne Bay and a line of thirty-three small, outlying coral islands—the northernmost reaches of the Florida Keys.

BISCAYNE NATIONAL PARK

History Note: Pirates of the eighteenth and nineteenth centuries lurked among the Florida Keys and attacked ships that had been crippled by storms and driven onto the reefs. Hawk Channel contains some of the wrecks.

Flora: Mangrove forests along the shorelines of the keys and the bay; tropical hardwood forests on the islands' interiors; lush beds of sea grass in the bay.

Fauna: More than three hundred species of fish, crabs, spiny lobsters, sea turtles, the endangered manatee, and many species of birds, including brown pelicans, egrets, and herons.

Visitor Tip: Set aside three hours to take the daily snorkel tour of the park's outstanding reefs. If swimming doesn't suit, consider a reef tour in a glass-bottomed boat.

BISCAYNE NATIONAL PARK
Black Point
RAGGED KEYS
BOCA CHITA KEY
Lewis Cut
Bowles Bank
Fender Point
SANDS KEY
Sands Cut
BISCAYNE BAY
Triumph Reef
Dante Fascell Visitor Center
Coon Point
Sea Grape Point
Elliott Key Ranger Station
Ott Point
Long Reef
Turkey Point
Billys Point
HAWK CHANNEL
WEST ARSENICKER
SANDWICH COVE
Petrel Point
RUBICON KEYS
ARSENICKER KEY
MANGROVE KEY
Adam's Key
Ajax Reef
Midnight Pass
LONG ARSENICKER
REID KEY
Christmas Point
Caesar Creek
TOTTEN KEY
OLD RHODES KEY
EAST ARSENICKER
Pacific Reef
SWAN KEY
GOLD KEY
Broad Creek
CARD SOUND
KEY LARGO
0 1 2 Kilometers
0 2 Statute Miles
0 2 Nautical Miles

Northerly Coral
A diver glides past the wreck of the Laguna. *The park encompasses the northernmost coral reefs in the United States.*

A Brilliant Queen
The queen angelfish shares Biscayne's coral reefs with other tropical fish like damselfish, butterflyfish, and parrotfish.

Muckraking Bird
A resident of Biscayne's shallow coastal habitat, the snowy egret uses its yellow feet to stir up mud in order to flush out prey.

Drop by Drop
A wide variety of calcite formations, including these delicate stalactites, adorn the walls of Carlsbad Caverns. They form slowly as calcite precipitates from drops of water.

CARLSBAD CAVERNS NATIONAL PARK

History Note: In the early 1900s, Jim White, cave guide and explorer, used to lower sightseers into Carlsbad Caverns in a giant bucket once used to haul bat guano from the cave.

Flora: Above ground, Carlsbad takes in a swath of the Upper Chihuahuan Desert, with its hardy grasses, junipers, cactuses, yucca, desert willows, gray oaks, and Texas madrones.

Fauna: Sixteen types of bats roost within the cave. Above ground live mule deer, raccoons, rock squirrels, snakes, lizards, javelinas, ringtails, and coyotes.

Visitor Tip: Consider a ranger-guided tour of Slaughter Canyon Cave, a subterranean wilderness without electricity, paved pathways, elevators, or rest rooms.

Cavernous Halls of Dripstone
Renowned for its dripstone formations, below, Carlsbad boasts the largest rooms of any cave in the United States, including the Hall of Giants area within the Big Room, right.

CARLSBAD CAVERNS

NATIONAL PARK IN NEW MEXICO

UNDERGROUND WONDER

Carlsbad Caverns National Park has been dissolved out of the same 250-million-year-old limestone reef that rises from the desert to form the Guadalupe Mountains. Twenty to thirty million years ago, after mountain uplifts cracked the layers of sediment, water seeped into the gaps and began the slow process of opening larger spaces. About ninety-four caves are known in the park's 73 square miles.

The fantasy world of caves has attracted and repelled us for ages. We savor the urge to explore, to unlock the mystery, to go somewhere no one has ever gone before. Against that urge, we weigh our fear of the unknown, our uncertainty over whether some things should ever be unlocked—and maybe a secret lurking creepiness about how dark it is down there.

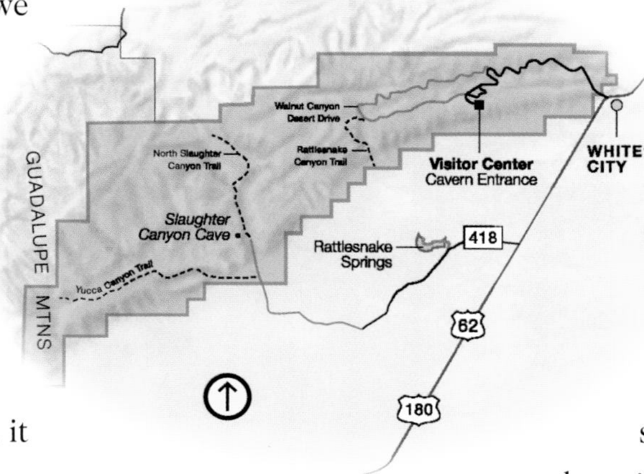

The cave parks are a particular blessing, then, because they allow for the adventurous while they readily accommodate the most timid. Carlsbad Caverns is nothing if it is not generous with its treasures. In a moment, you can travel by modern elevator to a depth of more than 700 feet and step immediately into a wonderland of unearthly delights. It is quite a lot like stepping into Jules Verne's classic, *Journey to the Center of the Earth*. A lot like that, except that you aren't alone, there are no monsters waiting for you, and you can return just as easily as you came (the movie version of that stirring and improbable novel was partly filmed in these very chambers).

Expect to see the famous large stalactites and stalagmites, of course. But there is much else, and the terminology of speleothems is especially vivid and apt. There are shelfstones, cave pearls, draperies, soda straws, cave popcorn, rimstones, totem poles, lily pads, trees, flowers, needles, balloons . . . more than enough marvels to make even the least intrepid Carlsbad Caverns explorer forget for a moment the unspeakably absolute darkness that is waiting at the flip of a switch.

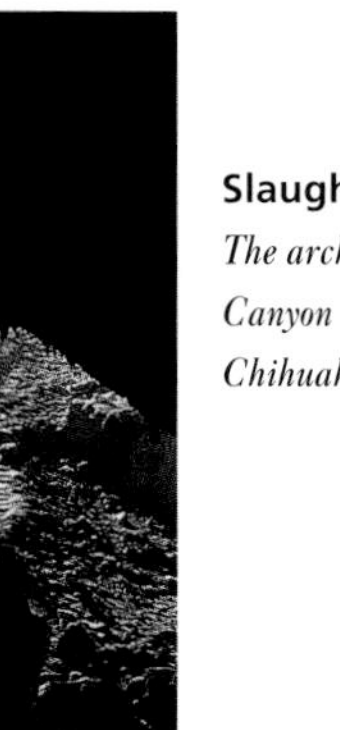

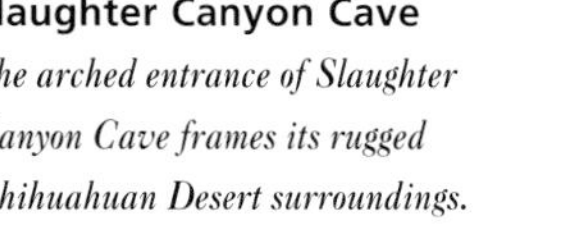

Slaughter Canyon Cave
The arched entrance of Slaughter Canyon Cave frames its rugged Chihuahuan Desert surroundings.

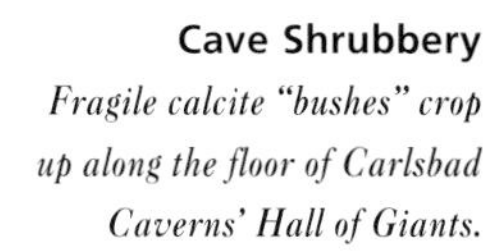

Cave Shrubbery
Fragile calcite "bushes" crop up along the floor of Carlsbad Caverns' Hall of Giants.

CHANNEL ISLANDS

NATIONAL PARK IN CALIFORNIA

ISLAND WORLDS

Geologists agree that the Channel Islands have a messy biography. As the North American and Pacific plates slide laterally past each other, surface features like the Channel Islands have slowly spun like wood chips caught in a riptide. But their significance as a national park has had much more to do with biology than geology. Most important, their extended isolation from the mainland has given them time to affect native life-forms in some surprising ways.

The Channel Islands have plant and animal inhabitants that are similar to those on the mainland but with slight variations. Islands are powerful forces in shaping their inhabitants—all they need is time.

Consider the mammoths that thrived in much of North America during the ice ages. Mammoths were accustomed to spending time on certain highlands along what is now the California coast. The mammoths who swam to the nearby Channel Islands made the best of their new situation. They adapted to their small new world that lacked threatening predators by becoming small themselves. Before they died out they were pygmies, only 5 feet high.

On islands, every biological development is a study in tricky chains of consequence. No doubt the native people who lived here for thousands of years had some serious effects too, but Euro-Americans quickened the pace of change. New plants and animals ate or preyed or outcompeted their way from shore to shore. Native species (there are sixty-five unique plant species here) took a lot of hits. Some disappeared completely. These are very tangled processes. When native bald eagles were driven from the islands by pesticides and harassment, it wasn't long before golden eagles showed up. Possibly the bald eagles had kept them out before, but the goldens have now established a breeding population. They concentrated on eating the introduced pigs that were running loose. That might not have been a bad thing, because feral pigs are notoriously destructive. Unfortunately, between pork dinners the eagles also began

Wave Power
Wave-erosional features, such as this sea arch, left, are common along the shore of Anacapa; so are seabirds, above.

Rugged Diversity
Largest and most rugged of the park's islands, Santa Cruz boasts six hundred types of native plants.

Battered Isles

Lit by sunrise and battered by waves, Anacapa Island, below, stretches west into the Pacific. Castle Rock, right, lies off the north shore of San Miguel Island.

picking off the native island foxes, another unique miniaturized form.

The foxes hadn't evolved to deal with this predation. They were used to being out and about in broad daylight—which, of course, was just fine with the eagles. Worse, the foxes couldn't hide very well anyway, because introduced sheep had overgrazed the vegetative cover. Now some islands may lose their foxes entirely. Introduced canid diseases and parasites might be making things even worse.

Volcanic Birth

Anacapa Island is part of a volcanic ridge that erupted from the floor of the ocean millions of years ago.

Ultimately, every lesson learned from these situations ends up seeming a little too simple. There are always more factors than anyone considered. There are always pieces of the puzzle nobody has noticed.

But one of the real blessings of parks like Channel Islands is that they do give us a chance to watch, and learn, and find ways to put things back together. And for all the damage they have sustained, the Channel Islands are still a great wonder. They are, in fact, ecologically significant enough to merit selection by the United Nations Educational, Scientific, and Cultural Organizations as an International Biosphere Reserve. There is still plenty here to be saved and cherished.

Yellow Giants

A field of tree sunflowers, left, blazes on Santa Barbara Island. Right: A humpback whale shows its flukes.

Anacapa Greenscape

Green vegetation cloaks the gullies and rolling hills of Anacapa Island. Dormant and brown for most of the year, the plants revive under winter rains.

Separated by the Sea

The isolated Channel Islands are home to plants and animals found nowhere else in the world. The nearest island lies 11 miles offshore.

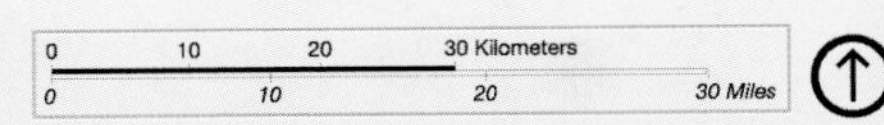

CHANNEL ISLANDS NATIONAL PARK

SANTA BARBARA

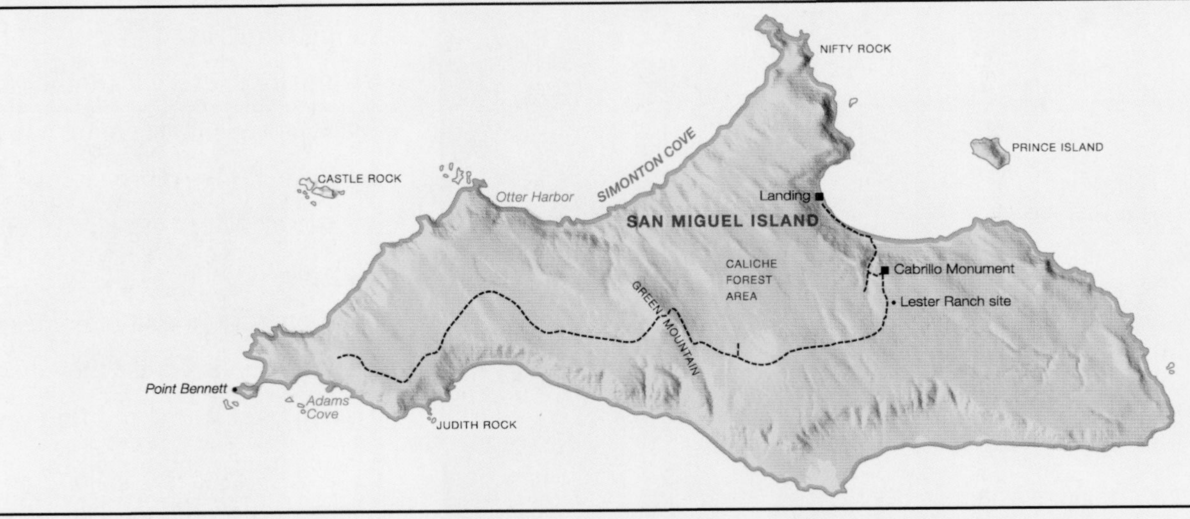

Carved by Waves

Powerful wave action has beaten most of Anacapa's volcanic shoreline into a procession of steep cliffs, sea caves, sea stacks, blowholes, sea arches, and surge channels.

A Panoply of Pinnipeds

Sea lions are one of four species of pinnipeds—fin-footed mammals—drawn to the remote beaches and rich feeding grounds of the Channel Islands.

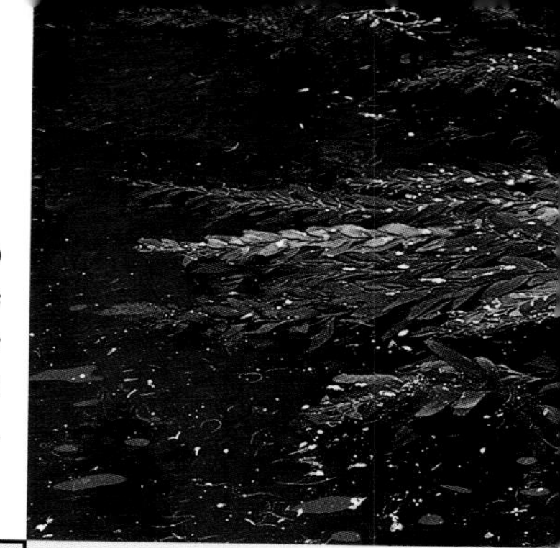

Strands of Kelp

Kelp beds, which flourish in Channel Islands waters, are one of the most biologically diverse ecosystems on the planet, harboring more than one thousand species of plants and animals.

Painted Cave
Scorpion Valley Ranch site
Mount Diablo
SANTA CRUZ ISLAND
CENTRAL VALLEY
SANTA CRUZ CHANNEL
Sierra Blanca
Punta Arena
GULL ISLAND

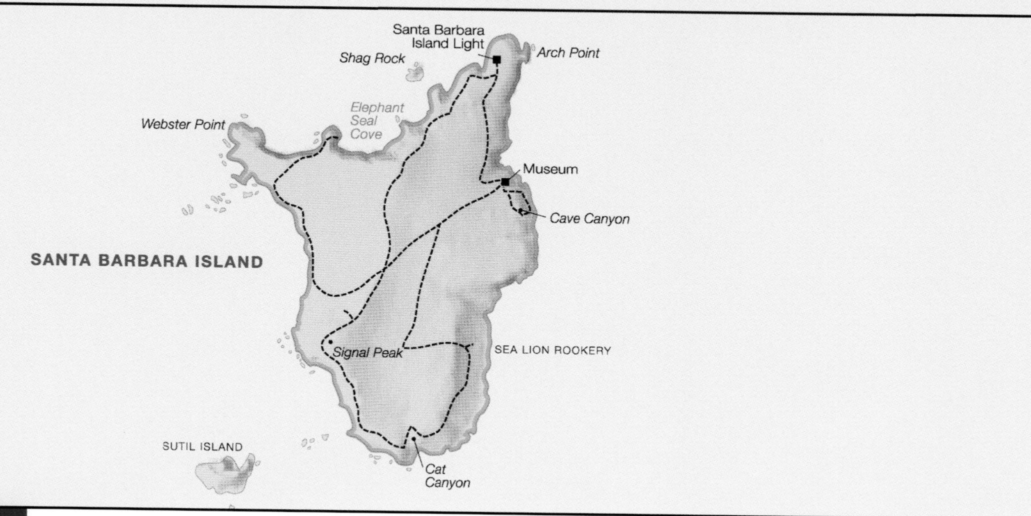

CHANNEL ISLANDS NATIONAL PARK

History Note: In 1959, the remains of "Arlington Woman" were discovered on Santa Rosa Island. The bones, dating back 13,000 years, are the oldest human remains yet found in North America.

Flora: More than six hundred species and subspecies from ten different families; sixty-five grow nowhere else.

Fauna: A cornucopia of marine mammals, including blue and humpback whales, elephant seals, and sea lions; abundant tidepool organisms; the cat-sized Island fox, 140 species of landbirds, and many seabirds.

Visitor Tip: Those with strong legs should consider taking the guided hike (15 miles roundtrip) to Point Bennett on San Miguel Island, where tens of thousands of sea lions and seals gather on the beach to bear and rear their young.

Varied Coastline

Formations along Santa Cruz Island's 77 miles of coastline vary from steep cliffs and enormous sea caves to quiet coves and sandy beaches.

Brown Pelican

A brown pelican folds its wings. Its commodious pouch serves as a fishnet, and its bill has a special hooked end to grip its slippery prey.

DRY TORTUGAS NATIONAL PARK

History Note: Fort Jefferson served as a Union prison during the Civil War and confined Samuel Mudd, the doctor who set the broken leg of John Wilkes Booth.

Flora: Few land plants, mostly mangrove and palms.

Fauna: Hundreds of fish species; loggerhead turtles; many birds, including tens of thousands of nesting terns.

Visitor Tip: Getting to the park can be expensive, but camping there is a bargain—just three dollars a person. Campers must pack in all provisions, including drinking water.

Historic Fort

Built over the course of thirty years but never completed, nineteenth-century Fort Jefferson, below and right, dominates Garden Key in the Dry Tortugas.

DRY TORTUGAS

NATIONAL PARK IN FLORIDA

UNDERWATER MAJESTY

The islands, reefs, and banks of the Dry Tortugas are about 70 miles west of Key West, Florida. Less than 1 percent of the park is dry land. There are seven islands, though the number has varied in historical times because the low-lying keys are occasionally subjected to being washed away and rebuilt—just enough to sink or raise them. The park's waters contain some of the most pristine coral reefs in the United States, while its islands are home both to wildlife and to important historic structures.

Ponce de León named this small group of islands "Las Tortugas" for the abundance of sea turtles in the area, and eventually they became known as the Dry Tortugas because there was no freshwater available. Since then, they have occupied a small but engaging niche in the course of American history.

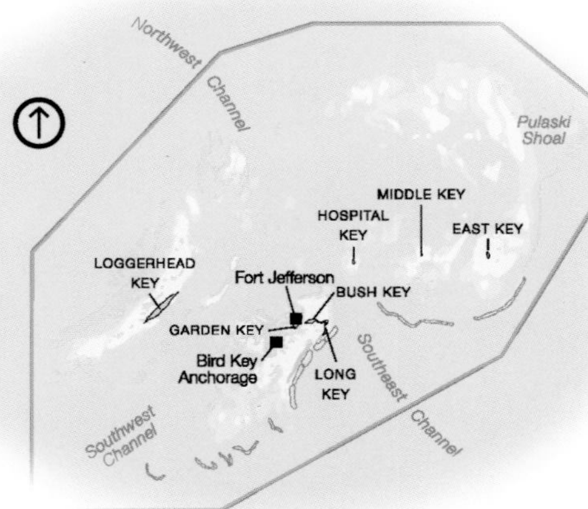

Their reefs and shoals were hazardous to shipping. One of the park's most unusual cultural resources is the collection of shipwrecks—more than three centuries' worth—scattered here and there. The first lighthouse was constructed on Garden Key in 1825, and another was built (and still remains) on Loggerhead Key in 1856.

The islands were ideally located to monitor shipping and other naval activity in the Florida Straits, so construction began on Fort Jefferson in 1846 and, despite formidable logistical challenges, went on intermittently until 1874.

Though it never underwent bombardment, the fort did play a role in the Civil War, perhaps most notably as a prisoner-of-war internment camp. Besides its 2,500 Confederate prisoners, the fort held four of the men involved in the assassination of President Lincoln.

The Dry Tortugas have accumulated value for such historical reasons. To their robust reef communities, tropical bird habitat, hospitality to imperiled sea turtles, and other obvious recreational and scientific values were added to the need to preserve the now-historic structures of earlier days. The area passed through periods as a wildlife refuge and national monument on its way to becoming a national park in 1992.

Longspine Squirrelfish
One of 442 fish species cataloged in the Dry Tortugas, a longspine squirrelfish hovers among the coral.

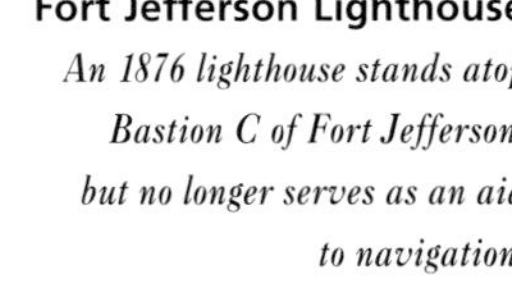

Fort Jefferson Lighthouse
An 1876 lighthouse stands atop Bastion C of Fort Jefferson, but no longer serves as an aid to navigation.

mangroves, and the maze of coastal waterways and ponds, and finally reaches Florida Bay and the Gulf of Mexico, where it supports yet more ecological communities on the many keys and in the sea itself.

All of this happened with the ease and beauty of wild nature for millennia, during which people came and took what they wanted but did not change the basics. The river still flowed, the plants and animals still thrived.

Bait-Fishing Bird
Green-backed herons sometimes lure fish into striking range by casting insects, berries, and twigs on the water.

But now people want more, much more. And there are more people all the time. Over the past fifty years, a complex system of canals and conservation areas have been constructed north of the park. They have catastrophically harnessed and reduced the river. Wading bird populations have declined by more than 90 percent, and every other part of the wild setting has been gravely affected. The Everglades are the most imminently endangered park in the United States, if not the world. The restoration of this magnificent place requires heroic actions by the American people. The river deserves nothing less. Nothing less will save it.

Boarded Over
A boardwalk, left, extends over an Everglades wetland. Red-shouldered hawks, right, patrol the park's wooded swamps.

Slender Trunks

Fire-resistant slash pines reach for the sky from an understory of saw palmetto. The diverse pinelands habitat boasts more than two hundred species of tropical plants.

Grudge Match

Roseate spoonbills compete for territory during mating season. Some two hundred pairs nest in the park.

EVERGLADES NATIONAL PARK

History Note: South Florida's post World–War II population explosion has led to a severe degradation of the Everglades' crucial freshwater supply. The decline in water quality and availability now threatens the very existence of the Everglades.

Flora: Nine distinct plant habitats, including estuarine, coastal marsh, mangrove forest, cypress swamp, coastal prairie, freshwater slough, pineland, freshwater marl prarie, and hardwood hammock; the largest continuous stand of saw grass prairie in North America; and the largest mangrove ecosystem in the Western Hemisphere.

Fauna: Fourteen endangered species, including the West Indian manatee, three sea turtles, and the rare Florida panther; more than three hundred species of birds, including the endangered wood storks and snail kites; dolphins, snakes, white-tailed deer; crocodiles and alligators.

Visitor Tip: For some of the best alligator and bird viewing in the park, take the tram tour from the Shark Valley Visitor Center.

29
EVERGLADES CITY
Gulf Coast Visitor Center
41
CHOKOLOSKEE
BIG CYPRESS NATIONAL PRESERVE
TEN THOUSAND ISLANDS
Lopez River
Lopez River
Huston River
Chatham River
Tree Snail Hammock
94
41
Shark Valley Visitor Center
SHARK RIVER SLOUGH
GULF OF MEXICO
Lostmans River
KEY MCLAUGHLIN
EVERGLADES NATIONAL PARK
Broad River
Rock Reef Pass
Pa-hay-okee Overlook
Long Pine Key
Harney River
9336
Ernest F. Coe Visitor Center
Park Headquarters
Ponce De Leon Bay
Shark River
Royal Palm Visitor Center
1
TAYLOR SLOUGH
Mahogany Hammock
Whitewater Bay
CAPE SABLE
Nine Mile Pond
West Lake
Flamingo Visitor Center
Eco Pond
KEY L
FLORIDA BAY
FLORIDA KE
NATIONAL MA
SANCTUAR
0 1 5 10 Kilometers
0 1 5 10 Miles
ATLANTIC OCEAN

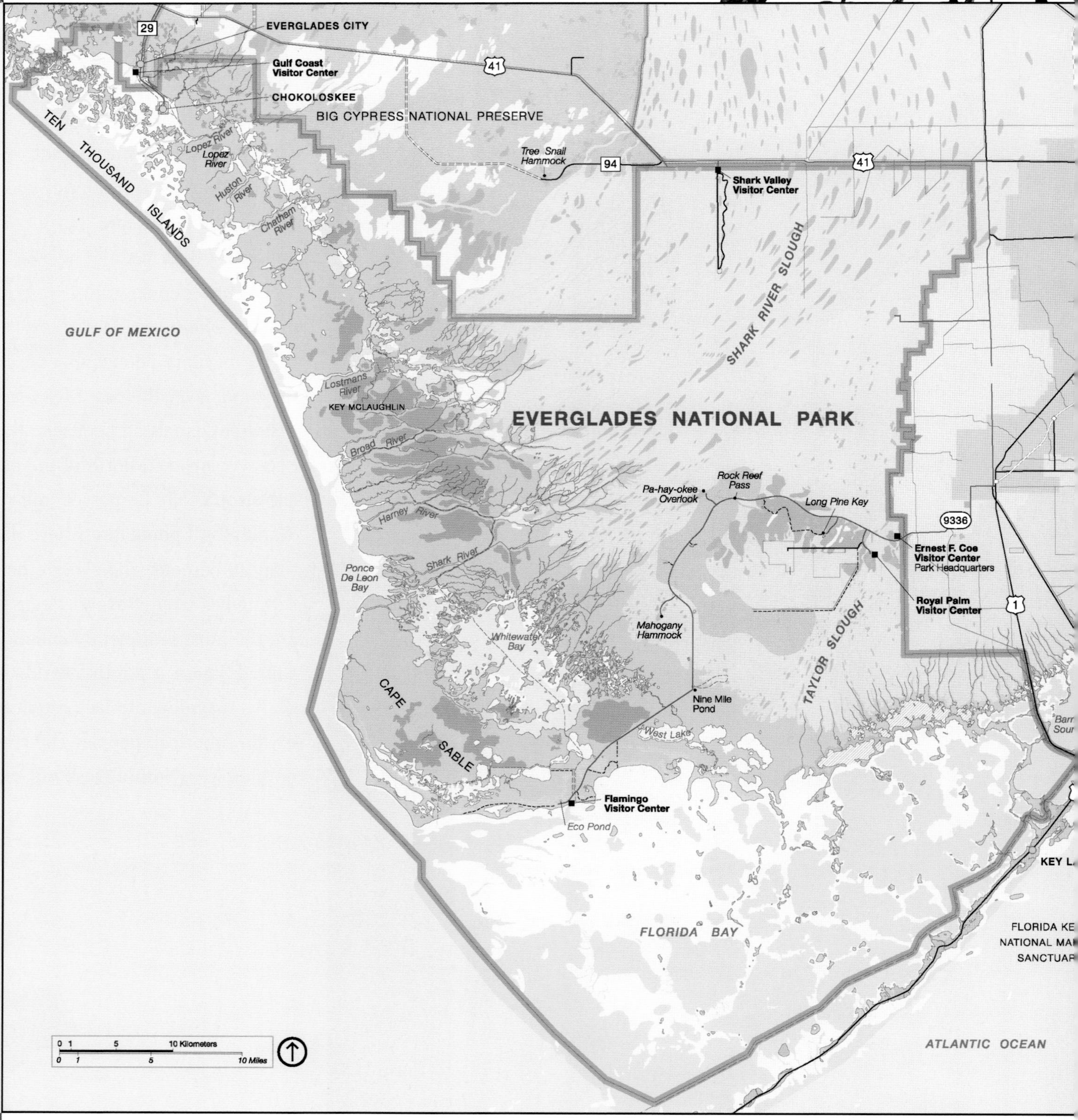

Snake in the Grass

A rough green snake mingles with the Everglades foliage. Its coloring camouflages it from prey and predator alike.

Bug Nets

Thousands of spider webs glisten across an Everglades landscape, right. Facing page: A viney tumble of Morning-glory flamingo.

SALTWATER HABITAT

Saltwater surrounds three sides of Everglades National Park and helps to define several major habitats. It extends south and east for a dozen miles or more and wraps around the park's irregular western shoreline, where it bathes Cape Sable, Key McLaughlin, and the Ten Thousand Islands. Close to shore, it mingles with the freshwater streams that pulse through the heart of the park.

Florida Bay is the largest body of water (salt or fresh) in the park. Dotted with hundreds of tiny mangrove islands, this marine habitat covers 800 square miles, averages just 4 to 5 feet deep, and supports extensive beds of sea grass. The sea grass shelters various types of fish and shellfish, including mangrove snappers and pink shrimp, and provides an important food source for the endangered West Indian manatee. Corals and sponges live on the bay's hard bottom areas.

Everglades also protects extensive areas of habitat, where saltwater blends with freshwater in the estuaries of the park's rivers and streams. Like the marine habitat of Florida Bay, the estuaries support mangrove trees and serve as breeding grounds, spawning grounds, and nurseries for many species of birds, fish, and reptiles, including crocodiles, brown pelicans, roseate spoonbills, and loggerhead turtles.

Forests of red, black, and white mangrove trees grow in the tidal zone of marine areas and in the transition zone between freshwater and saltwater in the estuaries. During dry seasons, the mangrove forests attract many wading birds that congregate here to feed on shrimp and fish. Mangroves actually extend the land as they spread along the coast, and they protect it from storm erosion.

Trees on Stilts
Red mangroves thrive in shallow tidal waters where freshwater mixes with saltwater.

Narrow bands of coastal prairie extend along the northwest shore of Florida Bay and the southwest shore of Cape Sable. Wind-blown, arid, and occasionally flooded by seawater during hurricanes, the prairie contains salt-tolerant succulents and other low-growing desert plants.

Endangered Manatees
West Indian manatees eat more than 100 pounds of aquatic vegetation daily.

On the Margin
Paurotis Pond lies along the margin of two important Everglades ecosystems—freshwater marl prairie and the mangrove zone.

Doors to the Underworld
A multitude of openings leads into the underworld throughout the Mammoth Cave region, including the maw of Sand Cave.

MAMMOTH CAVE NATIONAL PARK

History Note: During the War of 1812, Mammoth Cave was mined by slaves for saltpeter, a key ingredient in gunpowder. Later, a portion of the cave housed tuberculosis patients.

Flora: Diverse woodlands, including a remnant of Kentucky's old-growth forest of immense white and black oaks, tulip poplars, and sugar maples; white dogwood, hickory, mountain laurel, open barrens of prairie wildflowers and grasses.

Fauna: Over one hundred species of animals use the cave to some degree, including forty-two species of troglobites such as eyeless fish and eyeless crayfish, which live exclusively within the cave. Above-ground animals include many small mammals such as squirrels and raccoons, snakes, birds, fish, and fifty different freshwater mussels.

Visitor Tip: Wear hiking shoes and bring along a sweater or light jacket for touring the cool, damp interior of the cave system.

World's Longest Cave
Crystal Lake, right, lies near the Frozen Niagara entrance to Mammoth, the longest known cave in the world. Below: A beaver slaps an alarm signal.

MAMMOTH CAVE

NATIONAL PARK IN KENTUCKY

LIMESTONE PASSAGES

Starting about 350 million years ago, when much of North America was submerged beneath a large sea, several hundred feet of limestone were deposited on what is now west-central Kentucky. Groundwater worked its way down into vertical joints in the limestone beds until it met firm rock, then flowed along that rock layer to create long horizontal passages. These passages are uncannily similar to erosion-formed canyons, with added roofs.

Native Americans explored and used several miles of Mammoth Cave for a few thousand years before Euro-Americans arrived in the region and expanded human awareness and investigation of this immense labyrinth. By the early 1800s, the cave was a tourist attraction, though no one knew its total length. An early survey, in 1908, revealed 45 miles of passages.

Mammoth Cave was not the only cave attraction of the Kentucky limestone country. As others were discovered, the tourist business became stronger and more competitive. Operating with primitive equipment in perilous conditions, early guides and adventurers took heroic risks to enlarge knowledge of the caves. In 1925, explorer Floyd Collins, exploring a cave in Mammoth Cave Ridge, was trapped by a rockfall. His name became a household word during the two-week rescue effort that preceded his death from exposure. This dramatic tragedy no doubt increased awareness of the caves and interest in their exploration.

Over the next forty years, additional pioneering of new passages proved that the Flint Ridge caves were part of one gigantic system even larger than Mammoth Cave itself. Then, in 1972, spelunkers discovered a passage connecting the Flint Ridge system with the Mammoth Cave system. The label "Mammoth" seemed more apt all the time. Mammoth Cave, at over 350 miles in length, is now known to be three times longer than any other discovered cave in the world. Additional passages are assumed, and estimates of the cave's total length run as high as 600 miles.

River Mist
Mist rises from Green River in the rugged forest and bluff country above Mammoth Cave.

Spring Water
Underground water emerges from one of many springs in the park's Green River Valley.

VIRGIN ISLANDS

NATIONAL PARK

REMOTE PARADISE

The Virgin Islands have a complex geological history. During the past 100 million years, the region has been subjected to extended alternating periods of sedimentation and volcanic activity. As a result of these events, widely varying types of rock were deposited, many of them thousands of feet thick. Faulting, massive submarine rockslides, sea floor subsidence, and other distortions associated with the widening of the Atlantic Ocean further modified the regional topography.

The coral reef is proof of the curious axiom that "If you build it, they will come." Coral reefs have been under construction, deconstruction, and reconstruction for at least 200 million years—they are called "the world's oldest ecosystem"—and in that time have found an astonishing number of ways to support themselves.

It begins with a small animal, the polyp. Polyps, master colonists and unequaled team players, cooperate with microscopic algae that live in their tissue to secrete hard skeletons of calcium carbonate. In vast architectural partnerships, they build coral in its many treelike, antlerlike, brainlike, flowerlike forms.

A host of tiny organisms are not only attracted to but also nourished by the coral. Grazers and their predators are drawn to all the new opportunities. As the reef grows, its countless nooks, crannies, and caves are homesteaded by all manner of sea creatures, many specifically adapted to their chosen type of coral. Soon the relationships among these species of plants and animals become Byzantine in their convolutions.

For one example of many, some types of small fish and shrimps become "cleaners," who make part or all of their livings by carefully eating tiny parasites from the bodies of larger fish. Some even perform these duties inside the mouths of their patient clients. Specialization piles upon specialization. The more that life builds, the more new life comes. In the reefs of the Virgin Islands, this giddy pageant of colors, shapes, adaptations, lifestyles, and constructions is yours for the snorkeling.

Island Creatures
Foureye butterfly fish, left, and endangered hawksbill turtles, above, ply along the island's waters.

Coral Sand
Beaches of fine-grained coral sand adorn many of the island's bays, including Maho Bay.

Volcanic Islands

Built largely by volcanoes and thrust upward by tectonic forces, the Virgin Islands, below, lie between the Greater and Lesser Antilles. Right: **Palm trees.**

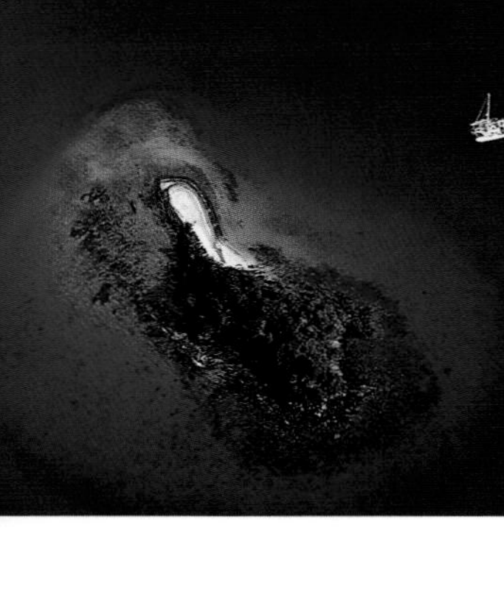

Snorkeler's Paradise

A coral reef rings Watermelon Cay off St. John's north side. Most of the Virgin Islands National Park's reefs are fringing reefs, closely aligned with the shore.

Harbor Town

The harbor town of Cruz Bay lies on the west shore of St. John. The island's original rain forests were destroyed to make way for sugar plantations.

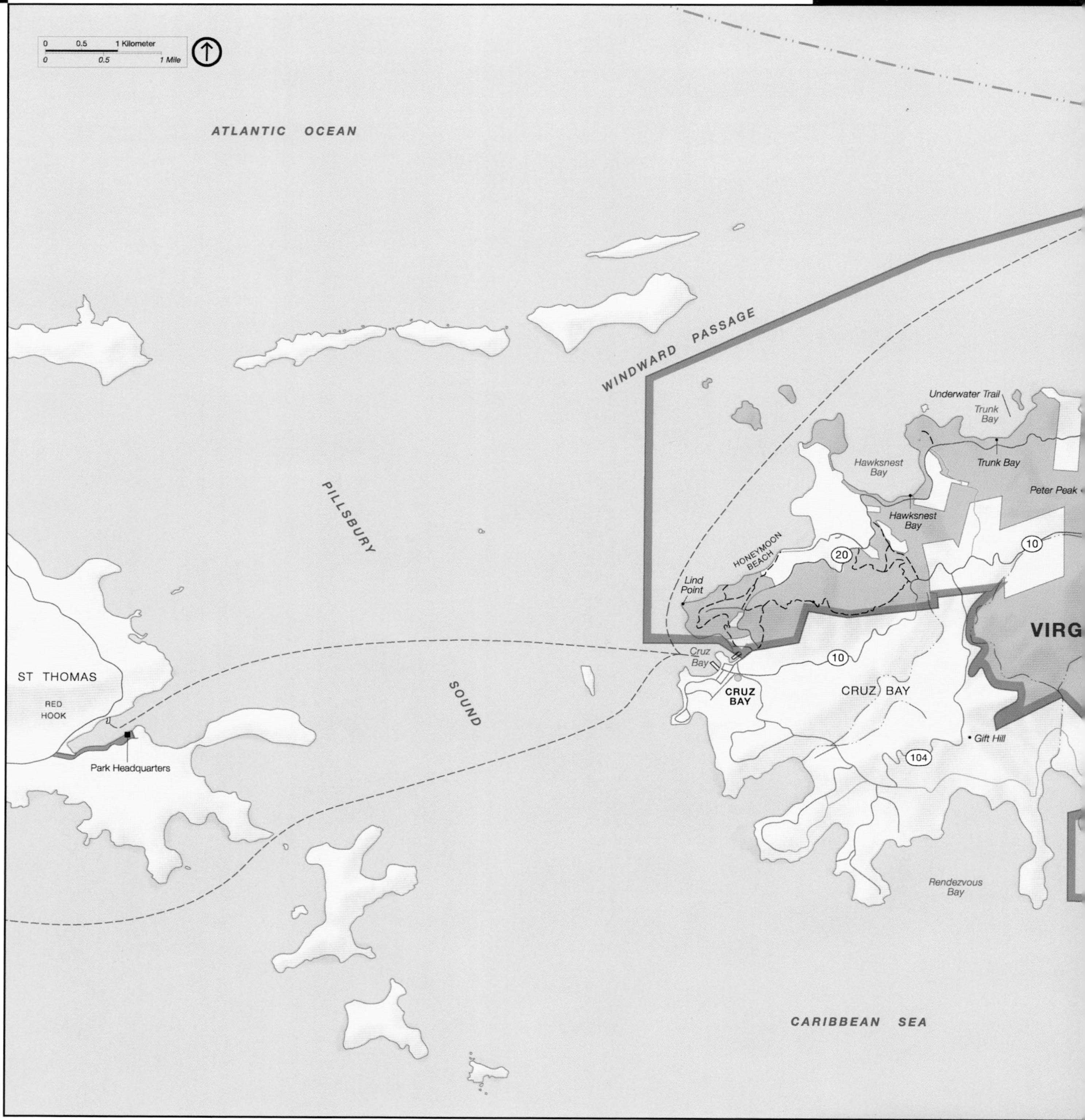

0 0.5 1 Kilometer
0 0.5 1 Mile
ATLANTIC OCEAN
WINDWARD PASSAGE
PILLSBURY SOUND
ST THOMAS
RED HOOK
Park Headquarters
Underwater Trail
Trunk Bay
Trunk Bay
Hawksnest Bay
Hawksnest Bay
Peter Peak
HONEYMOON BEACH
Lind Point
20
10
10
Cruz Bay
CRUZ BAY
CRUZ BAY
VIRG
Gift Hill
104
Rendezvous Bay
CARIBBEAN SEA

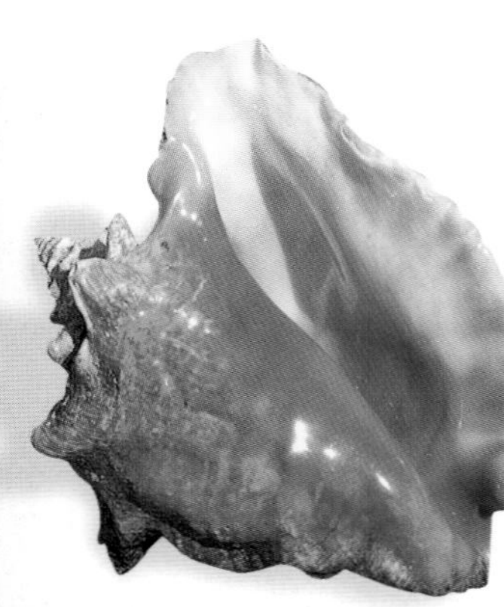

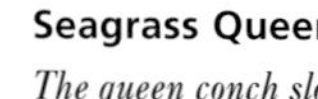

Seagrass Queen

The queen conch slowly roams the undersea beds of turtle grass and manatee grass that grow in St. John's calmer waters.

Trunk Bay

A strip of coral sand lines the shore of Trunk Bay. The bay's reef supplies the sand and protects the beach from wave erosion.

Rocky Beach

Cobbles smoothed by wave action lie along the rocky beach at Drunk Bay. Other rugged beaches on the island of St. John are made of coral rubble.

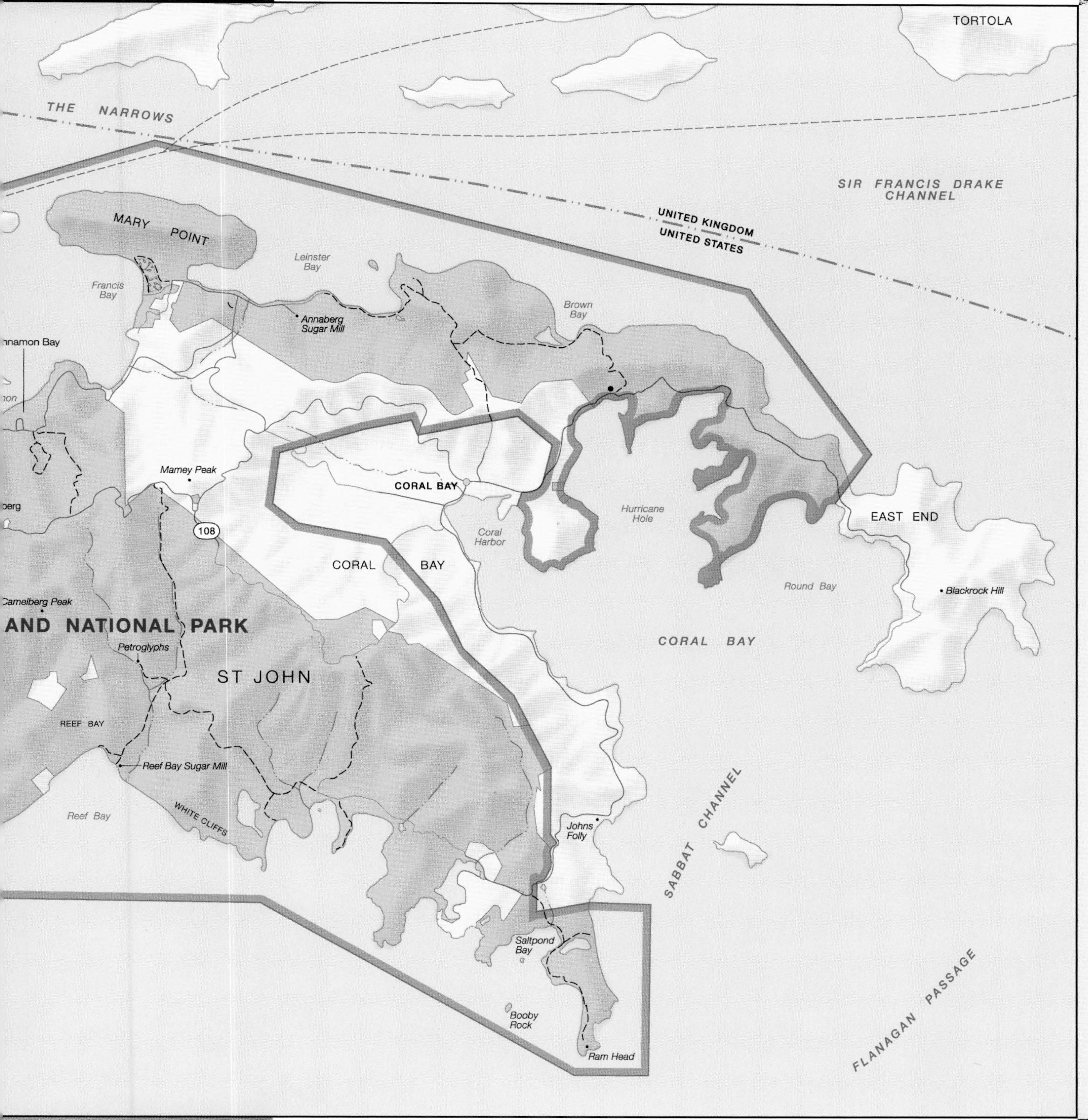

TORTOLA
THE NARROWS
SIR FRANCIS DRAKE CHANNEL
UNITED KINGDOM
UNITED STATES
MARY POINT
Leinster Bay
Francis Bay
Annaberg Sugar Mill
Brown Bay
nnamon Bay
Mamey Peak
CORAL BAY
108
CORAL BAY
Coral Harbor
Hurricane Hole
EAST END
Round Bay
Blackrock Hill
Camelberg Peak
AND NATIONAL PARK
Petroglyphs
ST JOHN
CORAL BAY
REEF BAY
Reef Bay Sugar Mill
Reef Bay
WHITE CLIFFS
Johns Folly
SABBAT CHANNEL
Saltpond Bay
Booby Rock
Ram Head
FLANAGAN PASSAGE

VIRGIN ISLANDS NATIONAL PARK

History Note: Danish planters claimed St. John Island in 1718, imported African slaves, and within twenty-five years cleared most of the island's ancient rain forests.

Flora: More than eight hundred species of plants, including kapok, bay rum, strangler fig, palm trees, orchids, century plants, and dildo cactus; mangrove swamps; subtropical forests; and semiarid cactus scrublands.

Fauna: Corals, two types of endangered sea turtles, bats, frogs, lizards, more than thirty species of tropical birds, and a cornucopia of reef creatures, including octopuses, parrot fish, grunts, moray eels, spiny lobsters, fireworms, trumpet fish, and squid.

Visitor Tip: For a terrific introduction to the reef ecosystem, take the weekly ranger-guided snorkel trip at Trunk Bay.

Reef Predator

Lightning fast and armed with a jawful of sharp teeth, the great barracuda cruises the island's reefs hunting for smaller fish.

Delicate Boxwork

South Dakota's Wind Cave is renowned for its intricate boxwork formations, below, which can resemble honeycombs. Left: Prairie dogs thrive in the park.

WIND CAVE

NATIONAL PARK IN SOUTH DAKOTA

SUBTERRANEAN LABYRINTH

The modern caves of Wind Cave National Park were created following the rise of the Black Hills about sixty-five million years ago. Portions of modern Wind Cave apparently follow ancestral cave passages from earlier building episodes. Wind Cave's maze of passages is known to reach more than 100 miles, but calculations based on the volume of air that moves in and out of the cave suggest that this may be only 5 percent of the total extent.

Caves aren't for everybody. Wind Cave is indeed one of the world's longest known caves, but don't assume that means its passages are all world-sized too. Among your group on a typical Wind Cave tour may be some people who, though at ease in the spacious chambers of Carlsbad Caverns or Mammoth Caves, find the long person-sized tunnels of Wind Cave a little close. Though the main tour routes are never truly squeeze-through tight, they do appear to have been designed to let fairly trim, calm people pass through—single file.

But that intimate acquaintance with the rock, even if you're trying your best not to brush against it and affect its delicate structures, is a good thing. Because Wind Cave is different in other ways, too.

The most significant difference is that its decorative formations, though as beautiful as any on earth, are not monumental in scale. They are miniature marvels, delicate and elegant almost beyond imagining, as if they'd been formed somewhere in deep space without even the restraints of gravity to moderate their creation.

Boxwork is the most prominent, evoking thoughts of avant-garde ice-cube trays. But coral-like helictites, cave popcorn, calcite rafts, dogtooth spar, and even limited quantities of dripstone and flowstone are here too. Boxwork fringed with popcorn and frostwork crosses the line between geology and magic. All you need to do to discover the magnificence of Wind Cave National Park is adjust your sense of scale, and give each small wonder a long, careful look.

Daybreak
Radiant dawn breaks over a prairie pothole full of rainwater, left. Above: Dames rocket flanks a stream.

Avian Diva
A meadowlark belts out a prairie oratorio. Male meadowlarks have up to a dozen songs in their repertoire.

Prairie Hills

Dames rocket blossoms beside a small creek flowing among the hills of Wind Cave National Park's prairie. The park brags five hundred plant species.

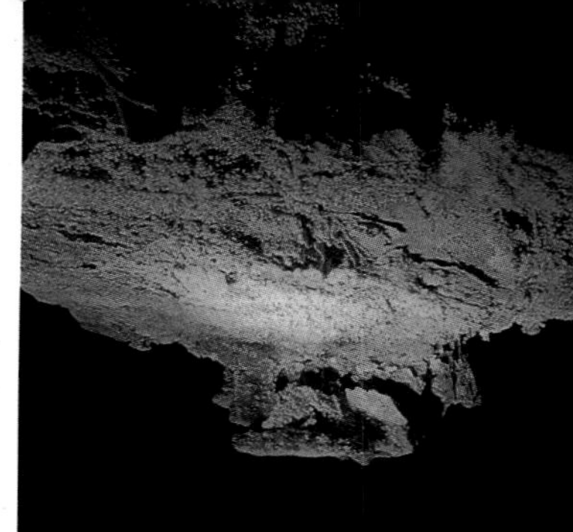

Stony Snack

Cave popcorn, a formation so named because it resembles the food, clings to the ceiling of Wind Cave National Park's Garden of Eden. It is formed by seeping water.

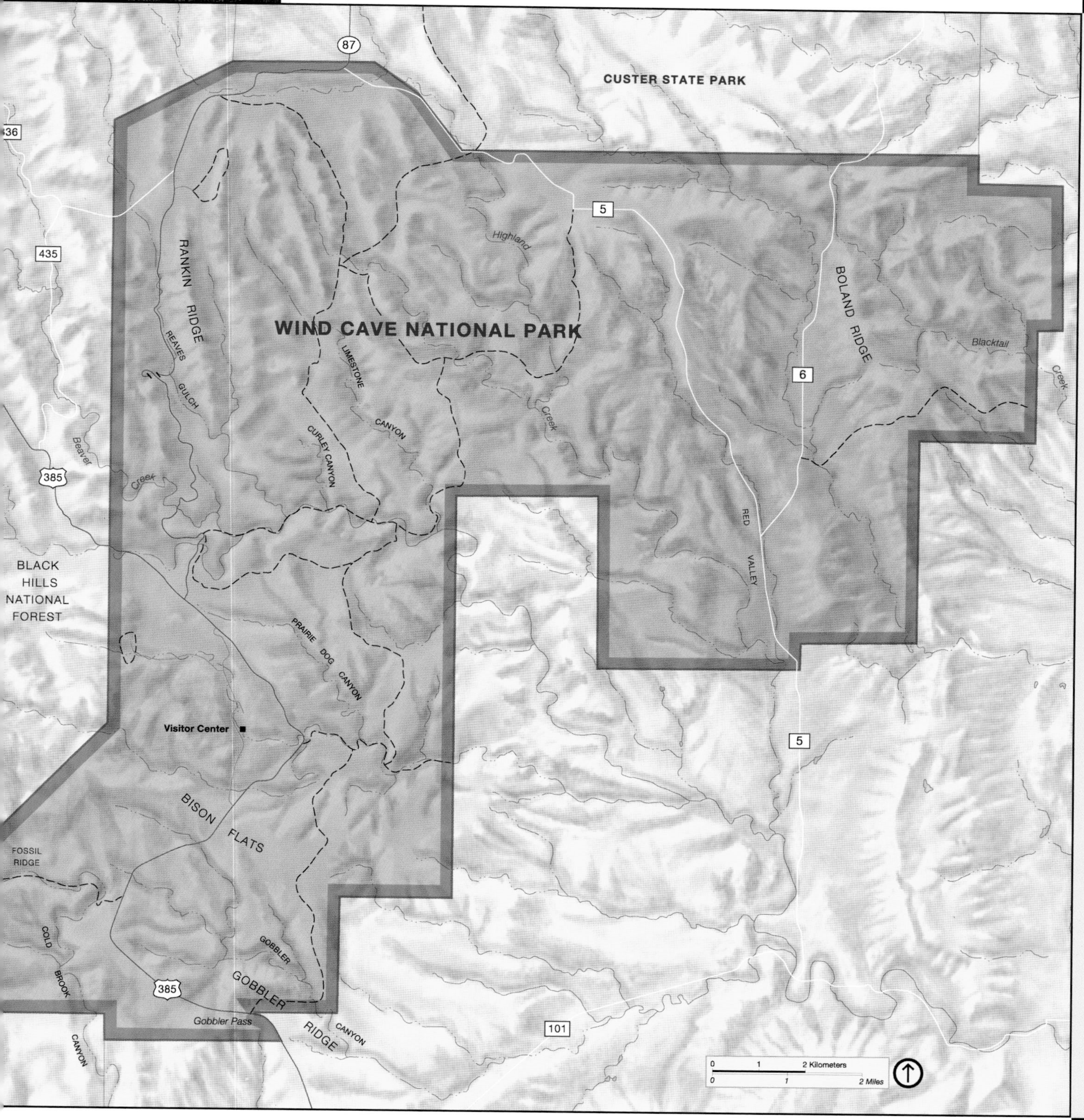

87
CUSTER STATE PARK
36
435
5
Highland
RANKIN RIDGE
BOLAND RIDGE
WIND CAVE NATIONAL PARK
REAVES GULCH
LIMESTONE CANYON
Creek
Blacktail
Creek
6
Beaver
Creek
CURLEY CANYON
385
RED VALLEY
BLACK HILLS NATIONAL FOREST
PRAIRIE DOG CANYON
Visitor Center
5
BISON FLATS
FOSSIL RIDGE
COLD BROOK CANYON
GOBBLER
385
GOBBLER RIDGE
CANYON
Gobbler Pass
101
0 1 2 Kilometers
0 1 2 Miles

WIND CAVE NATIONAL PARK

History Note: Known to the Sioux for generations as "Sacred Cave of the Winds," Wind Cave was billed as the "Great Freak of Nature" by local tourism boosters during the 1890s.

Flora: Mixed-grass prairie bursting with a variety of wildflowers, including black-eyed Susan, sunflowers, hairy golden asters, paintbrush, goldenrod, and wild blue flax; ponderosa pine forests.

Fauna: Large mammals, including bison, pronghorn, and mule deer; many rodents, including prairie dogs; badgers, coyotes, skunks, and diverse species of birds such as red-tailed hawks, eastern bluebirds, meadowlarks, and pinyon jays.

Visitor Tip: Explore the margin between Wind Cave's two dominant surface habitats—grassland and forest—by following the 1-mile Elk Mountain Nature Trail.

Prairie Remnant

Wind Cave preserves one of the last remnants of the original mixed-grass prairie, facing page, a diverse blend of tall and short grass species. Following spread: One of the park's primary missions as a wildlife sanctuary was to help restore bison populations.

Perching Pirate

Winter residents of the park, magpies sometimes mob a successful raptor in order to steal its meal. Such piracy is called kleptoparasitism.

Molded Boxwork

Wind Cave's boxwork probably predates the cave itself. The delicate calcite fins formed in cracks in the limestone, then remained as surrounding rock dissolved.

THE CARVING POWER OF GLACIERS

GLACIERS, MORE THAN any other great earth-shaping force, remind us of animate, almost sentient things. Some scientists cannot resist calling them "creatures" and imbuing them with intention and purpose. Glaciers grow, carve, sculpt, scrape, scour, scratch, surge, crush, pile, grind, retreat, and die. More daintily, they pluck, sort, and polish. They pick things up, carry them around for a while, and drop them somewhere else. More ominously, they remember. And if we ask them the right questions, they predict. This seems a lot to ask of a big blob of ice.

Ice Aplenty
More than three hundred glaciers glaze the peak of North Cascades National Park.

They begin as snow, somewhere high and cold enough that it can bank and deepen through the years. Given the right conditions, it doesn't take long for the snow to compress under its own weight, become ice, and begin to move.

Capped by Glaciers
Cloaked in ice, Mount Shuksan looms above Picture Lake in the North Cascades.

A glacier works in many directions, and no part of its bed is unaffected by its passage. The very weight of the ice actually compresses the land underneath. The glacier grinds rock into the fine "flour" that gives glacial rivers their distinctive milkiness, mounds up rock in huge moraines alongside, and bulldozes them along in front.

ICE SCULPTING STONE

In a hundred ways, the glacier reshapes the land, rounding off knolls, turning full-bodied mountain ridges into slender walls and turrets, trenching solid rock along its weakest joints, making lakes, and rerouting rivers. Glaciers have done all these things many times, and with variations beyond our imagining, and their legacy reaches far beyond the ice itself.

Grinding Ice
Exit Glacier grinds past a forested slope in Kenai Fjords.

A Valley Carved by Ice

No erosive force can match the power of glacial ice. Often thousands of feet thick and armed with gravel, rocks, and boulders, it carves out valleys, chisels away at mountain peaks, and helps to create fjords, lakes, and ribbony waterfalls. Yosemite Valley, once buried in ice,

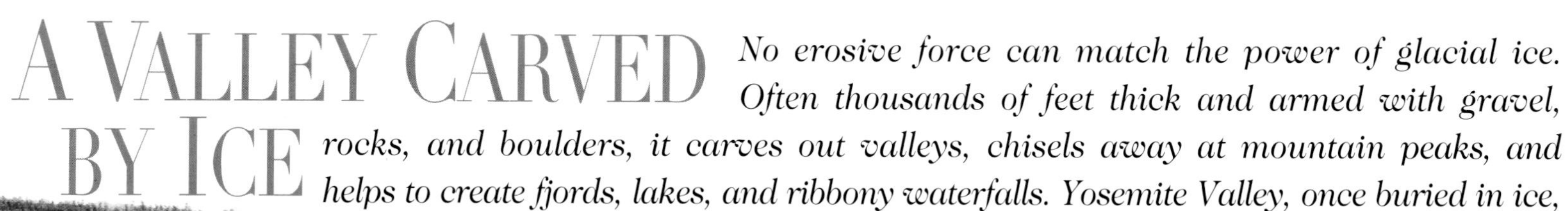

THE SHAPING OF YOSEMITE VALLEY

At least four major glaciations carved the walls of Yosemite Valley and helped to create its spectacular cliffs, hanging valleys, and precipitous waterfalls. Fed by heavy snowfall along the crest of the Sierra Nevadas, the glacial ice followed the course of the Merced River through Little Yosemite Valley, then coalesced with a glacier from Tenaya Canyon and continued down Yosemite Valley. The earliest glacial advance was the most extensive and most powerful, inundating virtually every landmark. Later glaciations, though less comprehensive, still managed to fill the valley with thick tongues of ice as far as Bridalveil Falls.

is a masterpiece of Pleistocene glaciation. It is also one of the first sites in America where the influence of glaciers was recognized and studied. Elsewhere throughout the Rockies, but particularly in Alaska, glaciers continue to practice their benevolent form of vandalism.

RIVERS OF ICE

Once a glacier forms and begins to flow down a mountain slope, it takes the path of least resistance by following the course of an existing stream valley. Prior to glaciation, the valley's profile in cross section will exhibit the characteristic contours of stream-cut valleys—narrow, V-shaped, and often zigzagging.

During glaciation, moving ice plucks and carries hunks of rock and other debris from the walls and floor of the valley and uses these abrasive materials to widen, deepen, and straighten the valley. The result is a broad, U-shaped glacial trough.

Tidewater Wastage
With tidewater glaciers, such as Glacier Bay's Reid Glacier, the zone of wastage extends into the sea, where large chunks of ice calve from the glacier and form icebergs.

HOW GLACIERS CARVE THE LAND

ANATOMY OF A GLACIER

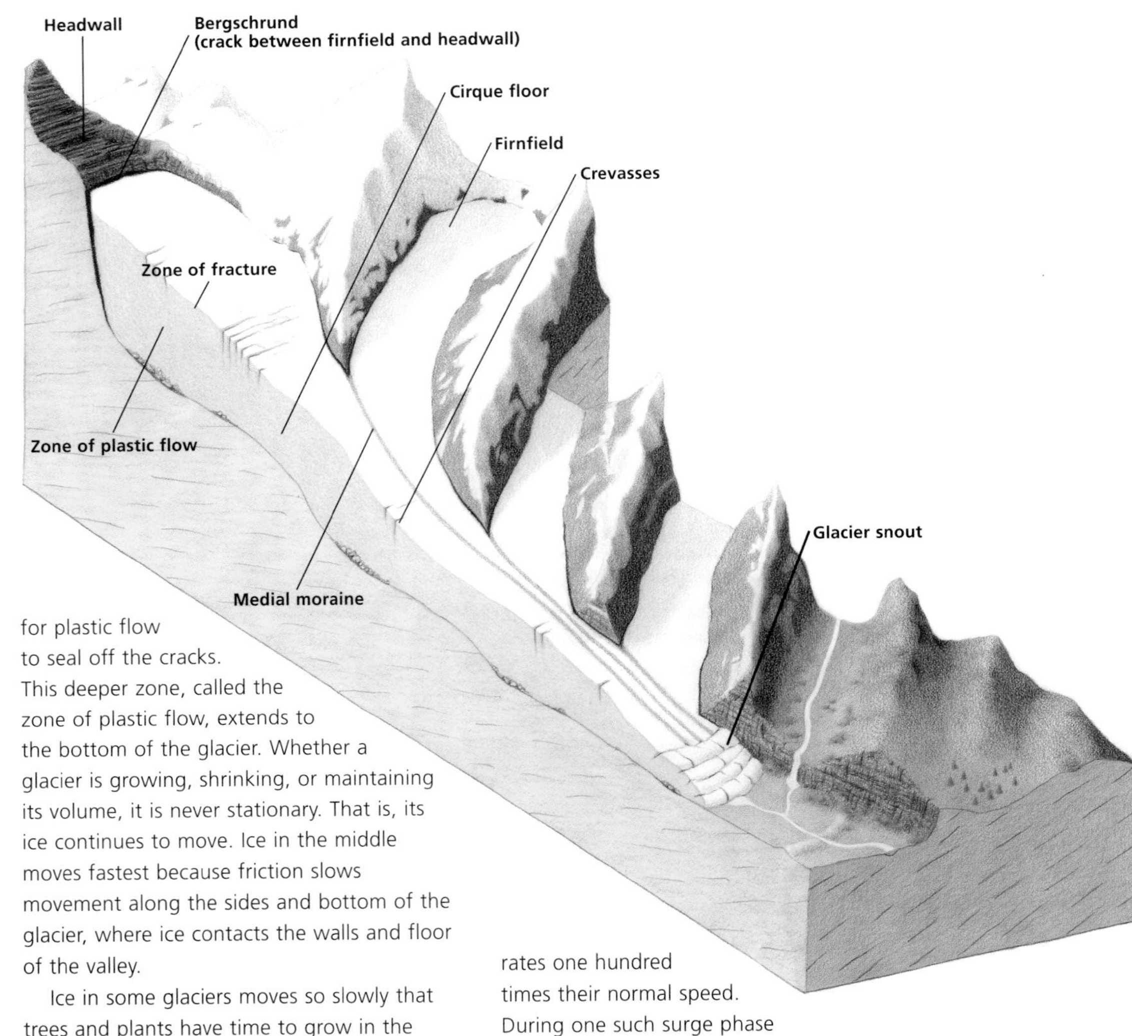

Glaciers are thick masses of ice that form on land from the accumulation, compaction, and recrystallization of snow. They form where more snow falls during winter than melts during summer.

As snow accumulates year after year, a perennial snowfield forms, grows, settles, and compacts under its own increasing weight. Light, powdery snow recrystallizes from angular, six-pointed flakes into ice grains that have the consistency of coarse sand. As more snow is added, pressure increases on the lower layers, and the ice grains fuse to form solid ice. Once the body of snow and ice exceeds a thickness of 165 feet, the weight is sufficient to cause ice in the lower layers to behave as a plastic material and to flow downhill. At that point, the whole mass of snow and ice is considered a glacier.

At the upper end lies the zone of accumulation, where more snow falls during winter than melts during summer, and where glacial ice is formed. Toward the lower end of the glacier lies the zone of wastage, where all of the previous winter's snow melts along with some of the glacier's ice. The balance—or lack thereof—between accumulation and wastage determines whether a glacier advances, retreats, or stays about the same size.

In the upper layer, called the zone of fracture, the ice is brittle and tends to break into deep cracks as the glacier rides over irregular terrain. Called crevasses, these cracks can reach depths of roughly 165 feet. But below that depth, pressure is sufficient for plastic flow to seal off the cracks. This deeper zone, called the zone of plastic flow, extends to the bottom of the glacier. Whether a glacier is growing, shrinking, or maintaining its volume, it is never stationary. That is, its ice continues to move. Ice in the middle moves fastest because friction slows movement along the sides and bottom of the glacier, where ice contacts the walls and floor of the valley.

Ice in some glaciers moves so slowly that trees and plants have time to grow in the debris that collects on the glacier's surface. Other glaciers move thousands of feet each year. Occasionally, advancing glaciers surge at rates one hundred times their normal speed. During one such surge phase in the 1980s, Alaska's Variegated Glacier advanced as much as 180 feet each day.

Moraines and Abrasions
Russell Glacier, in Wrangell-Saint Elias, left, bears long dark strips of glacial till known as medial moraines, formed when two or more valley glaciers coalesce. The scoured granite of Yosemite, right, and Acadia's Cadillac Mountain, far right, attest to the tremendous abrasive power of glaciers.

Glacier Bay

Less than three hundred years ago, Alaska's Glacier Bay was completely covered by a thick layer of glacial ice.

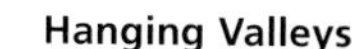

Hanging Valleys

Reynolds Mountain, a prominent horn, caps the rim of a hanging valley near Logan Pass in Glacier National Park.

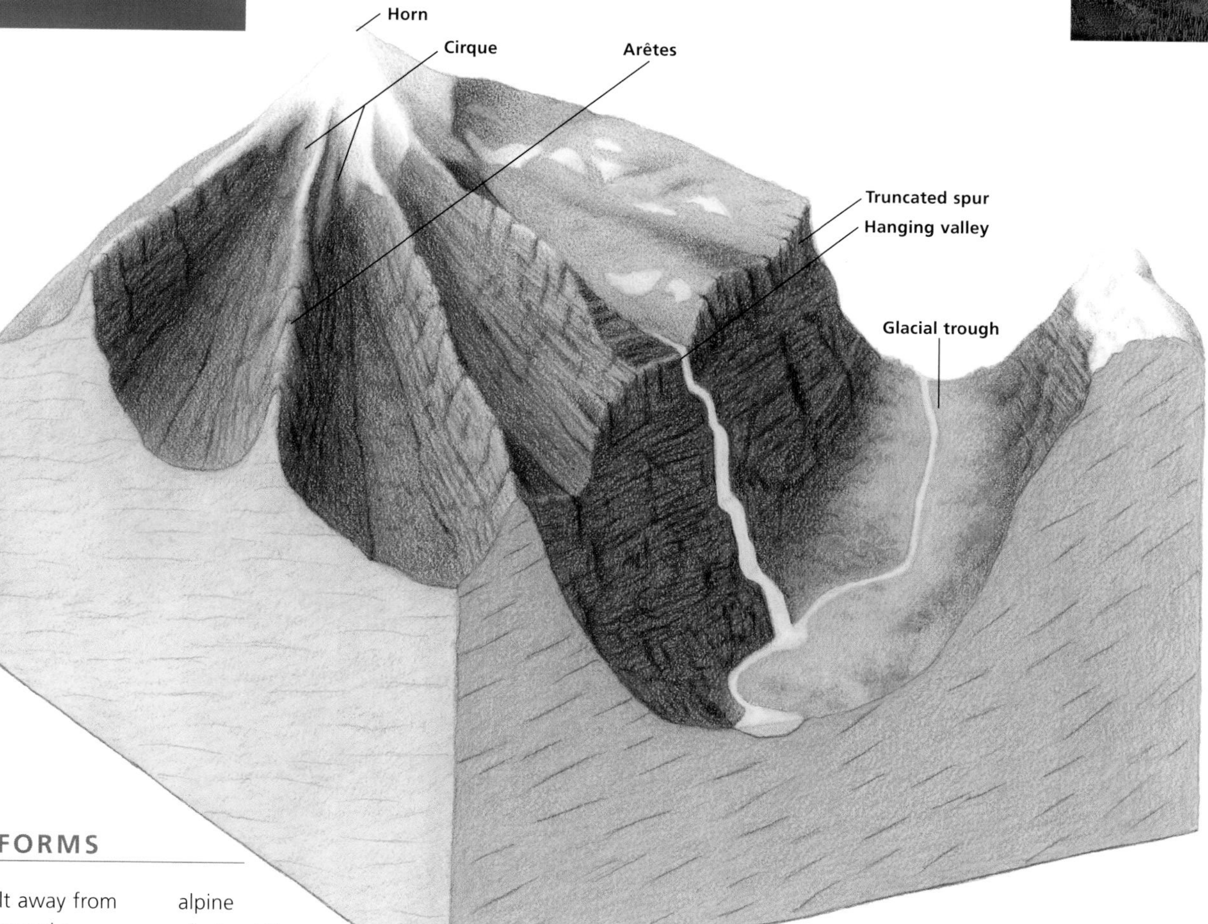

GLACIAL LANDFORMS

When valley glaciers melt away from a mountain range, they reveal a transformed landscape in which canyon walls have become steeper, peaks more jagged, and dividing ridges even more abrupt. The fact that this transformation occurs in solid rock attests to the matchless erosive power of glacial ice.

Starting at the crest of the range, small alpine glaciers form semicircular, bowl-shaped depressions called cirques. Where three or more alpine glaciers bite into a protruding summit, they carve the peak into a pyramidal form known as a horn. Where glaciers gnaw away on both sides of a dividing ridge, they can sharpen it into a knife-edged arête, or even bite through completely to form a gap, or pass, called a col.

As they flow down the range, these smaller glaciers often join and flow into much larger glaciers, called main, or trunk, glaciers. Since the intensity of glacial erosion depends partly on the thickness of the ice, the thicker trunk glaciers tend to cut their valleys deeper than their relatively thin tributary glaciers. When the ice recedes, the valleys of tributary glaciers are left standing above the main trough and are called hanging valleys.

When a trunk glacier straightens out a valley's sharp curves, it cuts away spurs of land that extend into the valley, thereby creating triangular cliffs called truncated spurs.

Glaciers also leave behind deposits of rock and other debris. They form ridges, called moraines, along the sides and leading edges of the ice. Streams running beneath, within, alongside, and over the ice deposit debris as valley trains, eskers, kames, and kame terraces.

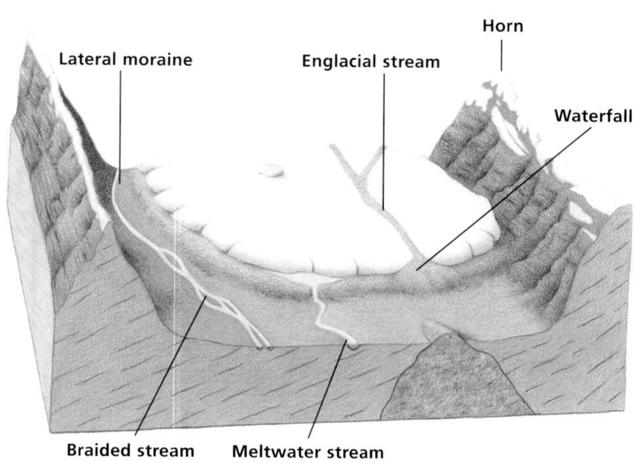

Valley Glacier

Postglacial Valley

Glacial debris

At Great Basin National Park, a rock glacier and piles of glacial debris occupy the floor of a glacial trough on Wheeler Peak.

RIVERS OF ICE, FIELDS OF SNOW

EARTH'S FROZEN FORCE

The glacial parks tell us a long, remarkable story about our changing continent. During the last ice age, as much as a million square miles of North America was smothered again and again in ice thousands of feet thick. At high elevations south of the main sheet there was also heightened glacial growth, and even huge local ice caps. In geological terms this icy realm vanished only yesterday, less than twenty thousand years ago. As the ice finally retreated it was for the first time followed by people—seeking out livings and homes in the raw, new landscape.

Glacier

Great Basin

At Acadia National Park, on Mount Desert Island on the Maine coast, the signs of the violence between ice and earth are everywhere. The granite put up a good fight, but the advancing ice found the weaknesses in its structure and dug deep, north-south-trending troughs across the island. The biggest, Somes Sound, has the distinction of being the only true fjord on the Atlantic Coast of the United States.

Isle Royale

A vast continental ice sheet submerged Isle Royale during the last ice age and scoured its Precambrian bedrock.

Along the midwestern border of the U.S. and Canada, Isle Royale and Voyageurs National Parks display the scars and redecorations left by continental ice sheets. Both parks are part of the ancient Canadian Shield, in a sense the basement or foundation rock of the continent. At Isle Royale, the weight of the ice sheets was so great that the whole island sank below the level of the lake. As the ice left, the island slowly bobbed back. A similar effect was had at Voyageurs, where very slow "rebound" from the weight of the ice is still occurring.

Beyond the southern reach of the great continental ice sheets, other glaciers grew. In the unlikely setting of the eastern Nevada desert, small alpine glaciers flourished above 8,000 feet in the Snake Range. In Great Basin National Park, it's possible to travel quickly from sagebrush desert to the bowl-shaped cirques carved around Wheeler Peak during the last glacial age. One small glacier from that era has even survived.

But the most spectacular display of glacial effects to be found south of the reach of the big ice sheets must be California's Yosemite National Park. In fact, Yosemite is twice important in glaciology, because it was here that mountaineer-conservationist John Muir convinced a doubting world that all of this magnificently domed, riven, polished, morained landscape showed evidence of "flowing, grinding, sculpturing, soil-making, scenery-making ice."

Many parks contain several kinds of glaciers, but most are best known for certain features. Glacier National Park, for example, was named more for what glaciers had done than for the glaciers that were still there (like many ice-rich areas in today's warming world, its small glaciers are retreating

Glacier Blue

Grinnell Lake gets its distinctive color from rock powder milled by a glacier.

Acadia

Glacier Bay

rapidly). Glacier is renowned for its glaciated peaks (many sculpted to narrow "horns") amid a welter of short, suspended valleys that are divided only by thin-walled ridges and narrow, beckoning passes.

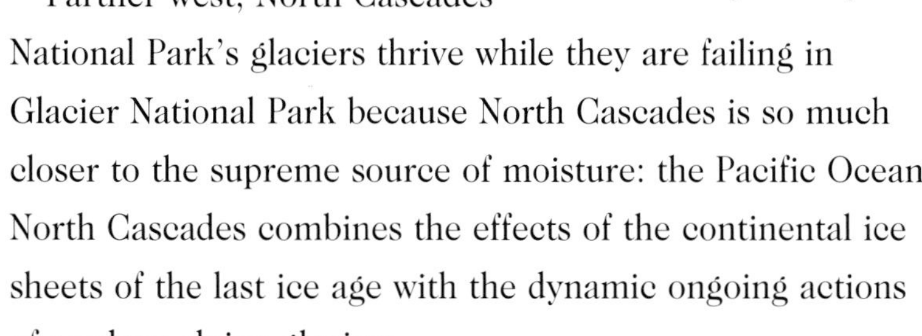

Tidewater Glacier
Holgate Glacier calves icebergs into Aialik Bay in Kenai Fjords.

Farther west, North Cascades National Park's glaciers thrive while they are failing in Glacier National Park because North Cascades is so much closer to the supreme source of moisture: the Pacific Ocean. North Cascades combines the effects of the continental ice sheets of the last ice age with the dynamic ongoing actions of modern alpine glaciers.

Isle Royale

Kenai Fjords

North Cascades

But it is in Alaska where the processes of glacial action can still be witnessed on the grandest scale. The rugged coastline of Glacier Bay and Kenai Fjords National Parks pours many tidewater glaciers directly into saltwater. Though the giant ice sheets and glaciers of the park's uplands are dramatically reshaping the landscape, it is where these ice rivers meet the sea and calve that has attracted most visitor attention.

Voyageurs

Wrangell–St. Elias

The glacial regime of Wrangell–St. Elias National Park encompasses the features of all the others combined, and adds more of its own. The scale here—the park is six times the size of Yellowstone—is stupendous, and so is the ice. The Malaspina Glacier, a piedmont glacier (one that flows out of the mountains onto a relatively flat plain), is by itself larger than Rhode Island.

Yosemite

Wrangell–St. Elias
Glaciated volcanoes cut the sky in Alaska's Wrangell Mountains.

ACADIA

NATIONAL PARK IN MAINE

RAGGED COASTLINE

Acadia National Park is classic coastal Maine. Most of the park is on Mount Desert Island, named by Samuel Champlain in 1604. Additional parklands are protected on the Schoodic Peninsula to the east, Isle au Haut to the southwest, and a dozen smaller islands. Mount Desert's surface, deeply gouged by glacial action, is defined by numerous troughs, inlets, coves, harbors, and lakes. There are more than 40 miles of coastline in this small park.

On the summit of Cadillac Mountain you stand 1,530 feet above the sea—not only the highest point in Acadia National Park, but also the highest point anywhere on the Atlantic Coast of the United States. From this unique eminence at dawn, look east to the open Atlantic and be among the first on the North American continent to see the sun. Or look just a little west of due north, and if the day is clear enough you can see a faint dome on the horizon. It is an even more famous Maine peak, mile-high Mount Katahdin, more than 100 miles inland.

But look down, in any direction, and you will not only see but also understand why the Wabanaki Indians, native to this island when Europeans arrived, called it Pemetic, which meant "the sloping land." Only along the coast, where the ocean is banging away at the cliffs and rocky shores, will you find much severe angularity. Everywhere else, the glacial legacy of smoothing and rounding endures.

Conservation writer Freeman Tilden once wrote that "this is a place where you can stand with one foot in the brine and one on the blossomy land." True, but your stride will cover many worlds. The intertidal zone, so rich in life, is bordered by dramatic seacliffs and rocky shorelines. Twenty percent of the park is wetland, every type from salt marsh to peatlands. The forests are a combination of northern boreal and eastern deciduous. The animals have enthusiastically embraced this smorgasbord of ecological niches.

There is a surprising and pleasant seamlessness of human culture and natural features here. Perhaps it is because of the smaller

Glacial Lakes
Like most of Acadia's lakes, Jordan Pond, left, occupies a basin carved by glacial ice. The "pond" is 150 feet deep and more than a mile long. Above: Blueberry thickets and sugar maples emblazon Cadillac Mountain.

Coastal Creature
Sea stars live in the park's intertidal zone.

Smoothed by Ice

Like much of the park's bedrock, this granite outcropping, right, was smoothed during the last ice age by a mile-high continental glacier that completely buried Acadia. Below: Bass Harbor Head Lighthouse overlooks the Atlantic from wave-battered granite cliffs.

size of the place, or because the glaciers provided the island with so many intimate little hideaways and corners. Or perhaps it is just because people have been living here for so long, and have such affection for Maine's peculiar beauty, that they and their workings seem to fit.

Lush Woods, Bare Granite
An understory of wild sarsparilla and wood fern girdles tree trunks in an Acadian woodland.

On one hand, Acadia features some charming attributes of early twentieth-century recreational planning such as its system of carriage roads and stone bridges. On the other hand, it is, after all, in good part still a wild place, its ecological nooks and crannies crammed with fertile worlds. In addition, the island's human population is largely concentrated in several handsome little harbor villages that seem a perfect fit with the wildness of the island and the sea.

The park is unique in that the land was neither public nor acquired by the government; the land was donated by the very people who most heartily believed the park should exist. With such generously demonstrated enthusiasm behind it, an unusually graceful combination of tame and wild survives in the park today.

The Bubbles
Rounded by glacial ice, the Bubbles stand at the north end of Jordan Pond, below. Left: A fractured dome of granite bulks high over the Atlantic.

Hand-Hewn Bridges

Sturdy stone bridges adorn park roads and connect a network of motorless carriage roads commissioned by John D. Rockefeller, Jr.

Mainland to Island

Broken granite along the Schoodic Peninsula offers a mainlander's view of Mount Desert Island, where most of the park lies. Acadia was created solely from donated private lands.

ACADIA NATIONAL PARK

History Note: A 1947 forest fire forced the evacuation of the island and burned most of its forests, many of its majestic summer homes, and 170 permanent residences.

Flora: Blueberry thickets; deciduous woodlands; coniferous forests of spruce, hemlock, fir, and pine; wildflower meadows; reedy marshes and ponds.

Fauna: Coyotes, black bears, raccoons, seven species of bats, many rodents, harbor seals and porpoises, seven species of salamanders, and 257 species of birds, including peregrine falcons.

Visitor Tip: For a primer on Acadia's native plants, drop by the Wild Gardens of Acadia at Sieur de Monts Spring, where more than four hundred species are labeled and displayed in appropriate settings.

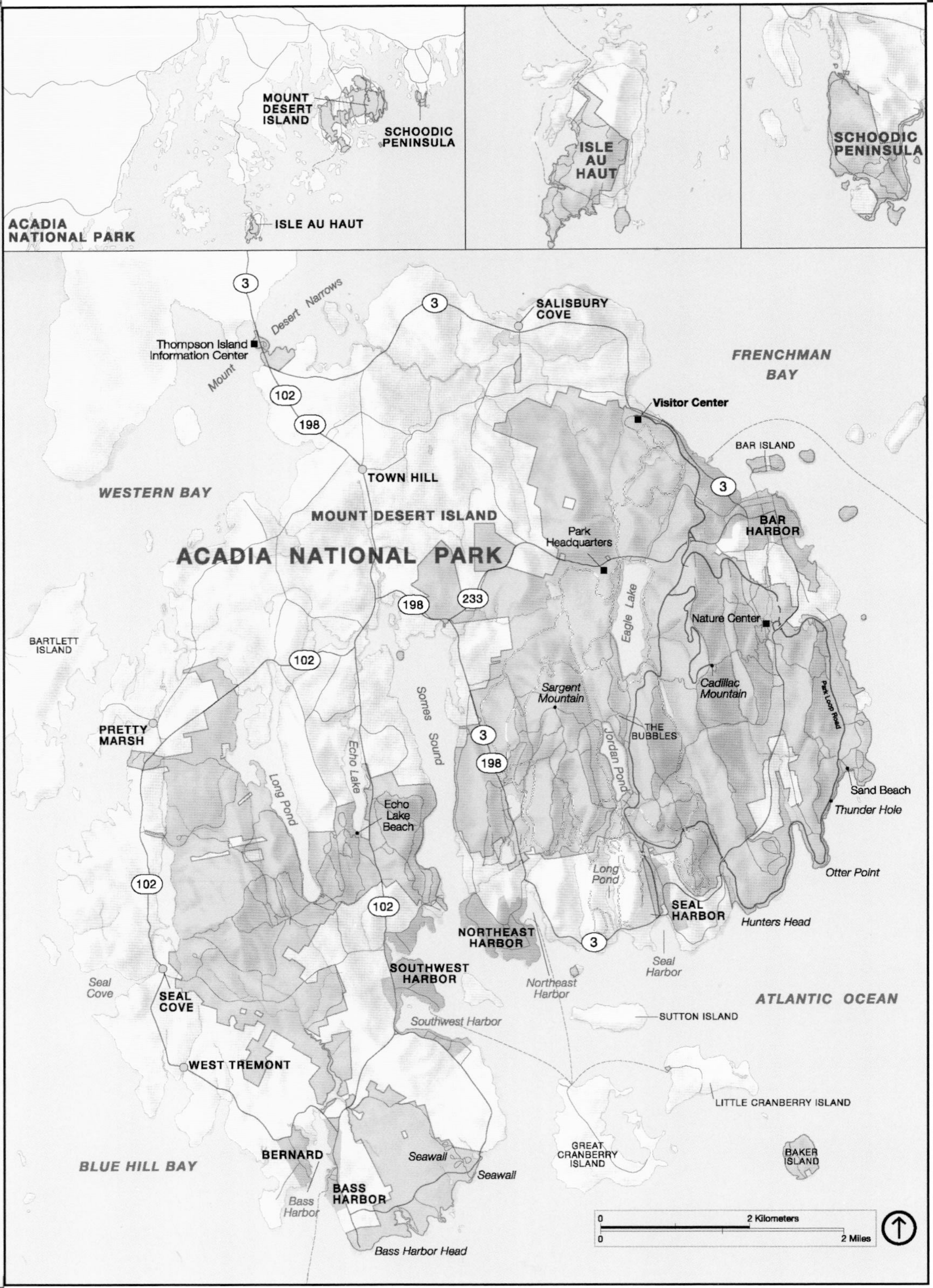

MOUNT DESERT ISLAND
SCHOODIC PENINSULA
ACADIA NATIONAL PARK
ISLE AU HAUT
ISLE AU HAUT
SCHOODIC PENINSULA

ACADIA NATIONAL PARK
MOUNT DESERT ISLAND
3
Desert Narrows
Thompson Island Information Center
Mount
102
198
SALISBURY COVE
FRENCHMAN BAY
Visitor Center
BAR ISLAND
TOWN HILL
WESTERN BAY
BAR HARBOR
Park Headquarters
233
Eagle Lake
Nature Center
BARTLETT ISLAND
Cadillac Mountain
Park Loop Road
Sargent Mountain
PRETTY MARSH
Somes Sound
THE BUBBLES
Jordan Pond
Echo Lake
Long Pond
Sand Beach
Thunder Hole
Echo Lake Beach
Long Pond
Otter Point
SEAL HARBOR
Hunters Head
NORTHEAST HARBOR
SOUTHWEST HARBOR
Seal Cove
SEAL COVE
Northeast Harbor
Seal Harbor
ATLANTIC OCEAN
Southwest Harbor
SUTTON ISLAND
WEST TREMONT
LITTLE CRANBERRY ISLAND
BERNARD
BLUE HILL BAY
Seawall
Seawall
GREAT CRANBERRY ISLAND
BAKER ISLAND
BASS HARBOR
Bass Harbor
Bass Harbor Head

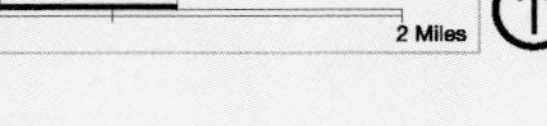

Deciduous Woodlands

Sugar maples and yellow birches scatter their leaves along Duck Brook. The park's deciduous woodlands also include aspen, beech, oak, and many shrubs.

Graceful Stream

A placid stream bends at the foot of a glacially rounded mountain in Acadia.

Coastal Gull

Gulls nest among Acadia's rocky cliffs and find plenty to eat nearby—fish, insects, crustaceans, mollusks, and carrion.

ACADIA'S ROCKY COAST

Crooked, wave-battered, and young, Acadia's rockbound shoreline bends around a multitude of coves, island-studded bays, and a long fjord that nearly bisects the park's main island. The shoreline's highly irregular shape reveals its youth: Erosion has had little time to beat it into a more uniform appearance.

In fact, the ocean has had less than ten thousand years to worry away at Acadia's cliffs, headlands, boulder beaches, and tidal pools. As continental glaciers melted at the close of the last ice age, sea levels rose worldwide. Here, the rising waters flooded a deeply glaciated landscape to create what is called a submergent, or drowned-coast. What appear today as arms of the sea were once river valleys, islands were the tops of mountains, and headlands and peninsulas were once rocky ridges.

Though it is young, the coast has already been altered by the staggering force of wave action. Cracks and crevices open quickly and widen under the thrust and pull of the surging water. Crashing waves also compress air trapped in the cracks. Between waves, the air expands rapidly and helps push apart the rocks.

Under such a concerted attack, the rock breaks apart, and fragments fall away, only to be hurled back at the cliffs as gravel.

Sunrise
Sunrise comes early to Newport Cove on the east shore of the island.

Chemical weathering—incorporating salt from seawater, spray, and mist—intensifies the effects of wave action, abrasion, and the freeze-thaw cycle.

Rocks that have broken away from the cliffs fall to the bed of the sea, where the waves roll them back and forth, rounding their sharp edges against one another and eventually polishing them smooth. Masses of them wash up as bars and shoals, others as beaches of boulders, pebbles, cobbles, and shingles. Sand, though, is rare in Acadia—again, a sign of the shoreline's youth.

Falcon Zone
Bird-rich berry thickets surrounding Jordan Pond, below, provide a reliable prey base for peregrine falcons nesting in nearby cliffs. Left: Cobbles were once angular rock fragments torn from Acadia's cliffs by wave action.

GLACIER

NATIONAL PARK IN MONTANA

JEWEL OF NATURE

Glacier National Park is formally part of Waterton/Glacier International Peace Park, a joint Canada–United States conservation reserve established in 1932. Less formally but more in keeping with ecological realities, it is the heart of what is called the Crown of the Continent Ecosystem, a large assemblage of public and private lands identified as crucial to the conservation of wildland values. The Native American name for the area was more vivid and personal—The Backbone of the World.

Take a trip across Glacier National Park. Start on the west side and head east on the perfectly named Going-to-the-Sun Road. Soon you are skirting the south edge of the long, glacially carved trench containing Lake McDonald. Ahead in the distance, fiercely steep mountains, ziggurat-shaped and striped with snowfields, distract you from the driving. To your right are occasional wetlands inhabited by moose. White-tailed deer and black bears are around, but might not be spotted. The mountains on this side of the park grab most of the moisture coming from the west, and along this road they nurture a genuine Pacific Northwest rain forest. Past Lake McDonald you have climbed little, but the mountain slopes are closing in. In early spring, the avalanche chutes—long, steep vertical meadow and shrublands—are inhabited by grizzly bears out exercising their ambitious appetites. As the road winds along McDonald Creek, you get your first good look at the spectacular Garden Wall up ahead. It is a ragged-topped dividing ridge left by the last great glaciation. In one long switchback, the road begins a steady climb across the lower slopes of the wall. The rain forest is gone, and the mixed vegetation—mountain maple, various berries, some lodgepole pines—is always worth scanning for animals. Park the car first.

Here nature is sorting out her priorities following a big fire in the 1960s. Elk and grizzly bears move in and out of cover, poking around for a snack. Farther up, bighorn sheep often descend from their favored "escape terrain" in search of a meal.

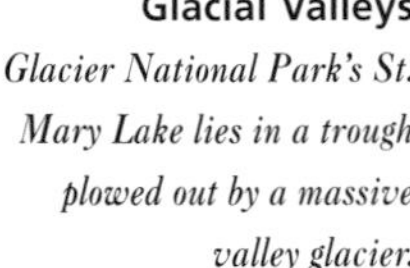

Maple and Moose
Rocky Mountain maple, left, grows in Glacier as a shrub or small tree and provides forage for moose, above, as well as deer and elk.

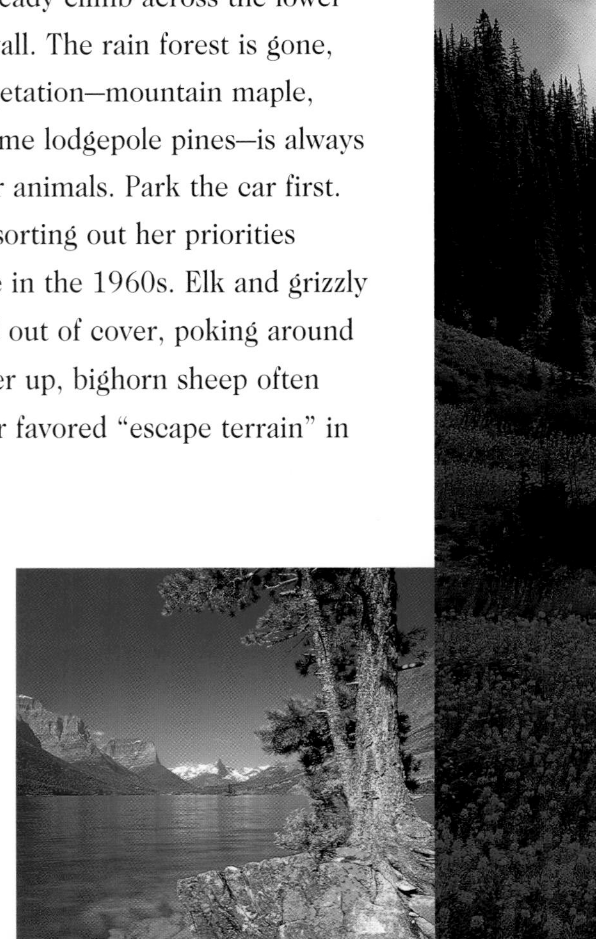

Glacial Valleys
Glacier National Park's St. Mary Lake lies in a trough plowed out by a massive valley glacier.

Cut for Cascades

The park's steep, glacially carved mountain slopes are tailor-made for waterfalls such as this stairstepping stretch of Haystack Creek along the Garden Wall, right. Clouded summits, below, enclose a hanging valley carved by small alpine glaciers.

As you angle across the slope, the Garden Wall moves in closer on your left, looming against the pavement. On your right, there is nothing but a low wall and a great deal of air. The faint of heart should have changed drivers back at McDonald Creek, for this cliff-hugging stretch of road is harrowing and tight.

Trumpeters
A trumpeter swan watches over its young cygnets. Trumpeters neared extinction in the 1930s, but find safe haven in Glacier.

There is more room at Logan Pass, the eroded ridge between two great glacial valleys. It is the gateway to an alpine wilderness of wildflowers, fantasy horizons, marmots, squirrels, and unanticipated grizzly bears.

Continuing east and down, you enter the drier realm of the rainshadow. But you descend through the same bands of wildlife habitats, and at the base of the mountains, where the prairie begins, bison once grazed.

You have just gone from the Pacific Coast to the Great Plains, by way of an alpine wonderland, in 50 miles. Just don't forget that the same magic, with infinite variations and without the road, awaits in valley after valley in both directions, north and south.

Logan Pass
Glacier lilies carpet an expansive alpine meadow at Logan Pass, below. Massive valley glaciers working in opposite directions gouged out the pass. Left: St. Mary Lake lies cradled within a deep, U-shaped valley carved by a glacier at least 2,000 feet thick.

Glacial Junction

Swiftcurrent Lake lies at the junction of two glacially carved basins. The ice bodies merged in front of Grinnell Point, the prominent summit on the photo's right side.

Lake Sherburne

Lupine and fireweed slope toward Lake Sherburne. The lakebed was gouged out by a glacier that stretched from the Many Glacier area to the plains east of the park.

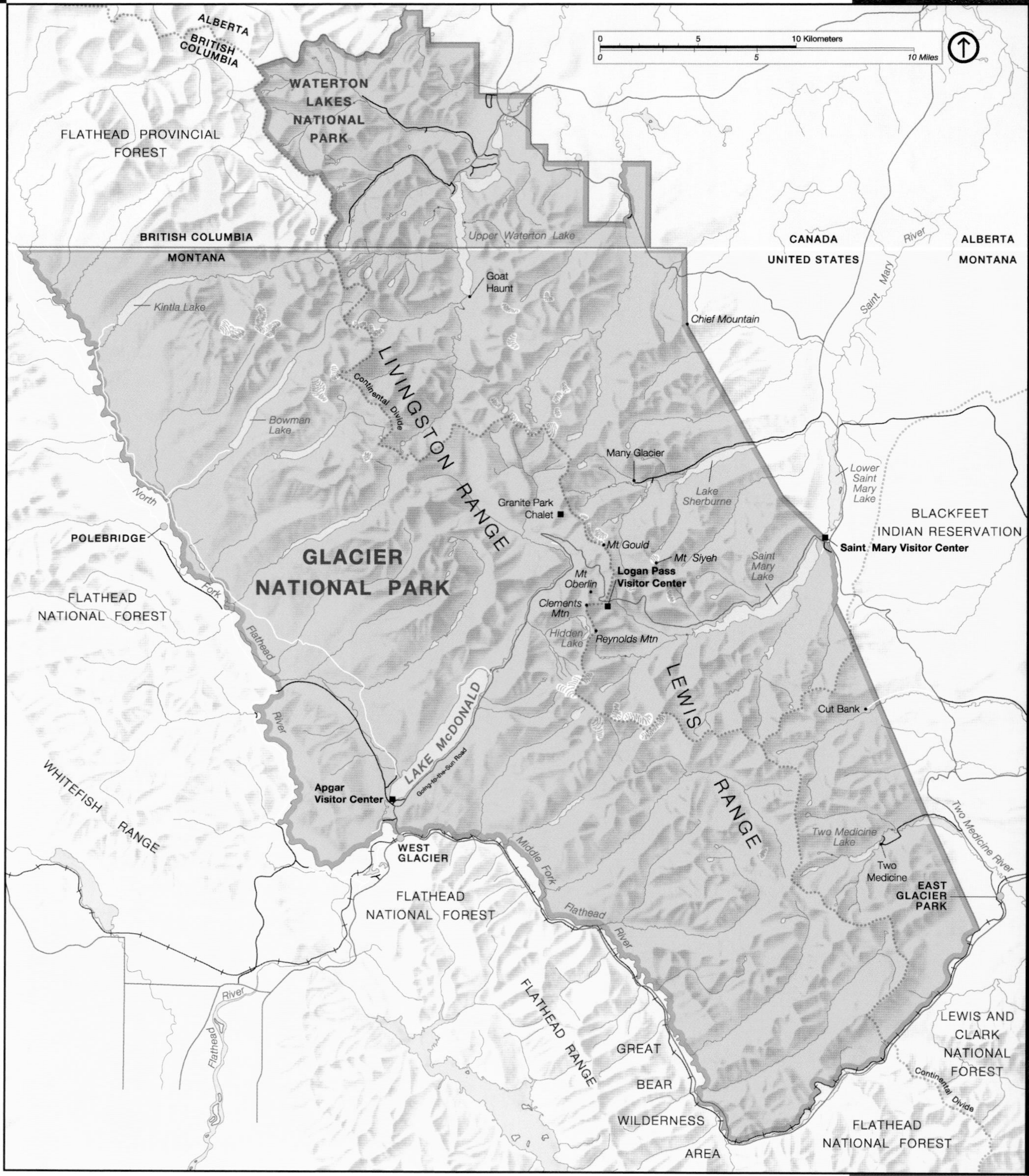

ALBERTA
BRITISH COLUMBIA
WATERTON LAKES NATIONAL PARK
0 5 10 Kilometers
0 5 10 Miles
FLATHEAD PROVINCIAL FOREST
BRITISH COLUMBIA
MONTANA
Upper Waterton Lake
CANADA
UNITED STATES
ALBERTA
MONTANA
Saint Mary River
Goat Haunt
Kintla Lake
Chief Mountain
LIVINGSTON RANGE
Continental Divide
Bowman Lake
Many Glacier
Lower Saint Mary Lake
Lake Sherburne
BLACKFEET INDIAN RESERVATION
North Fork Flathead River
Granite Park Chalet
POLEBRIDGE
Saint Mary Visitor Center
Mt Gould
Mt Siyeh
Saint Mary Lake
GLACIER NATIONAL PARK
Mt Oberlin
Logan Pass Visitor Center
FLATHEAD NATIONAL FOREST
Clements Mtn
Hidden Lake
Reynolds Mtn
LEWIS RANGE
Cut Bank
LAKE McDONALD
Going-to-the-Sun Road
Apgar Visitor Center
WHITEFISH RANGE
Two Medicine River
Two Medicine Lake
Two Medicine
WEST GLACIER
Middle Fork Flathead River
EAST GLACIER PARK
FLATHEAD NATIONAL FOREST
Flathead River
FLATHEAD RANGE
LEWIS AND CLARK NATIONAL FOREST
Continental Divide
GREAT BEAR WILDERNESS AREA
FLATHEAD NATIONAL FOREST

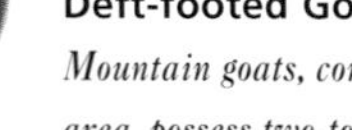

Deft-footed Goats

Mountain goats, common in the Logan Pass area, possess two-toed hooves with spongy central pads that enable them to leap nimbly among the park's highest crags.

Sunrise on the Garden

Sunrise paints the east face of the Garden Wall, which rises high above Glacier National Park's Many Glacier area.

Preening Eagle

A bald eagle preens its tail, right. Below: A steep ramp of wildflowers overlooks the park's McDonald Valley, a deep glacial valley that stretches west from Logan Pass.

GLACIER NATIONAL PARK

History Note: After the Great Northern Railway stalled for ten years in dismantling a sawmill it had used to build the Many Glacier Hotel, Park Service Director Stephen Mather lost patience. In 1925, he had crews place dynamite, then invited hotel guests to step outside and watch him blow it up. Quite an evening program!

Flora: Misty cedar-hemlock forests on the west side; prairie grasslands on the east; scattered wetlands; aspen groves; montane forests of lodgepole pine, spruce, and fir; subalpine forests of subalpine fir and Engelmann spruce; alpine meadows clogged with colorful wildflowers.

Fauna: All of the celebrity mammals of the Rockies such as mountain goats, bighorn sheep, grizzly bears, wolves, elk, and moose; a wide variety of birds, including trumpeter swans, eagles, peregrine falcons, and ospreys.

Visitor Tip: To catch the best light, drive Going-to-the-Sun Road from east to west starting in the morning and returning in the afternoon.

Uplifted Seabeds

Singleshot Mountain rises over the St. Mary River. Its colorful horizontal bands speak clearly of the rocks' sedimentary origin along the coastline of an ancient sea.

LAND OF HANGING VALLEYS

A sprawling testament to the power of moving ice, Glacier National Park's riveting landscape owes much to the work of immense ice-age glaciers that began gnawing into the mountains at least two million years ago. Glacier National Park's deep, U-shaped valleys and its cirques, arêtes, horns, moraines, hanging valleys, and long, fjordlike lakes were all formed by Pleistocene glaciers.

Today, thirty to forty small glaciers nibble away at the cliffs, but they are newcomers that formed during the "Little Ice Age" roughly four thousand years ago.

During the most extensive Pleistocene advances, alpine glaciers formed near the summits, coalesced, and filled the park's valleys. Much larger piedmont glaciers gathered along the eastern front of the mountains and extended onto the margin of the Great Plains. To the west, a gigantic belt of glacial ice 10 miles wide occupied the North Fork Valley.

Alpine glaciers at the crest of the mountains carved relatively small, bowl-like depressions where cirque lakes now lie nestled beneath semicircular amphitheaters of high cliffs. Avalanche, Hidden, Iceberg, and Upper Two Medicine Lakes are prime examples.

Horns, such as Reynolds and Clements Mountains near Logan Pass, are pyramidal summits formed by glaciers carving away on three or more sides of a mountain.

As the alpine glaciers coalesced and flowed downward, they joined much larger valley glaciers that carved more deeply into the earth. When the ice melted away, the shallower troughs carved by the alpine glaciers ended in abrupt drop-offs overlooking the main valley. It seemed as if they had been left hanging there; hence the name hanging valleys.

The large valley glaciers ploughed deep U-shaped troughs, some of which now harbor the park's major lakes: McDonald, Kintla, and Bowman lakes on the west side, and St. Mary Lake on the east.

Avalanche Lake
Waterfalls descend from high peaks above Avalanche Lake in western Glacier.

Iceberg Lake
Aptly named Iceberg Lake nestles beneath the soaring cliffs of the Ptarmigan Wall.

Bear Grass
Common bear grass blossoms in a meadow overlooking Grinnell Lake, left. Following spread: The ramparts of Mount Gould reflect on Lake Josephine.

Paintbrush

Scarlet bracts surround the tiny flowers of Paintbrush, left. Below: Lamplugh Glacier oozes into Glacier Bay. During the past two hundred years, the bay's glaciers have retreated 65 miles—the fastest retreat on record.

GLACIER BAY

NATIONAL PARK AND PRESERVE IN ALASKA

HIGHWAYS OF ICE

Glacier Bay, for which this national park is named, is a huge, many-forked fjord on the southeast coast of Alaska, just north of Cross Sound and Icy Strait. Its most momentous feature may be its gift for change. Only two hundred years ago, when Captain George Vancouver sailed by the mouth of the bay, its 65-mile length was under a single, unified ice mass. This 4,000-foot-thick glacier entirely melted by 1915, a world speed record for glacial retreat.

There is a way in which glaciers and volcanoes—seemingly as different as two earthly forces could be—are alike. Both have a thoroughly professional skill at sweeping a landscape free of all life. They do it in different ways, but the effects are very similar. And when the land is again hospitable to life—when the ice melts or the lava cools—a vast new field of play is suddenly exposed to the ambitions of all organisms. When the vacancy sign goes on, life rushes in.

It is, in fact, because of Glacier Bay's standing invitation to wildlife that it was first set aside as a national monument in 1925. Ecological researchers were engaged in studying both the remnants of former life (prior to the glacier's advance) and the rapid advance of new life that shadowed the retreating ice. Those researchers recognized the region for its scientific opportunities. It is lucky for us that they did. Glacier Bay today is still justifiably seen as a unique "natural laboratory," but it is also a great storehouse of Alaskan wonders, from the towering Fairweather range to all the far-ranging terrestrial and marine mammals who are easing into an inviting landscape (or in other parts of the park, retreating from other glaciers that are now advancing). On a large scale here, whether we are scientist or tourist, we can witness creation itself. Naturalist John Burroughs, who visited in 1899, did: "We saw the world-shaping forces at work; we scrambled over plains they had built but yesterday."

Marine Mammals
A humpback whale, left, breaches in Icy Strait. Above: Steller's sea lions bask on rocks in Glacier Bay.

A MARINE HIGHWAY

A highway of the marine sort, Glacier Bay allows waterborne visitors to get a close look at the park's celebrity features—tidewater glaciers hurling

A Hasty Retreat
Ice plunges from Margerie Glacier into Tarr Inlet.

massive hunks of ice into the sea. Summer weather permitting, tour boats depart daily from Glacier Bay Lodge at Bartlett Cove and travel up the west arm of the bay to take in the park's most active tidewater glaciers and to see its highest mountains.

As the boats travel up the bay, they retrace the path of glacial retreat and venture into progressively younger

A Passing Pod
A pod of orcas, also know as killer whales, surfaces in the bay.

landscapes. At the mouth of the bay, where a mature coastal forest now stands, glacial ice began retreating at the close of the eighteenth century. At the head of the bay, where algae, moss, and lichen may just be getting a start, the ice retreated just a few decades ago.

The route skirts the Beardslee Islands, which lay frozen in glacial ice in 1794. It passes Tlingit Point, which marked the leading edge of the ice as recently as 1860, then heads for Russell Island, still touched by glaciers in 1892. One of them, Johns Hopkins Glacier, has retreated roughly 10 miles up its inlet during the past century. Today, it calves so many icebergs that boats can rarely approach closer than 2 miles. At the head of Tarr Inlet, icebergs thunder from Margerie and Grand Pacific Glaciers, which reach the sea beneath the summit of 13,650-foot Mount Quincy Adams. Ice blocks up to 200 feet high plummet from the tidewater glaciers into the sea, where they bob around for a week or more as they melt.

Visitors are likely to catch glimpses of whales. Minke whales, which reach lengths of 33 feet, feed on Glacier Bay's cod and pollock. Pods of orcas, which can swim at a steady 29 mph, feed on fish, sea lions, seals, porpoises, sharks, squid, and other whales. Humpback whales, which feed only during summer, also ply the bay's waters, busily ingesting krill, shrimp, and salmon in order to store up enough fat to last the rest of the year.

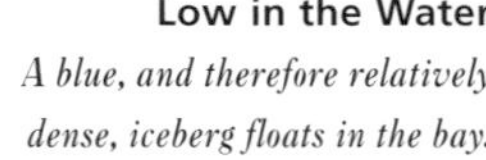

Low in the Water
A blue, and therefore relatively dense, iceberg floats in the bay.

Glacial Advance

During the spectacular, northwestward retreat of glaciers from Glacier Bay National Park, Brady Glacier advanced southeastward from the Fairweather Range.

A Land Reinhabited

Once the ice retreated from the shores of Glacier Bay, bears were among the first mammals to reinhabit the land by swimming around ice and rock across open water.

TATSHENSHINI-ALSEK PROVINCIAL PARK
SAINT ELIAS MOUNTAINS
ALSEK RANGE
TAKHINSHA
Melbern Glacier
Grand Pacific Glacier
GLACIER BAY NATIONAL PRESERVE
Alsek Glacier
Grand Plateau Glacier
BRITISH COLUMBIA
ALASKA
Margerie Glacier
Tarr Inlet
Rendu Glacier
Rendu Inlet
Carroll Glacier
Cushing Glacier
Muir Glacier
Riggs Glacier
Queen Inlet
Wachusett Inlet
Mt. Fairweather
Johns Hopkins Inlet
Johns Hopkins Glacier
Lamplugh Glacier
Reid Glacier
Fairweather Glacier
FAIRWEATHER RANGE
GLACIER BAY NATIONAL PARK
GLACIER BAY
BRADY ICEFIELD
GULF OF ALASKA
Laperouse Glacier
Brady Glacier
PACIFIC OCEAN
CROSS SOUND
0 5 10 15 Kilometers
0 5 10 15 Miles

Bartlett Cove

Buried by glacial ice as recently as 1780, the lands around Bartlett Cove have progressed through a succession of plant communities and now support a mature spruce-hemlock forest.

Newly Exposed

Margerie Glacier carves through a recently exposed landscape of naked rock. In 1890, its ice extended the length of Tarr Inlet, or roughly 10 miles farther than it does today.

The Retreat Slows

The retreat of the bay's glaciers, right, appears to have slowed. Below: Fairweather Range snow forms ice for all the glaciers between Glacier Bay and the Gulf of Alaska.

GLACIER BAY NATIONAL PARK AND PRESERVE

History Note: Tlingit Indians lived in Glacier Bay until they were driven out by glaciers during a general ice advance which began about four thousand years ago.

Flora: A showcase of plant succession, from moss and lichen colonizing bare rock to a mature Sitka spruce and hemlock forest.

Fauna: Moose, bears, otters, and mountain goats; porpoises, several different whales, seals, and sea lions; many shorebirds, including guillemots and grebes.

Visitor Tip: Be prepared for long periods of rainy, overcast, and cool weather. Raingear, including waterproof footwear, is highly recommended.

Cold Storage

Glaciers and polar ice like those found in Glacier Bay National Park store more freshwater than all of the world's lakes, rivers, groundwater, and atmosphere combined.

Mountain Island

Like an island rising from a sea of desert, the mountains of Great Basin National Park, left, stand 6,000 to 7,000 feet above the floor of Spring Valley. Ice-age glaciers formed on Wheeler Peak, below.

GREAT BASIN NATIONAL PARK

History Note: Rock art sites in the park were left by prehistoric peoples who lived in small agricultural villages near the present towns of Baker and Garrison from about 1100 to 1300.

Flora: Most of the major plant communities found in the Basin and Range Province, including sagebrush desert; juniper and pinion pine; mountain mahogany; forests of Englemann spruce, limber pines, and firs; alpine meadows; ancient bristlecone pines; and alpine tundra.

Fauna: Some sixty species of mammals, including bighorn sheep, elk, pronghorn, mule deer, skunks, jackrabbits, and many rodents; many birds, including golden eagles, hummingbirds, and Clark's nutcrackers; snakes and lizards.

Visitor Tip: Take a ranger-guided tour of Lehman Caves, an intricately decorated limestone cavern and a welcome respite from the desert heat.

Ground Squirrel

Often confused with chipmunks, golden-mantled ground squirrels hoard seeds and berries in their underground burrows.

GREAT BASIN

NATIONAL PARK IN NEVADA

DESERT GLACIERS

The Great Basin is a basin in the true sense of the word: It contains water without leaks, draining only into itself with no outlets to the ocean. The Great Basin includes 200,000 square miles of Nevada, California, Oregon, Utah, and Idaho; the national park protects 120 square miles of it. The park's glaciated mountains are accurately compared to an island in a sagebrush ocean. The park also protects several limestone caves, a variety of woodland habitats, and a monumental limestone arch.

Nature writer Barry Lopez accurately described the Great Basin as "one of the least novelized, least painted, least eulogized of American landscapes." Most people are only vaguely aware that there is such a place, though many more probably know that there must be something occupying all that space between the Rockies and the Sierras. Others probably assume that there is not. Once they have driven across it, they may proclaim that their earlier impression was correct: there is, indeed, nothing there.

In fact, there is everything here—everything life needs not only to get by but also to thrive in a thousand forms. Great Basin National Park is a testimonial to the extraordinary tenacity, inventiveness, and fascination of life. Get out of your car and walk into the "lifeless desert" you may think you see there. Even without a plant field guide you will immediately notice that the apparent monotony of faded shades is in fact many different plants, all hard at work, all thriving.

Or climb to the top of the mountains and meet the earth's elders—bristlecone pines thousands of years old that are so adapted to harsh environments that the longest-lived are those in the poorest possible sites. They survive through the millennia by letting most of their architecture go dry and by sending water through a narrow band of living bark up to a few tiny branches. The heroic adaptability revealed in that accomplishment justifies a national park by itself. Great Basin commemorates the heroism of many such accomplishments.

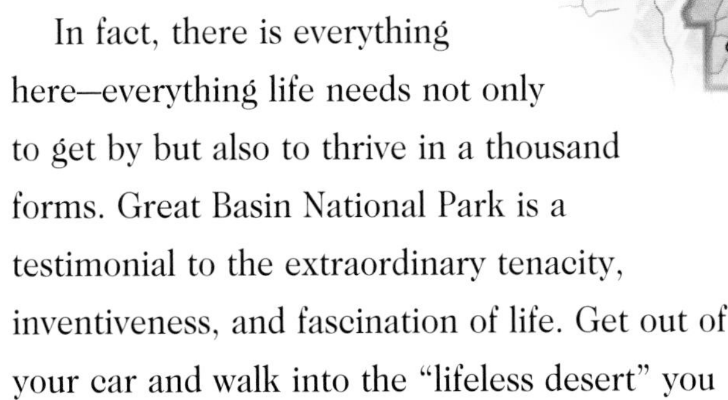

Ice-Age Remnants
Ice-age glaciers hollowed out a bowl-shaped depression where tiny glaciers survive today.

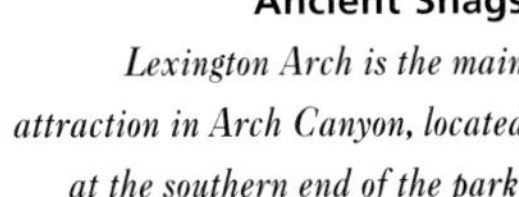

Ancient Snags
Lexington Arch is the main attraction in Arch Canyon, located at the southern end of the park.

ISLE ROYALE

NATIONAL PARK IN MICHIGAN

REMOTE SHORELANDS

The Isle Royale archipelago in northern Lake Superior has been important to humans for thousands of years. Native American and, later, Euro-American miners were attracted by the veins of copper in the island's weathered, glaciated rock. The Indian name of the island, "Minong," has been translated as "a good place to get copper," or, more simply, "a good place to be." The latter may be meaningful for modern visitors to this world-famous but lightly visited Biosphere Reserve.

In many national parks, the original intentions of the founders are often complicated and complemented by later events. Such has been the case in the wilderness of Isle Royale. Its remoteness, its robust forest community, its long, varied cultural heritage, and its rugged lakeshore beauty were all good reasons for creating a national park, but more was to come. About a decade after the park was established in 1940, persistent rumors of wolves were finally confirmed. Apparently, one winter day in 1948, a wolf pack of unknown size crossed the ice of Lake Superior from the Canadian shore, only 15 miles distant, and made themselves at home.

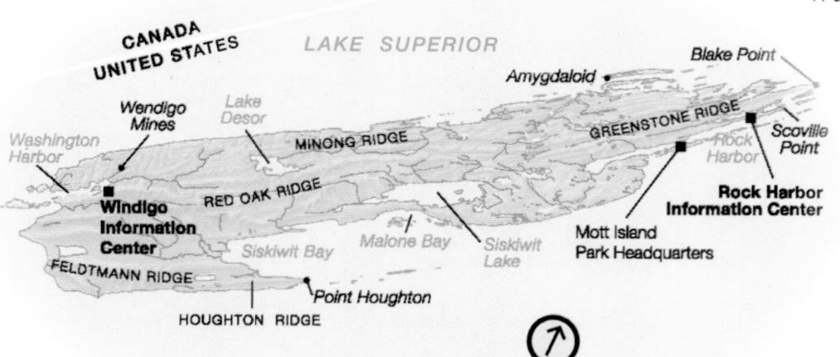

And what a home they found. Other animals—beaver, fox, snowshoe hare, some smaller rodents—had all somehow found their way across the water. Most important, around the turn of the previous century some moose had also made their way across, probably by swimming. The wolves and moose were, literally, made for each other, and soon scientists were taking notice of the drama being played out here. For half a century now, wolf and moose populations have been on a fascinating roller-coaster ride of growth and decline, boom and bust. This island has become one of the most important study sites for understanding predator-prey interactions. In the process, the wolves of Isle Royale have become, like the Serengeti lions, the Chinese pandas, and the Yellowstone bears, among the most famous wild animals in the world.

Isolated Shores
Isle Royale lies 15 miles from the nearest point on the mainland, isolating it from most mammals.

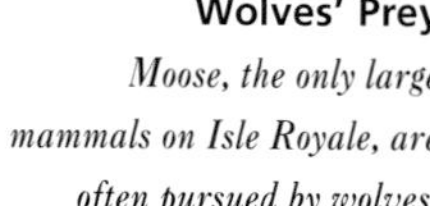

Wolves' Prey
Moose, the only large mammals on Isle Royale, are often pursued by wolves.

ISLE ROYALE NATIONAL PARK

History Note: Aboriginal copper mining pits date back 4,500 years, and the metal hammered from the pits was traded as far away as New York.

Flora: More than seven hundred species of vascular plants, including thirty-two species of orchids; pioneer stands of aspen and birch; boreal forests of fir, spruce, and birch; ridgetop forests of maple and birch.

Fauna: Moose, wolves, river otters, beavers, foxes, small rodents, and 120 species of birds.

Visitor Tip: A ferry boat circles the island once every two days, putting in at various points and making it possible to explore remote sections of the island by foot, canoe, or sea kayak.

Islands Great and Small
The cliffs of Split Island, left, reveal some of the Precambrian basaltic lava rock that form the foundation of Isle Royale and its islands. The park encompasses more than four hundred islands ranging in size from a tiny islet in Herring Bay, above, to Isle Royale itself, which is 45 miles long and 8.5 miles wide. Islands near Blake Point, below, stretch east into Lake Superior.

Streaming Cliffs
Fed by melting glacial ice and frequent summer rains, waterfalls stream down the steep rock walls of the Kenai Fjords National Park's fjords and bays.

KENAI FJORDS NATIONAL PARK

History Note: Native peoples have hunted and fished throughout the fjords for many generations. The area also drew Russian fur traders and American gold prospectors.

Flora: Where glaciers have retreated, Kenai is a showcase of plant succession, from moss and lichen to mature forests of Sitka spruce and hemlock.

Fauna: Sea lions, sea otters, seals, and whales; puffins, auklets, and storm petrels; moose, bears, mountain goats, and wolverines.

Visitor Tip: Little of the park can be reached by road or on foot, so plan to splurge a bit on scenic flights and boat charters.

Drowning Mountains
The Kenai Mountains, right, overlook a coastal labyrinth of glacially carved bays, inlets, coves, and lagoons that are flooding as the mountain range sinks into the Gulf of Alaska. Below: A sea otter reclines.

KENAI FJORDS

NATIONAL PARK IN ALASKA

ICE IN RETREAT

An Alaskan coastal park whose shoreline is slowly subsiding into the ocean, Kenai Fjords is the only park more than half-covered by ice. As the former mountains sink, visitors are treated to the incongruous sight of bowl-shaped bays flooding once-lofty cirques. Former river valleys have been transformed into long, steep-walled fjords. This tilting, settling shoreline, rich in cliffs and inaccessible heights, has attracted a tremendous aggregation of shorebirds and marine life.

This portion of the Kenai Peninsula, some 130 miles south of Anchorage, was of so little interest to settlers that its foremost feature, the Harding Icefield, was not even discovered by Europeans until the early twentieth century. Nearby residents saw the numerous glaciers extending down to the sea, but had no idea that all that ice was coming from the same gigantic source.

The Harding Icefield system covers about 300 square miles of the Kenai Mountains. Its expanse is broken by protruding nunataks, or mountain peaks, like islands in the ice. Though the glaciers it sends down to the coast are retreating, the high ice field, blessed with 40 to 80 feet of snow annually, is holding its own against the warming climate.

Tour boats take visitors along the coast for reasonable looks at a number of tidewater glaciers. You may be there just at the right time to watch icebergs slide and thunder into the sea, in the best tradition of glacial spectacle. But for a handy, up-close-and-personal meeting with a glacier, make the short stroll to Exit Glacier, in the northern end of the park near Seward. The approach road is posted with signs that give the dates and locations of various points where the ice once reached. The dates are surprisingly recent. The glacier is retreating before you, but you can easily catch up. Just follow its fresh tracks. Hop over the braided rivulets of its coldest, newest meltwater and walk right up to that weathered, blue-crevassed snout. It can't outrun you, but so far it's outrunning the sea.

Ice Burden
A lobe of the vast Harding Ice Field drapes from a Kenai Fjords National Park peak.

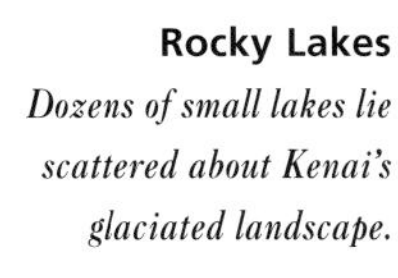

Rocky Lakes
Dozens of small lakes lie scattered about Kenai's glaciated landscape.

NORTH CASCADES

NATIONAL PARK IN WASHINGTON

REMOTE WILDNESS

The bounty of moisture provided by the Pacific Ocean enables the North Cascades to support glaciers when many other ranges are losing theirs. A third of all glaciers in the lower forty-eight states are found in the park and the attached Lake Chelan and Ross Lake National Recreation Areas. Besides their work of sculpting the mountains, glaciers play a key role in native plant and animal communities; roughly a quarter of the water in park streams comes from glaciers.

About 8,400 years ago, the people of the North Cascades started leaving us inadvertent messages about themselves. The oldest message that archaeologists have found was a quarry pit along the Skagit River, where people once extracted chunks of chert, a hard sedimentary rock suitable for making sharp edges and points. We don't know if that site was their first, but they seem never to have left since. For more than eight thousand years, people made their homes in these valleys, and wandered far into the high country during the summer months.

They came for many reasons that we can appreciate even today. There were tremendous salmon runs—like the precipitation, another gift from the Pacific Ocean. The Skagit's salmon came up into the park complex as far as Newhalem, a word derived from a Native American word meaning "goat snare." Goats were important for meat and for their exceptionally warm wool, which was widely traded. (Early park hunters used obsidian brought by trade all the way from Wyoming.) The high habitats of goats were thoroughly familiar to these early hikers, who knew all the passes, all the best berry patches, and all the places where elk, bears, marmots, and other prey could be found.

Today we hike through this great, roadless wilderness park and relish the feeling of remoteness—of distance from people. We search out the wonder and awe with a great feeling of discovery. But the thrill should only be heightened by knowing that we follow a long line of hunters on these trails.

Sculpted Peaks
Hundreds of alpine glaciers and a vast ice sheet nearly buried the North Cascades during the last ice age, sculpting peaks such as Mount Triumph, above, Mount Shuksan, below, and Cutthroat Peak, right.

Vascular Cornucopia

The extraordinarily diverse habitats of the North Cascades support more than 1,700 species of vascular plants, including these yellow glacier lilies near Heather Pass.

America's Alps

The North Cascades, sometimes called the American Alps, extend for hundreds of miles and exert enormous influence on the climate and vegetation of the Pacific Northwest.

Puzzling Range

With its many fault zones, anomalous fossils, diverse rock sources, and thick vegetative cover, the North Cascades Range comprises a baffling earth science puzzle.

NORTH CASCADES NATIONAL PARK

History Note: The Upper Skagit, Chilliwack, Nlaka'pamux, and Chelan peoples have lived in the North Cascades for thousands of years, fishing, hunting, and gathering throughout the mountains, river valleys, and lakes.

Flora: Misty old-growth forests of cedar, hemlock, and Douglas fir; stands of drought-resistant ponderosa and lodgepole pines; alpine wildflower meadows.

Fauna: Mountain goats, bears, deer, mountain lions; hundreds of bird species, including a nearby large winter population of bald eagles; salmon.

Visitor Tip: Consider taking the four-hour boat trip up Lake Chelan from Chelan to Stehekin. In places, the bed of this deep, glacially carved lake lies more than 400 feet below sea level.

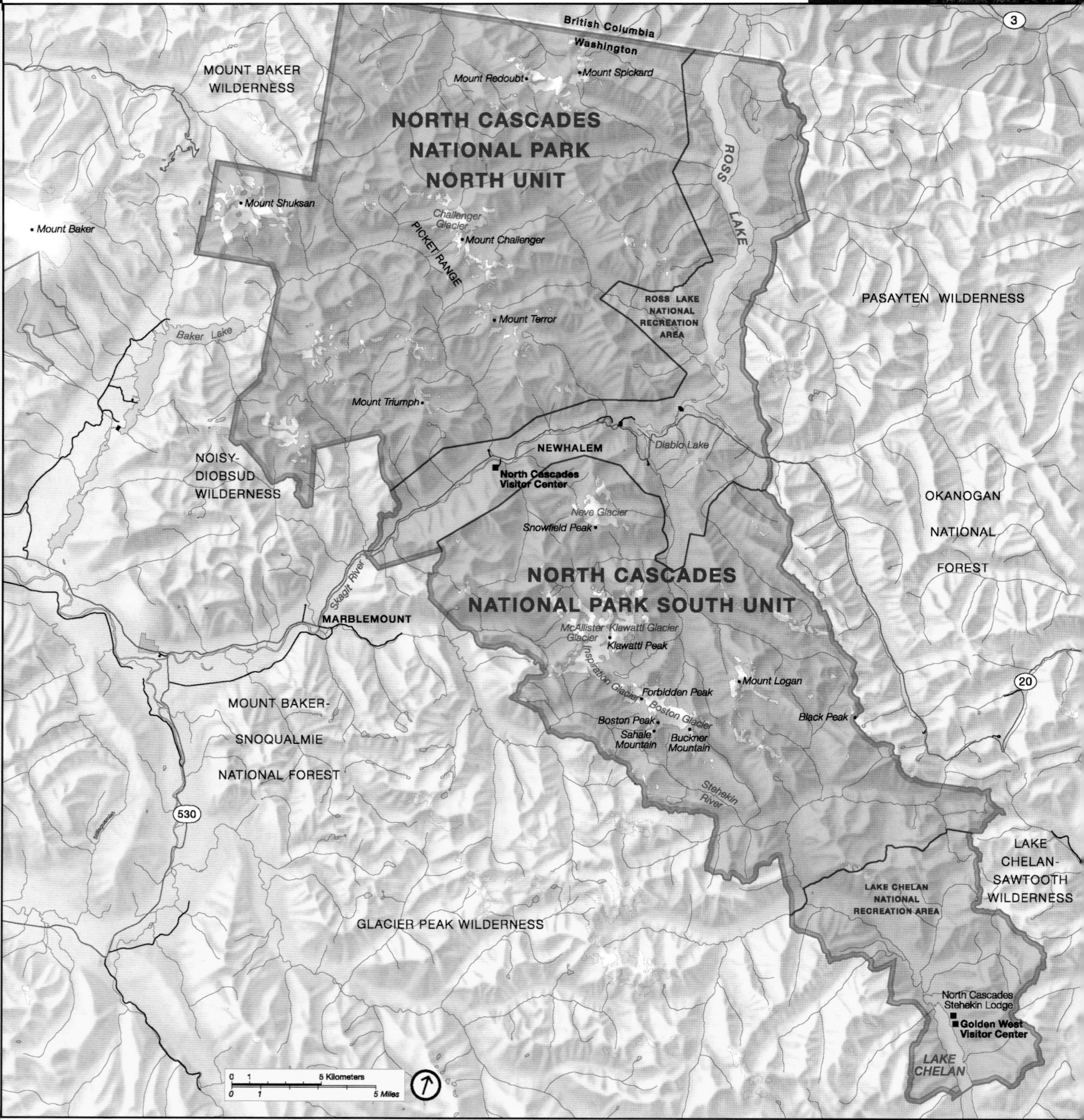

British Columbia
Washington
3
MOUNT BAKER WILDERNESS
Mount Redoubt
Mount Spickard
NORTH CASCADES NATIONAL PARK NORTH UNIT
ROSS LAKE
Mount Shuksan
Mount Baker
Challenger Glacier
Mount Challenger
PICKET RANGE
ROSS LAKE NATIONAL RECREATION AREA
PASAYTEN WILDERNESS
Mount Terror
Baker Lake
Mount Triumph
NEWHALEM
Diablo Lake
NOISY-DIOBSUD WILDERNESS
North Cascades Visitor Center
Neve Glacier
Snowfield Peak
OKANOGAN NATIONAL FOREST
NORTH CASCADES NATIONAL PARK SOUTH UNIT
Skagit River
MARBLEMOUNT
McAllister Glacier
Klawatti Glacier
Klawatti Peak
Inspiration Glacier
Forbidden Peak
Mount Logan
Boston Glacier
20
MOUNT BAKER-SNOQUALMIE NATIONAL FOREST
Boston Peak
Sahale Mountain
Buckner Mountain
Black Peak
Stehekin River
530
LAKE CHELAN-SAWTOOTH WILDERNESS
LAKE CHELAN NATIONAL RECREATION AREA
GLACIER PEAK WILDERNESS
North Cascades Stehekin Lodge
Golden West Visitor Center
LAKE CHELAN
0 1 5 Kilometers
0 1 5 Miles

Heavy Snow

Each winter, the North Cascades accumulates a deep mantle of snow, facing page. Moist Pacific storms sweep against the range, dumping 400 to 700 inches of snow on the park and its over three hundred active glaciers.

Jagged Crest

An icy stream rushes from a crest of jagged peaks in the North Cascades. Glacially carved cirques, arêtes, horns, and spacious U-shaped valleys abound within the park.

Rough Country

Steep, rocky, and often covered with nearly impenetrable vegetation, the park's rugged terrain can be a challenge for hikers.

Glacial Lakebeds

Continental ice sheets 2 miles thick scoured the Voyageurs region at least four times in the last million years, carving lake beds from rocks 2.7 billion years old, below. Left: A white-tailed deer.

VOYAGEURS

NATIONAL PARK IN MINNESOTA

GLACIAL ISLANDS

Voyageurs National Park, about a third of which is underwater, was created to protect a remarkable complex of lakes and islands along the Canada–United States border. Officials actually defined this stretch of the border as following the "customary waterway" of the French-Canadian voyagers who canoed through here on their fur-trade route. The park also exists to honor the cultural heritage of the voyagers, native people, and others who resided or visited here.

Few parks can match Voyageurs for the sense of participating in a tradition that you get when you leave the developed areas behind. There is in this landscape surprisingly little to differentiate what you will see as you round the next island, or slip into the next cove, from what was seen by similar travelers centuries ago.

It is a raw, young landscape. Little soil has built up in the past 10,000 years, and it only partly covers what north-country writer Sigurd Olson called "the bare bones of the continent." When the glaciers passed through here on their way to Iowa, they scoured and shaped this rock on a wholesale basis.

Wholesale isn't what most of us notice as we paddle along the island shores. What we will notice is more local, like the long scratches known as striations, caused when loose rocks frozen into the glacier were dragged heavily over the bedrock.

Sometimes a single area will have striations running in different directions because the ice coming back from Iowa passed at a different angle.

But our canoe takes us past more than rock. A moose emerges from a boggy forest, steps into the water, and dunks her head to feed on bottom vegetation. A bald eagle launches from a snag. A smallmouth bass swirls up and quietly pulls some hapless insect under. And later, just as we doze off in our tent, somewhere out on the lake something spooks a loon. Its tremolo alarm call rings hysterically through the mist to our island, and we wonder if that wild, maniacal sound made the voyagers shiver too.

North Woods

The park supports a boreal forest of deciduous trees such as maple and birch, above, and conifers such as jack pines on the Grassy Bay Cliffs, left.

The Lonely Land
A narrow strip of rock curves into the mist along Sand Point Lake. Lonely spots like this lure paddlers from all over the country.

Exclusively Precambrian
Autumn leaves decorate an outcropping along Rainy Lake. Every exposed rock in Voyageurs dates from early Precambrian time.

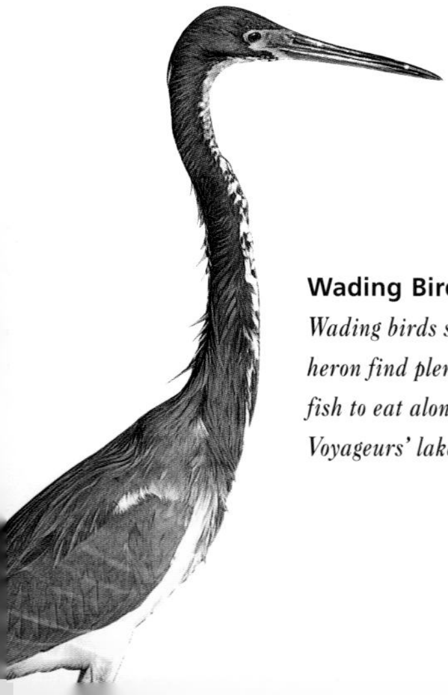

Wading Birds
Wading birds such as the great blue heron find plenty of frogs and small fish to eat along the shores of Voyageurs' lakes and marshes.

Lake Country Origins
The region's island-studded lakes formed on a nearly level surface of pockmarked bedrock that was smoothed by continental glaciers as recently as ten thousand years ago.

Timber Wolves

Wolf pups are born into packs of two to twelve in Voyageurs. Adults travel as much as 40 miles a night, hunting mainly for beaver and deer.

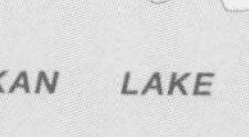

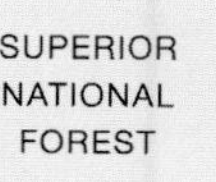

VOYAGEURS NATIONAL PARK

History Note: For more than two hundred years, French-Canadian voyagers paddled and portaged through the heart of the park as they shuttled furs and supplies along a 3,000-mile canoe route between Montreal and Lake Athabasca.

Flora: Boreal forests of birch, maple, cedar, spruce, and various pines; peat bogs; aquatic plants such as marsh grasses, reeds, cattails, and lily pads.

Fauna: Deer, moose, black bears, timber wolves, porcupines, skunks, and beavers; loons, grebes, ducks, cormorants, and kingfishers.

Visitor Tip: Never skimp on insect repellent.

Many Bays

Tongues of crystalline rock slope into the pristine waters of a small, wooded bay on Rainy Lake. Though Rainy is quite large, its irregular shoreline of bays and archipelagos conveys a deep sense of intimacy.

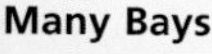

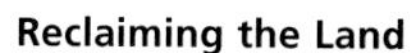

Reclaiming the Land

Vegetation, such as this handful of grass along Rainy Lake in Voyageurs National Park, continues to advance on rocks scraped bare during the last ice age.

WRANGELL–ST. ELI

NATIONAL PARK AND PRESERVE IN ALASKA

MOUNTAIN KINGDOM

At more than 13 million acres, Wrangell–St. Elias National Park is so enormous it strains the sense of scale established by all the other national parks. Nine of the United States' sixteen highest peaks and North America's premier collection of glaciers reside in this one park. There is a single piedmont glacier, the Malaspina, that alone is the size of Yellowstone National Park. It would take almost six Yellowstones to equal the size of Wrangell–St. Elias.

It has been described as more like a kingdom than a wilderness. And indeed, at such a size and with its great fortress of peaks dominating the horizon, there is something realm-like about Wrangell–St. Elias. The country is so suggestively Himalayan that it is easy to imagine that somewhere back in there, an inaccessible, secluded valley conceals a secret Shangri-la where people smile all the time and live forever.

If there are no hidden principalities, there are other wonders beyond counting. The park encompasses the convergence of several mountain ranges. Along its north, the Mentasta and Nutzotin Mountains represent the eastern end of the Alaska Range. Paralleling them across the park's northern third are the Wrangells; 14,163-foot Mount Wrangell is the park's only active volcano. The Wrangells end at Chitistone Canyon, and south across the canyon the St. Elias Mountains rise. They extend along the east side of the park to its southernmost corner, where they are the highest coastal range in the world. It is only 18 miles from Icy Bay to the peak of 18,008-foot Mount St. Elias, the second-highest peak in the United States. From the park's southeast, the Chugach Mountains branch from the St. Elias Range and wall in the park's southern border.

Thanks to these high ranges, Wrangell–St. Elias stands as a three-dimensional textbook on glaciers. Not only does it have some of the largest and longest (Nabesna Glacier is 75 miles long) but it also has some of the most active. Hubbard Glacier, which flows into Disenchantment Bay at the southeastern end of the park, can advance as much as 10

Fire and Ice

Medial moraines stripe Russell Glacier, above, as a dormant shield volcano, below, stands against the sky.

Soaring Heights

Carved by glacial ice, cliffs on Mount Drum, below, reveal some of the many layers of lava rock that compose the park's central mountains. Right: Dowitchers are among the first birds to fly south for the winter.

yards a day. In 1986, it advanced clear across a 30-mile-long fjord, damming it and turning it into a giant temporary lake. The water slowly rose behind the glacial wall and after a few months breached the dam.

Dormant Volcanoes
Like most of the Wrangell Mountains, Mount Drum, elevation 12,010 feet, is a massive shield volcano, now dormant.

The park's river system, almost entirely originating in the glaciers, also testifies to the landscape's immensity. On the west side, many streams and rivers drain to the Copper River, one of Alaska's largest, which constitutes much of the park's west boundary. To the north, the Nabesna, Chisina, and White rivers all are part of the Yukon River system. They will travel well over a thousand miles to reach the Bering Sea.

For the wilderness adventurer, there are several lifetimes of exploration here. But the park's value extends far beyond those hardy people who actually get there. A place like this exemplifies the term "existence value." Wrangell–St. Elias is important to us even if we only gaze in from the edge—even if we never see it at all. Just by the promise of its being there, it provides what one Alaskan has called "adventure for the soul."

The Wrangells
The broad, white summits of the Wrangell Mountains rise over Silver Lake, left. The Wrangells are one of four major mountain ranges that converge in the park. Below: Kennicott Glacier leaves a heap of morainal debris at the base of the Wrangell Mountains.

Snow-Fed Glaciers

Winter storms pile roughly 50 feet of fresh snow on the park's four mountain ranges, replenishing the world's largest subpolar ice field.

Bears of Wrangell

A male grizzly bear grasps a slender tree trunk. Both grizzly and black bears roam the park, feeding off the salmon that spawn in its lakes, rivers, and streams.

WRANGELL–ST. ELIAS NATIONAL PARK AND PRESERVE

History Note: During his friendly encounter with the Ahtna people in 1885, United States Army explorer Lt. Henry Allen was shown bullets the Ahtna had made from a copper-silver alloy they had produced from their own mines.

Flora: All major vegetation types found in south-central, southeastern, and interior Alaska, including coastal spruce-hemlock forests, closed spruce-hardwood forests, alpine tundra, and wet tundra.

Fauna: Large concentration of Dall sheep; also moose, caribou, black bears, grizzlies, and mountain goats; whales, sea lions, sea otters, and porpoises; trumpeter swans and eagles.

Visitor Tip: Several small, backcountry cabins with woodstoves and bunks are scattered throughout the park for visitors to use as bases for exploration. Access to most is by air.

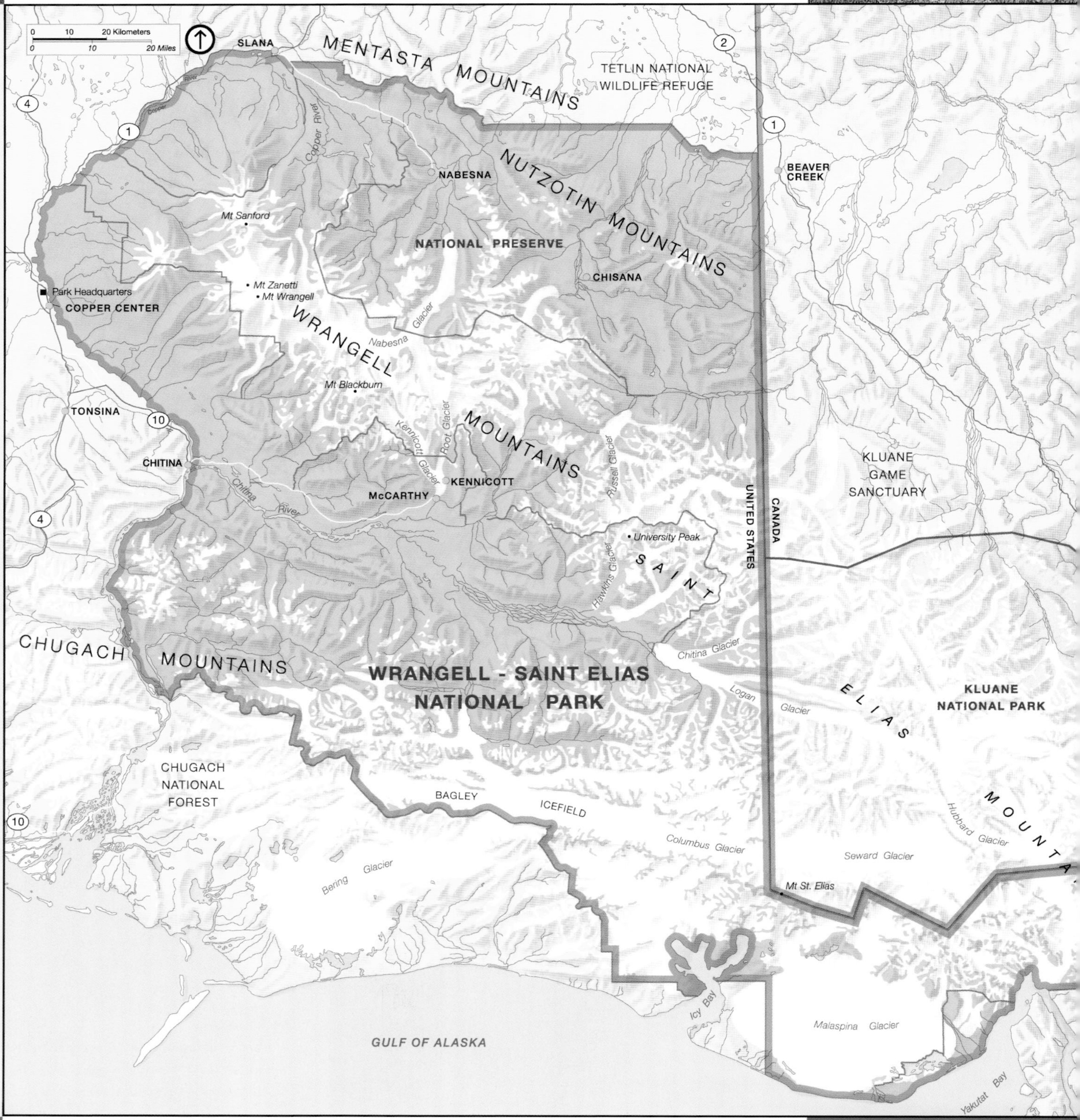

Spacious Valleys

Many of Wrangell–St. Elias National Park's river valleys were widened and straightened by glacial carving, *facing page.*

Valley Glaciers

Valley glaciers such as Kennicott gather ice from alpine glaciers near the tops of the mountains and bury entire valleys under thick tongues of moving ice.

Caribou

A set of shed caribou antlers lies silhouetted against the sun. Caribou feed on lichen and low woody plants around the Wrangell Mountains.

HISTORICAL KENNECOTT

The historic mining town of Kennecott sprang up during the early 1900s when prospectors discovered a fabulously rich lode of copper ore in a steep ridge overlooking Kennicott Glacier.

Rail Link
Trains leaving Kennecott's mill moved a billion tons of copper between 1911 and 1938.

Though the boomtown's working life was short, Kennecott today serves as a fascinating window to the past. Its mill and many of its other principal structures have been preserved and are considered the nation's best remaining example of early twentieth-century copper mining.

Heydays Past
Many of Kennecott's buildings are now historic landmarks.

Though the Kennecott discoveries made front-page news elsewhere, the presence of valuable metals here was nothing new to the region's native Ahtna people. For at least 1,400 years, they had been mining it, fabricating it, and trading it with other native inhabitants of the Far North. Then, as prospectors fanned out in the wake of the 1898 Klondike Gold Rush, the Ahtna helped them find copper ore in what is now the heart of Wrangell–St. Elias National Park.

By 1900, major deposits of copper ore, including the famous Bonanza Mine, had been located and the towns of Kennecott and McCarthy were laid out. Full production was delayed eleven years, however, while the Copper River and Northwestern Railway laid 169 miles of track between the Kennecott mill and the port of Cordova, on the Gulf of Alaska.

From 1911 to 1938, the mines produced an astonishing amount of chalcocite—a heavy, gray ore with a copper concentration of 80 percent. The ore was milled at Kennecott, then shipped to the sea by rail. When the ore played out, the Bonanza and four neighboring mines had produced a billion pounds of copper and nine million ounces of silver, which was recovered as a by-product.

Today, visitors to Wrangell–St. Elias National Park can wander historic Kennecott, take guided tours of the town's most important buildings, and stroll to the edge of its namesake glacier.

Early Autumn
Autumn comes early to one of Wrangell–St. Elias's river valleys.

Granite Faces

Sheer granite cliffs drop into the abyss of Yosemite Valley from Taft Point, left. Pleistocene glaciers transformed Yosemite Valley, below, from a tight, zig-zagging canyon cut by the Merced River into a spacious, flat-floored valley bounded by sheer cliffs.

YOSEMITE

NATIONAL PARK IN CALIFORNIA

REVELATION IN LIGHT

A beloved exemplar for the worldwide national park movement, Yosemite is a relentlessly enchanting landscape. There are deep, glacially sculpted valleys, beckoning alpine meadowlands, and groves of the largest living things, the giant sequoias. The abrupt topography and generous precipitation combine to create some of North America's most dramatic waterfalls. The combined drop of Yosemite Falls's two falls and one cascade is almost half a mile.

The view from the entrance of Yosemite Valley is one of the earth's most famous natural scenes. Wilderness prophet John Muir, Yosemite's foremost champion, said it was "a revelation in landscape affairs that enriches one's life forever." And yet for all its perfection of wild beauty, it is still hard to comprehend. It is bigger and more awesome than you imagine even as you gape at it in wonder.

But come to the valley in winter. In the morning, watch Yosemite Falls as the sun is warming and loosening the ice crust that has built up overnight on both sides of the arc of water. In a while, you will see bits of this ice fringe break away and drop hundreds of feet in a fine powder. But a couple of seconds later, you will hear a deep booming, as those tremendous masses of ice—not powder, but huge blocks—crash on the rocks below. Then you will begin to understand the magnitude of Yosemite.

It is that way throughout the park, a startling mixture of overwhelming setting and elegant subtlety. The sequoias are much more than the oldest and fastest-growing of living things. They are food, shelter, larder, and landmark to many other living things. They are, in short, a community on a very big stick. More than 180 species of insects and arachnids are known to use the trees themselves for one purpose or other, and many more rely on leaf litter and other debris in the rich soil ecosystem underneath. Several species hover in mating swarms directly above a tree, using it as a landmark to orient and gather their numbers.

Ascent and Descent
Purple lupine, above, bloom among the charred remains of a burn recovery area. Left: Yosemite Falls begins its 2,425-foot plunge.

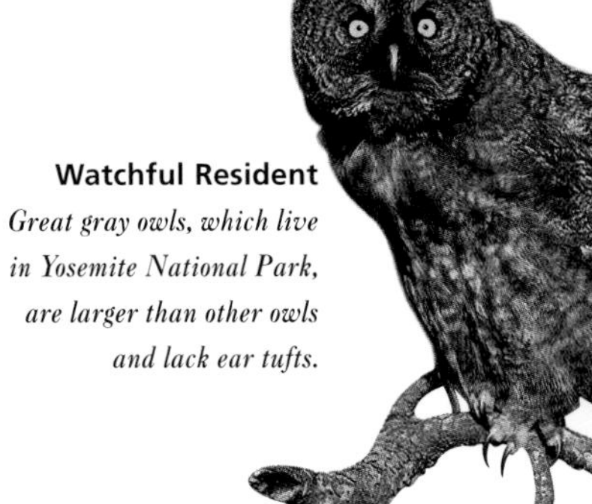

Watchful Resident
Great gray owls, which live in Yosemite National Park, are larger than other owls and lack ear tufts.

Many bird species are attracted by the insects. Warblers, vireos, flycatchers, and others pick the insects from the foliage or pluck them from the air. Sapsuckers and woodpeckers search the bark for burrowers. Several mammal species make themselves at home in the towering superstructure, most notably the squirrel known as the chickaree. The chickaree's persistent spreading of sequoia seeds, released as it eats the cones, may be vital to the regeneration of the great trees. The community's health depends upon the actions of its citizens.

Rising Above
El Capitan was a nunatak, a peak that once protruded through glacial ice.

Go to Tuolumne Meadows in late spring and early summer for the brief startling burst of wildflower blossoms, and think about the snow that piled high over your head right here, four months ago. Stroll, slowly, through the reconstructed Indian Village at the Valley Visitor Center, and think about life two hundred years ago in this hidden land—no cars, no stores, and no cell phones. Then, last, go to Glacier Point, 3,200 feet directly over the south side of Yosemite Valley, in time for sunset, and don't think about anything at all.

Glacial Track
Yosemite Valley bears the unmistakable, U-shaped track of glacial carving, right. Below: Rivers and waterfalls around Yosemite National Park reach their maximum flow in May and June.

Powdered Trunks

Fresh snow clings to the trunks of fir trees in Yosemite's Merced Grove. Here, too, stand giant sequoias, a species well adapted to wildfire.

Tallest Waterfall

The continent's tallest waterfall, Yosemite Falls drops 2,425 feet in three stages: an upper fall of 1,430 feet; a 675-foot cascade; and a lower fall of 320 feet.

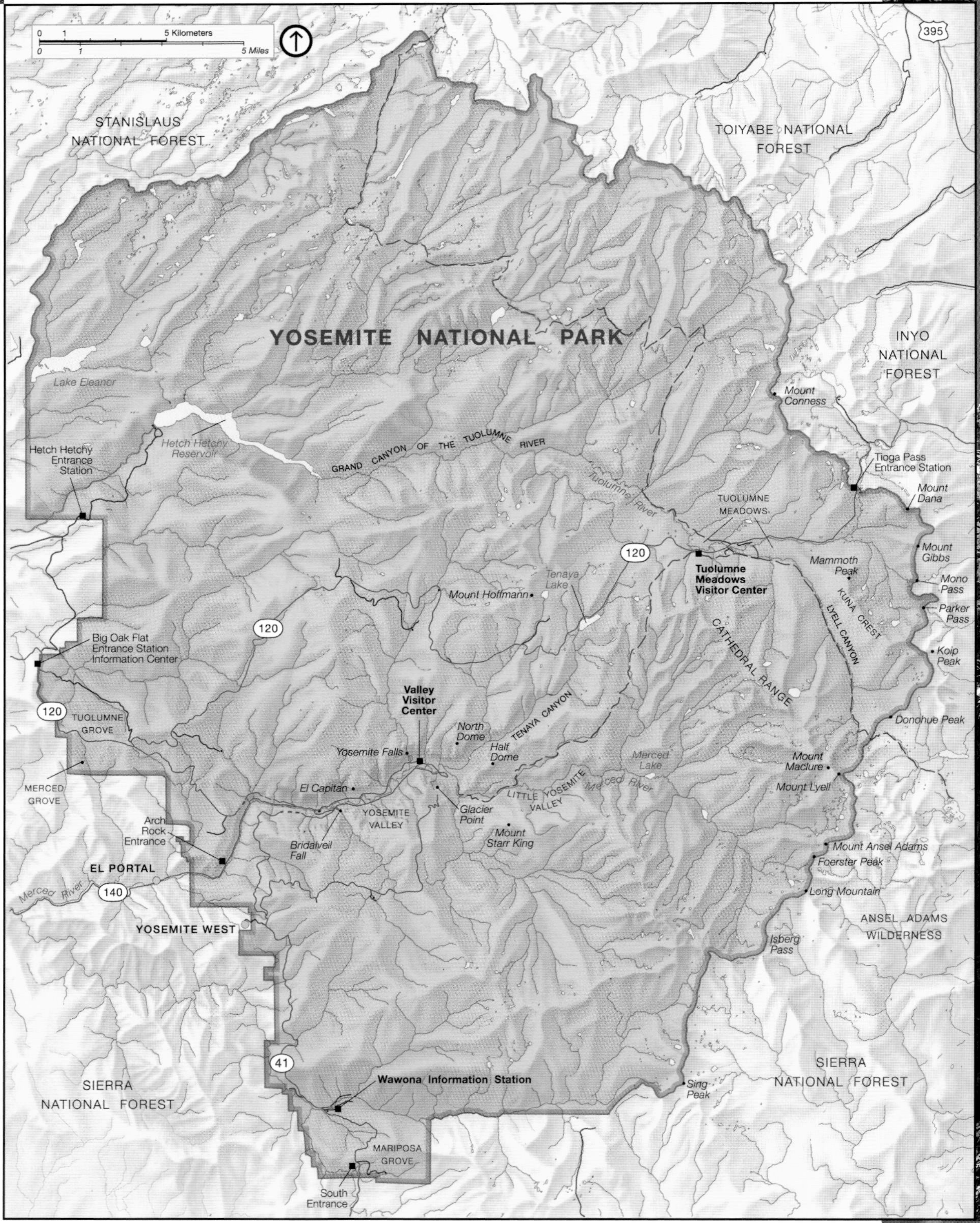

Mountain Aviary

A mountain bluebird checks traffic before flying off with a meal. Yosemite boasts 247 species of birds, including bald eagles and peregrine falcons.

Valley Bears

A black bear lumbers through a park meadow. Bears in Yosemite Valley also troll the parking lots, campgrounds, and picnic areas looking for food.

The Captain

El Capitan rises nearly 3,600 feet from the surface of the Merced River. It is highly resistant to erosion because its granite contains almost no joints or fractures.

YOSEMITE NATIONAL PARK

History Note: Nineteenth-century geologists scoffed at John Muir and called him an ignorant sheepherder when he suggested that Yosemite's dramatic landforms were the result of glaciation.

Flora: Three groves of giant sequoias; oak woodlands; montane and subalpine forests; expansive meadows; 1,400 species of flowering plants.

Fauna: Ninety mammal species, including mule deer, black bears, mountain lions, coyotes, and bighorn sheep; 250 species of birds.

Visitor Tip: To avoid road rage in Yosemite Valley, park your car, hail the park's shuttle bus, and stroll to the valley's landmarks.

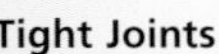

Tight Joints

Pillars, columns, and pinnacles such as Cathedral Spires form where closely spaced joints are attacked by the forces of weathering and erosion.

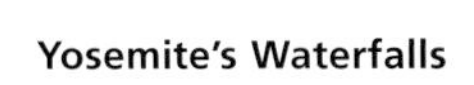

Yosemite's Waterfalls

Vernal Fall pours 317 feet from a wall at the east end of Yosemite Valley. Most of the nation's tallest waterfalls stream from Yosemite cliffs, and three rank among the five tallest on Earth.

GLACIAL POWER

One of the most dramatic glacial landscapes in the world, Yosemite was virtually buried in ice during the Pleistocene epoch. Its

Glacial Sheen
This outcrop of granite near Olmsted Point was polished smooth by ice-age glaciers.

spacious U-shaped valleys, sheer cliffs, bare rock walls, rounded monoliths, and plunging waterfalls attest to the incredible power of thick glacial ice flowing slowly across resistant granitic rock.

Four major periods of glaciation left their marks on Yosemite. The most recent ended ten thousand years ago, but the most extensive

Granite Bed
Glacially scoured slabs of granite form the bed of the Tuolumne River.

came much earlier (the dating remains obscure).

During the heaviest periods of glaciation, abundant snow along the crest of the range formed an enormous glacier that spread across the uplands for miles and sent trunk glaciers down the Tuolumne River Canyon, Tenaya Canyon, and Little Yosemite Valley.

The Tenaya and Little Yosemite ice bodies joined to carve out the main Yosemite Valley. At peak periods, only the highest points in the valley—Half Dome, El Capitan, Eagle Peak, and Sentinel Dome—projected above the ice as nunataks. Elsewhere, ice completely overrode existing domes such as Liberty Cap, Lembert Dome, and Mount Broderick and carved them into giant examples of roches moutonnées.

Armed with abrasive rock fragments plucked and scoured from the bedrock, the glaciers gouged down into existing stream valleys, widening, straightening, and deepening them, and hewing their slopes into precipitous cliffs. Small tributary glaciers carved out hanging valleys, which today end abruptly along the upper walls of the main valley and launch some of the world's tallest waterfalls.

In many places, the ice pressed fine-grained sediments against the rock, polishing the surface as smooth as a gravestone. Glaciers also transported surprisingly large rock fragments that fell from the ice as it melted and were left as "glacial erratics" throughout the park.

Path of the Glacier
The Tuolomne River snakes through Yosemite National Park near Glen Aulin.

FORESTS OF YOSEMITE

Thanks in large part to wide differences in elevation, Yosemite National Park embraces four distinct forest zones, each with characteristic plant and animal species. These zones overlap at the margins, and some of the birds and large mammals that live within them roam from one zone to another during the year.

Broadly speaking, though, among the park's foothills, visitors are likely to find gray pine, blue oak, interior live oak, scrub oak, chamise, and other chaparral plants. Mule deer browse here, and red-tailed hawks hunt for small rodents.

At the upper margin of the foothills zone, its species mix with and then give way to the lower montane forest, which characterizes the floor of Yosemite Valley and the flanks of the surrounding mountains. Here stands a mix of coniferous and deciduous trees: ponderosa pine, sugar pine, incense cedar, Douglas fir, California black oak, canyon live oak, bigleaf maple, and Pacific dogwood. Coyotes, black bears, ringtails, raccoons, mule deer, and squirrels all live here.

At about 6,000 feet elevation, tree species of the upper montane begin to take hold. They include red fir, Jeffrey pine, western white pine, lodgepole pine, and quaking aspen. Chipmunks and flying squirrels, marmots, and river otters are among the zone's residents.

Finally, subalpine species begin infiltration of the upper montane at around 8,000 feet and carry on to treeline, where expansive alpine wildflower meadows open up. Trees include lodgepole pine, but also mountain hemlock and whitebark pine. This is where the park's bighorn sheep live, along with pikas, pocket gophers, and other small rodents.

Whitebark Pine
One of the park's hardiest trees, whitebark pine grows in Yosemite's subalpine realm.

In addition to these four broad zones, the park protects three groves of giant sequoia trees. The largest of Yosemite's groves, Mariposa Grove, includes the Grizzly Giant, which is about 2,700 years old.

Sequoia Cone
Hundreds of giant sequoias drop their cones in Mariposa Grove.

Lifelong Embrace
The branches of a canyon live oak bend around the tree's lifelong companion, a giant boulder, left. Following spread: Spring aspens bask in the mist of Yosemite Falls.

WIND AND WATER EROSION

WE SEE EROSION everywhere, but there are very few places where we like it. It costs farmers and ranchers irreplaceable soil, undermines roadbeds, and topples hillside homes. But enter a national park, and take a look at this powerful natural force from a new angle. The partnership of water and weather has given us some of our most beautiful landscapes. When we can watch erosion without worrying, we discover that neither erosion nor the landscape being eroded is as simple as it seems.

Balancing Act
Arches National Park's Balanced Rock is a magnificent example of differential erosion.

When you stand in one of the famous erosion parks in the Southwest and feel the dry, gritty wind, it's hard to believe that water has much to do with what's going on there. But water, precious, rare, and ephemeral even when it comes, is as vital to the shapes of this landscape as it is to those hardy species of plants and animals who have adapted to life there.

Slip Stream
A narrow stream slips down a cliff carved by the Virgin River in Zion.

It couldn't get the job done alone. Weathering, by which wind and heat and cold and rain slowly fracture, dismantle, and disintegrate the rock, takes teamwork. One day these erosional forces may loosen only a few grains of sand, or ease a thin slab from the side of a boulder. The next day, they work their way along a weakened joint of some huge boulder and start the long, unhurried job of splitting it in two. On a rare banner day, they pull down the thin middle from some weary aged arch they've been nagging at for centuries. And even as the echoes of the collapsing arch fade, erosion starts to work on the new scars where the rock broke free.

THE PATIENT POWER

Black Canyon
The Gunnison River carved Black Canyon through resistant Precambrian rocks.

EROSION SHAPES THE LAND

Water, wind, and the freeze-thaw cycle have worked over time to wear down and remove the earth in many of the country's national parks. These forces can create formations that are mind-bogglingly massive or achingly

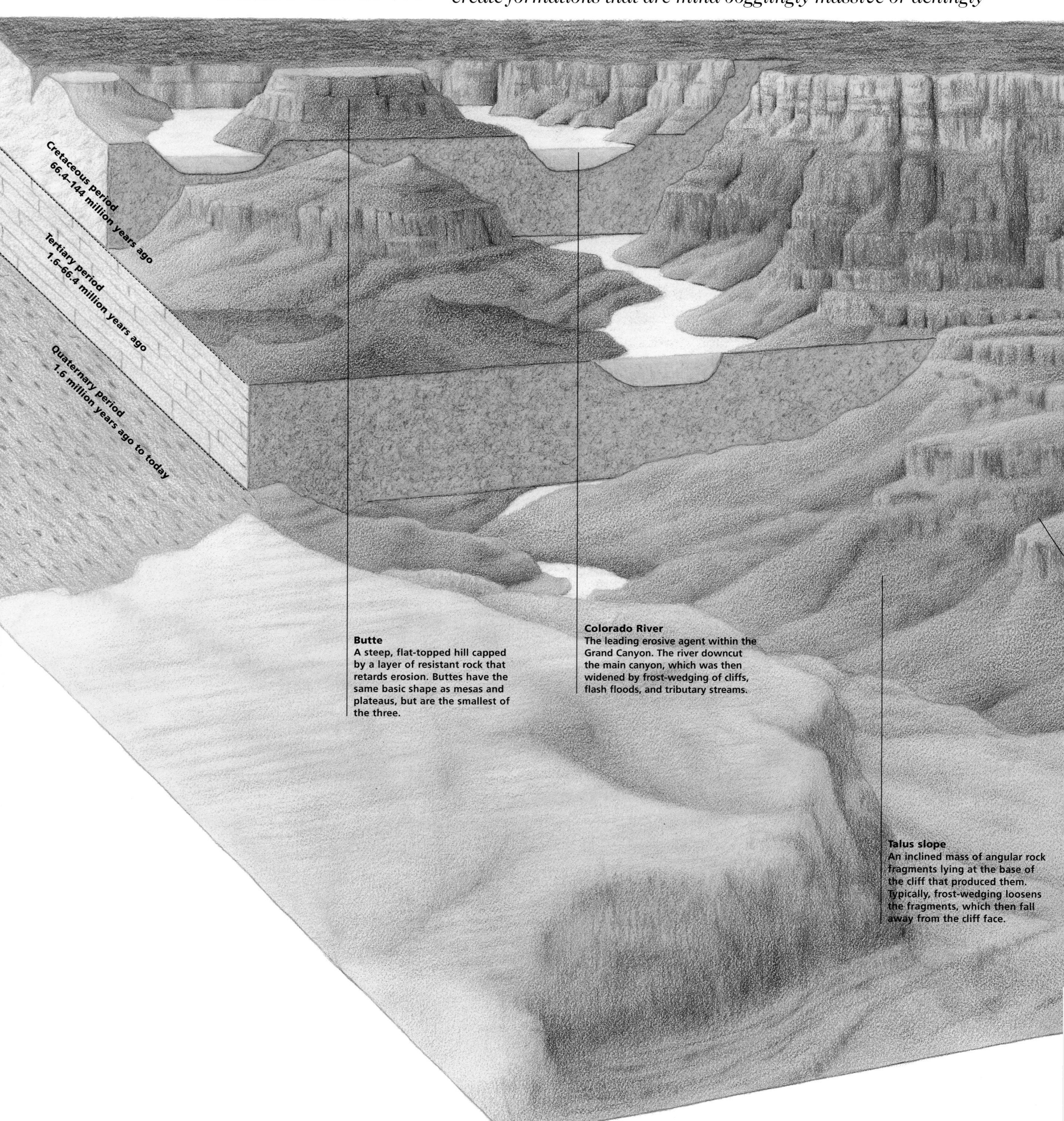

delicate. The aptly named Grand Canyon is perhaps the best-known example of the patient destruction of an erosive force, in its case, the Colorado River. Elsewhere, the power of erosion works to shape formations, polish exposed rocks to an eerie patina, or reveal fossils.

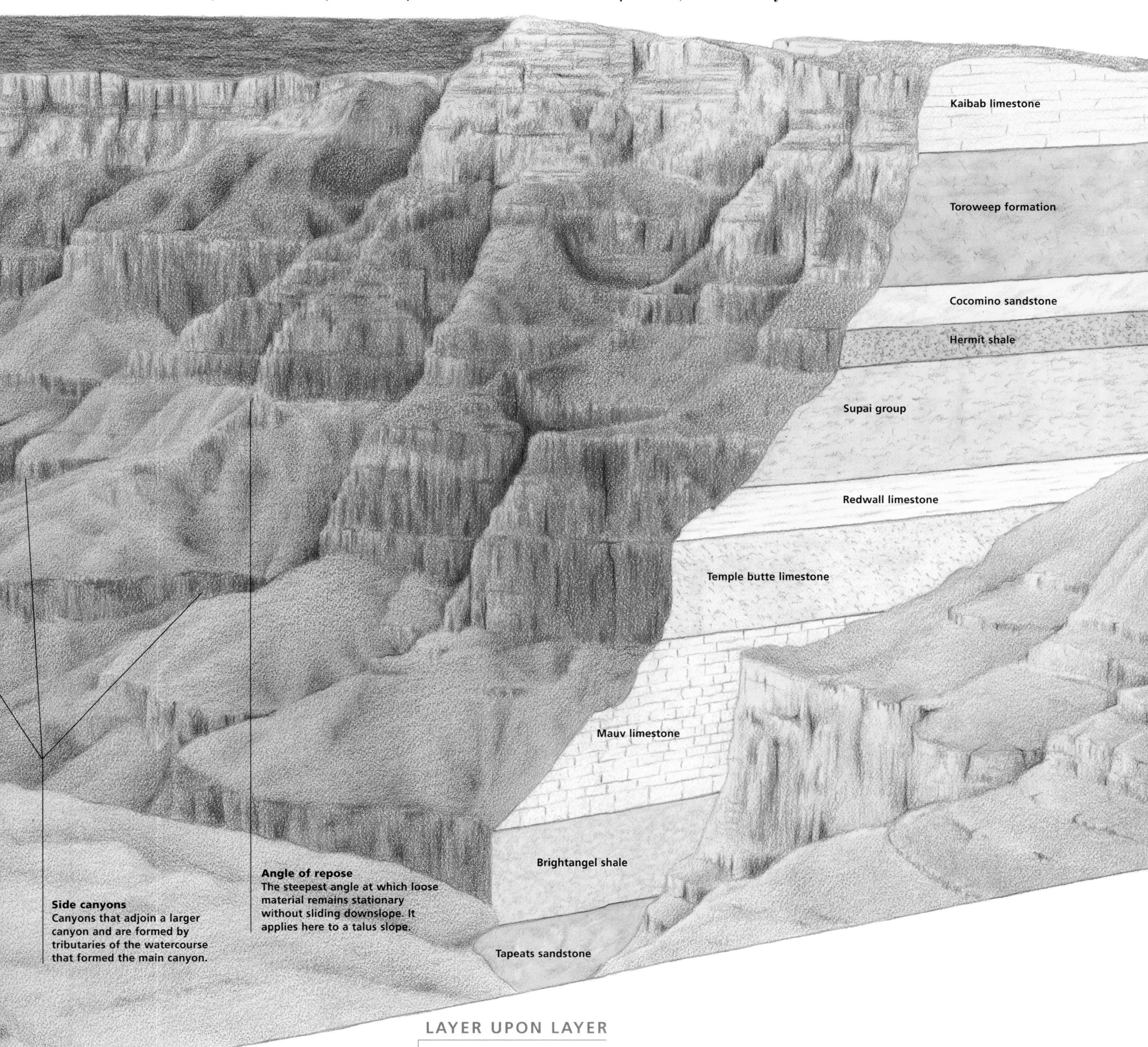

LAYER UPON LAYER

Built up over a period of more than 500 million years, sedimentary rock layers exposed in the canyons of the American Southwest record the major events of a planet in slow flux. Within the layers of limestone, sandstone, siltstone, mudstone, and shale lies evidence of ancient seas and deserts, the drift and collision of Earth's tectonic plates, the rise and fall of mountain ranges, the eruption of distant volcanoes, and the advance and extinction of various forms of life. In the depths of the Grand Canyon, above, erosion bites even deeper into Earth's history, exposing metamorphic "basement rocks" 1.8 billion years old.

All in a Row
This series of fins makes up part of the Fiery Furnace formation in Arches National Park. Fins are the first formation in the process of arch-building.

Work in Progress
Although it is made from the same layer of dune sandstone as other arches around Arches National Park, Navajo Arch is not yet as eroded.

BUILDING BLOCK FINS

Narrow fins of colorful sandstone and limestone often provide the basic building blocks for such intriguing rock formations as hoodoos and natural arches. In much of southeast Utah's canyon country, fins erode along deep, vertical joints that lie parallel to one another, like a sliced bread loaf. The joints were formed when movements deep within the Earth cracked the overlying layers of rock. Waterborne chemicals, the freeze-thaw cycle, rainwater, and wind combine to invade and enlarge the joints until a row of freestanding fins is created.

HOODOOS

Hoodoos are columns, pinnacles, or pillars of rock that have been eroded into shapes that strike the eye as incongruous, bizarre, strange, distorted, even grotesque. The canyon country of Utah is full of such structures, which are usually formed by differential erosion.

NATURAL BRIDGES

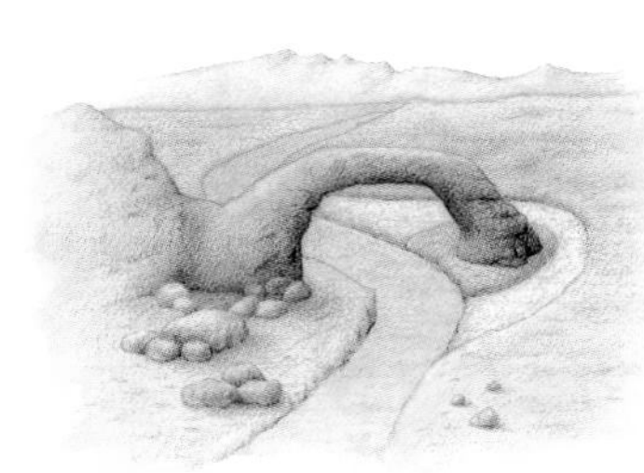

Unlike arches, natural bridges are carved by streams. They often form when a stream racing down a steep slope beats against a narrow rock fin that juts across its path. The current hurls sand, gravel—even boulders—against the fin and may also undermine it by carrying away an underlayer of softer stone. Eventually, the stream breaches the fin and may cut a small canyon beneath it.

Natural Bridge
When a stream tunnels through a fin, the resulting formation is a natural bridge. Bryce Bridge in Bryce Canyon National Park is an example of this action.

DESERT VARNISH

Ranging in color from red to black, desert varnish is a thin coating that streaks rock surfaces throughout canyon country. It is composed largely of clay minerals and sand grains colored by oxides and hydroxides of manganese and/or iron. Varnishes rich in manganese are black; those rich in iron, red to orange. They are emplaced by the physiological activities of microorganisms, which bond the clays and other particles to rock surfaces using manganese as a cement. These microorganisms use both organic and inorganic nutrition sources and thrive in desert environments unfit for organisms that rely solely on organic materials.

Desert Patina
Desert varnish is a thin coating of microorganisms and minerals that is seen on rocks throughout canyon country. Shiny, blue-black desert varnishes are rich in manganese.

CARVING ARCHES

Arches start as a series of fin forms that erosion continues to narrow. Often, the fins simply melt away or break up into columns and pinnacles before succumbing to the inevitable. But sometimes the right degree of balance and hardness is struck, and arches form. Water erosion may follow cracks (A) or some other weakness peculiar to that particular fin. Gradually, small flakes and chunks spall away until an alcove (B) and then an opening (C) appears. Arches in the southwest usually form in hard sandstone that lies on a bed of soft mudstone. Erosion carves the softer layer, thus undermining the harder, and ultimately reveals a window in the rock (D).

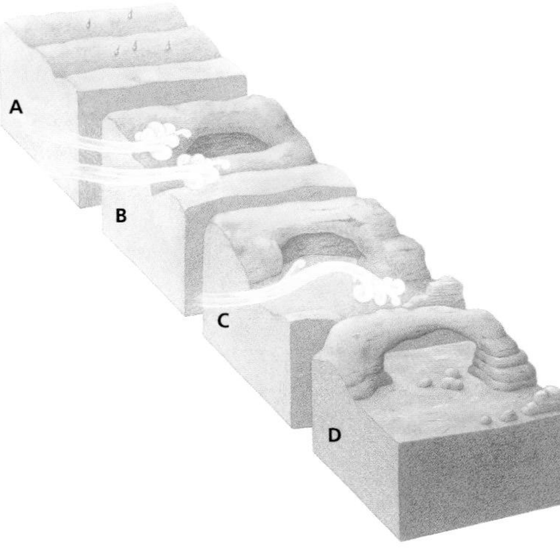

Balanced Rock
In a textbook example of differential erosion, the softer layers of Balanced Rock in Arches National Park have worn away faster, leaving a large bulb of more resistant rock perched on top, left. Eventually, erosion will thin Landscape Arch, right, each to the point of collapse.

Hoodoo Garden
Fins in the Fiery Furnace sector of Arches National Park erode into a garden of brilliantly colored hoodoos.

Rock Colors
Minute quantities of particular coloring agents are responsible for the brilliant pigmentation of rock layers in canyon country.

Warped Layers
The Waterpocket Fold is composed of sedimentary rock layers that were deposited horizontally (A). Later, mountain-building forces warped the layers into a thick monocline (B). Erosion gradually stripped away the upper layers and left today's spectacular bands of tilted rock (C).

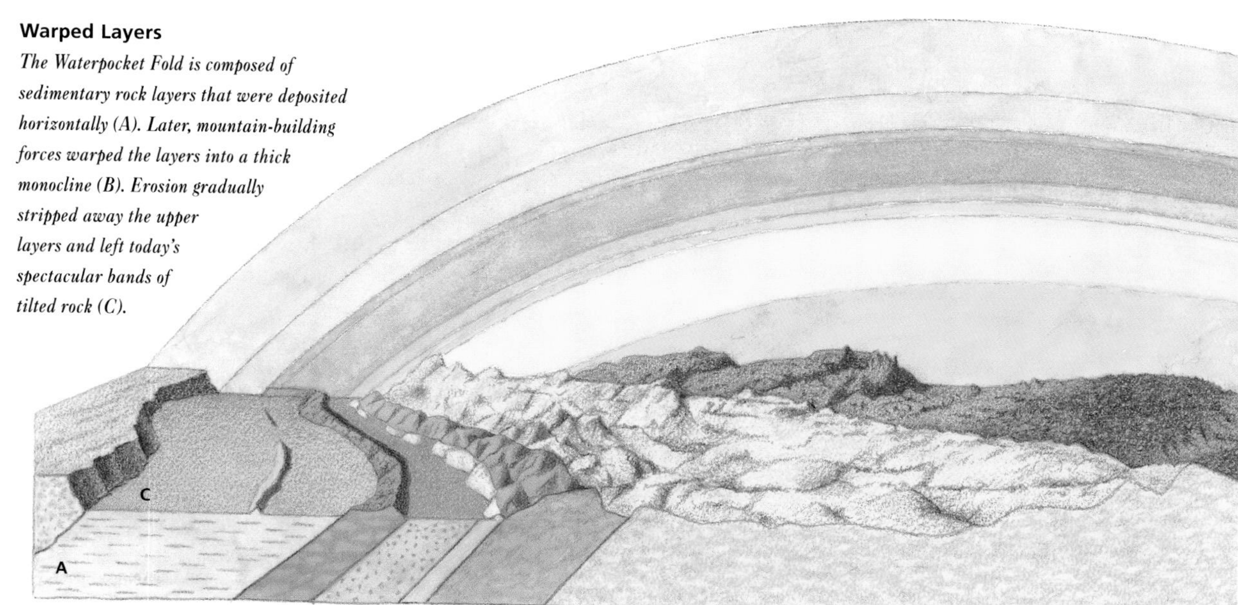

EXPOSING THE PAST

Throughout canyon country, erosion slices down through the rock layers as if they were pages in a book. Though the book is incomplete, and though one rarely gets more than a brief glimpse at a particular page, it vividly describes Earth history events both large and small.

The Waterpocket Fold, left, stretches across south-central Utah for 100 miles. It is the eroded remnant of a massive bulge, or monocline—thousands of feet high—that formed within the Earth's crust 50 to 70 million years ago, middle left.

On a more intimate scale, erosion of sedimentary rock exposes the fossilized remains of individual lives, such as a fish (A), bottom left. Two conditions are necessary for fossilization to occur: rapid burial (B), which removes the organism from the forces of decomposition; and the possession of hard body parts such as a fish's skeleton. Once buried and compressed by overlying layers of rock, fossils often become petrified, literally turning into stone (C). In other instances, minerals replace cell walls. Some fossils leave just an impression within the stone; others, a thin but intricately detailed layer of carbon. When erosion reveals such fossils (D), scientists are able to date geologic events around the world, shed light on the evolution of life, and sketch portraits of ancient ecosystems.

Fossils Revealed

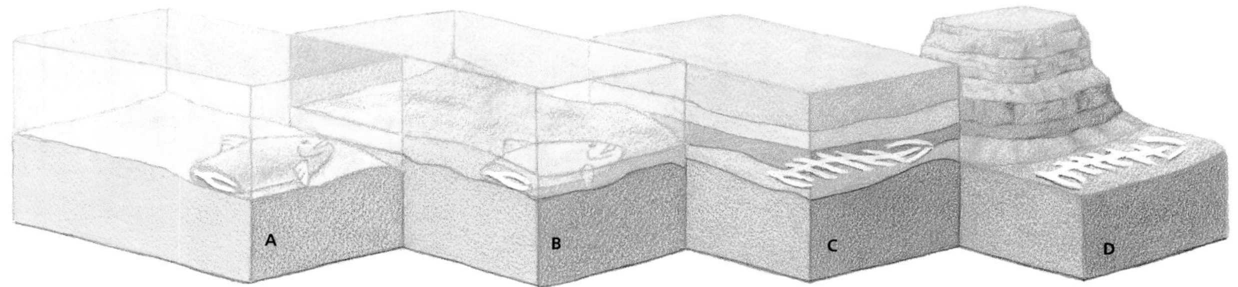

Uncovering History
Erosion in Theodore Roosevelt National Park has revealed deposits of bentonite, a blue-gray layer of clay that scientists believe is the result of ancient volcano ash.

TENACIOUS FORCES

At first, we were baffled and amazed by the arid badlands and canyon country of the West. Our European heritage did not prepare us for such sights—such forbidding and inhospitable landscapes, whose desert wilderness evoked a sense of evil that was nothing short of biblical. Erosion seemed almost to delight in getting in our way and defying our progress. The beauty eluded us, being almost as inaccessible as the land itself. Coming to terms with these lands was hard work, but few other American landscapes have taught us as much, or brought us as close to wild nature.

The erosion parks illustrate many things, including the vast, tortured haul of the planet's geological history. But they also illustrate erosion's path of most resistance. What is left is what would not erode, or what has not yet eroded. Erosion is a kind of test, and only the hardest rock passes it.

Rocky Perch
A pinyon pine stakes out a claim among the cliffs in Arches. It often grows in company with juniper.

The Grand Canyon proves that even the hardest rocks don't pass the test forever. The canyon's terraced walls and slopes have a ziggurat style, indicative of the "differential erosion" of the various strata. The rim is miles back from the Colorado River and its tributaries. But the river itself is often lost to sight, deep in its dark inner gorge. Down there, harder metamorphic and igneous rocks wear away more slowly, in sheer unsloping walls instead of terraced steps.

The Black Canyon of the Gunnison might be casually likened to an inner gorge without a higher canyon. The Gunnison River has cut straight down through the hard rock. On the other hand, a similar effect even appears in the softer sedimentary rocks of Zion National Park. The Virgin River has carved many sheer canyon walls, but the softer rock is more likely to slump, and in other places the canyon walls are wider and sloped.

Badlands and Theodore Roosevelt National Parks show us other slumping and sloping, in even softer siltstones, mudstones, and shales. Here and there, a top-heavy hill or mushroom-shaped spire reminds us that the hardest rock isn't always on the bottom. Caprocks of harder material may endure while softer rock underneath is worn away.

There are erosive features that are softer yet. Kobuk Valley National Park, north of the Arctic Circle in Alaska, contains hundreds of square miles of sand dunes, about as fluid a landform as is possible without adding water, which has little to do with their creation. For millennia, wind has been the primary force here and continues to engineer dune activity along the edges of some of the park's huge dune areas.

Capitol Reef National Park's spectacular Waterpocket Fold, a long, north-south trending dip in the sedimentary rock strata, has steeply tilted the strata that elsewhere we view by descending into a canyon. Here, we drive across it, and streams

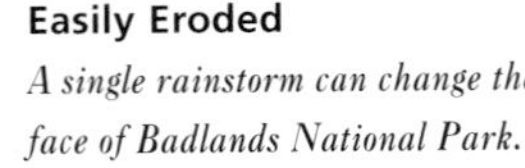

Easily Eroded
A single rainstorm can change the face of Badlands National Park.

Badlands

Bryce Canyon

Grand Canyon

Arches

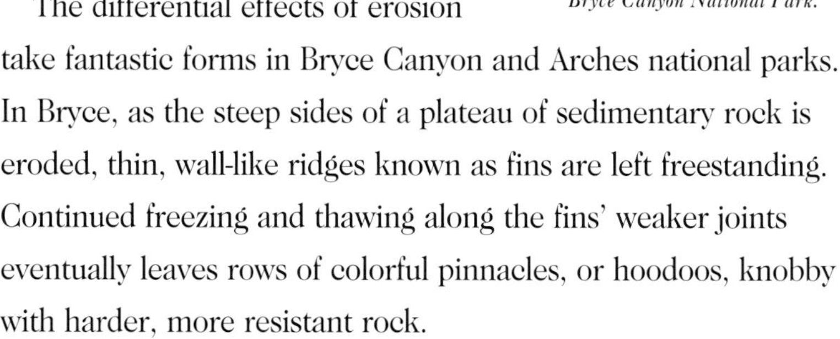

Snowy Canyon

Snow dusts the salmon-colored cliffs of Bryce Canyon National Park.

erode across or along it. The geological "layer cake" is turned on its side, so differential erosion turns one layer into spires, the next into a trench, the next into gullied domes, all more or less side by side.

The differential effects of erosion take fantastic forms in Bryce Canyon and Arches national parks. In Bryce, as the steep sides of a plateau of sedimentary rock is eroded, thin, wall-like ridges known as fins are left freestanding. Continued freezing and thawing along the fins' weaker joints eventually leaves rows of colorful pinnacles, or hoodoos, knobby with harder, more resistant rock.

Black Canyon of the Gunnison

Canyonlands

Capitol Reef

Cuyahoga

In Arches, the mountain-building era of the Laramide Orogeny left long, parallel stress fractures in the native sandstones. Weathering along these weak points eventually created separate, parallel fins, which are reduced to a variety of spires, balanced rocks, and, perhaps most famous, true arches, created by the gradual "exfoliation" of their sides by frost and other weathering processes.

Canyonlands protects the diverse wildlands around the confluence of the Green and Colorado rivers. When it comes to the distinctive erosive landscapes and landforms of the American Southwest, Canyonlands essentially has it all, from the huge, steep-walled river canyons to fins, domes, spires, arches, and other more localized phenomena beyond counting, including a legendary wilderness of smaller canyons, mesas, meadows, and potholes of incredible complexity.

Kobuk Valley

Theodore Roosevelt

Entrenched Meander

The Colorado River follows its entrenched course at The Loop in Canyonlands.

Zion

ARCHES

NATIONAL PARK IN UTAH

SLICKROCK WINDOWS

At Arches, Jurassic sandstones in lurid tints of red and orange, stressed and tilted by slow geological forces, were cracked deeply in long parallel patterns. Erosion gradually widened these gaps until only freestanding slab-sided ridges, or fins, remained. As weathering continues a window sometimes opens in the rock. Once open, the window's frame invites more weathering until nothing remains but a narrow arch of sandstone suspended over the slickrock.

Arches National Park must strike many visitors as eerily familiar, and no wonder. Thanks to some great storytellers and our own imaginations, we have all been here before. We may recognize it as a classic biblical wilderness—an old-fashioned sun-blistered "wasteland" in the very suburbs of hell. In our fantasy folklore, it is the Barsoom of Edgar Rice Burroughs, the Tatooine of George Lucas.

Here also we have met earthbound heroes. Under one looming fin, young Indiana Jones snatched the cross of Coronado from the greedy treasure hunters. And just down the road, environmental polemicist Edward Abbey, no less a romantic swashbuckler than Jones, sat in a hot little government trailer and unleashed his original blend of wonder, cynicism, and hope on the American West.

With this load of imagery in our heads, we are keyed up and ready for the wildest of shows when we enter this park, but the place can still reduce us to awestruck mumbling wonder.

Traveling through Arches, whether by car or afoot, is much like watching a really good fireworks show. You know that any second something wonderful is going to happen, but when it does you're still so surprised that you involuntarily ooh and aah with the rest of the crowd. Geology takes some of its happiest turns here.

Arches is an open invitation to our imaginations. But don't forget to set aside symbolism—there is plenty of wonder in the thing itself. As nature writer Terry Tempest Williams has put it, "Windows and arches ask you to recall what is no longer there, to taste the wind for the sandstone it carries."

Graceful Spans

Carved from massive beds of colorful sandstone, below, the landscape of Arches National Park contains the world's greatest concentration of natural stone arches. More than two thousand of these structures grace the park, including Turret Arch, above.

Paintbrush

Paintbrush, right, displays its brilliant color not from blossoms (which are usually yellowish-green) but from narrow, leaflike bracts. Below: Delicate Arch.

A Relentless Force

Though formations such as Double Arch may appear sturdy and permanent, erosion weakens all of the park's arches. More than forty have collapsed since the mid-1970s.

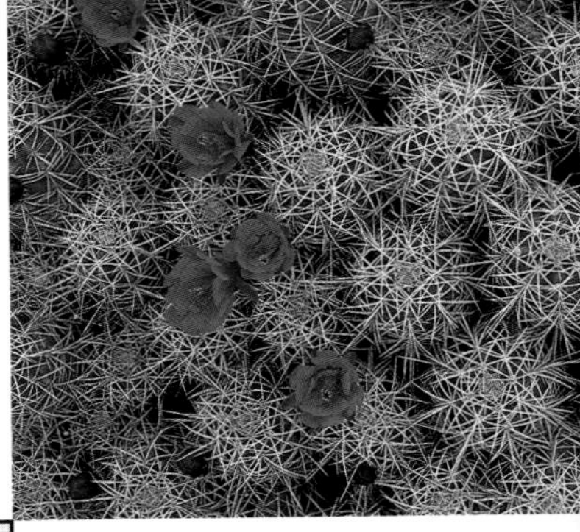

Cactus Garden

Various types of cactus thrive in Arches' desert climate, where surface temperatures can exceed air temperatures by 25 to 50 degrees Fahrenheit.

ARCHES NATIONAL PARK

History Note: The Old Spanish Trail, which linked the Spanish colonies of Santa Fe and Los Angeles, ran right past today's park visitor center.

Flora: Pinyon pine and juniper forest, cactuses, grasses, short-lived wildflowers, and, in moist microclimates, ferns, willows, cattails, columbine, and monkey flower.

Fauna: Lizards, snakes, jackrabbits, kangaroo rats, coyotes, mountain lions, mule deer, bighorn sheep, and foxes.

Visitor Tip: Set aside enough time to hike some trails. Easy walks lead to some of the most famous sights in the park, including Landscape Arch, Double Arch, and Balanced Rock.

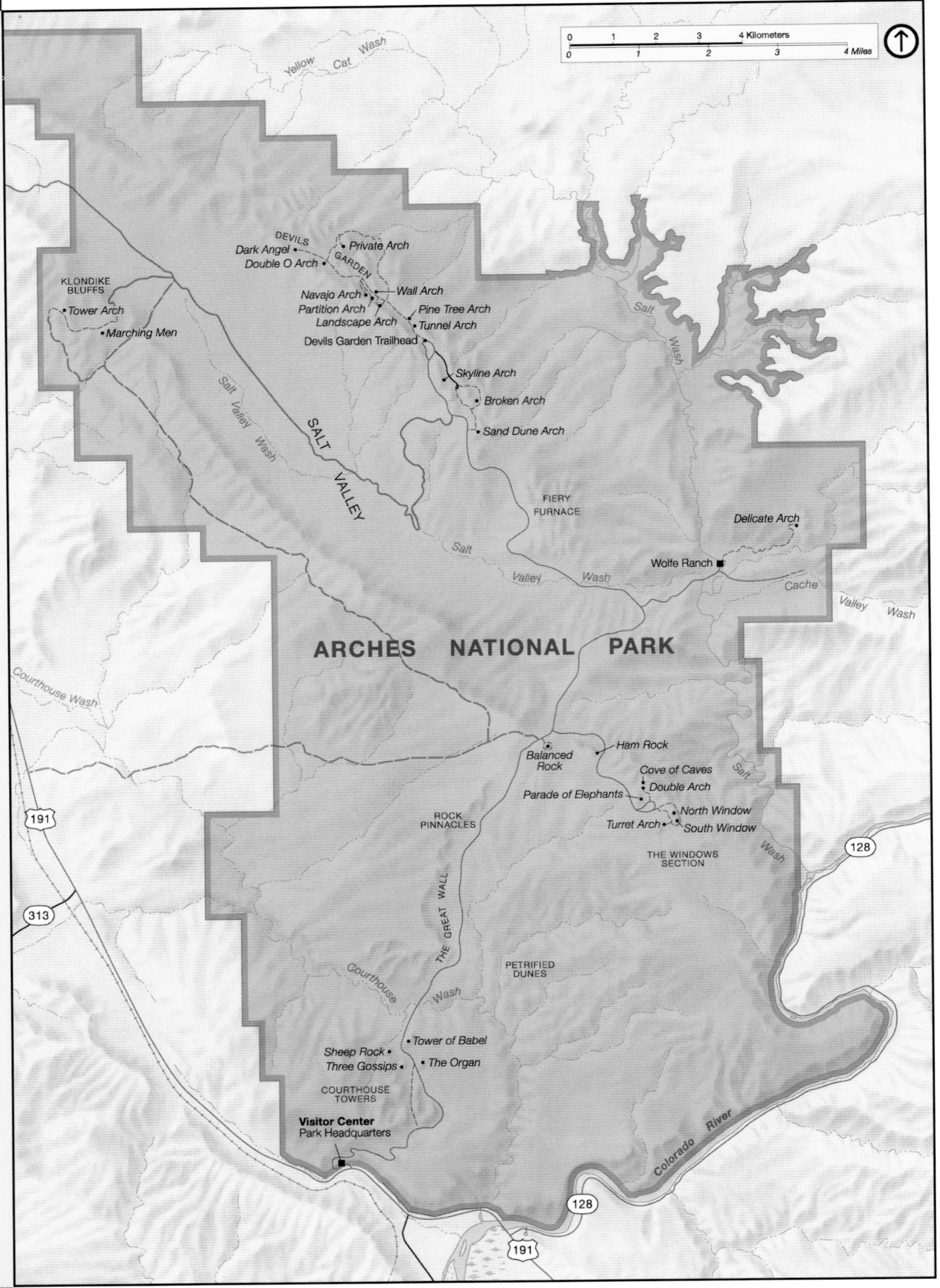

0 1 2 3 4 Kilometers
0 1 2 3 4 Miles

Yellow Cat Wash
DEVILS GARDEN
Dark Angel
Double O Arch
Private Arch
KLONDIKE BLUFFS
Tower Arch
Marching Men
Navajo Arch
Partition Arch
Landscape Arch
Wall Arch
Pine Tree Arch
Tunnel Arch
Devils Garden Trailhead
Skyline Arch
Broken Arch
Sand Dune Arch
Salt Wash
Salt Valley Wash
SALT VALLEY
FIERY FURNACE
Delicate Arch
Wolfe Ranch
Cache Valley Wash
ARCHES NATIONAL PARK
Courthouse Wash
Balanced Rock
Ham Rock
Cove of Caves
Double Arch
Parade of Elephants
North Window
South Window
Turret Arch
THE WINDOWS SECTION
ROCK PINNACLES
191
313
128
THE GREAT WALL
PETRIFIED DUNES
Courthouse Wash
Tower of Babel
Sheep Rock
Three Gossips
The Organ
COURTHOUSE TOWERS
Visitor Center
Park Headquarters
Colorado River
128
191

Dune Rock

Like most of the park's prominent formations, the Courthouse Towers are made of sandstone that formed when ancient dune fields were buried and compressed at depth.

Ute Rock Art

These petroglyphs are believed to include Ute images since some of them show people on horseback. Horses were introduced by the Spanish during the 1500s, when Utes lived in the Arches region.

Cozy Nester

Vermilion fly catchers build their nests with twigs, grass, forbs, rootlets, plant fibers, cocoons, and spider webbing, then line them with hair and feathers.

HIGH DESERT LIFE

As part of the Colorado Plateau, Arches lies within what is known as a cold, or high, desert. Here, plants and animals have evolved unique adaptations in order to live in a place where summer ground temperatures often reach lethal levels and winter lows drop below freezing. Just 9 inches of precipitation falls each year, and most of that sweeps by in the form of flash floods or quickly percolates down through lands ill-equipped for retaining water.

Still, 375 species of plants live here. How?

Some, including most of the showy spring wildflowers, complete their life cycles in just a few days or weeks during unusually wet periods.

Most perennials, though, must resist drought. Some have small spiny leaves or fuzzy layers that diffuse solar radiation and buffer the plants from hot air currents. Cacti protect stored water beneath a waxy outer layer. Yucca drives its roots down into deep water sources. Mosses tolerate complete dehydration, and Utah junipers conserve moisture by self-pruning—that is, they shut off water to one or more branches and allow them to die so the rest of the tree can live.

Other plants, such as monkey flower, columbine, and ferns, take advantage of microclimates in shady alcoves near seeps or springs.

Most of Arches' sixty-five species of mammals are nocturnal. They evade heat and conserve moisture by spending the day in cool burrows. Even diurnal mammals, such as mule deer,

Stone Windows
Utah juniper peppers a snowy slope beneath North Window and South Window.

bighorn sheep, foxes, and jackrabbits, are most active at dawn and dusk. Snakes and lizards also retreat from the heat of the day. Spadefoot toads can evade entire seasons of drought by becoming dormant. Large carnivores such as coyotes and mountain lions, as well as birds of prey, supplement meager sources of free

Radiator Ears
The ears of jackrabbits reflect harsh sunlight and radiate excess body heat.

water with fluids from the animals they eat. Kangaroo rats, though, never drink water. Their bodies metabolize all they need from dry plant food.

Rough Neighborhood
High desert valleys such as those surrounding Balanced Rock are intensely hot, cold, windy, and dry.

Fleet of Foot

Common in Badlands, pronghorns, left, are the fastest mammals in North America, capable of sprinting at 60 mph and cruising for several miles at 30 to 40 mph. A product of rain, wind, and frost, the White River Badlands of South Dakota, below, rise from the prairie as an anomalous barrier of pleated ridges, crumbling slopes, gullies, and ravines.

BADLANDS

NATIONAL PARK IN SOUTH DAKOTA

STRANGE TERRAIN

The vast treeless sea of grass we call the Great Plains in fact began as a vast sea of water. This warm ocean gathered and stacked sediments from many sources. Erosion carted in material and hauled off other material, again and again. Today's Badlands is the latest rendition of this continuing process. Water is still the primary creative and destructive force, furrowing the landscape with countless small, intricate gully drainages.

When scientists say "badlands," they mean a dry, easily erodible landscape with the kinds of features and contours you see here. Badlands National Park is the type specimen for a term now applied all over the world.

The only problem with calling them the badlands is that they're not. A hard place to cross on a horse—certainly. A hard place to farm or ranch—yes. A really hard place to do anything at all on a sunny August day—sure. But bad? No. In the midst of so much life, beauty, and wonder, the judgment seems hasty and poorly thought out. The first western meadowlark you hear will agree.

Spend some time in the exquisitely eroded drainages that spread from the Wall, a long scarp across the northern lobe of the park. You will wonder why they didn't call them the Weirdlands instead. In 1849, a stunned visitor described the Badlands National Park as "an immense city surrounded by walls and bulwarks, containing a palace crowned with gigantic domes and monuments of the most fantastic and bizarre architecture."

As if that weren't enough, it is a city inhabited by monsters, millions of years worth of nature's early experiments in its ever-popular product line of mammals. Fossils of clams, crabs, turtles, flying reptiles, and ancient fish have also been found in the park. And if even that is not enough for you, turn and walk out onto the mixed grasslands that occupy more than half the park. There you'll find the latest models in the same line—the pronghorn, prairie dogs, bison, and many other heirs to this prairie kingdom.

Parched Earth
A gumbo lily, left, finds a niche in the dry, cracked earth of Badlands, above.

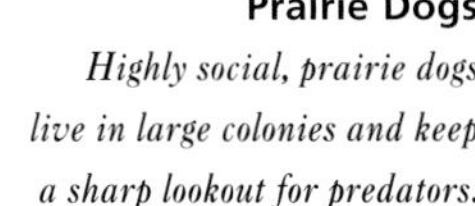

Prairie Dogs
Highly social, prairie dogs live in large colonies and keep a sharp lookout for predators.

BLACK CANYON OF THE

NATIONAL PARK IN COLORADO

MARBLED WALLS

The walls of Black Canyon of the Gunnison, composed of 1.7-billion-year-old basement rocks uplifted in a giant block dozens of miles long, are not black. Better, they are a mixture of slate grays, dark golds, and other somber shades. These are interlaced with huge, jagged bands of pink and tan granites that were injected as molten fluids into the joints and cracks of the older rocks. The effect is a gloomy beauty seen in dizzying vistas down past marbled cliffs to the Gunnison River.

It is hard to remember, in this day of fast roads and high bridges, what a canyon could do to your plans a hundred years ago. Hereabouts, wherever you came from and wherever you were headed, you went around the canyon. Those hard, sheer walls gave you no choice. Even the Utes, who lived nearby and knew the country best, found other trails. Among the early white travelers, Captain John Gunnison may never even have stood on its brink and looked in. Having heard about the canyon, he chose to travel through the region by a different route. It was only named to honor him after his death.

It is good for your perspective to recall what a canyon like this meant to earlier visitors. It heightens your appreciation of today's canyon visit. The rim drives, winding in and out along the top of each canyon contour, constitute a sort of marvel overload. At the viewpoints, only minutes apart, you step to the edge and catch your breath yet again at the inconceivable spaces. Canyon regulars emphasize that curiosity quickly overcomes those first shocks. Soon you are absorbed in the pattern of the erosion—the shady south side of the canyon is less steep because moisture has more time to work and erode there. Or the dwarfish little forest of oak and serviceberry charms you—such a tiny wood to border such an oversized spectacle. And perhaps after a while you even rise above your wonder, and take a moment to sympathize with all those earlier visitors who just wanted to get to the other side.

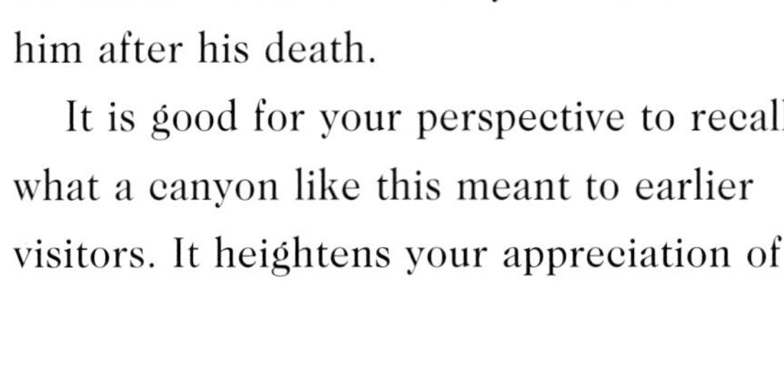

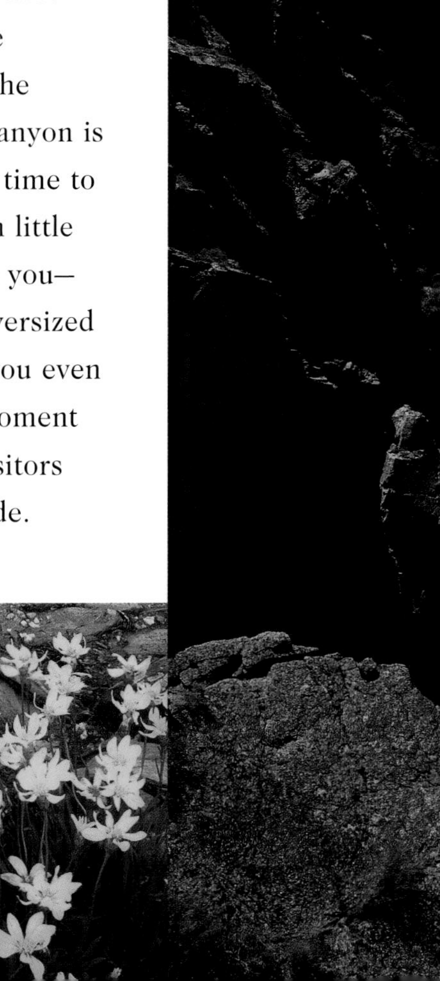

Bearly Seen
Black bears thrive along the rim of Black Canyon, where they feed on rodents, berries, and acorns.

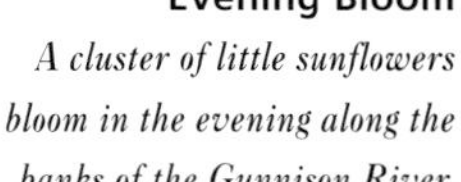

Evening Bloom
A cluster of little sunflowers bloom in the evening along the banks of the Gunnison River.

GUNNISON

Ancient Rock
The extremely hard gneiss and schist that compose the walls of Black Canyon were formed nearly two billion years ago.

BLACK CANYON OF THE GUNNISON NATIONAL PARK

History Note: The first people known to float through Black Canyon made the trip in 1901 on a rubber mattress. It took them ten days to travel 33 miles.

Flora: Thickets of Gambel oak with an understory of grass and wildflowers thrive along the rim, while chokecherry, box elder, cottonwood, and other water-loving plants hug the river in the shadowy depths of the canyon.

Fauna: Mule deer, black bears, chipmunks, bighorn sheep, peregrine falcons, golden eagles, beaver, ringtails, and lizards.

Visitor Tip: A fine paved road traces the south rim of the canyon, but the best vistas are from short trails that lead from the road to the brink of the cliffs.

Sheer Cliffs
The Gunnison River slips between the cliffs of Black Canyon, left and below. No other canyon in America is at once so deep, so narrow, and so sheer. Black Canyon measures 2,702 feet at its deepest, 1,100 feet at its narrowest. Following spread: The Gunnison River below East Portal.

Hoodoo Heaven

Known for its legions of crumbling rock pillars called hoodoos, below, Bryce Canyon National Park takes in the eroding ramparts of a high plateau. Left: A Douglas fir tree soars between the walls of a side canyon.

BRYCE CANYON

NATIONAL PARK IN UTAH

EERIE WEATHERING

Not formally a canyon at all, Bryce is a "break"—a place where a relatively level upland is being eroded. Erosion here has been accomplished not by the running water of rivers but by slope wash—rain draining down the sides of the features and gradually loosening their least resistant rock and soil. The effect on Bryce Canyon National Park is among nature's most serendipitous scenes, crowded with stone figures of every shape and silhouette.

Perhaps one reason why Bryce is so popular is that we love to name things. We love, specifically, to give things names that resonate—that associate the unfamiliar with what we know well. We also love to name things that are fun—that will make us laugh in recognition at the unlikely similarities we have found. If that is the portion of your imagination you most like to exercise, then you must go to Bryce. There you will find an open field for your gifts.

The objects of all this attention are the hoodoos—the countless towers, spires, cones, blobs, stubs, poles, knobs, and ribs eroded from the bright sedimentary rocks along the cliff faces that run the length of the park. Here, previous namers have filled the blanks on the map with a cathedral, a poodle, a fairyland, a hat shop, various walls, bridges, and tunnels, and many more official and unofficial names.

Take your turn, but with a knowing eye. Is that a row of goblins perched up on that ridge? Yes, it might be, and from another angle they may be baby owls, or toadstools. But see? They're always in a row. Viewed from some angles the hoodoos seem little more than a random maze of bizarre shapes, but get the right perspective and you begin to see the pattern even here. If you could look down on it all, you would see that the whole labyrinthine, amphitheatrical scene is constructed of ridges, with other ridges branching from them. The toads and derbies all stand in a line. Once in a while a ridge will mostly melt away, leaving only a single top-

Creative Force

At Rainbow Point, left, expansion of frost and ice wedges apart large blocks. Hoodoos, above, are formed by differential erosion.

Mule Deer

Bryce Canyon's mule deer rove throughout the park, browsing on shrubs and other foliage in the relatively cool periods of dawn and dusk.

heavy stalk or sleek obelisk. But far more often, the erosion is more consistent, and the ridge wears away more evenly along its ragged top. The ridge thus ends up peopled with a lineup of hobbits and gnomes, or decorated with castles and palaces.

High and Dry
A contorted ponderosa pine in Bryce Canyon National Park reflects the arduous climate of Utah's high plateaus.

You must go among them. Even the hastiest visitor to Bryce Canyon National Park has time for a quick stroll, and the luckiest are those who can go the farthest. The enchantment of this landscape increases the deeper you descend into it. Somewhere down in there among the trolls and orcs, there is a rounded red turret with a frosting like white cap. It is so appetizing you will suddenly need a snack.

Bryce is full of life, and even if you see no animals along the trail you will surely see their tracks. But you bring with you many more lives, in your imagination. With it you will animate this landscape and bring its stone to life in a thousand magical forms.

Badgers
Large weasels, badgers, below, have long claws that help them dig quickly into the burrows of ground squirrels, prairie dogs, and gophers. Right: The magnificent jumble of hoodoos in Silent City tower above gullies and ravines several hundred feet deep.

Freeze-Thaw

More than two hundred freeze-thaw cycles a year occur on south-facing cliffs, crumbling old hoodoos and creating new ones.

BRYCE CANYON NATIONAL PARK

History Note: Bryce Canyon was named for Ebenezer Bryce, a Mormon pioneer who homesteaded the area in 1875.

Flora: More than four hundred species of plants, including ancient bristlecone pine, Douglas fir, white fir, blue spruce, ponderosa pine, pinyon pine, manzanita, and—in season—many wildflowers.

Fauna: Elk, mule deer, rare Utah prairie dogs, porcupines, marmots, mountain lions, golden eagles, peregrine falcons, and the occasional California condor.

Visitor Tip: To avoid traffic and parking hassles, take the shuttle bus to the park's most popular viewpoints.

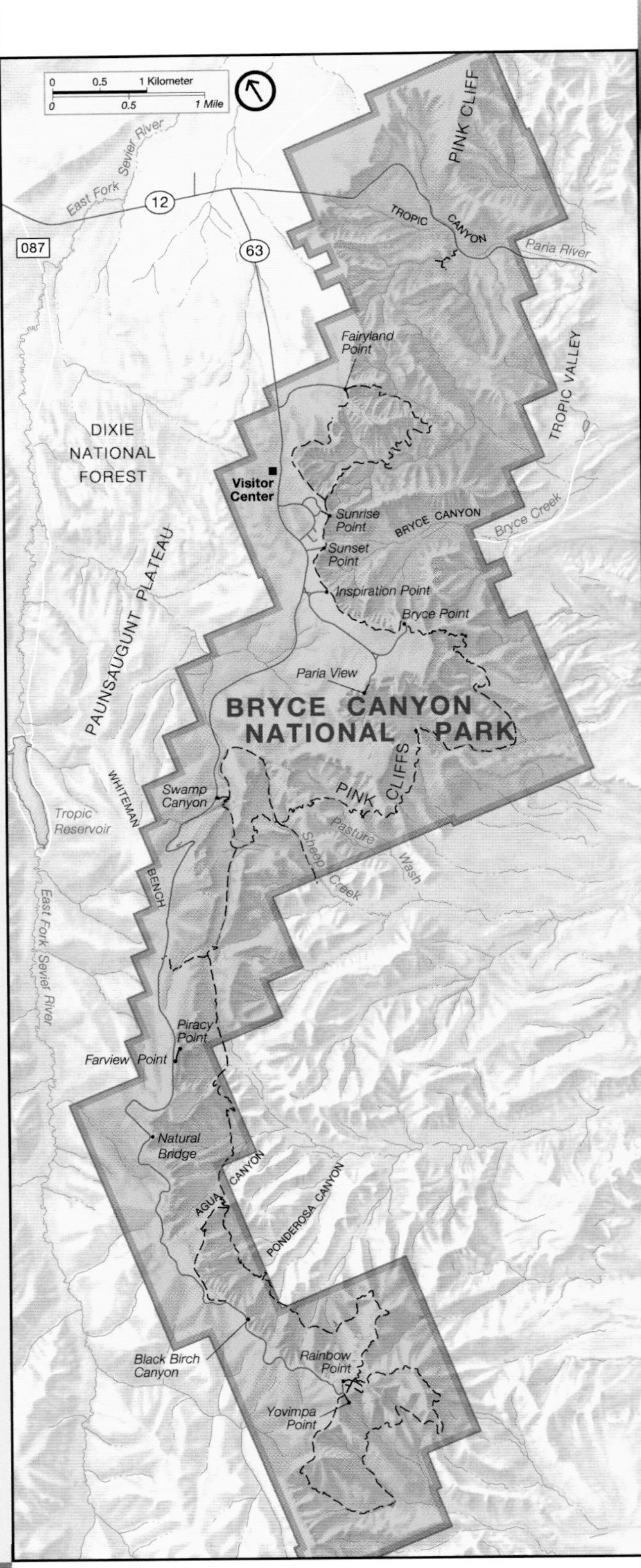

A Natural Misnomer

Technically speaking, Natural Bridge is actually a natural arch, formed from a narrow limestone fin by rain and frost erosion. Natural bridges involve stream erosion.

Faces of Erosion

Erosion undermines an outcropping of resistant rock by sweeping away the softer layer that lies beneath it.

CANYONLANDS

NATIONAL PARK IN UTAH

TANGLED EXPANSE

Centered on the junction of the canyons of the Colorado and Green rivers, Canyonlands National Park is a comprehensive sampler of the landforms and geological processes of the Colorado Plateau. Common features include a great variety of small and large canyons, baffling networks of eroded passageways, many arches and other distinctive geological forms beyond counting or naming, and hundreds of archaeological sites. The paved roads provide spectacular overlooks into the wilderness.

If you are new to the American Southwest and you go to Canyonlands, start at the long tableland known as Island in the Sky. You will look out on what seems an entire world, only it isn't any world you dreamed existed. The Colorado Plateau is such a treasure-land partly because even a scene this enormous can remain unknown to most people. They have all heard of the Grand Canyon, and probably of Bryce and Zion, but even after forty years as a national park, Canyonlands may be a surprise.

From Island in the Sky, at first all you see is overwhelming distance and an inconceivable variety of rock shapes. But the primary logic of the landscape comes into focus as you visit each Island overlook in turn. To the east is the Colorado River, to the west the Green River. From the southernmost tip of the Island, at Grand View Point Overlook, you can see their winding canyons join several miles south of you. About 1,200 feet below, you can trace the outlines of their steeper inner canyons by the distinctive White Rim sandstone. Besides skirting the brinks of the canyons for many miles, this relatively hard rock often forms bulbous caps and crowns on stems of the darker rock below.

Far off, southeast of the confluence, you can just see a tangled rockscape that demands your attention next. It's the Needles, and the park's other paved road takes you to its edge. But it takes a little unpaved driving or hiking to engage this setting fully. Get good maps, good advice, and good water. Head into one of the winding little canyons that dissect this landscape so bewilderingly. It is like entering a

Chipped Away
Eroded by water and the freeze-thaw cycle, Angel Arch and Molar Rock, left, stand against the desert sky. The same forces chip away at pinnacles and cliffs, above.

Collared Critter
A collared lizard pauses on a rock in Canyonlands.

Awesome Yet Intimate

A wilderness of canyons, mesas, and intricately eroded sandstone, Canyonlands combines vast erosional features such as the scalloped canyon of the Green River, below, with small-scale wonders such as sprays of purple desert asters, right.

small-scale model of the world you saw from Island in the Sky. The same forces prevailed, with the same results, but it's all whittled down to a cozy, inviting size.

Or take the plunge into bigger adventure. The Needles go on more or less forever beyond the easy hikes. Another rough road, into the park from the west, will take you into the Maze, perhaps this region's most challenging wilderness of convoluted rock. Float the rivers, either in their calmer upper reaches or through the legendary white water of Cataract Canyon.

Ancient Stores
Tucked into the hollow of a cliff, these granaries were built by Ancestral Puebloan farmers, who grew beans, corn, and squash.

Wherever you go, watch for traces of earlier Canyonlands people. Tucked under an overhang 40 feet up the wall of some back canyon is a crumbling granary made by Ancestral Puebloans. A mile farther on, a petroglyph speaks clearly in a language we don't understand about something that mattered to a people we will never know. Look around. How would you go about making a living here, and if you were successful, what message would you want to leave for later travelers through this rocky wilderness?

Window in the Sky
Perched along the edge of Canyonlands' Island in the Sky district, Mesa Arch overlooks canyons eroded by the Colorado River, left. Below: *These pictographs in Horseshoe Canyon were painted by nomadic hunter-gatherers who predated the Ancestral Puebloans.*

Confluence

The Green and Colorado rivers converge at the heart of the park after meandering slowly through their respective sheer-walled canyons.

Gleaming Ribbon

A thin, white layer of gypsum, sandwiched between layers of sedimentary rock, traces the course of the Colorado River deep within its canyon.

CANYONLANDS NATIONAL PARK

History Note: In 1869, the Powell expedition plunged through and named Cataract Canyon. The men swamped one boat and damaged the rest, and were then very nearly trapped by a flash flood.

Flora: Cactuses, desert wildflowers, juniper, and pinyon pine in dry areas; willows, cottonwoods, mosses, ferns, and small hanging gardens along the rivers and seeps.

Fauna: Bighorn sheep, deer, coyotes, bobcats, lizards, snakes, birds of prey.

Visitor Tip: Above their confluence, both the Green and Colorado rivers run smoothly enough for open canoe trips—a splendid way to see either canyon. A backcountry permit is required.

0 5 Kilometers
0 5 Miles
DEAD HORSE POINT STATE PARK
HORSESHOE CANYON UNIT
Great Gallery pictographs
Island In The Sky Visitor Center
Shafer Trail Road
Whale Rock
Upheaval Dome
ISLAND IN THE SKY
MEANDER CANYON
THE SPUR
White Rim Road
ANDERSON BOTTOM
WHITE RIM
Mesa Arch
GLEN CANYON NATIONAL RECREATION AREA
Orange Cliffs Overlook
Grand View Point Overlook
MONUMENT BASIN
Colorado River
Green River
CANYONLANDS NATIONAL PARK
Harvest Scene Pictographs
THE MAZE
ORANGE CLIFFS
Chimney Rock
Confluence
Lizard Rock
LAND OF STANDING ROCKS
CYCLONE CANYON
ELEPHANT CANYON
Pothole Point
Needles Visitor Center
The Golden Stairs
DEVILS LANE
DEVILS POCKET
Wooden Shoe Arch
Paul Bunyans Potty
CATARACT CANYON
THE GRABENS
THE NEEDLES
Druid Arch

Remote Corners

Isolated fins punctuate a ridge in Canyonlands National Park's Maze district, *facing page,* *one of the nation's most inaccessible tracts of land.*

Rock Garden

Princes (or desert) plume blooms among the rocks at the Green River Overlook in the park's Island in the Sky district.

Bighorn Sheep

Small bands of desert bighorn sheep roam throughout Canyonlands National Park.

Damp Pockets

Bulrushes and paintbrush, left, take advantage of a moist depression, one of many such small, eroded basins that dot the Waterpocket Fold. Stretching for roughly 100 miles across south-central Utah, the Waterpocket Fold, below, is the eroded remnant of a massive warp, or monocline, that formed in the Earth's crust 50 to 70 million years ago.

CAPITOL REEF

NATIONAL PARK IN UTAH

RIPPLED ROCK

Capitol Reef and the park for which it is named are defined by the 100-mile-long Waterpocket Fold, an abrupt upending of more than 200 million years' deposit of sedimentary rock. In the other Colorado Plateau parks, sedimentary layers are exposed vertically in deep canyons. In contrast, the Waterpocket Fold's layers spread out horizontally in narrow bands across the Earth's surface. Differential erosion has had a dramatic effect on Capitol Reef's landscape, exposing high cliffs, domes, and other shapes.

It is at first sight unnerving. The deeply eroded ridges of sandstone, each its own striking color, hump along together for miles, like so many partially exposed spinal columns. Though the rocks of Capitol Reefs National Park are the same as in other canyon country parks, they seem almost gaudy in this unorthodox arrangement. Pioneering geologist C. E. Dutton exclaimed, "so luminous are they, that the light seems to flow or shine out of the rock rather than to be reflected from it."

Perhaps the most intriguing search a visitor to Capitol Reef National Park can undertake is for water—especially the water that did all this. Where, for example, is the big river we always assume must run through a place like this? You know—the one that did all the heavy lifting?

Well, there isn't one, but there's evidence of water everywhere. Right along the roads you will see peculiarly rippled slabs of rock, legacy of a tidal flat millions of years ago (a few dinosaur footprints have been found). The Waterpocket Fold, a 100-mile wrinkle in the Earth's crust, got its name from its countless potholes, ground out of the rock by water and the abrasive rocks it carried. But where is the water now? The question is not where, but when. Some small streams do cut across the fold, or run along it, but they must save the serious landscape engineering for the rare rainstorm. Then, in incredibly violent bursts of thick, chunky liquid, they grind the rocks like crazy. It's only a part-time job, but you can tell from the results that they've been at it a long time.

Waterpocket Resident
A mountain bluebird makes his home along the Fremont River in Capitol Reef National Park.

Monoliths and Parapets
Freestanding monoliths such as the Temple of the Moon and Temple of the Sun, right, stud Cathedral Valley. Above: Resistant sandstone forms the upper ramparts of The Castle.

A Capitol Form

Formations such as this enormous sandstone dome reminded early visitors to the area now known as Capitol Reef of rotundas on capitol buildings.

CAPITOL REEF NATIONAL PARK

History Note: One of the rock walls in Capitol Gorge, called Pioneer Register, bears the inscribed names of many miners, settlers, and others who passed through the canyon beginning in 1871.

Flora: Juniper and pinyon pine, scattered wildflowers and shrubs, and cactuses in the desert; willows, cottonwoods, and ashes along the Fremont River.

Fauna: Mule deer, marmots, songbirds, migratory ducks, bighorn sheep, kangaroo rats, lizards, toads, golden eagles.

Visitor Tip: Fruita's orchards are open in season for visitors to pick apples, cherries, pears, peaches, and apricots free of charge. Harvest times vary. Call the park for details.

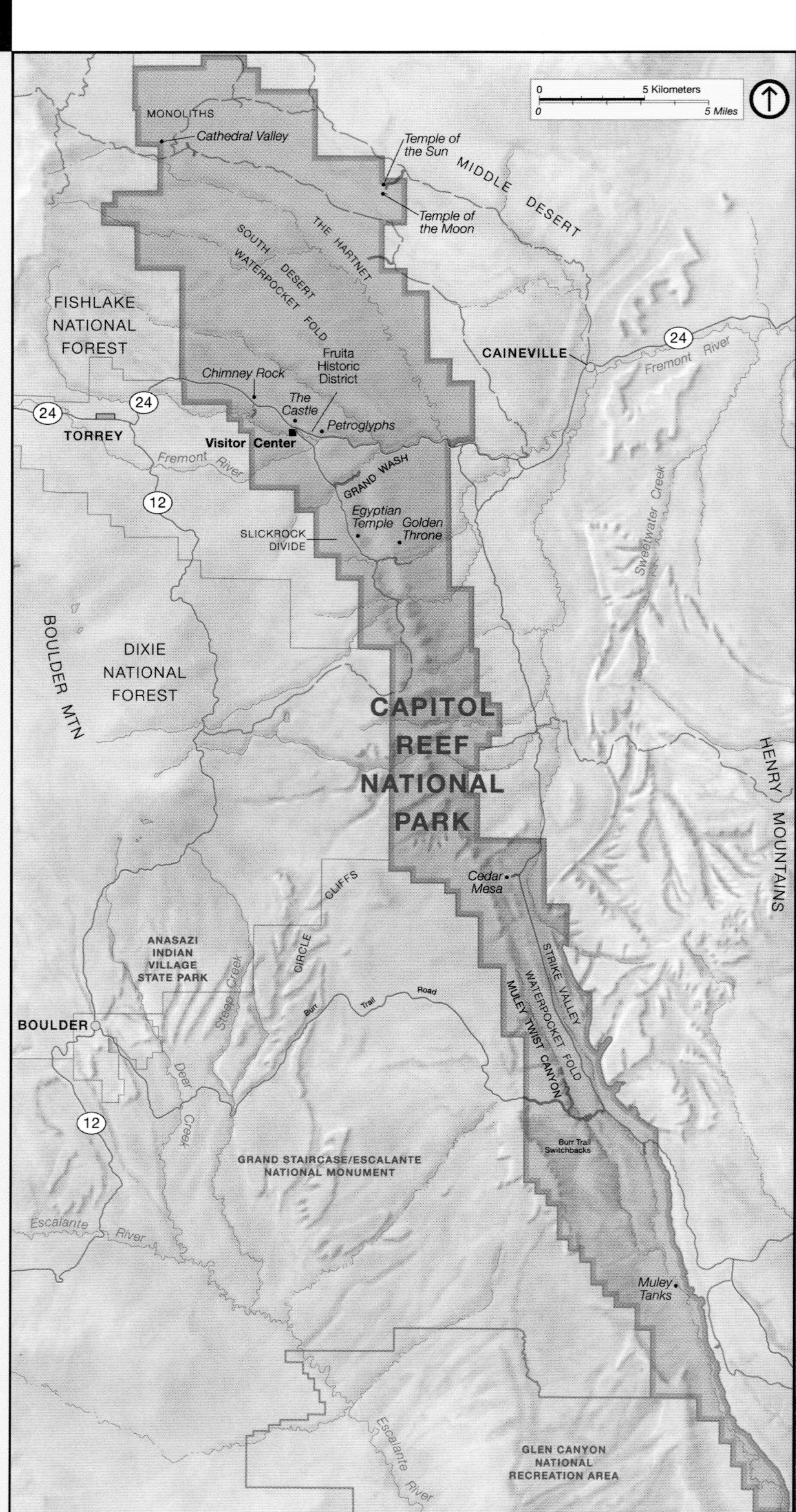

Eons in the Making

Nearly 10,000 feet of sedimentary strata are found in the Capitol Reef area and record nearly 200 million years of geologic history. The hard sandstone cliffs atop The Castle formed from dune sand.

Historic Fruita

One of the remaining barns of Fruita, a Mormon fruit-growing settlement, stands beneath sheer sandstone cliffs carved by the Fremont River. Following spread: A waterfall on the Fremont River.

Cuyahoga Valley

National Park in Ohio

Historic Waterway

The headwaters of the historic Cuyahoga River are only about 20 miles from the shores of Lake Erie, but the river drains southwest and then north in a great U, winding 90 miles before reaching the lake. Cuyahoga Valley National Park is astride the river for 22 miles of its northward course. One ancestral form of the Cuyahoga River is now 500 feet below the present river, buried under masses of till and sand left by glaciers.

Perhaps the foremost human interest in the Cuyahoga River over the past ten thousand years has been for travel. Native people could canoe up the river to its southern bend, make a portage of a few miles to the upper Tuscarawas River, and float from there all the way to the Ohio River. During the great canal-building era of the early 1800s, the Ohio & Erie Canal paralleled the Cuyahoga, finally making the venerable dryland portage unnecessary.

Cuyahoga Valley National Park honors all these heritages, and many more. It occupies a veritable island of rural land and small villages surrounded by the suburban sea of greater Cleveland and Akron, and that is precisely why it was first established, as a National Recreation Area, in 1974. Regional citizens, fearing the loss of this last enclave of both nature and historic community, found a way to protect and even enhance both. The park is actually a complex of areas managed by federal, county, and private authorities.

The canal and its towpath have become a charming 20-mile-long bike and foot trail. There are historic houses, farmsteads, and other structures from the canal era and later in the nineteenth century, many of which are actively interpreted. Mixed-oak forests and other native plant communities, as well as a surprising amount of native wildlife, make it easy for visitors to imagine what this landscape was like in the early days of settlement. There are still hidden corners where visitors to Cuyahoga Valley National Park may capture the feel of an even earlier, wilder, Ohio.

Peaceful Pond
Cattails ring Dover Pond, one of many small ponds and lakes that dot the park's forested landscape.

Great Blue Nester
Great blue herons nest in Cuyahoga Valley's treetop rookeries.

Water Features

Water spills from rock ledges above Blue Hen Falls. Foot trails lead to several such attractive waterfalls scattered throughout the park.

CUYAHOGA NATIONAL PARK

History Note: The Ohio & Erie Canal opened in 1827 and flourished for thirty years until it was replaced as a means of commercial transport by railroads.

Flora: Mixed deciduous forest with pockets of evergreens; wetlands and open fields; woodland wildflowers such as hepaticas and bloodroot, also asters, goldenrods, yellow and blue irises, and sweet-scented water lilies.

Fauna: White-tailed deer, beaver, coyote; more than one hundred species of nesting birds, including blue herons, warbling vireos, and eastern bluebirds.

Visitor Tip: Bike or hike a section of the Ohio & Erie Towpath Trail, which meanders through the heart of the park and follows the route of the historic canal along the river. It also connects at various points with the Cuyahoga Valley Scenic Railroad.

Cuyahoga Sunrise

Mist rises from the Cuyahoga River at dawn, *left.* *Below:* ***Beavers, absent from the park's ecosystem for 150 years, have returned.***

Side Canyons

While the Colorado River carved the Grand Canyon, below, a myriad of tributary streams such as the Little Colorado cut, left, spectacular side canyons.

GRAND CANYON

NATIONAL PARK IN ARIZONA

WONDROUS VOID

The Colorado River and its tributaries have here carved perhaps the most famous canyon in the world. By geological standards, the river is surprisingly young, having done most of this work in only two million years—and reaching two billion years into the past at its present depth. The distinctive terracing, or stairstep slopes, of the canyon walls depends on the durability of the layers of sedimentary rock, mostly sandstones, limestones, and shales.

The Grand Canyon has inspired a kind of literature of desperation. The world's great travel writers and naturalists, when confronted with this stupendous thing, have recruited their most ambitious adjectives and unleashed their most fervent raptures. One and all, they agree they were not up to the job.

Still, their failure was a heroic one. Moving far beyond such mundane approaches as actually describing the canyon, they launched a thousand gloriously hopeful metaphors. One early British visitor called the canyon "a sort of landscape Day of Judgment," even "Beethoven's Ninth Symphony in stone and magic light." The great western writer Owen Wister said it "seems like an avenue conducting to the secret of the universe and the presence of the gods." Naturalist John Muir declared that "it seems a gigantic statement for even nature to make, all in one mighty stone word." And Zane Grey said that to see the canyon was "to be elevated in soul."

It is all true, every word of it. And, as these and many other writers admitted, it is much more, and there is no substitute for seeing it. Our most brilliant artists have poured their hearts onto canvas, and at their best have caught a glimmer of what you see from the rims (Thomas Moran, the celebrated nineteenth-century master of western landscapes, may have come closest, but only by using a canvas the size of a barn). Photographers beyond counting have made film processors wealthy with about the same level of success.

Canyon Hunters
Mountain lions join bobcats, coyotes, and birds of prey as the park's top predators.

All the Amenities
The gaping maw of the Grand Canyon, above, cuts across northern Arizona for 277 miles and reveals 1.7 billion years of Earth history. Havasu Falls, right, is on the Havasupai Reservation.

Admittedly, this same claim—that there is no substitute for being there—could be made for any national park. But the shortfall between our verbal and artistic portrayals and the reality of the place somehow seems greater with the canyon.

North Rim Larder
Wild buckwheat blossoms along the North Rim. The seeds of this hardy plant provide important nutrients for mice and chipmunks.

A story may help explain the magnitude of the problem. In the 1930s, a scientific expedition made the first official climbs of Shiva Temple and Wotan's Throne, two prominent flat-topped "sky islands" in the canyon. They wanted to learn what happened to natural life there over the millennia since being isolated from the main rim. They expected obscure differences in similar organisms, but the story hit the press as a latter-day Lost World extravaganza. Sure enough, so great was the canyon's mystifying power that the public was eager to imagine that dinosaurs could still live in its remote corners. All the expedition found on their "pioneering" ascents was a familiar, if isolated, plant and animal community—and some litter left by other recent visitors who beat them to the top.

Water-Thrifty Scorpions
To conserve moisture, scorpions have a waxy coating on their exoskeletons and very slow metabolisms.

So go see it. Go to both rims. Take the shuttles to every view point. Find the trails into the junipers on the south rim and the ponderosa pines on the north. And then *you* try to describe it.

Mighty Excavator
Before Glen Canyon Dam was built, the Colorado River at flood stage swept an average 500,000 tons of sand, silt, and gravel from the canyon every day.

Wotan's Throne

Separated from Grand Canyon National Park's North Rim near Cape Royal by erosion, Wotan's Throne stands as a colonnaded island surrounded by open space.

Erosion's Swift Hand

It took just five to six million years to erode this 277-mile-long, 4-to-15-mile-wide, and 3,500-to-6,000-foot-deep canyon known as the Grand Canyon.

Hanging Garden

Water streams down Elves Chasm, hydrating a hanging garden of maindenhead ferns.

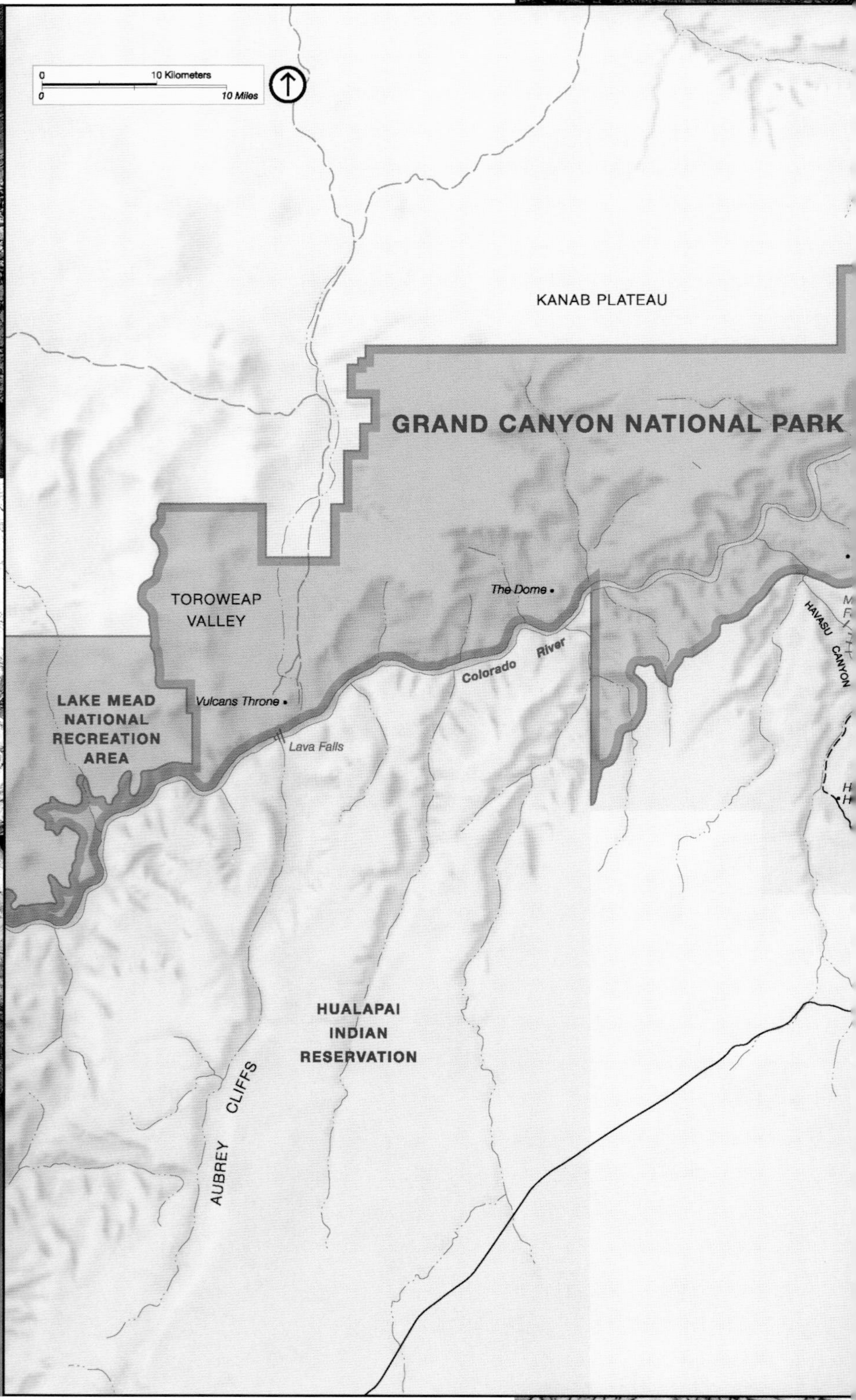

Sandblasted Alleys

Narrow side canyons such as Matkatamiba Canyon are periodically scoured by high-velocity flash floods that blast the walls and streambeds with sand, gravel, and stones.

Snowy Roost

A bald eagle finds a roost among snow-dusted foliage. Each winter, dozens of the birds gather at the mouth of Nankoweap Creek to feast on spawning trout.

Rim Rock

Resistant Kaibab limestone forms the uppermost layer of rock along both the North and South rims of Grand Canyon National Park.

KAIBAB NATIONAL FOREST
67
KAIBAB PLATEAU
SOUTH CANYON
MARBLE CANYON
NAVAJO INDIAN RESERVATION
KANAB CANYON
Colorado River
GRANITE NARROWS
GREAT THUMB MESA
Stanton Point
MIDDLE GRANITE GORGE
POWELL PLATEAU
North Rim Entrance Station
Colorado River
Apache Point
AZTEC AMPHITHEATER
Havasupai Point
HAVASUPAI INDIAN RESERVATION
Point Sublime
Shiva Temple
Grand Canyon Lodge
Bright Angel Point
Siegfried Pyre
Temple Butte
Jupiter Temple
UPPER GRANITE GORGE
Osiris Temple
Isis Temple
Bright Angel Creek
BRIGHT ANGEL CANYON
Zoroaster Temple
Cape Royal
Diana Temple
Phantom Ranch
Wotans Throne
GRANITE GORGE
Vishnu Temple
Pima Point
Hopi Point
Yavapai Point
Yaki Point
Solomon Temple
Visitor Center
Park Headquarters
GRAND CANYON VILLAGE
Desert View
Lipan Point
Moran Point
Grandview Point
Tusayan Ruin and Museum
TUSAYAN
64
COCONINO PLATEAU
KAIBAB NATIONAL FOREST
180
64

GRAND CANYON NATIONAL PARK

History Note: People have lived in Grand Canyon more or less continuously for the past four thousand years. The first Europeans to see it were Spaniards, who were guided to the South Rim by the Hopi in 1540.

Flora: Ponderosa pine, pinyon pine, juniper, Gambel oak; drought-resistant shrubs such as cliffrose, fernbush, serviceberry; cactuses, yucca, isolated riparian grottos stuffed with ferns and moss.

Fauna: Mule deer, desert bighorn sheep, bobcats, coyotes, mountain lions, ringtails, beavers, squirrels, rabbits, bats, snakes, frogs, salamanders, lizards, scorpions, and more than three hundred species of birds.

Visitor Tip: Even experienced hikers get overambitious in the canyon, where descents are easy and the way up is difficult. Set modest goals and turn around before your water runs out.

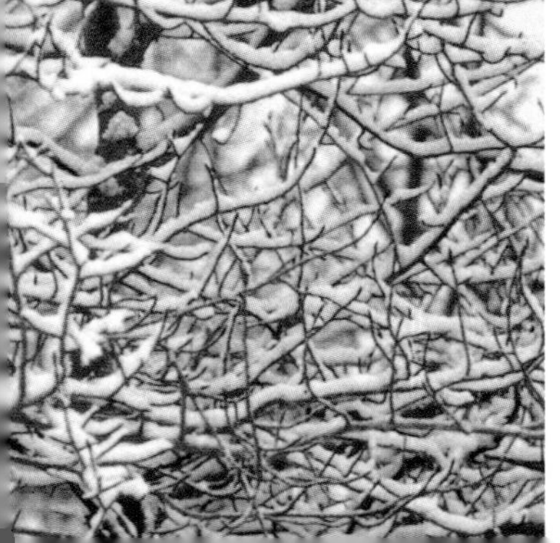

Winter Rim

Winter comes to Grand Canyon in late October or early November, when the first heavy snowfalls pile up along the cliffs and close the North Rim to visitors.

DEPOSITION AND EROSION

Built up over a period of roughly 300 million years, the colorful rock layers exposed in the walls of Grand Canyon lie neatly stacked upon a deep bed of much older Precambrian rocks, some of which are 1.7 billion years old.

The stack tops out at the rim with a layer of limestone that formed 240 million years ago. Above it, there once lay roughly 5,000 feet of additional rock layers, but they have been worn away by erosion. At the base of the stack lies evidence of another void where the geologic record skips hundreds of millions of years.

There, a layer of sandstone 550 million years old stretches across a complex mass of quartzite, shale, limestone, schist, and granite more than a billion years old. The point of contact—the skip—is called the Great Unconformity.

The story between the Great Unconformity and the Canyon rim is largely one of deposition. Thick layers of sandstone, shale, and limestone gradually accumulated as ancient seas advanced and retreated, deserts formed, and streams from distant mountains carried in mud, silt, and more sand.

Then, during a mountain-building phase roughly 65 million years ago, the Rockies began to rise. So did the Colorado Plateau and, with it, the stack of rocks that would eventually form the walls of the Grand Canyon.

Higher, Moister, Cooler
Grand Canyon's North Rim stands about 1,000 feet higher than the South Rim.

Precisely how the Colorado River descended from the Rockies and began to flow across the site of the Grand Canyon is a

Sea Lilies
Fossilized sea lilies lie embedded in limestone on the Shivwits Plateau.

complicated puzzle for today's geologists, with few firm solutions. But it is known that erosion of the present canyon began five to six million years ago, and that the Colorado accomplished all but 500 feet of the downcutting in just two million years.

With upstream dams now in place, downcutting by the Colorado River has largely

Canyon Plateaus
The Grand Canyon cuts through a cluster of adjoining Kaibab limestone plateaus.

ended. However, Grand Canyon continues to be widened by tributary streams, the freeze-thaw cycle, flash floods, and rockslides.

The Great Dunes
Built from sand milled by ice-age glaciers, the Great Kobuk Sand Dunes cover 25 square miles of the Kobuk River Valley in northwest Alaska.

KOBUK VALLEY NATIONAL PARK

History Note: Every autumn for the past ten thousand years or more, Inuit hunters have gathered at Onion Portage to wait for the caribou herds to swim the Kobuk River.

Flora: Boreal forest, taiga, and three distinct types of tundra—wet, moist, and alpine.

Fauna: Caribou, moose, grizzly and black bears, wolves, wolverines, foxes, weasels, lemmings, and eagles.

Visitor Tip: A boat trip on the Kobuk River is the best way to see the park, which has no roads or trails.

Midnight Sun
Though plant species such as mountain avens, below, and spruce trees, right, face harsh arctic winters, they benefit from long, relatively warm summer days under the midnight sun.

KOBUK VALLEY

NATIONAL PARK IN ALASKA

ARCTIC WILDERNESS

The Kobuk River flows through Kobuk Valley National Park on its way to the Chukchi Sea and Arctic Ocean. Its whole length, as Arctic Circle. Along the park's north side, on the slopes of the Baird Mountains, the tundra of the high arctic replaces the last trees. Several streams drain southward from the Baird Mountains, in the northern part of the park, into the Kobuk. The park is all wilderness, with no roads or trails.

Though a great arctic wilderness blessed with many ecological, geological, paleontological, and cultural values, the park is perhaps most noted for its dune fields, the largest in arctic North America. The climate, a relic of ice-age times, is dry—16 inches of precipitation annually. The polar winds, east in summer and west in winter, are almost as unrelenting as they are strong. The raw material for making sand—fine rock fragments left over from past glaciations, river sandbars, and existing dunes—is ample.

This combination of forces and circumstances has led to the creation of more than 500 square miles of dunes, but not all of that area is "alive." Much of the dune region consists of now-anchored sand that is covered to some degree by vegetation. Only 30 to 40 square miles is vegetation-free and likely to shift or to move around.

Kobuk might better be appreciated as a key piece in a much larger drama that occupies much of northwestern Alaska—the caribou migrations. The Western Arctic Herd, over 400,000 strong, winters south of the Arctic Circle. But its annual migratory route takes it north through Kobuk and Noatak National Preserve, over the Brooks Range to the North Slope calving grounds. The caribou spend the summer primarily on the north side of the Brooks Range, and then return to their wintering areas in mid- to late August. The success of this epic journey, across more than 140,000 square miles of Alaska, has been of vital interest to humans here for thousands of years.

Advancing Sand
Kobuk National Park's sand dunes advance an inch a year on the spruce forests that surround them.

Caribou Thoroughfare
Every autumn, thousands of caribou cross the Kobuk River at Onion Portage. Following spread: Kavet Creek.

THEODORE ROOSE

NATIONAL PARK IN NORTH DAKOTA

PRARIE BADLANDS

Theodore Roosevelt National Park preserves large tracts of distinctive and colorful North Dakota badlands. These badlands differ in composition from those in Badlands National Park but have similar landscape characteristics, which Roosevelt once described as "a chaos of peaks, plateaus, and ridges." The park protects these geological and paleontological features, and honors as well the experiences of the twenty-sixth president during his ranching days here in the 1880s.

This is a landscape of both order and confusion. The order is in the generally neat, horizontal layering of the sandstone, siltstone, shale, and lignite that can be seen on the weathered hillsides and cutbanks.

Roosevelt said that the Little Missouri River, which traverses all three units of the park, "twists down through the valley in long sweeps." The twisting river and its more intermittent system of tributaries have given the land a crazy gullying, and that is where the confusion comes in.

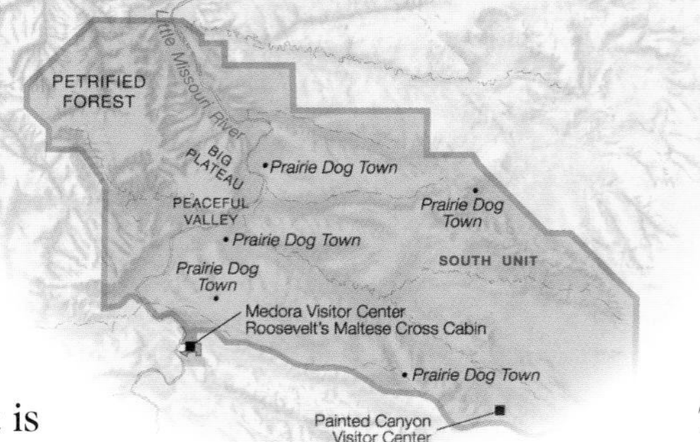

Roosevelt, with the obvious exasperation of a horseman who had somewhere to go, liked to use the word "chaos" to capture the mood of the badlands. He complained that "the whole country seems to be one tangled chaos of canyon-like valleys, winding gullies and washouts with abrupt, unbroken sides, isolated peaks of sandstone, marl, or 'gumbo' clay, which rain turns into slippery glue."

Roosevelt's career as a ranchman was short. Even he knew that, for all the risks and hardships, he was playing at the ranchman's life. But forever after he proclaimed that it was his time in the Dakota badlands that gave him the will and strength to become president.

The wildness that contributed to Roosevelt's presidency is still there. From the beautiful and infuriatingly difficult topography, to the wild horses, bison, and deer, to the western meadowlark whose brilliant song he loved, it's all still there. Perhaps it's making another president right now.

Namesake's Description
Theodore Roosevelt once described the park's badlands as "barren, fantastic, and grimly picturesque."

Center Stage
The Little Missouri River meanders through the park and plays a leading role in the erosion of the park's badlands.

VELT

Prairie Earth

The creases, folds, open slopes, and buttes of North Dakota's badlands, below, expose sediments that began washing eastward from the Rocky Mountains roughly 65 million years ago. The park's wildlife includes meadowlarks, right, and herds of bison.

THEODORE ROOSEVELT NATIONAL PARK

History Note: The park's namesake first visited the region in 1883 and immediately joined two other men in establishing the Maltese Cross Ranch.

Flora: Grasslands; a profusion of prairie wildflowers, including bastard toadflax, snakeweed, and crested beardtongue; many shrubs, including skunkbush, wild plum, and chokecherry; and a scattering a trees, including junipers, cottonwoods, box elders, and American elms.

Fauna: Bison, pronghorn, deer, mountain sheep, elk, wild horses, and prairie-dogs; more than two hundred species of birds; snakes, lizards, and salamanders.

Visitor Tip: Take a good long look at the prairie-dog town north of Medora to discern patterns in how the animals communicate through barks and body language.

Sharply Eroded

Sharply eroded rocks jut into the sky and reveal thin layers of more resistant stone. *Following spread:* *Wild horses populate parts of the park.*

ZION

NATIONAL PARK IN UTAH

VARNISHED WALLS

Zion is a high plateau that has been deeply eroded—incised might be a more precise word, considering the narrow nature of the canyons today. The fractured beds of sedimentary rock provided water and other weathering forces with weak joints in which to start their work. Most visitors confine their attention to Zion Canyon, but the park's 229 square miles feature many other canyons, domes, towers, and hoodoos as beautiful as, and far wilder than, the famous ones.

The novelist Thomas Wolfe, on a trip through Zion in 1938, described the pageant of the canyon's scenery with appropriate breathlessness. He rhapsodized as the mountainous, vividly tinted rocks went by, "striped with strange stripes of salmon pink—scrub dotted, paler—Now in the canyon road and climbing, and now pink rock again, strange shapes and scarrings in the rock, and even vertices upon huge swathes of stone, and plunging down now in stiff canyon folds the sheer solid beetling soaplike block of salmon red again . . ." Well, that's how it feels—one towering wonder after another. Zion is a canyon, yes, but the canyon is a hall of walls, slabs, and blocks. It is, in the words of one geologist, a "sculpturesque terrain."

Let's say you don't have time for an extended visit or a long hike. You can still find the spirit of Zion. First, take the shuttle as deep into the canyon as it goes, to the parking area beneath the Temple of Sinawava. Here the river emerges from the many miles of the Narrows, a wildly unlikely canyon often only a few yards wide.

If the river is low and the rangers approve, walk even a short distance, just a few hundred yards, into the Narrows. As you leave the sunlight and enter the slot of rock, you can feel the walls loom in above you. Imagine the trickling river in full flood, a thick churning mass of silt, sand, and boulders rolling along through this tight stone hallway. Think of the terrific beating it must give these walls each time it roars through.

For a better feel for how long the river has been at this work, backtrack a few river bends

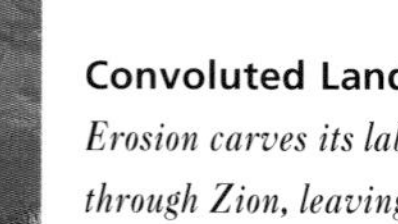

Convoluted Landscape
Erosion carves its labyrinthine course through Zion, leaving a complex of gullies and tight canyons, above, separated by forested tablelands and curving, snakelike ridgetops, left.

Work in Progress
Differential erosion, where some layers of sandstone sediment erode faster than others, continues to carve hoodoos in Zion like this one.

Cliffs of Dunes

Like most of Zion's rock, the West Temple and Towers of the Virgin, below, are composed of sandstone made from dunes that formed 150 to 250 million years ago. Right: Autumn maples edge Zion's Clear Creek.

downstream to the Hidden Canyon trail. Switch back and forth up the rock face until you're too tired to go on, or until the almost vertical dropoff finally gives you the willies. (Several hundred feet up, a cliff-gripping stretch of foot-trail with chain handholds serves to separate the hikers from the fanatics.) Look around and imagine when the canyon was only this deep, and the far wall was a lot closer. Think how much rock the river must have hauled out of all that space.

Versatile Predator
Coyotes generally hunt for small rodents but have been known to bob in creeks for crayfish and suckers.

For a gentler finale, hike the somewhat less vertiginous little trail up to Emerald Pools, just across from Zion Lodge. Everything about erosion and canyons seems to take on a more comprehensible scale in the smaller side canyons. The North Fork has carved so fast—half a mile from top to bottom in about 13 million years—and so furiously that it has outrun its tributaries. They just can't keep up, and are literally left hanging (with their mouths open), suspended above the canyon floor.

Two-Faced Virgin
Gentle most of the year, the Virgin River, left, becomes a furious erosive force during the summer rainy season. Below: Curved slabs of Navajo sandstone walls sometimes peel away and leave rounded overhangs such as Double Arch Alcove.

Navajo Sandstone

Navajo sandstone is made of fine quartz sand with a pinch of iron oxide for color. Wherever it is cemented with silica, the rock can stand in tall, vertical cliffs.

Kolob Snows

A snowstorm veils South Fork of Taylor Creek in the park's Kolob Canyons district. Each year, ice invades joints in the cliffs and helps sheer away blocks of rock.

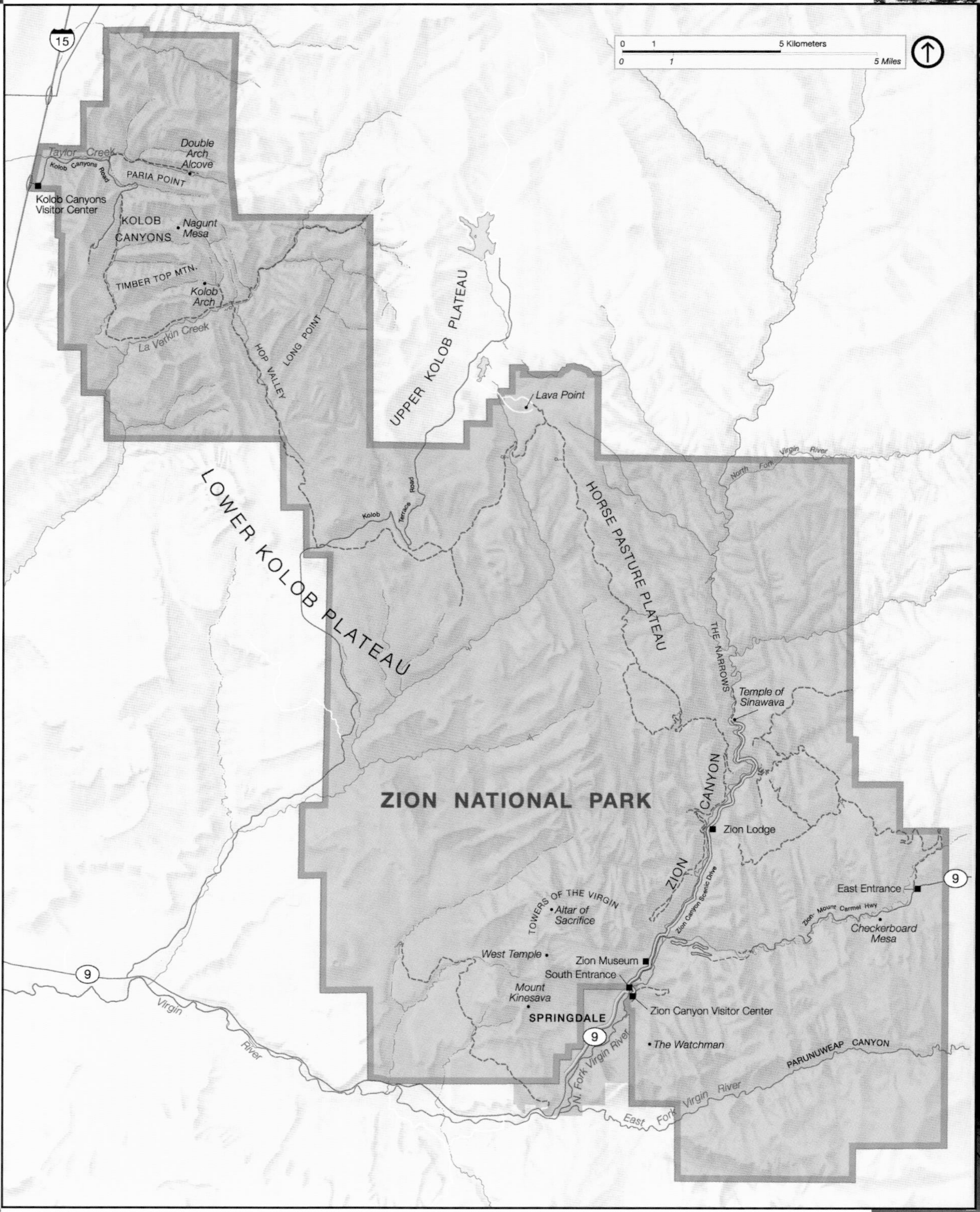

Just Browsing

A mule deer buck browses the foliage. Mule deer are abundant in Zion National Park, commonly seen throughout, especially at dawn and dusk.

Stony Wilderness

Zion's sprawling wilderness of sinuous cliff and canyon provides a home for such rare birds as peregrine falcons and Mexican spotted owls.

Cross-Bedded Stone

Checkerboard Mesa, right, shows the combined effects of cross-bedding of dune sand and the vertical erosion of rainwater. Below: A tributary stream spills into the Virgin River.

ZION NATIONAL PARK

History Note: Euro-Americans began settling the Zion area in the 1860s. Within a generation, the native Paiute people had been decimated by disease and starvation. Some communities lost 75 percent of their population.

Flora: Nine hundred species of plants, including pinyon pine and juniper in the canyons; ponderosa pine, fir, and aspen on the plateau surface; cottonwood, willow, and ash at the riverside.

Fauna: Mule deer, bobcats, mountain lions, foxes, squirrels, rabbits, lizards, and many bird species, including hawks, wild turkeys, and hummingbirds.

Visitor Tip: Get your feet wet on a short dayhike through Zion Narrows, where the "trail" is actually the Virgin River. In some places, the walls of the canyon are just 18 feet wide. Allow one to five hours.

Garden Among the Cliffs

A field of oxeye daisies blooms, right, within sight of Zion National Park's cliffs. Following spread: Cross-bedded Navajo sandstone can be seen through a shroud of mist.

THE EFFECT OF EXTREME CLIMATES

ALL WEATHER, LIKE all politics, is local. Whatever juggernaut of wind and moisture, heat or cold, the global weather patterns may cook up to send your way, some portion of the landscape near you is probably going to get in its way, customize it for your neighborhood, or sidetrack it altogether.

Dry Dunes
Expansive fields of sand dunes stretch across the arid landscape of Death Valley.

The atmosphere is yet another Theater of the Really Big. Air masses collide like tectonic plates. They flow like glaciers. They rage like rivers. They flop down like layers of sediment, and just sit there. They even uplift or subside like mountain ranges. They are as unpredictable as volcanoes, guaranteeing only that eventually they will do something we won't like.

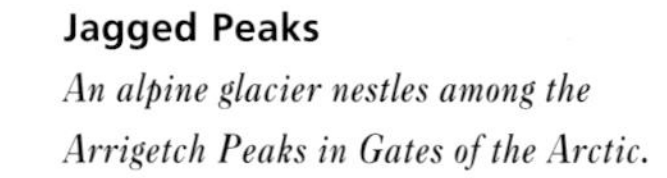

Jagged Peaks
An alpine glacier nestles among the Arrigetch Peaks in Gates of the Arctic.

For most people, all the geographical and topographical legacies of the Earth's billions of years of business matter only for giving life a chance. Whatever else the volcanoes, glaciers, faults, and oceans may or may not have achieved, and no matter how impressed we are with that action, what we really care about is what life is made of the opportunities the land provides.

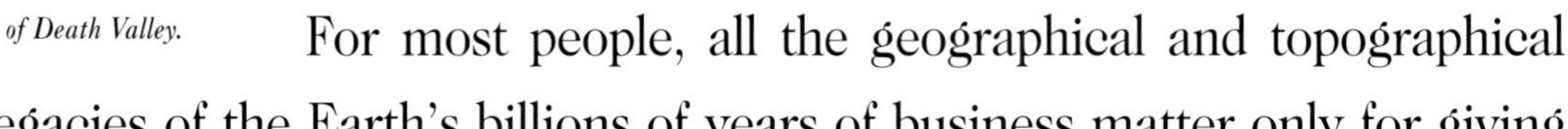

WEATHER SHAPING LIFE

Life, on the other hand, suggests that we needn't worry about it, because it makes its own opportunities. There is no question that life will find ways to exploit every environment—at least, every place short of actual flowing lava (even glacial ice has its inhabitants). Life will not merely survive but flourish in the most hostile places, and it will run riot in the more welcoming ones. And the biggest factor affecting hostility or welcome will be climate.

Lush Rain Forests
Abundant rainfall on the Olympic Peninsula sustains lush rain forests.

BREATH OF LIFE

Governed by latitude, topography, prevailing winds, and proximity to land and water masses, climate largely determines what sorts of plants and animals live in any given location. Its influence can be widespread, as in the deserts of the Southwest or the grasslands of the Great Plains. But climate also affects smaller, more isolated areas. Along a narrow strip of California's coast, for example, we find the ideal climate for lush, primeval forests of coast redwood trees.

COOL, MOIST WEATHER PATTERNS

In the redwoods country of northern California and southern Oregon, prevailing winds sweep in from the Pacific, carrying moist air inland. Clouds jam against the Coast Range and drop abundant amounts of rain during winter. In summer, thick fog often envelopes the coast and helps keep the ancient forests damp. Proximity to the ocean also moderates average temperatures, which range from 40 to 60 degrees year round. Salt-tolerant shrubs and Sitka spruce, occupying their own climatological niche, form a buffer zone along the immediate coast and protect the redwoods from salt spray and powerful winds.

Finding a Home

Whether home is a moist alpine meadow, left, or a semiarid plateau, right, life must adapt to the local climate to survive.

EXTREMES OF LUSH AND ARID

SEVEN CLIMATIC ECOLOGICAL ZONES—FROM SEA LEVEL TO ABOVE TIMBERLINE

In mountainous areas, abrupt differences in elevation profoundly influence the local climate and account in large part for the spectacular diversity of life found within relatively small areas.

On Washington's Olympic Peninsula, elevation varies from sea level to nearly 8,000 feet and spans seven distinct ecological zones: coast, temperate rain forest, lowland forest, montane forest, subalpine forest, alpine meadow, and barren, ice-clad summits. Here, damp Pacific air stalls against the west slope of the mountains, then rises into cooler elevations, where moisture condenses into rain or snow. An average of 140 inches falls in Olympic's rain forests; 200 inches on its glaciers. The peaks also cast a rainshadow to the northeast, where some areas receive as little as 17 inches annually.

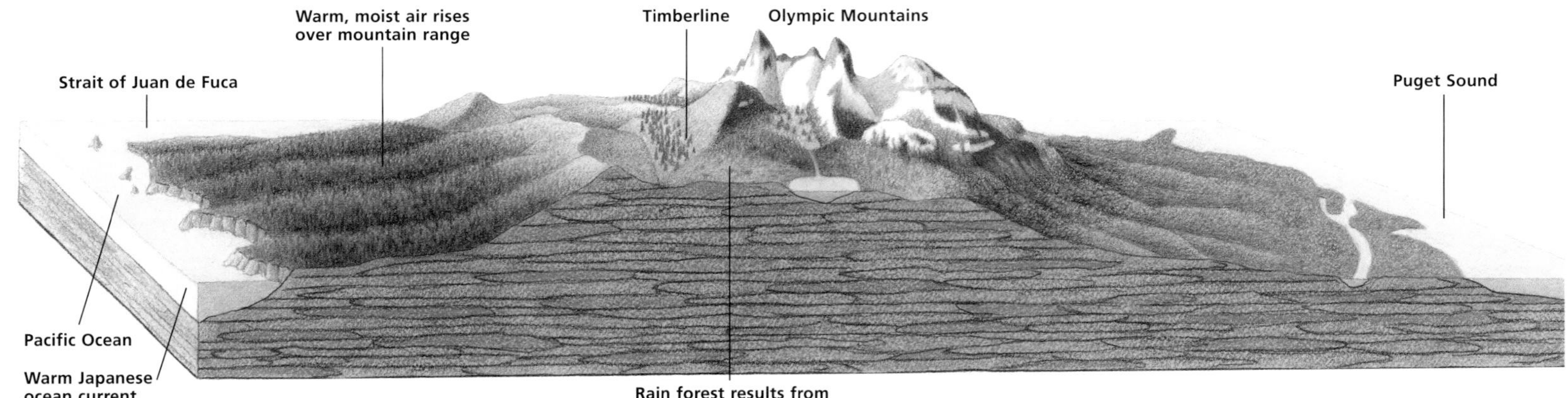

ADAPTING AND SUCCUMBING TO CLIMATIC FORCES

For more than seven hundred years, Ancestral Puebloans, also known as Anasazis, thrived in a semiarid climate atop Mesa Verde, a plateau that juts 2,000 feet above the parched floors of the Mancos and Montezuma valleys in southwestern Colorado. They dry-farmed fields of crops, built stone dams and reservoirs to conserve water, and hunted deer and small game.They abandoned the mesa during the late thirteenth century, perhaps due to drought, overpopulation, and depleted natural resources.

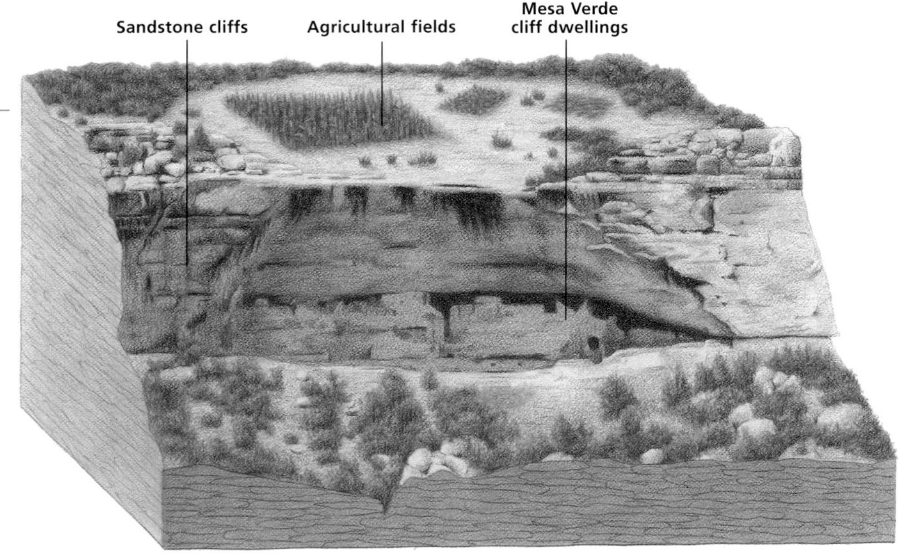

Dry Side

Mount Angeles rises 6,454 feet above the Strait of Juan de Fuca, on the drier northeast side of the Olympic Peninsula.

RAINSHADOW EFFECT

The downwind side of a mountain range often receives far less precipitation than the windward side. This is because as damp air blows against the windward side, it is pushed up into cooler elevations where the moisture condenses and falls as rain. Little moisture is left, then, for the downwind side, creating what is called a rainshadow.

California's Sierra Nevada Range casts perhaps the most striking rainshadow in North America. The range wrings precipitation from damp Pacific air, providing abundant water for the giant sequoia groves of Sequoia and Kings Canyon national parks and other west slope forests. It also blocks moisture from desert parks farther inland, including Death Valley, the driest spot on the continent.

Cold and Dry

Though winter brings intense cold to the Brooks Range in Gates of the Arctic National Park, little snow falls there. A polar desert extends north of the peaks.

Bristling with Character

Confined mostly to the Mojave Desert of California, Arizona, Utah, and Nevada, Joshua trees gather scarce water through a widespread, but shallow, root system.

PLANTS REFLECT DIVERSE CLIMATES

Stalwart manifestations of their own distinct climates, trees and other conspicuous plants reflect conditions from a variety of settings. Whitebark pines typically grow near tree line in wind-hammered, alpine conditions. Red firs grow in cool, moist locations. Sugar pines tolerate shade and grow well among other conifers. Ponderosa pines, resistant to drought and fire, are often found in dry, grassy locations. Redwoods grow along the fog-shrouded coast of northern California and southern Oregon. Giant sequoias find their niche along the western slope of the Sierra Nevada Range. Joshua trees grow in the Mojave Desert above 3,000 feet; saguaro in the Sonoran.

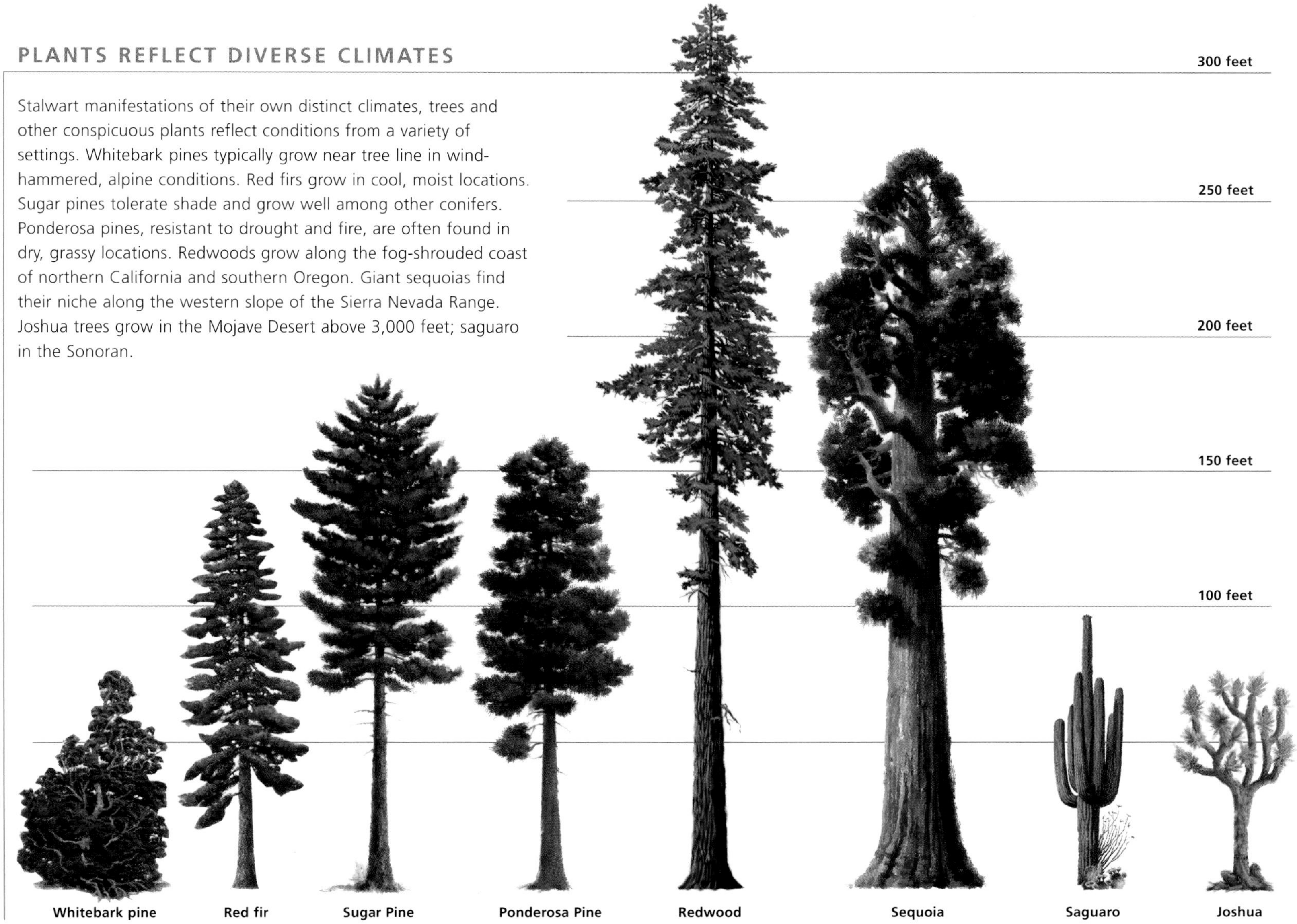

300 feet
250 feet
200 feet
150 feet
100 feet

Whitebark pine | Red fir | Sugar Pine | Ponderosa Pine | Redwood | Sequoia | Saguaro | Joshua

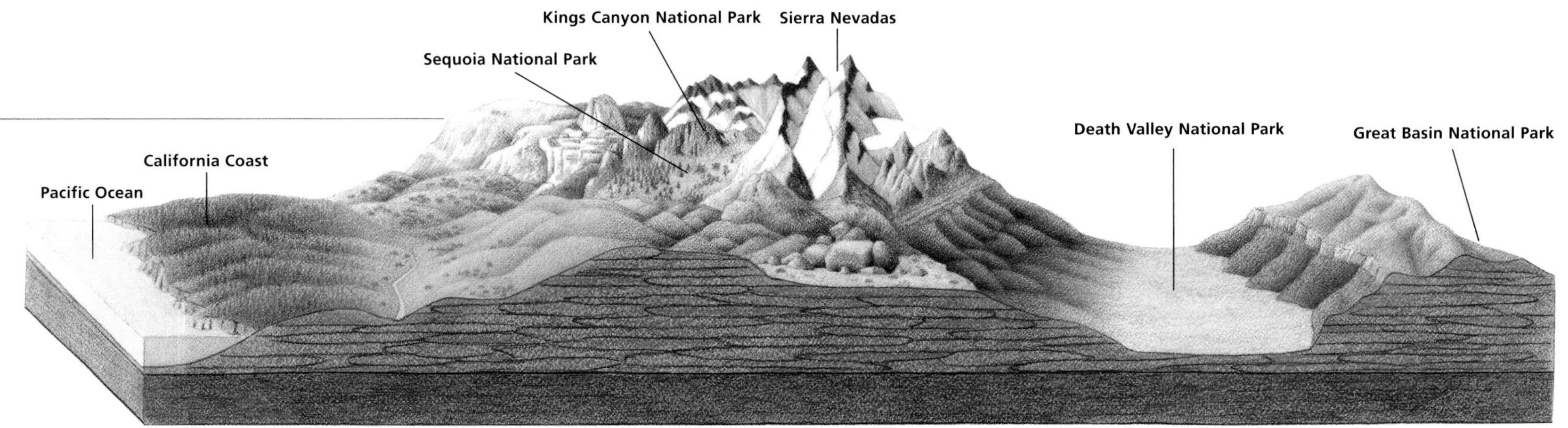

LANDS, LUSH AND ARID

Thanks in good part to climate, the national parks featured in this chapter are all in some way monuments to the immoderate. Whether arid, lush, bitterly cold, or sweltering, climatic extremes encourage biological extremes in the national parks they affect. This is not simply a matter of life scrambling for a foothold, or growing to its biggest, or surviving in the hottest or coldest or wettest or driest place, or developing weird, photogenic adaptations. The interplay of climate and biology is simply a matter of life making the most of each situation.

Gates of the Artic

Mesa Verde

Usually there is not one extreme but several. Gates of the Arctic National Park, for example, combines extreme northern latitude with extreme cold and extreme dryness. Northern latitude provides the varying sunlight regime—endless summer days, endless winter nights—that encourages extreme seasonality in life, a seasonality heightened by the very short and flashy growing season of the arctic summer. Extreme dryness (less than a foot of precipitation a year) and cold (the north side of the Brooks Range is called a polar desert) may test life's adaptive capacities even more than dryness and heat would.

Giant Sequoias
Giant sequoia trees, Earth's largest living things, grow only along the west slope of California's Sierra Nevada Range.

But dryness and heat are test enough. Joshua Tree, Saguaro National Park, and Death Valley demonstrate the breadth of tests possible. All three are caught in the rainshadow of mountain ranges to their west, which block the prevailing westerlies that might otherwise bring them moisture. Joshua Tree and Saguaro get about the same amount of precipitation as Gates of the Arctic. The lowest, hottest, driest part of Death Valley barely gets a tenth of that, less than 2 inches a year. But even at that, and despite their searing temperatures, these deserts are able to respond to another kind of climatic extreme—brief seasonal flushes of violently delivered moisture—with vivid, even lush, displays of vegetation.

Under such a stern and unforgiving regime, life has learned a hundred ways to get its water, whether by localizing near water sources, developing extraordinary storage capacity, putting most of its growth into long, thirsty roots, or just hunkering down and waiting for better days. The saguaro cactus and the Joshua tree do most of these. For all the gloom of its name, Death Valley National Park, from its sub-sea-level floor to its highest peaks, hosts more than nine hundred species of plants.

Petrified Forest National Park, though similar in climate to these other desert parks (and similar in geology to many of the parks in the Erosion chapter), has a different climatic theme. It protects a forest that gives the term old growth a whole new meaning: fossilized logs, chunks, and chips left from a 225-million-year-old coniferous forest. Inhabitants of a much wetter world, the trees, some as much as 200 feet tall, appear to have been

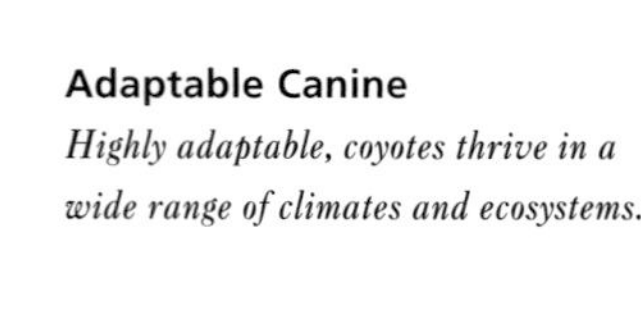

Adaptable Canine
Highly adaptable, coyotes thrive in a wide range of climates and ecosystems.

Death Valley

Joshua Tree

Olympic

Petrified Forest

Redwood

Saguaro

Sequoia and Kings Canyon

the victims of various local catastrophes. Erosion or earthquake or some other force toppled them and pushed them into moving water, where the trees were securely buried and then fossilized.

Castles in the Cliffs
Ancestral Puebloans built magnificent dwellings among the cliffs of Mesa Verde.

Mesa Verde is likewise dry country. The foremost saga celebrated in this park is human, and much of it is tied to climate. The ancient cliff dwellings and mesa-top settlements of Mesa Verde are a testament to adaptability in a dry environment. But it was adaptability that finally failed the test some eight hundred years ago when an extended drought drove these superb architects from the area entirely.

The extreme in environmental conditions is also represented by two extreme life forms, the giant sequoia and the coast redwood. Both are prisoners of a fairly constricted set of habitat requirements, of which climate is clearly a key constituent. The giant sequoias of the Sierra Nevada have long thrived in only a small number of groves between 5,000 and 7,000 feet in elevation. They are blessed with precipitation that the Sierras stop before it can reach Death Valley. The coast redwoods inhabit a similarly narrow strip of land along the California coast, where rainfall amounts to as much as 80 inches a year. Fog off the sea mists the trees during the dry summers.

Olympic National Park offers a kind of ecological synthesis of nearly the full range of extremes already represented by the other parks. Its Pacific Coast shores and associated rain forest receive ten times the precipitation of Gates of the Arctic (and a thousand times that of Death Valley), but thanks to the high wall of the park's mountains, the northeastern side of the Olympic Peninsula is not much wetter than some deserts. In this one setting, coastal rain forests give way to progressively higher plant communities that have adapted to cooler and cooler conditions, until trees are mere stunted shrubs, and wildflowers blossom hastily in the lee of glaciers.

Gates of the Arctic
North of the Arctic Circle, an August snowfall dusts Alaska's Endicott Mountains.

DEATH VALLEY

NATIONAL PARK IN CALIFORNIA

ARID WONDERLAND

The portion of the Mojave Desert contained in Death Valley National Park is the driest and hottest place in the United States. Near Badwater, in the long trench of desert between the Panamint Range on the west and the Black Mountains on the east, is the lowest dry land in the Western Hemisphere—282 feet below sea level. A showcase of desert extremes, the park includes one of the largest salt pans on Earth, dramatically faulted landscapes, young volcanic craters, and dune fields.

The desert is a difficult place to survive, but it has been an even more difficult place to understand, much less enjoy. Even John Van Dyke, whose book *The Desert* (1901) helped pioneer an aesthetic for such hostile landscapes, began by admitting that "there is not a thing about it that is 'pretty,' and not a spot upon it that is 'picturesque.'" Thanks to Van Dyke and others who opened our eyes, we know better now. Death Valley, approached in the right frame of mind, is wall-to-wall beauty.

The right frame of mind is, by most accounts, a very cautious one. Virtually all advice given to photographers, sightseers, and hikers here emphasizes avoiding the middle of the day. The National Park Service recommends against hiking at all in the heat of the summer, when it is sometimes 120 degrees on the valley floor. The heat is oppressive, yes, but the beauty is still there.

For people expecting only barren sand dunes and endless flats of baked mud, the park's badlands may be the biggest surprise. There are stretches of badland topography along the Artists Drive, just south of Furnace Creek, where the colors are truly unbelievable. It looks as if some ancient tribe of industrialists dumped their most shocking chemical waste here, to be eroded into the jumbled network of gullies we see today. And the eroded country around Zabriskie Point puts on a much better, and more convincing, show in real life than did Antonioni's 1970 movie of the same name.

But Death Valley also does offer plenty of old-fashioned desert at its most stereotypical. The drive along the edge of the lowest portion

Rare Blossoms
Rock mimulus, a rare plant, blossom in one of Death Valley National Park's many canyons, left. Above: Barrel cactus.

Prickly Lizard
The desert horned lizard is one of Death Valley's forty-one species of reptiles and amphibians.

Low Point

Badwater Basin, right, includes the lowest point in the Western Hemisphere, 282 feet below sea level. Below: Eroded mudstone hills and gullies.

of the valley, from Artists Drive to Badwater, features just this sort of hell-on-earth country. At Devil's Golf Course, you stand on uncounted layers of salt and sediments from lakes that have intermittently occupied the area. Badwater was in fact named by an early surveyor, who discovered that the small pool here was so saline that his mule refused to touch it.

Dune Fields

In addition to mountains, basins, and playa lakes, Death Valley takes in several large dune fields.

For contrast—at least as much as this valley bottom can provide—hike the little Salt Creek Interpretive Trail, north of Furnace Creek. Salt Creek emerges from the ground, flows about 2 miles, and disappears. The unusually thick plant life along its banks reveals how eager even the desert is to bloom given the slightest encouragement. The creek is as salty as the ocean and is inhabited by tiny Salt Creek pupfish, which live nowhere else. Twenty thousand years ago, the valley contained a huge lake with many species of fish. As the lake dried and shrank, only the pupfish held on in the increasingly salty water. They settle into the mud in the "cooler" winter months, and emerge to reoccupy their tiny realm when spring returns.

Early Bloomers

Desert sunflowers, left, are among the first wildflowers to bloom during Death Valley's brief spring. Their seeds require just an inch of rain to germinate. Below: Like many other park creatures, desert woodrats forage during the cool of the night.

Racetrack Rocks

Snail-like tracks left by moving rocks criss-cross a mudflat in Racetrack Valley. It is thought the rocks are pushed by strong winds after rain slicks the surface of the mudflat.

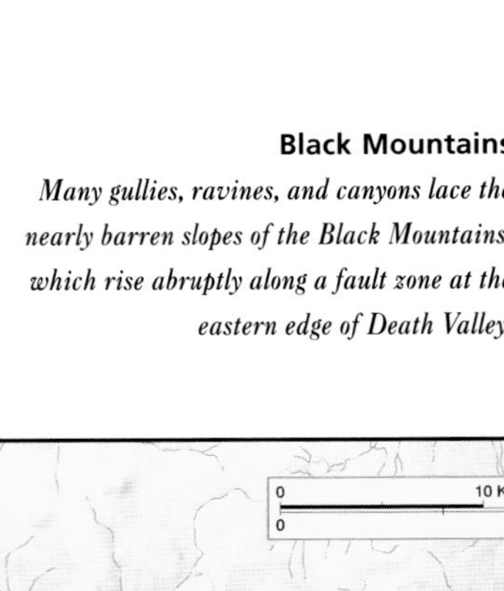

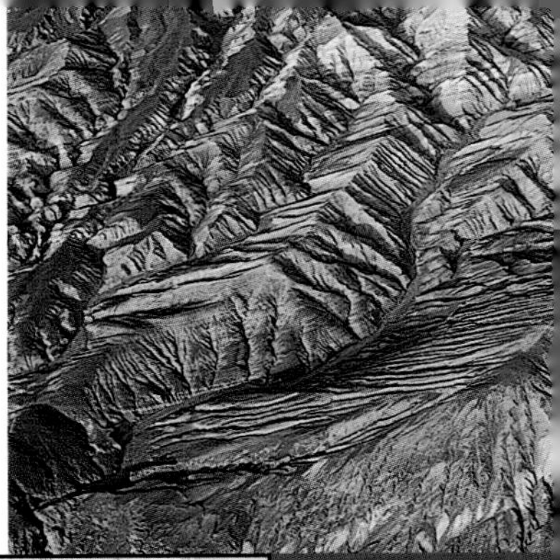

Black Mountains

Many gullies, ravines, and canyons lace the nearly barren slopes of the Black Mountains, which rise abruptly along a fault zone at the eastern edge of Death Valley.

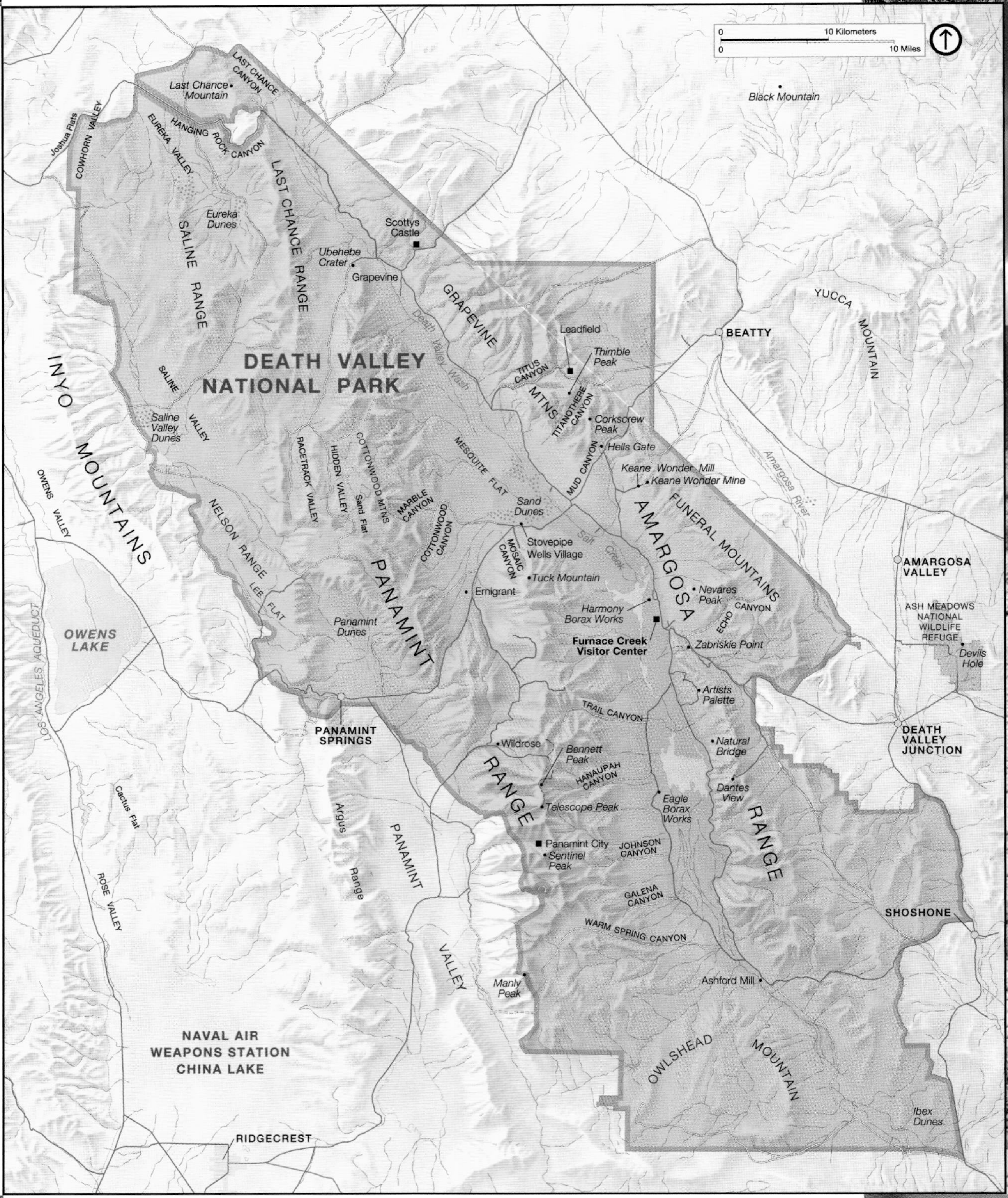

Volcanic Craters

Part of a cluster of volcanic craters, Little Hebe Crater, in the foreground, and Ubehebe Crater, in the background, were created by explosive volcanic eruptions.

Cholla Cactus

Cholla, one of thirteen species of cactuses within the park, adds a splash of yellow to the desert. Certain packrats use joints of the cholla to build their dens.

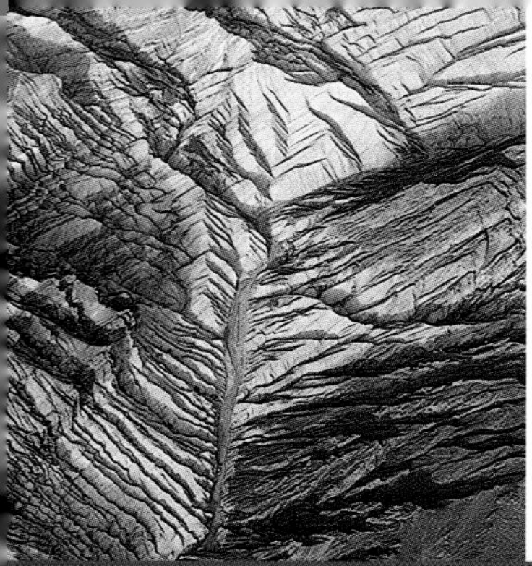

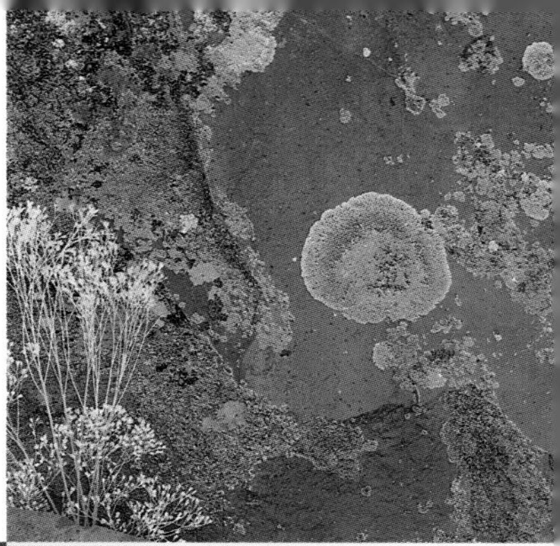

Hardy Lichens

Lichens mottle a volcanic rock in Death Valley. One of the hardiest life forms on the planet, lichens can remain dormant through long periods of unfavorable conditions.

DEATH VALLEY NATIONAL PARK

History Note: Death Valley was named in 1849 by a group of prospectors hoping to find a shortcut to the California gold fields. One of the party died, and the rest came close.

Flora: Nine hundred and seventy plants, including Joshua trees, bristlecone pines, mountain mahogany, creosote bushes, and thirteen species of cactuses. Fifty of the park's plants are endemic to Death Valley.

Fauna: Three hundred and forty-six species of birds; several species of rare desert pupfish; five amphibians; thirty-six reptiles; and fifty-one mammals, including kangaroo rats, kit foxes, and desert bighorn sheep.

Visitor Tip: Never underestimate the power of heat. Death Valley has the highest daily maximum temperature in the world, and dehydration is the second most common cause of death in the park.

Coming Storm

Storm clouds gather over the dried mud and creosote bushes in Death Valley National Park.

Salt Creek

Salt Creek bends toward the Panamint Range. Snipes, killdeer, and herons frequent its grassy banks, and a type of pupfish found nowhere else in the world lives in the stream.

Schwatka and Endicott Mountains

Steep, glacially carved, and remote, the Schwatka Mountains, left, include the highest peaks in the Brooks Range. The Alatna River, below, meanders south through the Endicott Mountains.

GATES OF THE ARCTIC

NATIONAL PARK AND PRESERVE IN ALASKA

FRIGID BACKCOUNTRY

This is an enormous wildland, without roads and trails for its 200-mile width, with no access but by foot, boat, or air. During the last ice age, extensive glaciation sculpted the peaks of the Brooks Range—the extreme northwestern end of the Rocky Mountains—and created the wide, rounded contours of the lowland valleys. The present dry climate provides no more than 18 inches of precipitation a year in the park's wettest regions, so the glaciers are almost gone.

In the finest spirit of democracy, which insists that we each earn our own way, Gates of the Arctic is yours for the earning. It is there for those willing to make the extra sacrifices, take the extra time, and do the extra work required by such complete wilderness. From the moment of its establishment, the park was envisioned as a refuge not only for wildness and wildlife but also for that rarest of human qualities—self-sufficiency. Indeed, the park's creators reaffirmed the continued use of the area by America's most self-sufficient citizens, the subsistence hunters and fishermen, both native and non-native, who were already here. So don't go unless you're prepared to take care of yourself. If you are, there are few better places on earth for you.

Even in many roadless areas and parks in the lower forty-eight states, backcountry enthusiasts have become a little spoiled. We expect a fair number of streams to be provided with footbridges. Trails are marked with blazes of one kind or another. Backcountry ranger patrols show up in the nick of time. Now that much of the planet is reachable by cell phone, there is always a safety net of sorts if we get into serious trouble.

Northern Interior Alaska, as preserved in Gates of the Arctic, ups the ante on wilderness responsibility. There are still airplanes, boats, and other modern technological backup, but the purity of the wildness and the great distances you can get from that backup make this a different kind of wilderness. Those who are attracted to such distances would agree with Robert Marshall, whose writings influenced the creation of this park. He said that, "Life without the chance for such exertions

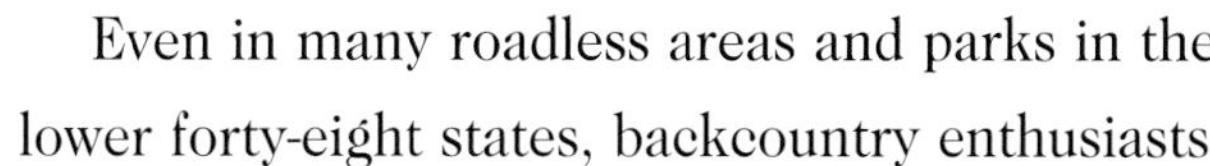

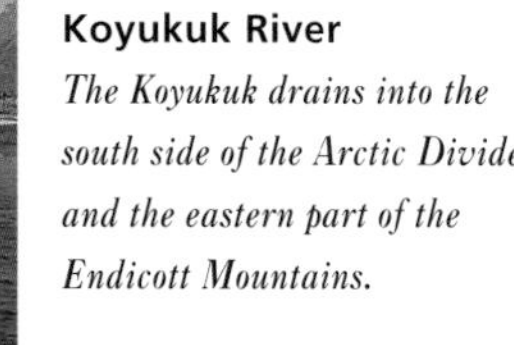

Koyukuk River
The Koyukuk drains into the south side of the Arctic Divide and the eastern part of the Endicott Mountains.

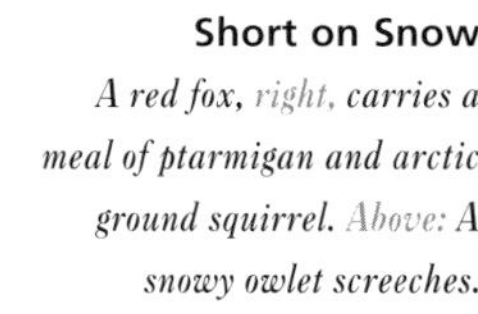

Short on Snow
A red fox, right, carries a meal of ptarmigan and arctic ground squirrel. Above: A snowy owlet screeches.

would be for many persons a dreary game, scarcely bearable in its horrible banality."

But exertion for its own sake misses the point here. Gates of the Arctic is wilderness opportunity personified. There are mountains, lakes, streams, and rivers—by the hundreds. There is the vast and subtle world of the tundra, with all its mattressy, boggy variations and its miniaturized habitats so full of life in the summer and so stiff and still in the winter. There is the whole Arctic cast of characters—bears and wolves, moose and sheep, birds from three or four continents.

Kobuk River
The Kobuk River flows through boreal forest, drains the Arrigetch Peaks and Walker Lake, then flows west of the park.

Most of all, there are the caribou in all their hordes, obeying a deep and unifying herd wisdom as they make their subcontinental migrations. These movements are not random. Nor are they optional. Caribou need every square mile they use, and by moving so much they use it all so lightly it lasts forever. Conservation writer Margaret Murie, watching them here half a century ago, called them "the living, moving, warm-blooded life of the Arctic."

Landmark Spires
Autumn emblazons a meadow at the foot of the Arrigetch Peaks, a spectacular cluster of black granite spires designated as a National Natural Landmark, right. Below, Caribou are the only deer in which both sexes have antlers.

Nunamiut Handiwork
A hand-carved mask lies on gravel at Anaktuvuk Pass, a year-round Nunamiut village where people continue to live in the traditional manner.

Migration Corridor
An important route for large herds of migrating caribou, the spacious John River Valley leads north to the Arctic Divide at Anaktuvuk Pass.

Tundra Lichen
Arctic tundra lichens mingle with the red leaves of mounain avens in the Endicott Mountains of Gates of the Arctic National Park and Preserve.

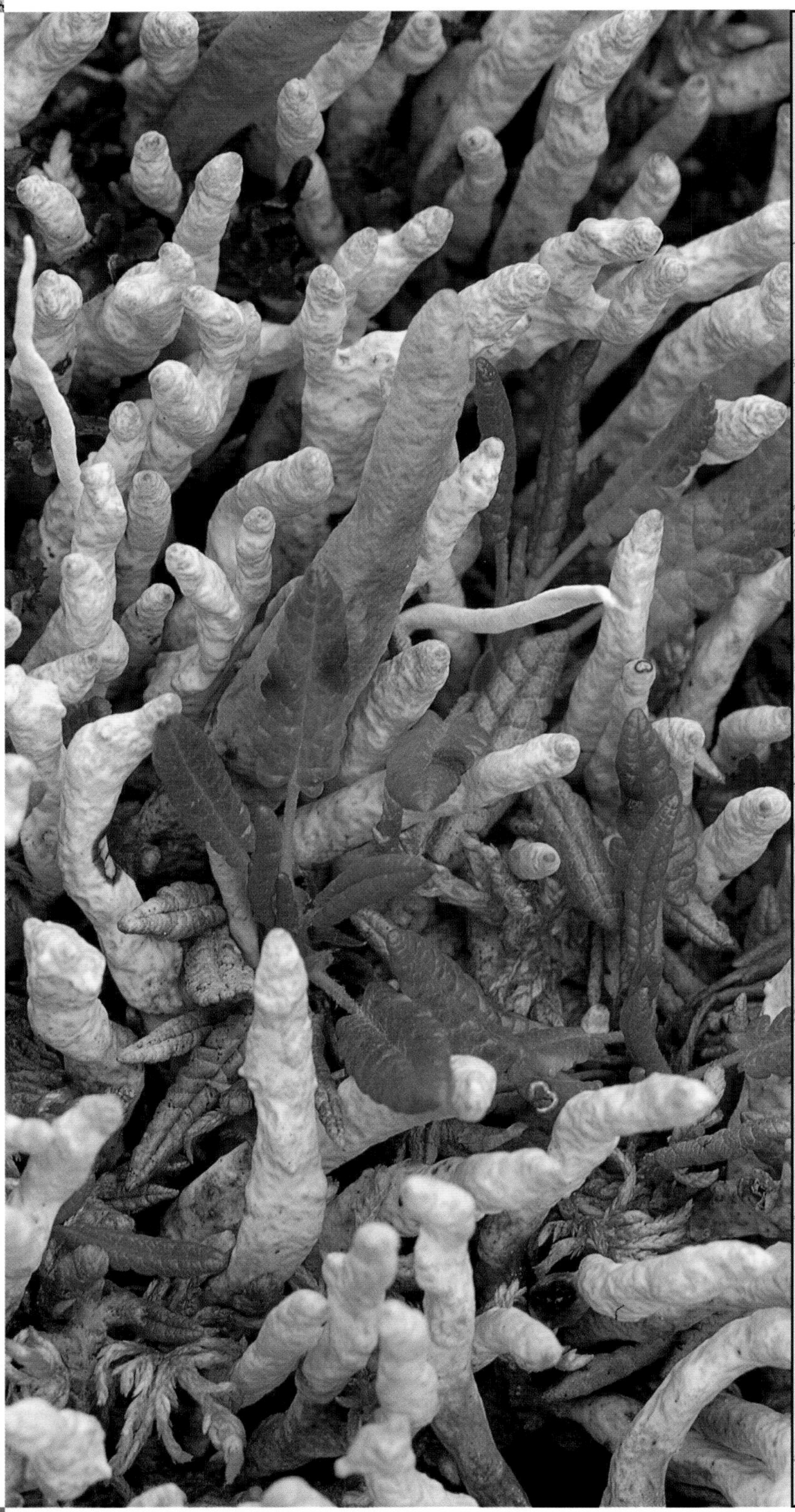

Vivid Vegetation
Vivid red bearberry leaves brighten up the park's shrub thickets during autumn. Bears do eat the berries, but prefer to fatten up on the park's abundant blueberries.

Noatak River
Flowing north and west from the Arctic Divide, the Noatak River meanders through moist tundra, where cotton-grass tussocks are the predominant form of vegetation.

Fuzz Protection

A fuzzy layer on the leaves of one-flowered cinquefoil diffuses visible light rays, traps heat rays, and reduces water loss—all of great value in the park's climate.

GATES OF THE ARCTIC NATIONAL PARK AND PRESERVE

History Note: In 1929, Bob Marshall—founder of the Wilderness Society and an indefatigable backcountry traveler—applied the name Gates of the Arctic to a place on the east side of the park where the Koyukuk River Valley squeezes between two high mountains.

Flora: Boreal forests of spruce, aspen, birch, and poplar; shrub thickets of dwarf and resin birch, willow and alder; alpine tundra, with its characteristic low, mat-forming heather vegetation; and moist tundra, where cotton grass predominates.

Fauna: Large herds of caribou, wolves, brown bears, black bears, Dall sheep, moose, lemmings, voles, and arctic ground squirrels; 133 species of birds, including eagles, hawks, owls, jaegers, and waterfowl.

Visitor Tip: The park is accessible only by air taxi or on foot from the Dalton Highway. There are no maintained trails or roads, but floating on one of the park's six designated Wild Rivers makes for easy travel and opens up many possibilities.

Wolverine

The largest member of the weasel family, wolverines are quick, tenacious carnivores that have been known to harass even feeding grizzly bears.

Cat's Eyes

Furtive, nocturnal, and rarely seen, bobcats have short, powerful bodies and excellent night vision, left. The park's namesake plants, below, are giant members of the agave family that grow 30 to 40 feet tall.

JOSHUA TREE

NATIONAL PARK IN CALIFORNIA

DESERT FOREST

The rocky, long-eroded topography of Joshua Tree National Park is bordered on the north and south by low mountain ranges. Much of what visitors see in the current shapes on this landscape, especially in the erosion of Joshua Tree's wide assortment of metamorphic and igneous rocks, is a legacy of colder and wetter climates. The strange rock formations provide an exotic backdrop for the equally striking vegetation the park was created to protect.

Joshua Tree National Park protects representative portions of two distinct desert worlds. The lower, eastern portion of the park, mostly below 3,000 feet in elevation, is warmer and drier. This Colorado Desert plant community includes mesquite, yucca, creosote bushes, and ocotillo and cholla cactus "gardens."

The higher elevations to the west are both wetter and cooler, with plant communities popularly classified as Mojave Desert. Various locations favor pinyon pine, scrub oak, and California junipers, but this portion of the park is most notable for its forests of Joshua trees.

Joshua trees do not need much moisture, but they seem to have retreated from many other southwestern habitats as the Southwest has grown drier over the millennia since the last ice age. Fossilized droppings from the long-extinct giant ground sloth, found near Las Vegas, Nevada, were composed mostly of Joshua tree leaves. As you see these trees, picture a huge, lumbering sloth reaching up among their tufted arms to feed.

Like most deserts and their specially adapted life forms, the area around Joshua Tree got its share of mixed reviews from early Euro-American observers. Spanish visitors probably saw the trees as early as the 1770s, but the first American to visit, Captain John C. Fremont, was decidedly unimpressed. In the 1840s, having just come from the lush, well-watered San Joaquin Valley farther north, Fremont was apparently not up to the shock of this dry new country. He said the Joshua tree was "the most repulsive tree in the vegetable kingdom." To someone unfamiliar with the needs and ways of

Claret Cup

The park's high desert region is home to claret cup cactus, left, and piles of smooth monzogranite boulders 100 million years old, above.

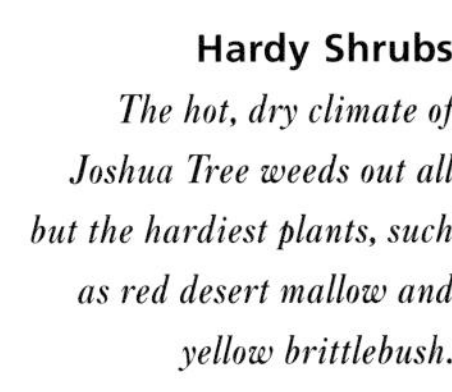

Hardy Shrubs

The hot, dry climate of Joshua Tree weeds out all but the hardiest plants, such as red desert mallow and yellow brittlebush.

desert life it certainly would look odd, but even an enlightened modern ecologist, A. Starker Leopold, described it as "a spooky-looking yucca."

Juniper Frame
A gnarled California juniper tree frames one of the park's striking monzogranite monoliths that dot the upland desert.

Native people found abundant reasons to inhabit the Joshua Tree area for thousands of years. The fan palm oases are still among the most hospitable of places in California. But Euro-Americans were attracted to the park area in greater numbers after the Civil War. Prospectors dug everywhere. By the 1870s, stockmen brought longhorns to feed on the grasses. Homesteaders zeroed in on the oases.

After the turn of the century, desert plants like the Joshua tree became more fashionable in urban gardens—a reversal of taste since Fremont's time. By the 1930s, there were so many people coming just to haul off the handsome trees and other plants that concerned citizens organized a campaign to prevent the complete destruction of the spooky-looking trees. They succeeded in 1936, when Joshua Tree National Monument was created. In 1994, the monument was enlarged and reclassified as a national park, a more prestigious classification reserved for the most significant and distinctive of landscapes. No doubt John Fremont would be appalled.

Poised Rattler
A prairie rattlesnake coils, poised to flee or strike.

Low Desert Thicket
A hallmark of the park's low Colorado Desert ecosystem, teddy bear (or jumping) cholla forms thickets on sandy flats and rocky slopes.

Scarlet Beauty
A patch of scarlet paintbrush dangles from a rock crevice in Hidden Valley. Most types of paintbrush fasten themselves to the root structures of host plants such as grasses.

Mojave Trademark
Each Joshua tree supports a complex web of life that includes birds, insects, and tiny yucca night lizards that may spend their entire lives in a single Joshua tree.

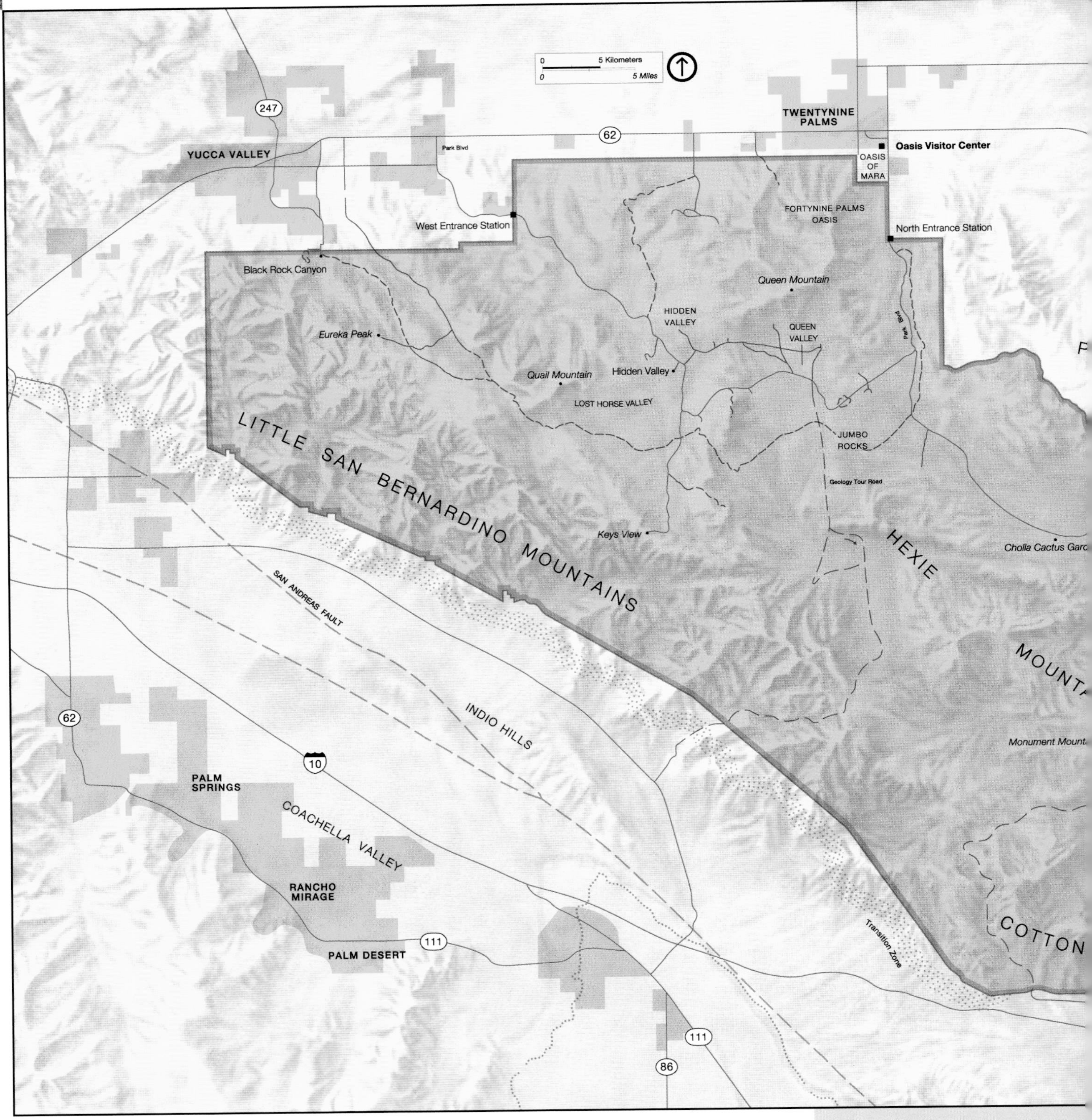

0 5 Kilometers
0 5 Miles
247
62
YUCCA VALLEY
Park Blvd
TWENTYNINE PALMS
Oasis Visitor Center
OASIS OF MARA
West Entrance Station
FORTYNINE PALMS OASIS
North Entrance Station
Black Rock Canyon
Queen Mountain
HIDDEN VALLEY
QUEEN VALLEY
Eureka Peak
Park Blvd
Quail Mountain
Hidden Valley
LOST HORSE VALLEY
JUMBO ROCKS
LITTLE SAN BERNARDINO MOUNTAINS
Geology Tour Road
Keys View
HEXIE MOUNTAINS
Cholla Cactus Garden
SAN ANDREAS FAULT
INDIO HILLS
62
10
PALM SPRINGS
COACHELLA VALLEY
Monument Mountain
RANCHO MIRAGE
111
PALM DESERT
Transition Zone
COTTON
111
86

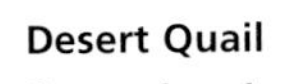

Desert Quail
Better adapted to deserts than any other quail, the Gambel's quail lives in coveys of twenty to forty birds and roosts in shrubs and low trees.

Weathered Rockpiles
Contorted clusters of weathered monzogranite formed as underground intrusions of crystallized magma and weathered while still buried beneath the surface.

Indigo Bush

Like all of Joshua Tree's plants, indigo bush must cope with a harsh desert climate of widely fluctuating temperatures, sudden torrents of rain, and high winds.

SHEEP HOLE MTNS

MOUNTAINS

Transition Zone

COXCOMB MOUNTAINS

JOSHUA TREE NATIONAL PARK

MOJAVE DESERT

COLORADO DESERT

PINTO BASIN

Pinto Basin Road

EAGLE MOUNTAINS

Eagle Mountain

Visitor Center

Cottonwood Spring

Lost Palms Oasis

MTNS

62

177

DESERT CENTER

10

195

JOSHUA TREE NATIONAL PARK

History Note: During the more verdant era of the Pleistocene, a slow-moving river wound through the now-dry Pinto Basin and helped to support one of the Southwest's earliest cultures—the hunters and gatherers known as the Pinto people.

Flora: Two large, distinct desert ecosystems: the Colorado Desert, characterized by creosote bushes, teddy bear cholla, and ocotillo; and the Mojave Desert—higher, moister, cooler—home of the Joshua tree. Spring rains bring a host of wildflowers into vivid bloom.

Fauna: Desert bighorn sheep, coyotes, jackrabbits, kangaroo rats, snakes, lizards, burrowing owls, golden eagles, roadrunners, termites, tarantulas, and stinkbugs.

Visitor Tip: For a taste of how ingenuity and hard work could carve out a family niche in the desert, take a ranger tour of the Desert Queen Ranch, where Bill and Frances Keys raised five kids and lived for sixty years.

Desert Dawn

Early light catches the crest of a rocky ridge in Joshua Tree. The park is esteemed for its unique transition zone between the Mojave Desert and Colorado Desert ecosystems.

MESA VERDE

NATIONAL PARK IN COLORADO

ANCIENT DWELLINGS

A combination of uplift and erosion has cut away the south-facing 2,000-foot-high cliffs of Mesa Verde in a series of long deep canyons. For centuries, precipitation percolated through sandstone layers, gathering in springs. The emerging water, assisted by freezing and thawing, gradually eroded alcoves, caves, and low-ceilinged shelves out of the cliff face. In the thirteenth century, the alcoves were the site of some of the most impressive architectural achievements in the New World.

Beginning about 1,500 years ago, people colonized the flat top of Mesa Verde and moved into some of the alcoves. We don't know what they called themselves, but we have long called them the Anasazi, which is Navajo for "the ancient ones." It is now believed more accurate to call them Ancestral Puebloan, but the name Anasazi has a mystique that will not easily be discarded.

There are two reasons for that mystique. The first is what they created here. Around 1200 A.D., after about seven hundred years of farming and building mostly on the mesa top, these people began a brief but spectacular period of construction in the cliff alcoves. This alone would have assured the admiration of modern people, but to this achievement the builders added a mystery. About 1300 A.D., within a generation's time, they abruptly abandoned the whole mesa.

It now appears that their disappearance was a dispersal to more hospitable regions following a relentless two-decade drought. Perhaps soil exhaustion or some other form of resource depletion, caused by the several thousand people inhabiting the mesa, also contributed to their departure. In any event, the legacy of these "lost cities" and their mysterious builders has been a richly conjectural one. Since the late 1800s, several generations of researchers, native people, and other admirers of Mesa Verde have puzzled over these buildings and wondered where the builders went.

It is now assumed that some moved south, and were the ancestors of some of today's

Pincushion on Legs
Roughly thirty thousand quills cover the typical porcupine and protect it from all but the most determined predators.

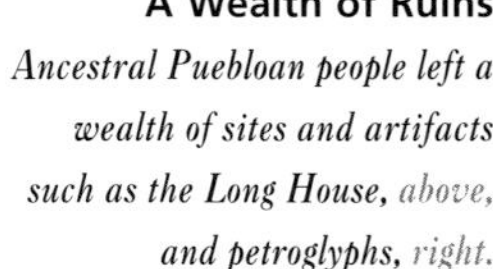

A Wealth of Ruins
Ancestral Puebloan people left a wealth of sites and artifacts such as the Long House, above, and petroglyphs, right.

Mesa Snow

Snow, right, and the occasional summer thunderstorm supplied water for the Ancestral Puebloans who left Cliff Palace, below, probably due to an extended drought.

Pueblo Indians. But knowing that seems not to have reduced the mystery surrounding the reasons they abandoned their lovely homes in Mesa Verde.

Balcony House
A narrow defile leads to the entrance of Balcony House, one of the largest and best-known cliff dwellings in the park.

It is both fun and instructive, when visiting Mesa Verde's sites, to especially remember that this was someone's home. For one thing, it will remind you not to do things you wouldn't do in any other person's home—sit down without being invited to, or climb on the walls, or take things, or make a racket.

But by thinking of the sites as a home you will also see them more clearly. Look around. Imagine you lived here. Why would you build your rooms so small? On a busy summer day in 1250, where would you go to butcher a turkey? To sit down and have a snack? To relieve yourself? To find some rock to patch a broken wall? Or just to be out of the way in a quiet corner? What we honor here is more than architectural achievement; we also honor humanity's singular gift for making ourselves at home.

Atop the Mesa
Snow blankets Far View, a cluster of pueblos near the center of the mesa, where the best growing conditions existed and the highest concentrations of people lived, left. Below: *A wooden ladder protrudes from the roof of a kiva at Spruce Tree House.*

Balsamroot Blooms
A cluster of balsamroot, nestled among the juniper and pinyon pine of the mesa, overlooks the Montezuma Valley from the North Rim of Mesa Verde National Park.

Sun Temple
Sun Temple was intended to be a ceremonial structure before construction apparently stopped when people began moving away from Mesa Verde.

MESA VERDE NATIONAL PARK

History Note: Euro-Americans got their first glimpse of Mesa Verde's cliff dwellings in 1874, when William H. Jackson photographed Two Story Cliff House in what is now Ute Mountain Tribal Park.

Flora: Juniper and pinyon pine and thickets of Gambel oak on top of the mesa; Douglas fir and ponderosa pine in northern elevations; many wildflowers, sagebrush, yucca, serviceberry, and rabbitbrush.

Fauna: Mule deer, coyotes, ringtails, prairie dogs, mountain lions, bats, chipmunks, mice, and other rodents; snakes and lizards; and many birds, including golden eagles, kestrels, hawks, and magpies.

Visitor Tip: To put the dwellings and other archaeological sites into context, begin your visit with a stop at the Chapin Mesa Museum, which presents an overview of what is known about the Ancestral Puebloans and exhibits exceptional examples of basketry and weaving.

Sacred Chamber
A ladder descends into a kiva through a roof of mud-covered beams, facing page. Kiva is a Hopi word for ceremonial room.

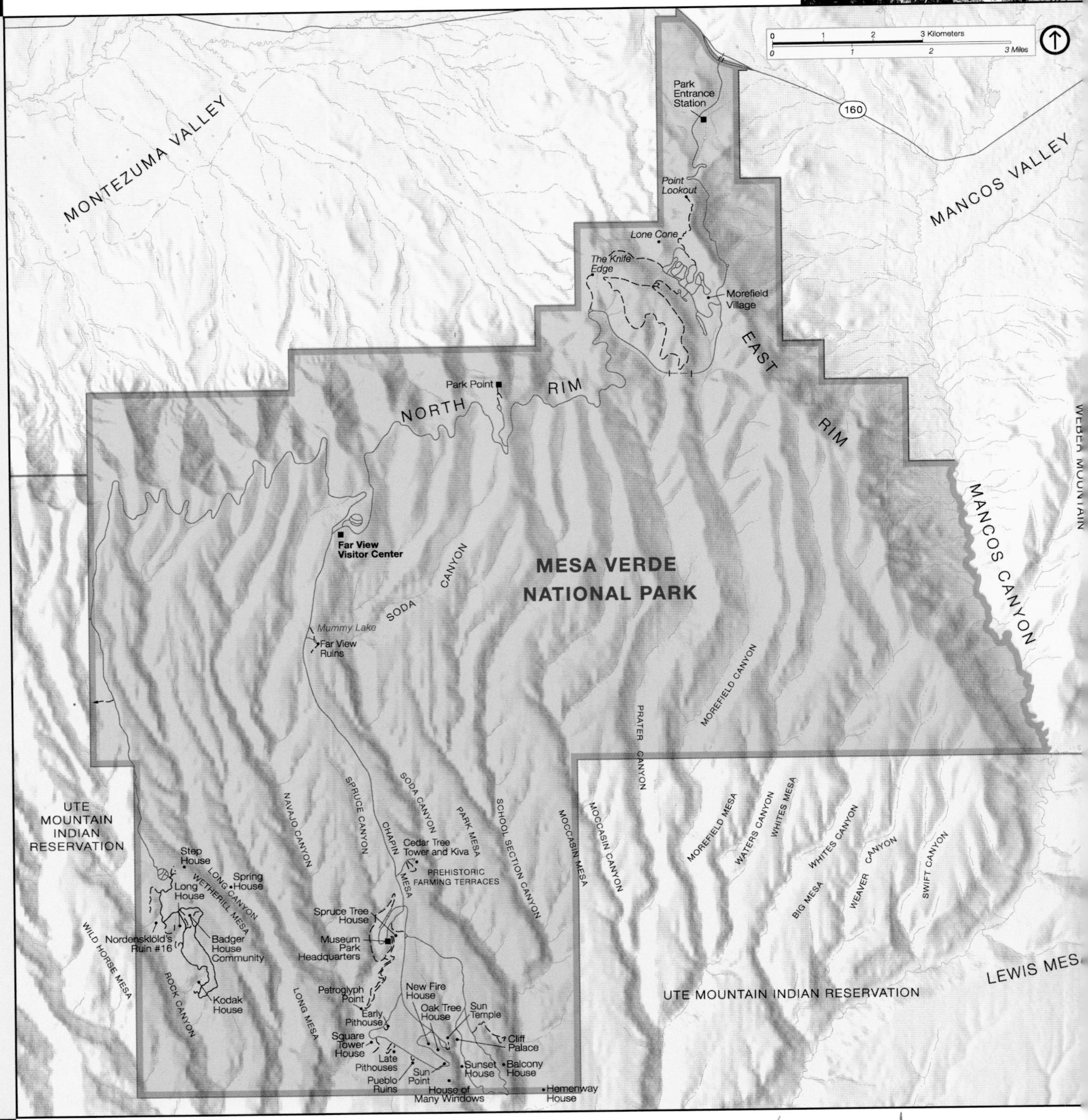

MESA VERDE NATIONAL PARK
0 1 2 3 Kilometers
0 1 2 3 Miles
160
MONTEZUMA VALLEY
MANCOS VALLEY
Park Entrance Station
Point Lookout
Lone Cone
The Knife Edge
Morefield Village
EAST RIM
NORTH RIM
Park Point
WEBER MOUNTAIN
MANCOS CANYON
Far View Visitor Center
SODA CANYON
Mummy Lake
Far View Ruins
MOREFIELD CANYON
PRATER CANYON
UTE MOUNTAIN INDIAN RESERVATION
NAVAJO CANYON
SPRUCE CANYON
SODA CANYON
CHAPIN MESA
PARK MESA
SCHOOL SECTION CANYON
MOCCASIN MESA
MOCCASIN CANYON
MOREFIELD MESA
WATERS CANYON
WHITES MESA
WHITES CANYON
BIG MESA
WEAVER CANYON
SWIFT CANYON
LEWIS MES
Step House
Long House
Spring House
LONG CANYON
WETHERILL MESA
WILD HORSE MESA
Nordenskiöld's Ruin #16
Badger House Community
ROCK CANYON
Kodak House
LONG MESA
Cedar Tree Tower and Kiva
PREHISTORIC FARMING TERRACES
Spruce Tree House
Museum
Park Headquarters
Petroglyph Point
Early Pithouse
Square Tower House
Late Pithouses
Pueblo Ruins
Sun Point
New Fire House
Oak Tree House
Sun Temple
Cliff Palace
Sunset House
Balcony House
House of Many Windows
Hemenway House
UTE MOUNTAIN INDIAN RESERVATION

Ruins
The Ancestral Puebloans built and occupied large cliff dwellings such as this site only during the last century they occupied the mesa.

Dietary Supplement
The Ancestral Puebloans hunted mule deer and other of the mesa's animals to supplement their crops of beans, squash, and corn.

Shrouded in Fog

A veil of fog drifts over the hills and forests of the Elwha River Valley on the park's north side.

Abundant Water

Olympic's 12 to 14 feet of annual precipitation produces extensive temperate rain forests, right, while its several thousand feet of abrupt vertical relief creates a multitude of waterfalls, including Marymere Falls, below.

NATIONAL PARK IN WASHINGTON

LUSH ECOSYSTEMS

The rugged landscape of the Olympic Peninsula, a by-product of the collision of the Pacific and North American plates, has over time been shaped and scoured by glaciers, some sixty of which remain at the highest elevations of the park. Though many national parks are home to diverse sets of ecosystems, Olympic National Park's combination of Pacific Coast, several distinctive forest types, and extensive mountain ranges make it extraordinary among American national parks.

Forget for the moment that Olympic National Park is connected to the continent, at the end of a thick, rather stubby peninsula. Forget also that it's only a short drive from Seattle. Remember instead that this park is celebrated as an island—and that it more strongly bears the characteristics of an island than many places that are entirely surrounded by water.

The most easy and obvious comparison with an island comes when we consider the park's wildness. Satellite photographs of the Olympic Peninsula show the park as a vaguely oval mass of unmarked land entirely surrounded by the tidy geometry of settlement. Clear-cut forests, communities, agricultural lands, and other traces of human use clearly outline the park, and are even visible from Earth's space.

So whenever you enter Olympic you may have a strong feeling of crossing a threshold, from a busy human landscape to an equally busy wild one. The contrast is made all the more striking by the magnificence and scale of the wildness. Here is the largest surviving old-growth forest in the Pacific Northwest. Over here is the largest undisturbed temperate rain forest in North America. Over there are miles of wilderness coastline to be explored.

But Olympic has been islanded in other ways. During the last glaciation, when much of the neighboring mainland was covered in ice, the peninsula was at times a true, water-encircled island. In biological terms, the ice has not been gone very long, and it shows. There is no evidence that grizzly bears, wolverine, and several other animals ever made

Sun and Shade Lovers
A butterfly pauses on an alpine aster, left: Above: Shelf fungus find a moist, shady home.

Coastal Islands
A weathered driftwood log frames the James Island group, which lies offshore of La Push.

the long trek to the Olympics, while other species, both animals and plants, exist only here.

Consider these "missing" species as you drive or hike along. What if we hadn't come along and thoroughly settled the country between the Olympics and the Cascades? Would a few grizzly bears have eventually lumbered on over to the peninsula, just to check it out?

Blooming Alder
An alder tree blossoms in the Elwha River Valley, which winds through the heart of Olympic National Park.

Olympic also superbly represents the idea of parks as "islands of hope"—places that promise a secure future for the wild things we love. At Olympic, this hope has recently taken some thrilling forms. Two dams, near the mouth of the Elwha River, may soon be removed, reopening that long park-spanning watershed to salmon that once spawned there by the hundreds of thousands. There was even cautious talk about restoring the gray wolf to the park's predator- prey system. With dreams like these, the defenders of Olympic might well consider hope itself one of their most important natural resources.

High Country Meadow
Autumn comes to a high country meadow in Olympic, right. At this elevation, conditions begin to discourage tree growth and favor ground-hugging plants. Below: Giant green anemones.

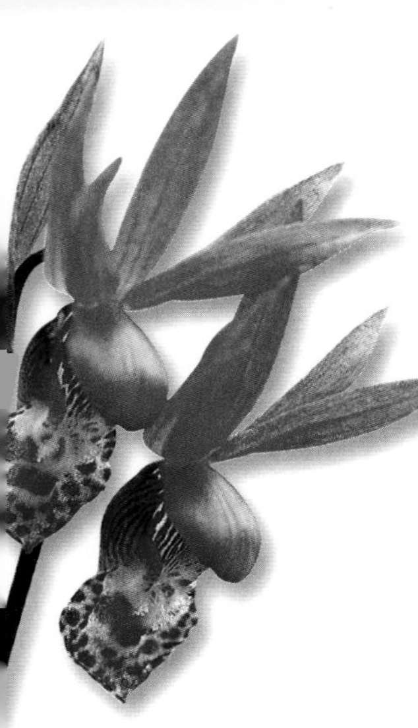

Calypso Orchids

One of the most beautiful and striking of Olympic's many wildflowers, the calypso orchid, or fairy slipper, grows in the shade of deep coniferous forests.

Temperate Rain Forests

A spongy understory of mosses, ferns, ground cover, and shrubs thrives in the park's temperate rain forests, where 12 to 14 feet of precipitation falls annually.

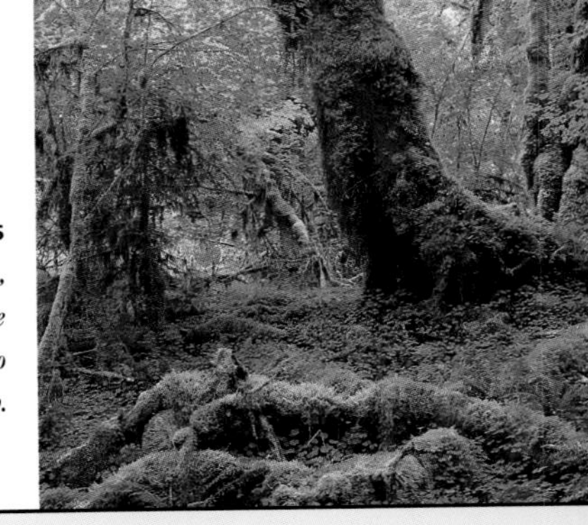

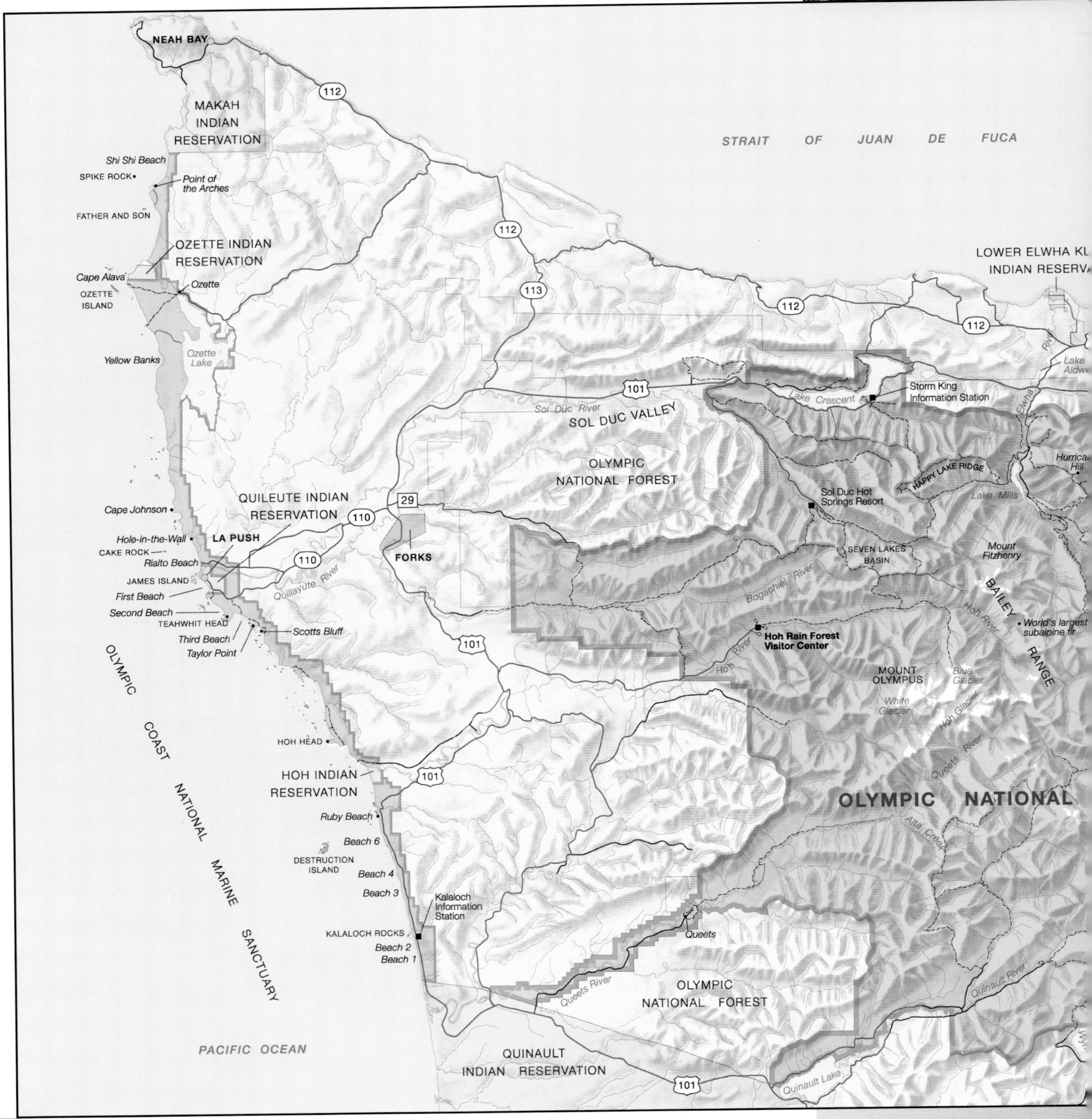
NEAH BAY
112
MAKAH INDIAN RESERVATION
STRAIT OF JUAN DE FUCA
Shi Shi Beach
SPIKE ROCK
Point of the Arches
FATHER AND SON
112
OZETTE INDIAN RESERVATION
LOWER ELWHA KL
INDIAN RESERV
Cape Alava
Ozette
OZETTE ISLAND
113
112
112
Yellow Banks
Ozette Lake
101
Storm King Information Station
Lake Crescent
Sol Duc River
SOL DUC VALLEY
Elwha
Lake Aldw
OLYMPIC NATIONAL FOREST
HAPPY LAKE RIDGE
Hurrica Hill
Sol Duc Hot Springs Resort
Lake Mills
Cape Johnson
QUILEUTE INDIAN RESERVATION
29
110
Hole-in-the-Wall
LA PUSH
CAKE ROCK
FORKS
Rialto Beach
110
SEVEN LAKES BASIN
Mount Fitzhenry
JAMES ISLAND
First Beach
Quillayute River
Bogachiel River
BAILEY RANGE
Second Beach
TEAHWHIT HEAD
Hoh River
World's largest subalpine fir
Scotts Bluff
Hoh Rain Forest Visitor Center
Third Beach
Taylor Point
101
Hoh River
MOUNT OLYMPUS
Blue Glacier
White Glacier
Hoh Glacier
OLYMPIC COAST NATIONAL MARINE SANCTUARY
HOH HEAD
HOH INDIAN RESERVATION
101
Queets River
OLYMPIC NATIONAL
Ruby Beach
Alta Creek
Beach 6
DESTRUCTION ISLAND
Beach 4
Beach 3
Kalaloch Information Station
KALALOCH ROCKS
Queets
Beach 2
Beach 1
Quinault River
Queets River
OLYMPIC NATIONAL FOREST
PACIFIC OCEAN
QUINAULT INDIAN RESERVATION
101
Quinault Lake

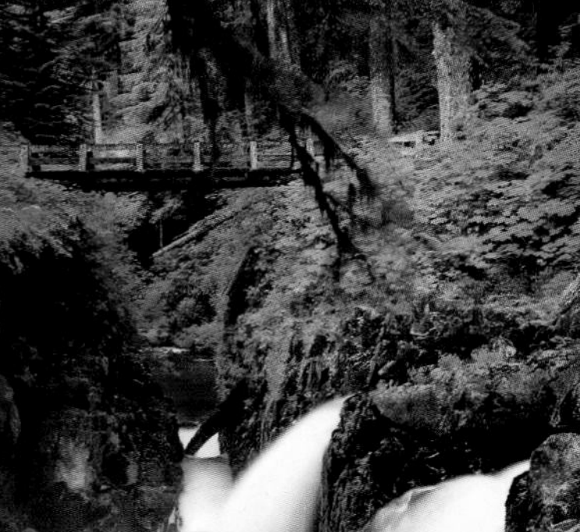

Sol Duc Falls

Thundering in the heart of one of Olympic's major northwest slope old growth forests, Sol Duc Falls crashes into a narrow, rock-lined chasm overhung with ferns and shrubs.

Fog-Shrouded Coast

Pacific rollers sweep onto Rialto Beach. Most of Olympic's coastline looks the same today as it did when various bands of Native Americans built their first villages here.

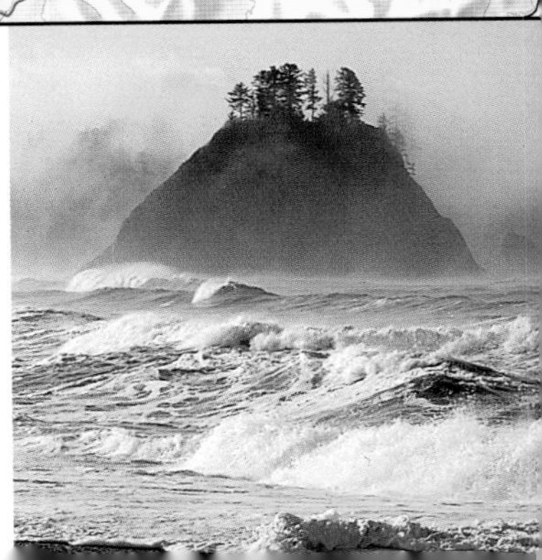

Deadly Beauty

An amanita mushroom, also known as fly agaric, bursts from a layer of leaf litter, right. Below: Monkey flowers in Seven Lakes Basin.

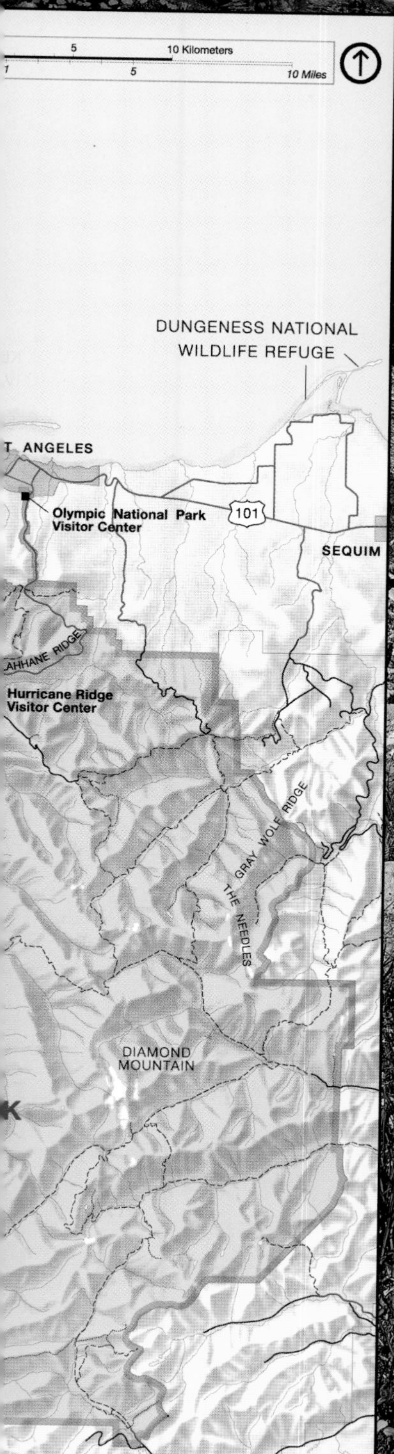

OLYMPIC NATIONAL PARK

History Note: In December 1889, an expedition sponsored by the Seattle Press set off on the first recorded trek across the rugged Olympic Range. It took six grueling months of hiking to succeed in crossing from Port Angeles to Aberdeen, a straight-line distance of just 80 miles.

Flora: Four distinct forest types, including temperate rain forest, lowland, montane, and subalpine; about 1,200 plants overall, including wildflowers such as Sitka columbine, western pasqueflower, and Flett's violet.

Fauna: Roosevelt elk, black-tailed deer, river otters, sea lions, seals, whales, porpoises, frogs, salamanders, lizards, and snakes; and several animals found nowhere else, including the Olympic marmot, Olympic snow mole, and Crescenti trout.

Visitor Tip: While in the area, don't pass up the chance to learn about the rich cultural life of the Makah Indians, who have lived along the coast for thousands of years and who operate a fascinating anthropological museum at Neah Bay.

Alder Grove

Members of the birch family, alders are unique among Northwest trees in that they convert atmospheric nitrogen into soil nitrogen, thus enhancing soil fertility.

OLYMPIC'S MULTIPLE ECOSYSTEMS

Rising abruptly from the Pacific Ocean and topping out at nearly 8,000 feet, the Olympic Peninsula takes in a stunningly diverse range of ecosystems.

Start at the edge of the ocean, where the park takes in 65 miles of wilderness coast. Here, whales cruise offshore, seals bob in the surf, and giant sea stacks provide nesting sites for seabirds and shorebirds.

In the intertidal zone, sea level fluctuates at least 6 feet daily, alternately exposing and submerging tidepools and rock outcroppings crammed with life forms. As many as four thousand organisms may live within a single square foot of any given tidepool, including sea stars, barnacles, urchins, snails, crabs, and limpets.

Along the west slopes of the mountains, abundant rainfall supports four distinct types of forest. At low elevations along the coast and in western-facing valleys, you'll find Olympic's famous temperate rain forests, where Sitka spruce, western red cedar, Douglas fir, and other trees rise from a spongy floor of moss and ferns.

Farther inland and a bit higher, you'll find lowland forests of grand fir and western hemlock. Red cedar grows here, too, but gradually thins and disappears as elevation increases and the trees make a subtle shift to the montane forest, marked by the presence of silver fir.

In higher climes, average temperatures drop, more snow falls, and growing seasons shorten. In the subalpine zone, tree species shift to subalpine fir, mountain hemlock, and Alaska cedar. In its upper reaches, the trees begin to give

Verdant Land
A thick cloak of moss and lichen drapes the limbs and trunks of a big-leaf maple.

out, and meadows of wildflowers open up.

As conditions become more challenging, trees shrink away entirely and you'll find yourself in the heady realm of the alpine zone, where tiny gardens of wildflowers blossom among rocks, crevices, and patches of gravel. Here, too, large glaciers grind away among bare rock cliffs and pinnacles, and, in summer, add a generous volume of meltwater to the rain that sustains the lower forests.

The "AKA" Lily
Known by many names, including glacier lily, Erythronium grandiflorum *is one of the park's early bloomers.*

Mainland Remnants
Recently part of the mainland, sea stacks, left, *jut from a wave-cut platform along the Olympic coast.* Following spread: *The snow-covered peaks of the Olympic Range rise above a valley filled with clouds.*

PETRIFIED FOREST

NATIONAL PARK IN ARIZONA

FROZEN REMNANTS

In the geographic region known as the Painted Desert, at the southern edge of the Colorado Plateau, thousands of petrified logs have been exposed by erosion. The trees, reptiles, dinosaurs, and other life-forms represented in this fossil kingdom thrived during the Triassic Period, more than 200 million years ago. The trees seem to have been torn from their original sites, probably by floods, and carried long distances before coming to rest and being buried in mud and volcanic ash.

The movie version of Petrified Forest National Park would be called, not surprisingly, *Triassic Park*. The protagonists would be trees—really big trees. In this script, they live out their slow, leafy years on broad floodplains for many generations. Little dinosaurs poke around in the underbrush, hoping for a bigger role in their next film. Suddenly, a tremendous flood comes along, drags the trees around for a while, and buries them in mud. Insensitive volcanoes choose this time of deep personal disappointment to erupt, spreading thick, silica-rich ash over our heroes. The muddy water dissolves the silica and wicks it deep into the cellular structure of each tree.

This part of the movie goes by pretty fast, because not even Steven Spielberg knows exactly how petrification works. As we fast-forward through millions of years, the soggy logs magically turn into brilliantly colored stone. In some, quartz blossoms, adding even more color. More movie millennia zoom by until erosion again exposes these natural masterworks. They litter the desert with a kind of battlefield glory. A vivid desert sunset glints from a thousand random facets. Geology upstages Tiffany's.

So what if the plot is kind of sluggish, and the character development is weak? Here in the last act, we even have genuine villains—the people who, after all these years of knowing better, steal a ton of this precious beauty from Petrified Forest National Park every year. So maybe it's a blockbuster after all. At the very least, you have to admit that the special effects are fabulous.

Painted Desert
Shadows lengthen on the Painted Desert near Kachina Point. The desert's harsh climate lays the land open to erosion.

Old Wood
The park contains one of the greatest known concentrations of petrified trees, which continue to emerge from the bedrock, right. Above: Coyotes roam the park.

Carved by Water

From the air, the region's landscape bears the clear imprint of water erosion, right. Below: Blocks of petrified wood 225 million years old lie scattered in a badlands gully.

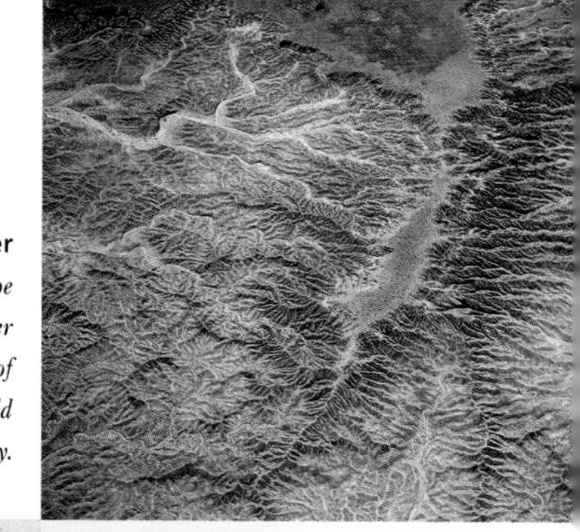

PETRIFIED FOREST NATIONAL PARK

History Note: In the late nineteenth century, an enterprising company built a stamp mill near today's park in order to crush the petrified logs for use as abrasives. This, along with years of wholesale plundering by collectors, led to the establishment of the park.

Flora: Mainly plants of the high desert shortgrass prairie, such as yucca, cactus, various shrubs and grasses; narrow riparian corridors shaded by cottonwood trees; and scrubby woodlands along the rim of the Painted Desert.

Fauna: Pronghorn, coyotes, rabbits, rodents, snakes, and lizards.

Visitor Tip: Take the short stroll to Agate House, a partially restored pueblo built from petrified wood. Other cultural sites include Puerco Pueblo, a one-hundred-room pueblo built before 1400, and the petroglyphs of Newspaper Rock.

Climate Change

A cholla cactus, reflecting the region's semiarid climate of today, bristles against a cross section of a petrified conifer tree, which grew here when the region was dominated by a tropical climate.

Extreme Desert

Sunlight glows on the profoundly eroded landscape of the Painted Desert, where temperatures range 71 degrees between maximum highs and lows.

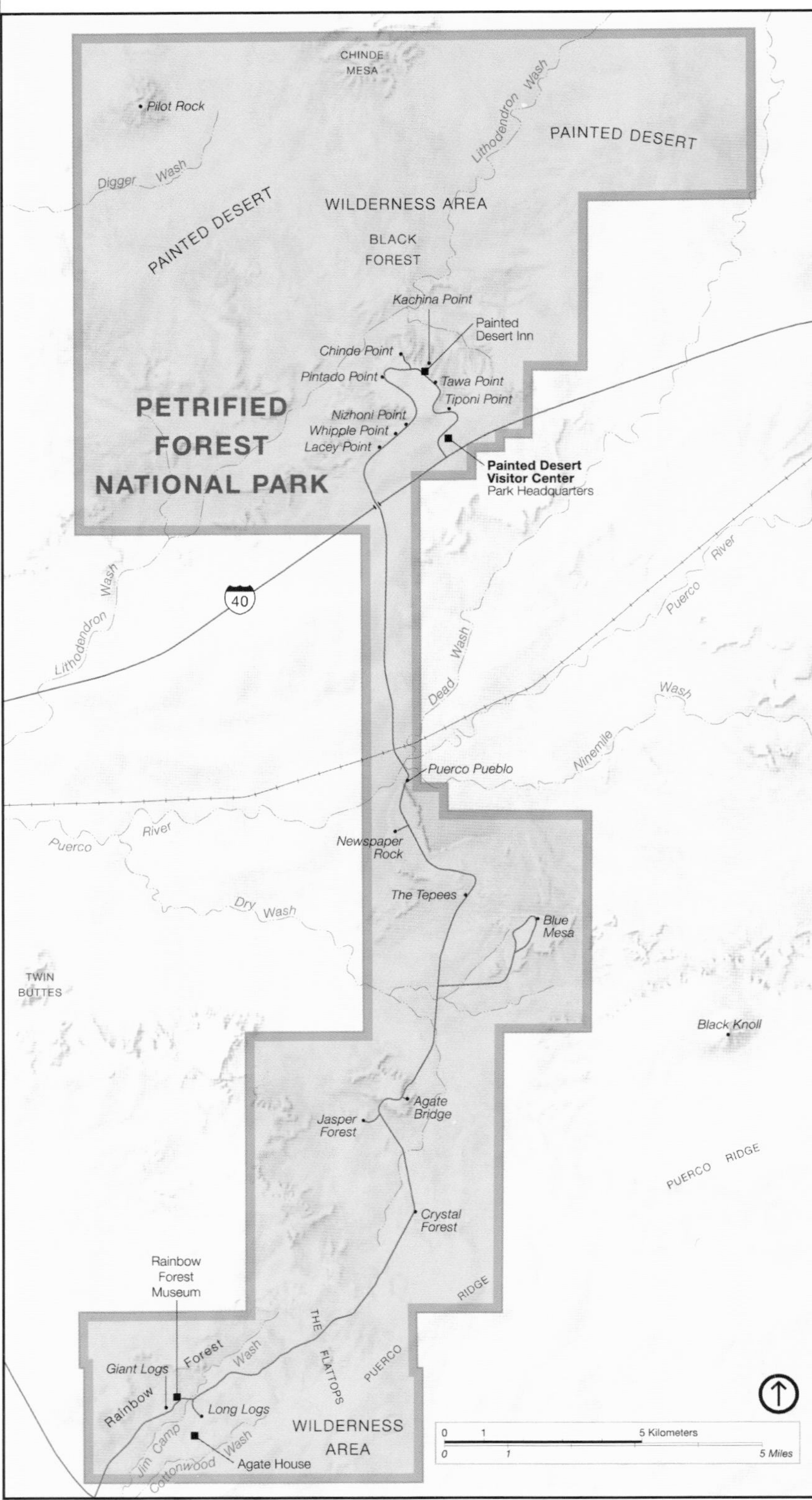

Vivid Fossil

A section of petrified log in the park's Jasper Forest retains its original texture, right down to the knot. The park's fossil trees derive from three now extinct species.

Rumpled Land

Rumpled, bulbous, and colorful, the badlands of the Painted Desert are shaped by the presence of bentonite clay, which swells when wet, then slumps.

REDWOOD NATIONAL PARK

History Note: During the century prior to 1965, loggers cleared 85 percent of the original 2 million acres of coastal redwood forest. Today, the park protects less than half of what is left.

Flora: The park contains the three tallest trees in the world; old growth redwood groves in a variety of microclimates; open prairie meadows; a buffer zone along the coast occupied by hardy beach, dune, and scrub plant communities; and mixed evergreen communities farther inland.

Fauna: Roosevelt elk, black-tailed deer, black bears; whales, seals, and porpoises; slugs and snails; tidepool creatures, including sea anemones, tiny crabs, and sea stars; and more than 370 species of birds.

Visitor Tip: If you want to visit the spectacular Tall Trees Grove, plan ahead and get there early. The park issues just fifty permits (free) each day to use the grove's access road.

Verdant Sheaths

Moss and lichen sheathe every available inch of redwood branches, *above. Right:* ***Park tree tower above an understory of ferns and bushes. Redwoods have thrived along the northern California coast for 20 million years,*** *below.*

REDWOOD

NATIONAL PARK IN CALIFORNIA

CATHEDRAL OF TREES

The geological origins of Redwood National Park belie the cathedral tranquility of the forest groves and the seeming permanence of the cliff-lined beaches. The land under this verdant coastline is a complex mixture of sedimentary and volcanic materials with a restless, earthquake-prone foundation. The redwoods position themselves to make the most of coastal streams, and reach extraordinary heights to comb additional moisture from the sea winds and seasonal fogs.

The Redwoods have paid a perilous price for the specialization that permitted them to grow so tall. They are native to only a very narrow band of habitat, along a few hundred miles of Pacific Coast. Within that band, much of which is protected by Redwoods National Park, they are restricted on both sides.

On the Pacific Ocean side, redwoods are held back from the water's edge by their vulnerability to salt, which is carried on shore by spray and wind. They must depend upon other plants that inhabit the dunes and bordering scrub communities to absorb that shock.

Inland, they are likewise confined. It is said that they will live no farther from the sea than the coastal fog reaches—only about 30 miles. Most rain here falls in the winter and spring, so the dense fogs of summer seem essential to keep the forest saturated. The biggest trees of all make eloquent statements of the redwood's preference for this sopping atmosphere—only along streams and in the most protected, well-watered lowlands do they pass 300 feet in height.

It is hard to be disappointed by the "smaller ones," though, if only because from the ground it is often hard to tell the gigantic from the merely huge. Redwoods are such an imposing presence, and such a stately, even regal, expression of nature's ambitions, that at any age and height you are awed. You drive through their groves as though you are driving through some dim and sheer-walled canyon. You stand among these magnificent trees as in some gargantuan shrine where it would be rude to speak above a whisper.

Meadow and Beach
Fog drifts over a prairie meadow bursting with lupine, left. Above: A rhododendron blooms.

Coastal Inhabitant
A pelican takes wing.

Nursery Logs

When one of the great trees falls in Redwood National Park, it rots and often acts as a nursery for all manner of understory plants, including tree seedlings.

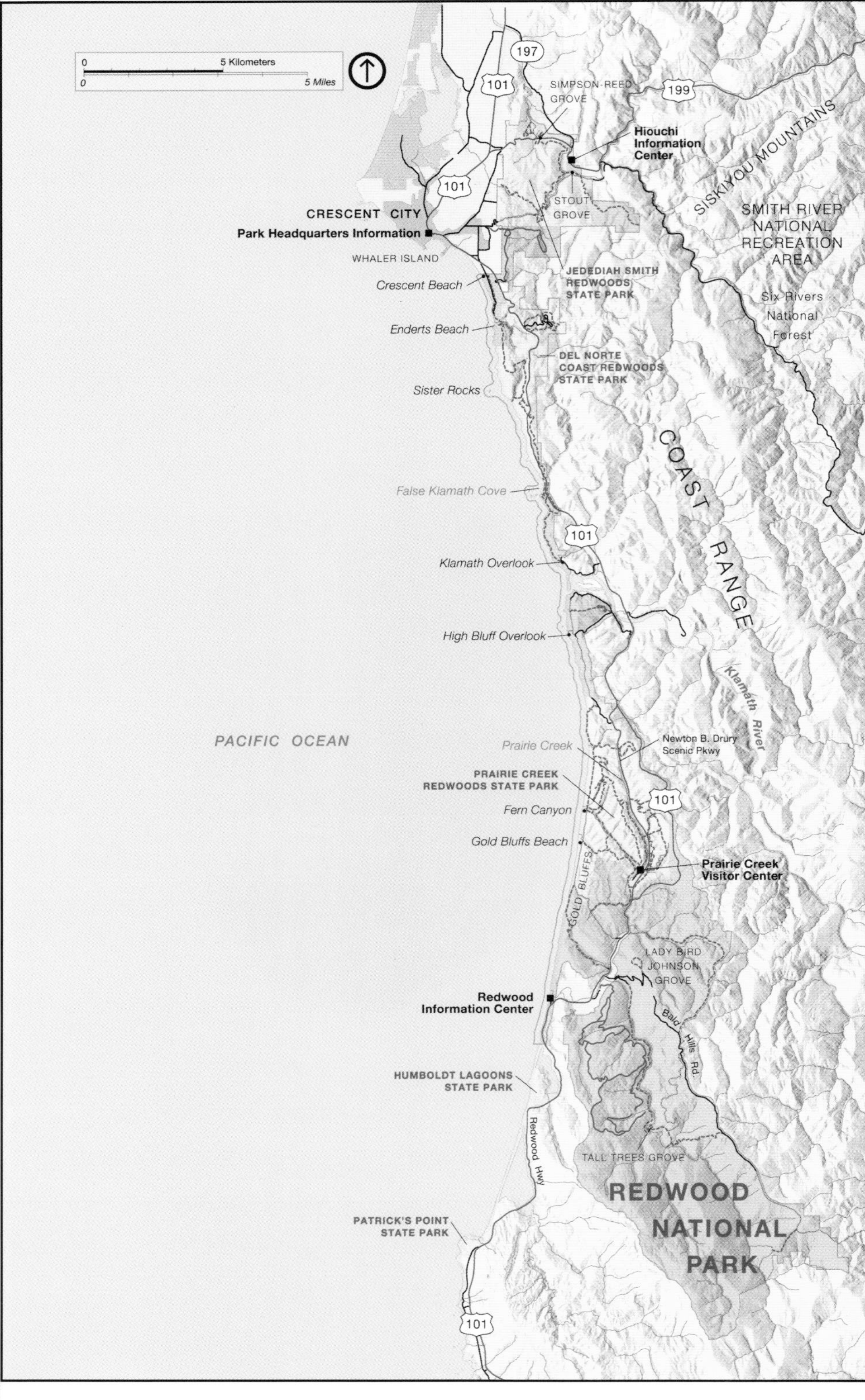

Pristine Coast

Driftwood rests along a beach in Redwood National Park. The park preserves 37 miles of coastal land in northern California.

Tangled Understory

A footbridge crosses a stream deep in the heart of a redwood forest, where mosses, ferns, and azaleas make up the tangled understory.

SAGUARO

NATIONAL PARK IN ARIZONA

WESTERN ARCHETYPE

The two units of Saguaro National Park are separated by a flat lowland occupied by the city of Tucson. The Tucson Mountains, in Saguaro West, are composed of uptilted ancient sedimentary rocks mixed with a profusion of ancient igneous, metamorphic, and more recent volcanic materials. The Rincon Mountains, in Saguaro East, are the result of equally complicated processes, in which metamorphic rocks "domed" up under younger sedimentary rocks.

You have almost certainly seen the very landscape that dominates Saguaro National Park dozens if not hundreds of times. For more than sixty years, the Tucson area's ruggedly picturesque mountains have appeared in hundreds of old-West movies and television shows. These movies—to say nothing of legions of cartoons and comic strips—sold us the saguaro as the quintessential cactus. Other species of cactus are much more common and widespread, but ask any child to draw you a cactus and you'll see that it looks like the national park namesake.

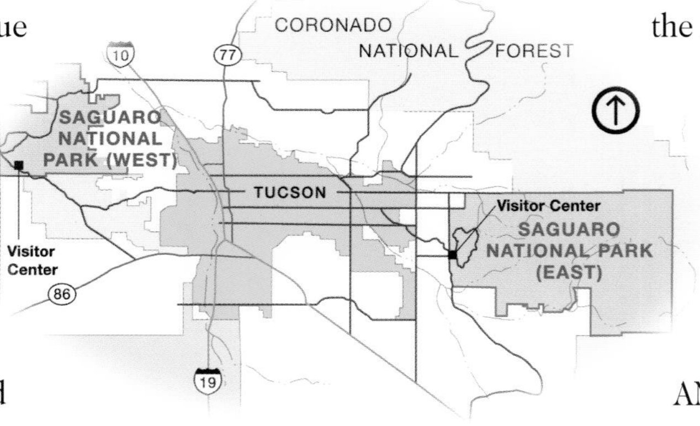

What it looks like, of course, is us. The great tree folklorist Donald Culross Peattie said the upturned "arms" of saguaros give them an "exclamatory expression, as if they were shouting 'hosannah' and testifying to the miracle of their existence upon the desert." Ethnobotanist Gary Paul Nabhan heard an old Tohono O'Odham (formerly known as Papago) woman react in alarm when asked if the fruit of the saguaros could be harvested by throwing rocks at them. "The saguaros—they are Indians too. You don't EVER throw ANYTHING at them."

Native American uses of the saguaro have been so diverse that it is tempting to see the cactus as a big green buffalo—provider of food, shelter, and spiritual support in one tall package. And if you get a close look at a few saguaro, you'll see that they serve a variety of wild animals, mostly birds, with comfortable, well-insulated high-rise dwellings. Only a few species of birds actually drill holes in them, but a crowd of other birds and insects are eager to move in once the holes are made.

Rincon Mountains
The Rincon Mountains support scrub oak woodlands and forests of pine and fir similar to those found in more northerly climes.

Desert Tortoise
Desert tortoises sit out the heat of the day by confining most of their activities to the early morning and evening hours.

SAGUARO NATIONAL PARK

History Note: Ancient peoples living in Box Canyon bored conical holes into solid rock and used the holes as mortars to pulverize mesquite pods.

Flora: Many types of cactus, including hedgehog, fishhook, teddy bear cholla, and prickly pear; creosote bushes and mesquite trees, ocotillo, and paloverde.

Fauna: Javelinas, jackrabbits, cactus mice, kangaroo rats, and other small mammals; snakes, lizards, desert tortoises, and Gila monsters; two hundred birds, including Gila woodpeckers and gilded flickers, elf owls, Harris hawks, kestrels, cactus wrens, and Lucy's warblers.

Visitor Tip: Don't miss the extraordinary Arizona-Sonora Desert Museum, an expansive showcase of Sonoran plants and animals just south of the park's western unit.

Classic Cactus

The saguaro, above, and topped by a ringtail, below, is the largest cactus in the United States. Each saguaro blossom, left, opens after sunset and withers away by the following afternoon. Following spread: A petroglyph at Signal Hill.

Small Things, Big Things
Raccoons, left, rummage for food in the scrubby chapparal of the parks' foothills. Below: Sequoia trees are the world's largest living things.

SEQUOIA

AND KINGS CANYON

NATIONAL PARKS IN CALIFORNIA

SIERRA TREASURES

Sequoia and Kings Canyon National Parks present a geological and ecological spectacle. The massive Sierra uplift has tilted a block of the Earth's crust to the west; the mountains drop off steeply on their east side, but slope more easily to the west. The parks are crisscrossed with steep canyons and include many peaks more than 12,000 feet high. Upon this extreme range of topography many ecological communities have settled, perhaps most notable among them the forests of giant sequoia.

To those few visionaries and conservationists who fought so hard to create the first American national parks, it must have all seemed quite simple. Draw the lines on a map, declare it protected, and relax—it's safe forever. But the very first national parks soon gave them pause, and made them wonder what they'd gotten into. Sequoia, established in 1890, was second after Yellowstone. In its long and stormy life, this park has been a classroom in conservation. When you stand in the sequoia groves of Sequoia and Kings Canyon, you are in the presence of some of the most influential teachers in that classroom.

Perhaps you'll be lucky enough to visit on a day that fires are being set. Nothing provides a quicker awakening to how things have changed in the management of wild country than to see park service fire crews actually starting fires in the forest. It's been a long road from 1890. The founders would have been as shocked as if someone had set fire to their churches. It took the first half of this century for professional foresters and park managers to realize just how essential fire was in a wild setting. For thousands of years, fires, caused by lightning or set by Native Americans, recycled nutrients, created a mosaic of different-aged tree stands, and maintained wildlife habitats. In some tree species, fire was needed to release seeds from the cones. In some types of forests, occasional small fires kept natural "fuel" levels low.

But think of it—after so many years of thinking of fire as completely evil, who was going to stand up and say that we should actually let fires go, or even start them ourselves? A few people, but not many.

Giant Domes

Giant domes of granite protrude from canyon walls, left. Above: The confluence of the middle and south forks of the Kings River.

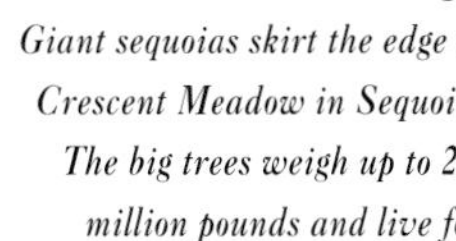

Meadow's Edge

Giant sequoias skirt the edge of Crescent Meadow in Sequoia. The big trees weigh up to 2.7 million pounds and live for more than three thousand years.

Luckily, the national parks, especially Sequoia and Kings Canyon, were a perfect laboratory for just such an experiment. The sequoias, able to withstand the heat of small fires, provided one opportunity. In the early 1960s, scientific studies in the groves confirmed that carefully set fires on the forest floor would substantially reduce the risk of much bigger fires that might roar up into the canopy of the big trees by getting rid of much of the fuel a large fire would need.

Granite Cascade
A narrow cascade slips behind a cedar trunk and streams over one of the parks' many slopes of rounded granite.

This type of fire management is still being tested, and is often controversial. But as you wander through the groves of Sequoia and Kings Canyon national parks you will notice the occasional black scar under an old sequoia's arching base. Think of the tree as a teacher, and the fire as a test—of our growing wisdom in how wild nature works, and of our willingness to give these trees the conditions they need to survive.

High Country
A full moon, right, rises over Mount Whitney, elevation 14,495 feet, and highest point in the contiguous United States. Left: A pika.

Stout Fellows

Rivaled by the coast redwood for height, giant sequoias beat out the redwoods for overall bulk thanks to their much thicker trunks.

SEQUOIA AND KINGS CANYON NATIONAL PARKS

History Note: In 1872, the great rambler and conservationist John Muir began exploring and writing about the Kings Canyon and Sequoia region. As he lobbied for the protection of the Sierras, Muir conceived and articulated many of the fundamental precepts of the wilderness preservation movement.

Flora: Giant sequoias, in the company of Jeffrey and sugar pines, white firs, and incense cedars; foothills chapparal; dry alpine in the highest reaches of the mountains.

Fauna: Mule deer, mountain lions, black bears, pine martens, wolverines, and squirrels; and many birds.

Visitor Tip: Visit the world's largest tree, the General Sherman tree, which stands just east of the Generals Highway 2 miles south of Lodgepole. A short walk leads to the great sequoia, 275 feet high, 36.5 feet thick at the base, and containing 52,500 cubic feet of wood in the trunk alone.

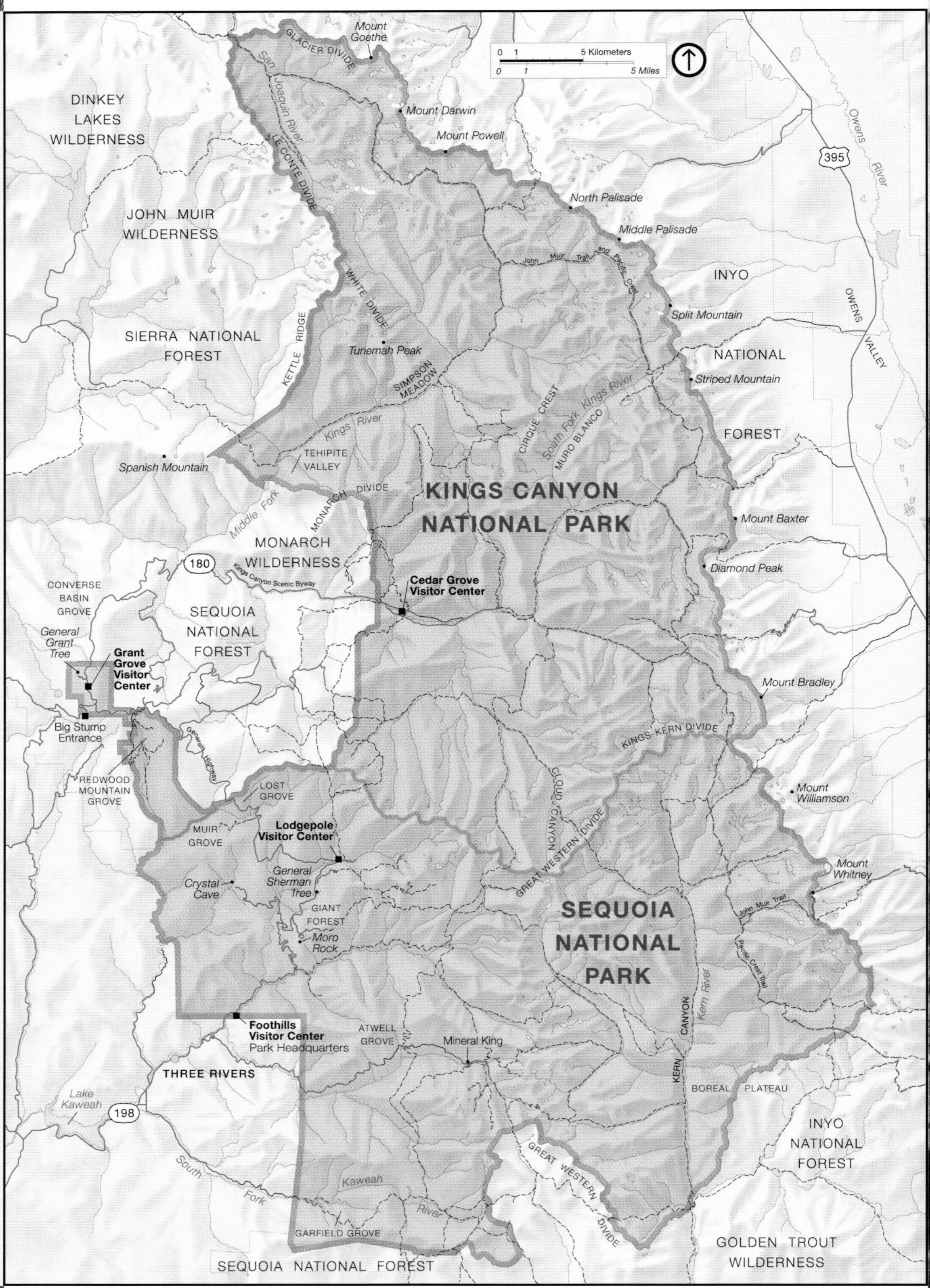

Sierra Crest

The crest of the Sierra Nevada forms the eastern border of the parks, cutting along at elevations of roughly 11,000 to 14,500 feet.

Pounding Force

Grizzly Falls in Kings Canyon National Park is just off the Kings Canyon Scenic Byway, an easy summertime drive.

THE GIANT SEQUOIAS

Giant sequoias, the world's largest living things when measured by volume, grow in scattered groves along the well-watered western slopes of the Sierra Nevada and nowhere else. Some reach the heights of thirty-story buildings, but it is the tree's stupendous trunk diameter that dwarfs all rivals for overall size. The General Sherman Tree, for example, rises just 275 feet, which is nearly one hundred feet lower than the tallest redwood. But the General Sherman weighs nearly three times as much thanks to its thick trunk, which boasts a base diameter of 36.5 feet.

These biggest of trees are also among the longest lived. The oldest sequoia on record sprouted sometime during the Trojan War, 3,200 years ago, and other living specimens have stood for well over 2,000 years.

Sequoias grow in the company of other evergreen, their deeply furrowed, cinnamon brown trunks rising above Jeffrey and sugar pines, white firs, and incense cedars.

Armored with fire-resistant bark as much as two feet thick, they easily tolerate small, frequent wildfires. Indeed, fire plays a crucial role in their reproduction by clearing and enriching soils, scattering seeds, and creating clearings where seedlings can gain a foothold. Each year, mature trees produce two thousand cones that dangle from the tree for as long as twenty years, waiting for fire to dry them, break them open, and disperse their seeds. The sequoias' thick bark also protects them from insect infestation.

Since logging of sequoias has largely stopped and since they don't seem to die from old age, either, the most common cause of death is from toppling. The big trees simply get too top heavy for their root systems to support, and they fall over, usually pushed by heavy winds.

Bit Part
A Douglas squirrel, also called a chickaree, hefts a cone.

Oak Woodland
A carpet of common madia blossoms on a grassy hillside shaded by blue oak trees, below. Left: Visitors view an exhibit at Grant Grove. Following spread: A bend in Kings Canyon Scenic Byway overlooks a stretch of the South Fork Kings River.

Glossary

Alluvial fan: A fan-shaped body of earth that has accumulated where a stream moved from a steep gradient to a flatter grade.

Angle of repose: The maximum angle at which loose earth will come to rest when added to a pile of similar material.

Arête: A narrow, saw-toothed mountain ridge separating adjacent glacially carved valleys.

Basaltic rock: A hard, black volcanic rock derived from the solidification of fluid lava.

Bar: A raised area (fractions to several feet high) composed of sand or gravel deposited on the bed of a lake, stream, or sea.

Barrier reef: A relatively continuous body of coral separated from an adjacent mainland by a lagoon.

Braided stream: A stream composed of a maze of interconnected channels around sandbars or islands.

Calcite: A mineral composed of calcium carbonate ($CaCO_3$) that is the main mineralogical component of limestone.

Caldera: A volcanic depression that is many times larger than a crater. Calderas are created when the summit of a volcano is destroyed during an eruption.

Calving: The breaking away of ice from a glacier into lakes or oceans, creating icebergs.

Cave: A natural opening extending underground that is large enough for a person to enter.

Cinder cone: A conical volcano formed by the accumulation of pyroclastic materials erupted out of a central vent area.

Cirque: A steep-walled, half-bowl-shaped depression occurring at the head of a glacial valley. A cirque is the place of origin for mountain glaciers.

Climate: The characteristic temperature and precipitation for a given region.

Column: A pillar formed in a cave when a downward-growing stalactite and an upward-growing stalagmite meet.

Continental drift: The slow movement of continents produced by seafloor spreading across the surface of the Earth.

Convection currents: Currents in the air or water or within the interior of the Earth caused by a difference in temperature.

Crater: A steep-walled depression, usually at the summit of a volcano. The vent, or the opening through which lava or pyroclastic material is erupted, may or may not coincide with the crater.

Crevasse: A crack in a glacier.

Delta: A body of sediment deposited by a stream where it flows into a body of water such as a lake or an ocean.

Dripstone: Calcium carbonate deposited from a solution as water enters a cave. Dripstone forms stalactites and stalagmites.

Ecosystem: A community of animals, plants, and bacteria and their interrelated physical and chemical environment.

Erratic: A stone or boulder moved by a glacier from its place of origin to an area of different bedrock composition.

Erosion: The gradual wearing away and transportation of materials by water, wind, or ice.

Estuary: The area where a river meets a sea.

Fault: A surface or set of surfaces across which there has been displacement of one side relative to another.

Fjord: A glaciated valley that has been flooded by the sea.

Flowstone: Deposits formed by dripping and flowing water on the walls and floors of caves.

Fumarole: A hole in a volcanic region from which highly heated gas and vapors escape.

Geology: The study of physical nature and history of the Earth.

Geothermal: Of or relating to the Earth's internal heat.

Geyser: A hot spring that intermittently erupts water and steam.

Glacial till: A heterogeneous mix of materials transported and deposited by a glacier.

Glacier: A body of ice that moves due to its own weight.

Hanging valley: A tributary valley cut by a glacier whose mouth is elevated high above the floor of its main valley, which was also cut by a glacier.

Hoodoo: A column or pillar of rock produced by differential weathering.

Hot spot: A region of high heat flow on the Earth's surface, thought to lie above a column of rising hot mantle material.

Ice cap: A dome-shaped cover of ice over a mountain summit.

Ice field: An extensive area of connected glaciers or pack ice.

Igneous rock: Rock that is the result of the crystallization of a liquid composed of silicate material.

Lava: A liquid composed of silicate material that flows out onto the Earth's surface.

Lava dome: A bulbous mass inside a volcano crater formed by highly viscous lava squeezed out of a vent.

Levee: A bank of sand and silt along a stream built over time by deposition during floods.

Lithosphere: The rigid outer shell of the Earth, including the crust and the outermost mantle.

Longshore drift: The movement of sand parallel to the shoreline caused by waves that carry sand at an angle up the shore face. When water has reached its most shoreward position, it and the sand that it carries are pulled straight back out to sea, resulting in a net longshore displacement.

Magma: The molten rock that comprises the inner layer of the Earth.

Mantle: The thick shell of dense, rocky matter that surrounds the magma core.

Moraine: An accumulation of earth carried and ultimately deposited by glaciers. Medial moraines are formed when two glaciers coalesce.

Mudpot: A bubbling mix of clay and silica that has been dissolved by sulfuric acid. Mudpots are found in thermal areas such as Yellowstone National Park.

Nunatak: A hill or mountain completely surrounded by glacial ice.

Orogeny: The process of mountain building.

Piedmont glacier: A glacier that spreads out at the foot of a mountain, formed by the coalescence of two or more valley glaciers.

Pleistocene: The epoch that extended from about 1.8 million years ago to 10,000 years ago, when most recent glaciers occurred.

Precambrian: A term that refers to all geological time from the formation of the Earth to the beginning of the Cambrian period 545 million years ago.

Rain shadow desert: A desert formed by the blocking of moisture-bearing winds by mountain barriers.

Reef: A ridge- or mound-like structure, resistant to waves, that is built by the remains of calcareous organisms.

Sediment: (1) Pieces of pre-existing rocks and minerals. (2) Particles such as shells that are secreted by organisms. (3) Minerals precipitated from solutions such as alkaline lakes in desert regions.

Sedimentary rock: Consolidated sediment such as limestone or sandstone.

Shield volcano: A broad, relatively low relief volcano built by very fluid lava flows that commonly crystallize to form basalt.

Sinkhole: A depression in the ground caused by the collapse of underlying rock into a cave below.

Speleothem: A deposit formed in a cave when minerals precipitate from dripping or thin films of water.

Stalactite: A downward-growing speleothem created by the precipitation of calcite from downward-dripping water in a cave.

Stalagmite: A mounded speleothem that grows up from a cave floor, created by the precipitation of calcite from water dripping from the ceiling above.

Stratovolcano: A volcano that is composed of alternating layers of different kinds of lava and pyroclastic material. Stratovolcanos are sometimes referred to as composite volcanoes.

Striations: The scratches or small lines on a rock surface caused by a geological agent, such as a glacier.

Tectonics: The theory that the Earth's lithosphere is broken into mobile plates that are in slow, constant motion.

Travertine: A general term for calcite deposited in layers by hot or cold spring waters.

Tundra: A treeless area, usually in the northern hemisphere or at high altitudes, dominated by a long, bitterly cold winter.

U-shaped valley: The steep-walled, broad-floored valley that is indicative of mountain glaciation.

Volcano: A vent or opening in the surface of the Earth through which magma erupts, or the landform created by such eruptions.

Wetland: A lowland area, such as a marsh or swamp, that is saturated with water.

Contacting the Parks

Acadia National Park
PO Box 177
Bar Harbor, ME 04609-0177
(207) 288-3338
www.nps.gov/acad

Arches National Park
PO Box 907
Moab, UT 84532-0907
(435) 719-2299
www.nps.gov/arch

Badlands National Park
25216 Ben Reifer Rd.
PO Box 6
Interior, SD 57750-0006
(605) 433-5361
www.nps.gov/badl

Big Bend National Park
PO Box 129
Big Bend National Park, TX 79834-0129
(432) 477-2251
www.nps.gov/bibe

Biscayne National Park
9700 SW 328 St.
Homestead, FL 33033-5634
(305) 230-7275
www.nps.gov/bisc

Black Canyon of the Gunnison National Park
102 Elk Creek
Gunnison, CO 81230-9304
(970) 641-2337x205
www.nps.gov/blca

Bryce Canyon National Park
PO Box 170001
Bryce Canyon, UT 84717-0001
(435) 834-5322
www.nps.gov/brca

Canyonlands National Park
2282 South West Resource Blvd.
Moab, UT 84532
(435) 719-2313
www.nps.gov/cany

Capitol Reef National Park
HC 70 Box 15
Torrey, UT 84775-9602
(435) 425-3791
www.nps.gov/care

Carlsbad Caverns National Park
3225 National Parks Hwy.
Carlsbad, NM 88220-5354
(505) 785-2232
www.nps.gov/cave

Channel Islands National Park
1901 Spinnaker Dr.
Ventura, CA 93001-4354
(805) 658-5730
www.nps.gov/chis

Crater Lake National Park
PO Box 7
Crater Lake, OR 97604-0007
(541) 594-3100
www.nps.gov/crla

Cuyahoga Valley National Park
15610 Vaughn Rd.
Brecksville, OH 44141-3018
(216) 524-1497
www.nps.gov/cuva

Death Valley National Park
PO Box 579
Death Valley, CA 92328-0570
(760) 786-3200
www.nps.gov/deva

Denali National Park and Preserve
PO Box 9
Denali Park, AK 99755-0009
(907) 683-2294
www.nps.gov/dena

Dry Tortugas National Park
PO Box 6208
Key West, FL 33041
(305) 242-7700
www.nps.gov/drto

Everglades National Park
40001 State Road 9336
Holmstead, FL 33034
(305) 242-7700
www.nps.gov/ever

Gates of the Arctic National Park and Preserve
PO Box 26030
Bettles, AK 99726
(907) 692-5494
www.nps.gov/gaar

Glacier National Park
PO Box 128
West Glacier, MT 59936
(406) 888-7800
www.nps.gov/glac

Glacier Bay National Park and Preserve
PO Box 140
Gustavus, AK 99826-0140
(907) 697-2230
www.nps.gov/glba

Grand Canyon National Park
PO Box 129
Grand Canyon, AZ 86023-0129
(928) 638-7888
www.nps.gov/grca

Grand Teton National Park
PO Drawer 170
Moose, WY 83012-0170
(307) 739-3300
www.nps.gov/grte

Great Basin National Park
Baker, NV 89311
(775) 234-7331
www.nps.gov/grba

Great Smoky Mountains National Park
107 Park Headquarters Rd.
Gatlinburg, TN 37738
(865) 436-1200
www.nps.gov/grsm

Guadalupe Mountains National Park
HC 60, Box 400
Salt Flat, TX 79847-9400
(915) 828-3251
www.nps.gov/gumo

Haleakala National Park
PO Box 369
Makawao, Maui, HI 96768
(808) 572-4400
www.nps.gov/hale

Hawaii Volcanoes National Park
PO Box 52
Hawaii National Park, HI 96718-0052
(808) 985-6000
www.nps.gov/havo

Hot Springs National Park
PO Box 1860
Hot Springs, AR 71902-1860
(501) 624-2701
www.nps.gov/hosp

Isle Royale National Park
800 E. Lakeshore Dr.
Houghton, MI 49931-1895
(906) 482-0984
www.nps.gov/isro

Joshua Tree National Park
74485 National Park Dr.
Twentynine Palms, CA 92277-3597
(760) 367-5500
www.nps.gov/jotr

Katmai National Park and Preserve
PO Box 7 #1 King Salmon Mall
King Salmon, AK 99613
(907) 246-3305
www.nps.gov/katm

Kenai Fjords National Park
PO Box 1727
Seward, AK 99664-1727
(907) 224-2132
www.nps.gov/kefj

Kobuk Valley National Park
PO Box 1029
Kotzebue, AK 99752
(907) 442-3890
www.nps.gov/kova

Lake Clark National Park and Preserve
1 Park Place
Port Alsworth, AK 99653
(907) 271-3751
www.nps.gov/lacl

Lassen Volcanic National Park
PO Box 100
Mineral, CA 96063-0100
(530) 595-4444
www.nps.gov/lavo

Mammoth Cave National Park
PO Box 7
Mammoth Cave, KY 42259-0007
(270) 758-2180
www.nps.gov/maca

Mesa Verde National Park
PO Box 8
Mesa Verde, CO 81330
(970) 529-4465
www.nps.gov/meve

Mount Rainier National Park
Tahoma Woods, Star Route
Ashford, WA 98304-9751
(360) 569-2211
www.nps.gov/mora

National Park of American Samoa
National Park of American Samoa
Pago Pago, AS 96799-0001
011-684-633-7082
www.nps.gov/npsa

North Cascades National Park
810 State Route 20
Sedro-Woolley, WA 98284
(360) 856-5700
www.nps.gov/noca

Olympic National Park
600 East Park Ave.
Port Angeles, WA 98362
(360) 565-3130
www.nps.gov/olym

Petrified Forest National Park
PO Box 2217
Petrified Forest National Park, AZ 86028-2217
(928) 524-6228
www.nps.gov/pefo

Redwood National Park
1111 Second St.
Crescent City, CA 95531-4198
(707) 464-6101
www.nps.gov/redw

Rocky Mountain National Park
1000 Hwy. 36
Estes Park, CO 80517-8397
(970) 586-1206
www.nps.gov/romo

Saguaro National Park
3693 South Old Spanish Trail
Tucson, AZ 85730-5601
(520) 733-5100
www.nps.gov/sagu

Sequoia and Kings Canyon National Parks
47050 Generals Hwy.
Three Rivers, CA 93271
(559) 565-3341
www.nps.gov/seki

Shenandoah National Park
3655 US Hwy. 211 E
Luray, VA 22835-9036
(540) 999-3500
www.nps.gov/shen

Theodore Roosevelt National Park
PO Box 7
Medora, ND 58645-0007
(701) 623-4466
www.nps.gov/thro

Virgin Islands National Park
1300 Cruz Bay Creek
St. John, VI 00830
(340) 776-6201
www.nps.gov/viis

Voyageurs National Park
3131 Hwy. 53 South
International Falls, MN 56649-8904
(218) 283-9821
www.nps.gov/voya

Wind Cave National Park
RR 1 Box 190
Hot Springs, SD 57747
(605) 745-4600
www.nps.gov/wica

Wrangell–St. Elias National Park and Preserve
106.8 Richardson Hwy
PO Box 439
Copper Center, AK 99573
(907) 822-5234
www.nps.gov/wrst

Yosemite National Park
PO Box 577
Yosemite National Park, CA 95389-0577
(209) 372-0200
www.nps.gov/yose

Yellowstone National Park
PO Box 168
Yellowstone National Park, WY 82910
(307) 344-7381
www.nps.gov/yell

Zion National Park
SR 9
Springdale, UT 84767-1099
(435) 772-3256
www.nps.gov/zion

INDEX

Boldface indicates pages with photos.

Photo Credits

Alan Kearney/The Viesti Collection, Inc., 206a.

Alan Majchrowicz/Peter Arnold Photography, Inc., 201f, 232–233, 235, 378a.

Bud Nielsen, 140a, 143a, 143b, 145c, 156b, 160d, 201c, 244b, 230a, 238b, 288a, 302b, 322–323, 324b, 377c.

Butch Dill/Proto, Inc., 126a.

Carl Rosenstein/The Viesti Collection, Inc., 170b.

Carol Polich, 85c, 278a, 279a.

Cathy & Gordon Illg, 20a, 86a, 116a, 118b, 132, 137b, 175b, 189c, 241, 249c, 272c, 272d, 290c, 297b, 352b.

Charles Gruche Photography, 20–21a, 30d, 38, 72a, 73a, 74–75, 76a, 78–79, 82, 140b, 142–143, 145a, 145d, 146–147, 192c, 233, 266e, 266f, 268a, 270b, 298a, 305c, 325a, 337d, 341a, 362–363, 367c, 368–369.

Chlaus Lotscher/Peter Arnold Photography, Inc., 231b, 346–347.

Claudia Dhimitri/The Viesti Collection, Inc., 137a.

Clyde H. Smith/Peter Arnold Photography, Inc., 240–241, 201h.

Craig Lovell/The Viesti Collection, Inc., 162a.

Dan Peha/The Viesti Collection, Inc., 356c, 260b.

David Jensen, 4–5, 24c, 26/31, 33b, 39a, 72–73, 33h, 74a, 101b, 114–115, 210c, 234a, 324–325b, 336a, 351c, 354–355b, 355a, 355b, 384–385, 337h, 385a, 386–387, 386a.

Debbi Adams, 107c, 131a.

Debi Field/Wheeler Photography, 388–389.

Dennis Flaherty, 31, 100b, 100d, 122–123, 130a, 155, 174–175, 178–179, 199b, 201i, 227b, 248–249, 253b, 254a, 262–263, 328a, 340–341, 336d, 351a, 352a, 356–357, 359b.

Dennis Frates, 39b, 70–71, 76–77b, 77b, 116b, 118–119c, 210b, 266b, 284, 323b, 334a, 363a, 366b, 370–371, 377a.

Douglas Peebles, 24b, 25, 32a, 32d, 44a, 44b, 45a, 48–49, 48a, 48b, 48c, 49, 51b, 51a, 52–53b, 53a.

Erwin & Peggy Bauer, 22–23, 59, 62b, 65c, 89b, 102a, 109b, 113b, 172b, 175a, 220, 221a, 222–223, 236, 239b, 384.

Fred Hirschmann Photography, 8–9, 18a, 54b, 65a, 65b, 66–67, 163a, 201e, 230–231, 269g, 312–313, , 312a, 312b, 313a, 314–315, 328c, 335, 336c, 337i, 344, 344–345, 346a, 348–349b, 348b, 349a.

Fritz Prenzel/Peter Arnold Photography, Inc., 68b.

G. Alan Nelson, 42–43a, 98c, 102–103, 101a, 102b, 106–107b, 106a, 122b, 124a, 124b, 200a, 201d, 201g, 205b, 214a, 218–219, 228–229, 229b, 236–237, 237b, 238a, 239c, 239a, 277b, 291, 316b, 317b, 328b, 330–331, 334b, 343b, 354–355a, 363c, 376b, 378b.

G. Brad Lewis, 20–21b, 52b, 53b.

Galen Rowell/Peter Arnold Photography, Inc., 16, 214–215b, 269f, 302–303.

George H. H. Huey Photography, 20b, 33c, 44–45, 46–47, 50–51, 164–165, 157b, 166–167, 260a, 261, 269a, 269d, 269i, 270–271, 274–275, 290–291, 292–293, 320–321, 324–325a, 382–383.

Inge King/Peter Arnold Photography, Inc., 198d.

J.C. Leacock, 150–151, 187a, 187b, 189a, 190–191, 193, 398–399.

Jack Dykinga, 12–13, 20c, 81c, 98a, 205a, 210–211, 200c, 212–213, 214–215a, 269c, 296, 304, 306a, 308c, 308b, 309a, 309b, 311a, 337e, 337g, 342a, 343a, 366–367a, 372c, 372–373, 373b, 374b, 377b, 380–381, 381a, 391b.

Jason & Jody Stone/Leeson Photography, 72b, 386b.

Jeff Foott/Jeff Foott Productions, 2–3, 10–11, 18b, 19c, 30b, 29–30, 33j, 35b, 60–61, 80–81, 84–85a, 85a, 90–91, 121a, 145e, 155b, 157c, 167b, 168–169b, 171a, 179b, 202b, 208–209, 215a, 225b, 225c, 226a, 250a, 252–253b, 256–257, 257a, 258–259, 267a, 279b, 286–287, 298b, 308–309b, 320a, 324a, 376a.

Jeff Garton Photography, 266c, 329, 362a, 364b, 364a, 367b.

Jim Wark/Peter Arnold Photography, 99.

Joe Englander/The Viesti Collection, Inc., 109c, 112–113b, 118–119, 194–195, 249a, 385c.

John Barger, 40a, 40b, 42–43b, 73b, 73c, 76–77a, 77a, 80b, 84–85b, 199a, 211, 213b, 217a, 217b, 227b, 267, 270a, 278b, 278–279a, 297a, 300–301, 337a, 338–339, 362b.

John Hyde/Wild Things Photography, 92a, 92c, 100a, 114, 198a, 199, 221b, 222a, 222b, 224–225a, 224–225b, 225a, 406–407.

John Kieffer/Peter Arnold Photography, Inc., 280–281, 281b, 269b.

John W. Warden/The Viesti Collection Inc., 18–19b.

Jonathan A. Meyers, 268d, 284–285, 285a, 286a, 288b, 289–289, 293a, 293b, 305a, 308a, 310–311, 359a.

Joseph Kayne/ Willard Clay Photography, 84a, 84b, 260c, 321.

Kathleen Norris Cook, 257b, 392–393.

Kathy Clay, 30c.

Keenan Ward, 33f, 62–63a, 64–65, 112–113a, 113a, 165, 168–169a, 224b, 231a, 345a, 346b, 408–409.

Kevin Schafer Photography, 58a, 61a, 62–63b, 63c, 76b, 99b, 183, 198c, 232a, 232b.

Kim Heacox/Peter Arnold Photography, Inc., 109a, 224a, 244a, 313b, 345b, 348c.

Lee Foster, 43a, 43b, 64a, 66b, 68a, 68–69, 33g, 82, 93, 110a, 126–127a, 154a, 164a, 168b, 169a, 176a, 179a, 182a, 184–185a, 206d, 228b, 254–255, 308–309a, 348a, 390–391.

Marilyn Kazmers/Peter Arnold Photography, Inc., 366–367b.

Mark Bowie, 254b.

Mary Clay/The Viesti Collection, Inc., 138–139.

Mary Liz Austin/Donnelly-Austin Photography, 19a, 42–43, 88–89, 104–105, 118a, 119b, 201a, 202–203, 203, 209b, 278–279b.

Michael Collier/Collier Photographics, 30a, 32c , 38–39, 81b, 94-95, 98d, 98b, 101d, 105a, 112a, 116–117, 118–119a, 126–127b, 130–131, 134–135, 136–137c, 154c, 169b, 192b, 267b, 269e, 269j, 277a, 282–283, 296–297, 324–325c, 326–327, 338b, 342–343a, 342b, 373a, 374a.

Michael J. Doolittle/Peter Arnold Photography, Inc., 334c.

Michele Burgess, 32b.

Nik Wheeler, 69b, 157h, 164b, 167a, 168a, 249b, 250–251, 253a, 306–30, 311b, 388b.

Patricia Caulfield/Peter Arnold Photography, Inc., 173.

Paul & Shirley Berquist, 101g, 106–107a, 115a, 130b, 139a, 186, 214b, 275b, 276, 294d, 305b, 306b, 336b, 341b, 354b, 372a, 381b.

Peter Arnold/Peter Arnold Photography, Inc., 229a.

Ray Pfortner/Peter Arnold Photography, Inc., 182c, 184a, 185a.

Robert Mackinlay/Peter Arnold Photography, Inc., 145b, 200b, 252a.

Robert Mitchell/The Viesti Collection, Inc., 55b, 56–57.

Robert Winslow/The Viesti Collection, Inc., 136–137a, 361.

Roland Seitre/Peter Arnold Photography, Inc., 19b, 156c, 162–163, 163b.

S.J. Krasemann/Peter Arnold Photography, Inc., 164c.

Scott R. Avetta/Willard Clay Photography, Inc., 136b, 139b.

Scott West/The Viesti Collection, Inc., 101c, 127a.

Stephen Frink/Waterhouse Marine Images, 6–7, 148c, 158–159, 157a, 158c, 158b, 159, 160c, 160a, 161, 182b, 185b.

Steve Kaufman/Kaufman Photography, 18c, 58b, 61b, 62b, 62a, 63a, 66a, 100c, 108–109, 108, 113c, 126b, 176c, 198b, 216–217, 230b, 238–239b, 240b, 243a, 244c, 246a, 348–349a, 367a.

Steve Kaufman/Peter Arnold Photography, Inc., 201j.

Steve Mulligan Photography, 119a, 133b, 134a, 136a, 154b, 157d, 157g, 158a, 160b, 172–173, 172a, 177, 186–187, 189b, 202a, 228a, 266d, 266a, 268b, 271, 272a, 272b, 275a, 281a, 285b, 290b, 294a, 294b, 295, 302a, 320b, 360b, 376–377, 337f.

Susan Cole Kelly, 192a, 206c, 214–215c, 240a, 242–243, 245, 248, 252–253a, 380a.

Terry Donnelly/Donnelly-Austin Photography, 18–19a, 33d 33i, 40–41, 42a, 42b, 54–55, 80a, 85b, 89a, 101e, 123a, 123c, 124–125, 127b, 132–133, 144, 206b, 207, 209a, 215b, 234c, 234d, 234b, 267c, 279c, 320c, 335, 337b, 339, 350–351, 351b, 352–353, 354a.

The Viesti Collection, 149, 156a.

Tom & Pat Leeson/Nature Wildlife Photography, 1, 15, 21b, 33e, 39c, 58–59, 64b, 69a, 74b, 77c, 81a, 106b, 123b, 127c, 134b, 141b, 148b, 170a, 172c, 176b, 180b, 187c, 200d, 210a, 213a, 226–227, 226b, 243b, 244d, 252b, 252–253c, 269h, 277c, 280a, 285c, 286b, 303b, 316–317, 317a, 318–319, 323a, 338a, 338c, 342–343c, 345c, 349b, 350, 356b, 360d, 363b, 364–365, 366a, 369b, 380b, 388a, 391a, 402–403.

Tom Till Photography, 24a, 33a, 34a, 34b, 34–35 , 35a, 36–37, 45b, 54a, 92b, 99a, 110–111, 112b, 122a, 128–129, 140c, 141a, 148a, 154a, 156d, 157e, 157f, 162b, 170–171, 171b, 180a, 180–181, 181b, 181a, 182–183, 184–185b, 184b, 188, 189d, 201b, 204–205, 220–221, 237a, 238–239a, 246–247, 246b, 250b, 268e, 273, 280b, 290a, 294c, 297c, 298–299, 304–305, 325b, 337c, 356a, 357, 358–359, 360a, 385b.

Walter Bibikow/The Viesti Collection, Inc., 202c.

Willard Clay Photography, 55a, 86–87, 101f, 103, 107b, 115b, 120–121, 121b, 131b, 133a, 136–137b, 140–141, 176d, 268c, 276–277, 303a, 316a, 342–343b, 369a, 372b, 374–375, 378–379.

William D. Adams, 21a, 52–53a, 52a, 53c, 86b, 105b, 107a, 360c.

Yogi, Inc./Peter Arnold, Inc., 110b.

WARNING
RESTRICTED
WILDLIFE AREA
FOR NEXT 5 MILES PHOTOGRAPHY
AND OBSERVATION OF WILDLIFE
PERMITTED FROM ROAD ONLY

"There can be nothing in the world more beautiful than a Yosemite, the groves of giant Sequoias and Redwoods, the Canyon of the Colorado, the Canyon of Yellowstone, its three Tetons. And our people should see to it that they are preserved for their children and their children's children forever." –Theodore Roosevelt, 1905

The Benefits of Being a Partner of the National Park Foundation

$50—National Park Contributor: You will receive the *GoParks* quarterly newsletter that puts you at the forefront of park activities and events.

$75—National Park Supporter: The above, plus an attractive National Park Foundation lapel pin.

$100—National Park Friend: All of the above, plus the unique *Passport to Your National Parks™*, which provides fascinating information about your National Parks and space for you to record your visits.

$125—National Park Benefactor: All of the above, plus a personalized National Parks Pass™ you can use from Maui to Maine, Alaska to the Everglades, for free admission for one year to all National Parks requiring entry fees.

$250—National Park Defender: All of the above, plus a special memo from the Foundation President mailed to you quarterly to provide detailed information about the latest initiatives to preserve, protect, and enhance your National Parks.

$1,000—National Park Preservation Society: All of the above, plus a certificate of appreciation (suitable for framing) and Park Privileges™, a unique service to help you plan your trips to your National Parks.

PLEASE DETACH THIS FORM, PLACE IT IN AN ENVELOPE, AND MAIL IT TO:

National Park Foundation
1101 17th Street NW, Suite 1102
Washington, DC 20036

Visit us online at www.nationalparks.org/npf

CREDIT CARD INFORMATION:

Please bill my: ❑ Visa ❑ MasterCard ❑ American Express

Card No. ______________________

Exp. Date ______________________

Signature ______________________

❑ My employer will match my contribution to the National Park Foundation. My company's matching gift form is enclosed.

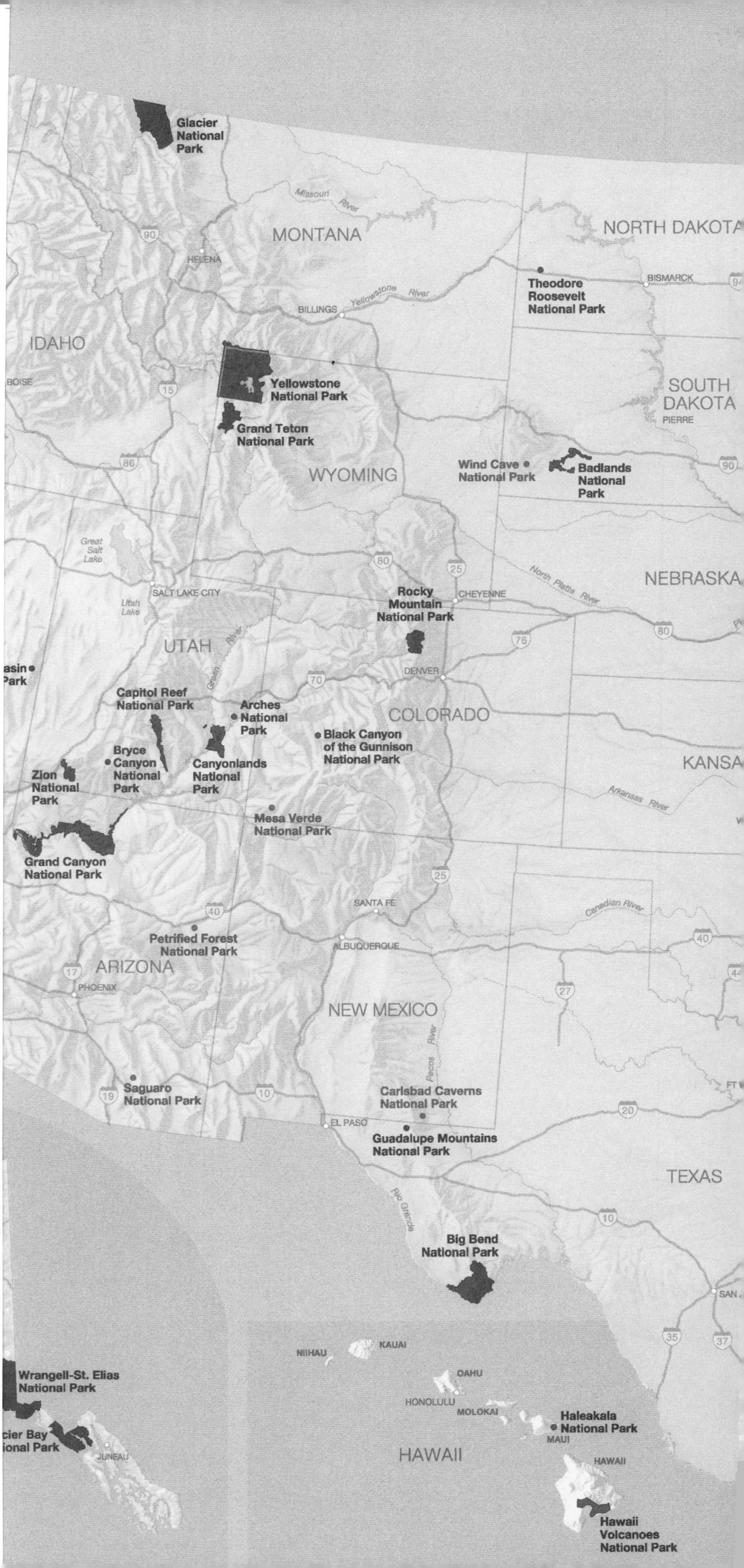

Glacier National Park
MONTANA
NORTH DAKOTA
Theodore Roosevelt National Park
IDAHO
Yellowstone National Park
Grand Teton National Park
SOUTH DAKOTA
WYOMING
Wind Cave National Park
Badlands National Park
NEBRASKA
Rocky Mountain National Park
UTAH
Capitol Reef National Park
Arches National Park
COLORADO
Black Canyon of the Gunnison National Park
Bryce Canyon National Park
Zion National Park
Canyonlands National Park
KANSAS
Mesa Verde National Park
Grand Canyon National Park
Petrified Forest National Park
ARIZONA
NEW MEXICO
Saguaro National Park
Carlsbad Caverns National Park
Guadalupe Mountains National Park
TEXAS
Big Bend National Park
Wrangell-St. Elias National Park
Glacier Bay National Park
HAWAII
Haleakala National Park
Hawaii Volcanoes National Park